SIDE EFFECTS AND COMPLICATIONS

The Economic Consequences of Health-Care Reform

CASEY B. MULLIGAN

THE UNIVERSITY OF CHICAGO PRESS

CHICAGO AND LONDON

Casey B. Mulligan is professor of economics at the University of Chicago. He is the author of *The Redistribution Recession: How Labor Market Distortions Contracted the Economy* and *Parental Priorities and Economic Inequality.*

The University of Chicago Press, Chicago 60637
The University of Chicago Press, Ltd., London
© 2015 by The University of Chicago
All rights reserved. Published 2015.
Printed in the United States of America

24 23 22 21 20 19 18 17 16 15   1 2 3 4 5

ISBN-13: 978-0-226-28560-3   (cloth)
ISBN-13: 978-0-226-28574-0   (e-book)
DOI: 10.7208/chicago/9780226285740.001.0001

Library of Congress Cataloging-in-Publication Data

Mulligan, Casey B., author.
  Side effects and complications : the economic consequences of health-care reform / Casey B. Mulligan.
        pages   cm
  Includes bibliographical references and index.
  ISBN 978-0-226-28560-3 (cloth : alk. paper)—ISBN 978-0-226-28574-0 (e-book)
1. Health care reform—Economic aspects—United States. 2. United States. Patient Protection and Affordable Care Act.   I. Title.
  RA395.A3.M86 2015
  330.973—dc23

                                                                    2015011404

♾ This paper meets the requirements of ANSI/NISO Z39.48-1992 (Permanence of Paper).

To Maeve!

With thanks to the others enrolled in the University of Chicago Maroon plan in the year she was born.

CONTENTS

PREFACE

In a way, this book is an unplanned sequel to the 2012 *The Redistribution Recession*, where I looked at new assistance programs primarily for the unemployed and poor and their effects on labor market aggregates. Most of the programs were supposed to be temporary measures to help people endure the recession. I was writing shortly before their sunset, looking back at labor market dynamics as the programs came on line and making projections for the path of the labor market through the end of 2013 as the last of the temporary provisions expired. Sure enough, by the end of December 2013 the final expiration occurred with the termination of the last long-term unemployment benefit package. Also as expected, the labor market had only partly recovered, more by some measures than others.

But last year it became clear that safety net programs were not getting back to what they used to be. The Affordable Care Act is going ahead with relatively little modification, and it is going to be a lot more than a Medicaid expansion. The generous middle-class premium assistance provision in the 2009 federal stimulus law is reemerging larger, permanent, and more ambitious as a combination of health insurance assistance and employer penalties that help not only people laid off from work but also early retirees, part-time workers, and people who quit their jobs.

New and better data are always welcome, but having seen and analyzed the 2009 premium assistance provision as well as several other safety net measures, I felt there was little reason to wait before seriously analyzing the labor market incentives in the health reform. Moreover, in writing and talking about the first book I learned a lot about clearly explaining the basic labor economics and public finance without sacrificing the numerical accuracy of the conclusions.

Anyone interested in economic performance over the next several years has to understand the contents of the Affordable Care Act from a labor market perspective—it's vastly more important than, say, the interest rate on fed funds—and the first half of this book is, so far, the only comprehensive and user-friendly introduction to the topic. It is about recognizing a tax as economics does, regardless of what politicians call it. It is about detecting the difference between large taxes and small ones. None of this is technical: it just requires data about the structure of our labor market, which I present in a sequence of tables and charts, and arithmetic. But it is conceptual in that the reader sometimes has to dispense with conventional terminology and look at what provisions in the law actually do to create rewards and punishments. Withholding benefits from people because they work and earn is hardly different from telling them to pay taxes on their work and earnings.

The second half of the book looks at the economic consequences of all of the new taxes, also with attention to distinguishing small effects from large ones. Sometimes, as with the application of Adam Smith's equalizing differences, arithmetic and measurement can be enough to do the job. Other times, as in chapter 6, more mathematical analysis is required. The rewards are several surprises about our economy, regardless of the reader's level of technical sophistication.

I thank my family, Tsega Beyene, and Mekdes Yohannes for helping me dedicate the time needed to write a book—yet again! I would understand if they asked Congress to take a break from creating big social programs for a while. And not to repeal any, either! As readers will notice, Sherwin Rosen did a lot to make Adam Smith's equalizing differences ready for quantitative policy analysis. Gary Becker taught economists at the University of Chicago and elsewhere to pay attention to what economics has to say, regardless of how inconvenient or ignored it might be, and encouraged me to finish this book.

Matt Kahn, Glen Weyl, Jorge Garcia, and Saachi Gupta carefully read early drafts of the manuscript. I benefited from comments by Trevor Gallen, Josh Archambault, Jeff Brown, James Broughel, John Cherf, John Cochrane, David Cutler, Bill Dougan, Merle Erickson, Diana Furchtgott-Roth, John Goodman, Robert Graboyes, Paul Gregory, Joe Jackson, Pamela Kelly, Dan Kessler, Arnold Kling, Amanda Kowalski, Eddie Lazear, Kristen Lepore, John McDonough, Bruce Meyer, Jared Meyer, Magne Mogstad, Jack Mulligan, Derek Neal, Matt Notowidigdo, Tomas Philipson, Yona Rubinstein, Rob Shimer, Kosali Simon, Don Taylor, Kevin Tsui, Rob Valletta, Paul Winfree, several economists at the Congressional Budget Office, several anonymous referees, and graduate students, undergraduate students, and seminar participants at the University of Chicago; Hoover; Suffolk University; Texas A&M; UNC-Chapel Hill; the Federal Reserve Banks of Atlanta, Chicago, Minneapolis, and St. Louis; and Western Kentucky. Clemson University even held a seminar while I was absent.

Kevin McKenna and Josh Mills also helped with their comments and suggestions on my posts at nytimes.com about related topics. I also appreciate the assistance of Ada Barbosa and Getfriday's Nithin, the financial support of the George J. Stigler Center for the Study of the Economy and the State, and support from the University of Chicago's Division of Social Sciences during a part-year leave of absence that allowed this book to get started.

A technical version of this book was completed in May 2014 and released as a self-published e-book three months later. In preparing the manuscript for the University of Chicago Press, I rewrote much of the prose to include more examples and cut out technical derivations. Chapter 6 was especially transformed from an algebraic analysis to a graphical presentation (readers wanting the algebra should look back to the 2014 e-book). However, I did not change any of the datasets, impact calculations, or quantitative conclusions about the ACA. An anonymous referee recommended that I present alternative demographic adjustments (i.e., labor market changes that would occur even without the ACA). Following that recommendation, and auditing the forecasting formulas, slightly changed a couple of entries in table 7.4, table 7.5, table 9.3, table 9.4, table 9.5, figure 9.3, and figure 11.2. The final manuscript preparations were finished in November 2014.

Additional appendixes, updates, and bonus features related to this project are available at www.acasideeffects.com.

1 | The Paradox of Affordability

In our unbelievably rich land, the quality of health care available to many of our people is unbelievably poor, and the cost is unbelievably high.
—Senator Edward M. Kennedy (December 9, 1978, speech at the Democratic National Committee midterm convention)

As the nation has become richer and health technologies have advanced, health care has become capable of delivering results ranging from new knees and hips for the elderly to a good chance at a long life for premature babies, to peace of mind for patients and their families. At the same time, spending on health care has grown faster than the economy itself. Millions of people pay a significant portion of their income, often in the form of voluntary deductions from their paychecks that go toward health insurance premiums, so that they and their families can access good doctors, hospitals, pharmaceuticals, and medical devices when needed. Many people take jobs solely for the purpose of paying for their health insurance. The magnitude of their sacrifices demonstrates the importance that people ascribe to health care.

Take Mike Smith, who was working long hours in California as a district manager for a national auto parts retailer. Despite wanting to help care for his grandchild and elderly in-laws, Mr. Smith kept the manager job into his 60s because he and his wife wanted the health insurance that came with it.

In order for the Smiths and others to receive the health-care results that they value, society has to dedicate workers to diagnose illnesses, administer treatments, think of and experiment with ways to improve health care, manufacture medical devices, adjudicate disputes, administer payment systems, and produce structures, equipment, and software to assist with these tasks. Those working in health care and supporting industries are workers who cannot instead be producing goods and services such as food, transportation, and entertainment.

Because people differ in terms of their income, health status, family situation, and priorities, invariably a segment of the population is unable or at least unwilling to pay for their own health care. After Senator

Kennedy's speech, the share of the population without health insurance continued to grow, at least in part because health care continued to get more expensive (Cohen et al. 2009).

In many other markets, it is tolerated and maybe even welcomed when a customer segment stops buying in response to high costs. Many households, for example, have stopped subscribing to cable television as the monthly cable bill grows more expensive and they are no longer able or willing to dedicate the funds to such an expense. The trend toward dropping a cable subscription is not universally viewed as a serious problem. But health care is said to be different: people are supposed to get quality health care even if they have not taken steps to purchase health care themselves.

In the past, the federal government stepped in to deliver health insurance to populations that were least likely to get it on their own. In the 1960s it created the Medicare insurance program, which heavily subsidizes payments to health providers on behalf of elderly patients. But the Smiths did not qualify for Medicare because they were too young. Medicaid is another public health insurance program created in the 1960s and expanded in recent decades, in this case by federal and state governments on behalf of poor families, especially those with children. The Smiths, who do not have young children at home, did not qualify for Medicaid either. The Affordable Care Act of 2010 (hereafter, ACA) is for people like the Smiths to get health insurance without necessarily having a full-time job with benefits.

Medicaid and Medicare help poor and elderly individuals avoid some of the tough sacrifices that would be necessary for them to purchase health insurance without assistance. On average, Medicaid and Medicare permit beneficiaries to work less, spend more on nonhealth-related goods and services, or both. But no program can change the fundamental reality that society has to pay for health care with more people in the workforce, fewer nonhealth goods and services, more productivity, or all of the above. Thus, while Medicare and Medicaid help their target populations and give them a bigger slice of the economic pie, the programs also diminish the pie itself. The programs reduce, among other things, how much program participants work on average, exacerbating the societal problem that the economy as a whole cannot expand its health sector without giving up something else of value. In effect, people who are not receiving assistance from Medicare or Medicaid are paying twice for the programs: once as the total economic pie gets smaller and a second time as they receive a smaller piece.

A reasonable person might conclude that Medicare and Medicaid do relatively little to shrink the economic pie, because even without the programs the vast majority of work would be done by people who are neither poor nor elderly. But the economic effects of the ACA are a different matter since the program involves the bulk of the U.S. population that has been excluded from Medicare and Medicaid, and thereby the people who have been doing most of the work in the economy. Indeed, before the Affordable Care Act, both Mike and Laura Smith were together contributing as much as 100 hours per week to economic activity. But, according to National Public Radio (NPR), they both retired in 2014 because the law gave them health insurance for just $200 per month.

When NPR broadcast its story, it portrayed the Smiths' experience as an economically healthy development because the law had allowed them to "leave unfulfilling jobs," enjoy "leisurely lunches," and Mike to practice guitar. This book explains that, although NPR's conclusion contains a grain of truth because the health-insurance market before the ACA was tilted in the direction of employer-provided plans, a complete economic analysis must also recognize the taxpayer burdens created by retirements, unemployment, and other cases in which able people are not working. Because Mike retired, the federal government was paying four to six times as much for the Smith's insurance premiums as the Smiths were. We also must account for the extra taxpayer-financed Social Security benefits that early retirees may receive, and the income and payroll tax revenues that both California and federal governments lost when the Smiths stopped working.

Other economic stories put in motion by the ACA bear little resemblance to the Smiths'. Among others, workers at many schools, restaurants, and municipal offices are having their hours cut so that the new law does not recognize them as full-time workers (Pear 2014b; Graham 2014). Or take Mr. Ben Winslett, a Baptist pastor, husband, and father of five from Alabama, who describes himself as "securely in the middle class earning nearly the exact average US income each year." His family's health insurance was "taken care of on my own in the previous system," but the ACA outlawed their $250-monthly policy, leaving them with far more expensive options. As he describes it, the ACA "has placed an enormous financial burden on normal, everyday people quite literally forcing us onto government assistance we didn't need before."[1]

Although anecdotes help to illustrate economic ideas, they cannot be the foundation for careful economic analysis. People sometimes get carried away when relaying their stories to a radio-show microphone, television camera, or newspaper reporter. Anecdotes invite overattributing results like the Smiths' retirements or fast-food workers' schedule changes to the new law, when economics tells us that the ACA is just one of many forces affecting decisions by an individual or business and sometimes a law is just the straw that broke the camel's back. Anecdotes are rarely put in a market context, and thereby risk obscuring regular market patterns with excessive individual details. The purpose of this book is to use comprehensive economic reasoning and large representative samples to measure the taxes in the ACA—including both positive and negative taxes—and to offer quantitative predictions about the law's effects on the labor market, capital accumulation, and total production in the U.S. economy.

A. Hidden Taxes

At first glance it might appear that the ACA helps people get access to health care and disproportionately benefits low-income households without many new taxes. By one estimate, the ACA's tax increases are less than 0.5 percent of gross domestic product, and less than several other hardly memorable tax increases of the postwar period (Klein 2012). The White House suggested that health reform would largely pay for itself, without mentioning taxes that, individually or in combination, would have more than a "little effect" on the labor market (Council of Economic Advisers 2009a).

Politicians and journalists use the term *tax* more narrowly than economists do, but the economic definition is needed to understand the effects of the ACA. Suppose, hypothetically, that the government provided a "universal" $2,000 health benefit to every person and paid for it with a tax, in the narrow sense of the word, of $4,000 per employee. Employees are half the population, so the employee taxes average $2,000 per person and are enough to pay for the universal benefit.

Now consider an alternative "targeted" approach that pays the $2,000 health benefit only to people who do not work and gets the revenue from a $2,000 tax per employee. By excluding workers from the benefit, the targeted approach appears to spend and tax less: only $1,000 per person. But the economic result is the same because, in both systems, employees pay $2,000 more than they receive. In both systems, people who are not employed receive more than employed people do; in the universal system their lack of employment exempts them from a large tax whereas in the targeted system it exempts them from a smaller tax plus it gives them access to a benefit that is withheld from workers.

Withholding benefits from people who work or earn is hardly different than telling them to pay a tax. For this reason, the field of economics refers to benefits withheld as "implicit taxes." What really matters for labor market performance is the reward to working inclusive of implicit taxes, and not the amount of revenue delivered to the government treasury according to economically arbitrary distinctions between implicit taxes and other taxes. The targeted system gives the same economic results, including the economic harms from taxes, as the universal benefit system does but without the (politically ugly) appearance of bringing significant revenues to the government treasury.

The ACA resembles the targeted approach because it is full of implicit taxes, including implicit taxes on employment and income. Mike Smith's district manager job, and tens of millions of other full-time positions, are subject to the ACA's implicit employment tax because anyone employed in it is (together with spouse and dependents) expressly prohibited from getting the ACA's assistance until the employee quits, retires, is laid off, or otherwise ceases that employment. Mike's retirement made it possible for him and Laura to get the law's new and generous benefits.

Many of the law's implicit taxes have remained hidden "in the fog of controversy" surrounding the law and their effects excluded from economic analyses of it. As of 2014, essentially the only place to find an economic analysis of the ACA's large and hidden employment taxes is this book (or drafts of its chapters). No investigation of the economic effects of the ACA should be considered accurate unless it accounts for the ACA's implicit taxes.

Figure 1.1 puts the ACA's new taxes in perspective of federal tax increases over the past 70 years. The taxes include federal personal income taxes (Form 1040, shown in pink), social insurance payroll taxes (gray), and various employment and implicit taxes (red). The figure does not show revenue for the U.S. Treasury—that statistic is vulnerable to some of the arbitrary distinctions noted above—but instead shows the effect of various tax laws on the incentives for workers to earn more labor income rather than less as measured by a marginal labor income tax rate (by marginal labor income tax I mean the extra taxes paid, and subsidies forgone, as the result of working). During a period that included more than a dozen tax increases, the ACA is arguably the largest as a single piece of legislation, adding about six percentage points to the marginal tax rate faced, on average, by workers in the economy. The only way to cite larger marginal tax increases would be to combine multiple coincident laws, such as the Revenue Acts of 1950 and 1951 and the new payroll tax rate that went into effect in 1950. The four payroll tax rate increases between 1970 and 1980 are another example of a large rate increase if we also include the personal income tax rate changes that occurred during the decade owing to inflation causing taxpayer incomes to creep into higher tax brackets without any new legislation. Even with these adjustments, the ACA is still the third largest marginal tax rate hike during the 70 years. Another feature of the ACA that distinguishes it from other large marginal tax rate rises is that the former is, by law, entirely permanent whereas essentially the only other permanent ones shown in figure 1.1 are the payroll tax rate changes.

Figure 1.1 represents the ACA as a single number, but underlying that number are multiple economically distinct taxes. Chapter 2 of this book is an introduction to a dozen or so provisions in the law and offers some indicators of their relative importance. The employer penalty is explained and measured in chapter 3. Chapter 4 features the *employee* penalties that are hidden in the ACA's arrangements for subsidizing health insurance assistance. The subsidy rules also include a couple of new implicit income taxes, which are discussed and measured in chapter 5.

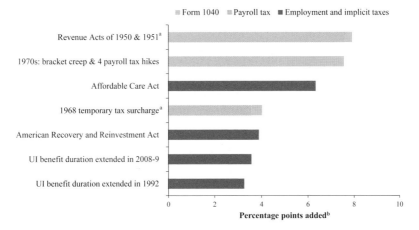

FIGURE 1.1. The largest marginal labor income tax rate increases during 1946–2016, by type of federal tax increase.

[a] Includes contemporaneous payroll tax rate increases.
[b] Average marginal percentage of wages and salaries, excluding untaxed fringes.
Sources: Barro and Sahasakul (1986), Mulligan (2012b), National Bureau of Economic Research (2012), U.S. Department of Labor (2012).

Economists generally acknowledge that taxes have side effects, and this book is not unusual in terms of its representation of the amount of unintended consequences per dollar of taxation. The real surprises are the wide range and astonishing size of the taxes measured in chapters 3, 4, and 5. Each of the chapters shows how the ACA's new taxes can put millions of workers in a "100 percent tax" situation in which full-time work pays less than part-time work, or less even than not working at all. This is without counting the workers who can raise their disposable income by working less and thereby climbing one of the "cliffs" that are part of the ACA's rules for determining federal assistance on the basis of household income. Anyone interested in the evolution of the labor market in the United States has to understand the ACA's new taxes—they're vastly more important than, say, the interest rate on fed funds—and the first half of this book is so far the only comprehensive and user-friendly introduction to the topic.

B. Using Economics to Forecast Policy Consequences

A complicated law like the ACA has forces pushing in multiple directions. For example, the ACA contains an implicit tax on unemployment benefits. This by itself tends to reduce unemployment and increase employment, which is the opposite result of some of the other taxes in the law. But it does not mean that anything is possible, or that we must wait for more data before having any idea as to which forces dominate. The ACA's various taxes can be quantified individually and collectively. Chapters 2 through 5 show that the law's employment taxes far outweigh its employment subsidies, and its income-earning disincentives far outweigh its income-earning incentives. When the government redistributes by taxing something, the usual result is to get less of it, which is why I expect national income per person and hours worked per person to be less than they would be if the ACA had not been passed.

In writing this book, my exemplar was *The Economic Consequences of the Peace*, in which John Maynard Keynes (1919) offered his predictions for the effects of the 1919 Treaty of Versailles (between World War I Allied Powers and Germany) on the German economy. Keynes believed that several economic consequences of the treaty were knowable ahead of time, and he wrote his book after the hotly debated document was written but before it was fully executed. He carefully quantified the economic provisions of the treaty, and the economy that would be affected by them. Keynes wrote little about "the ideal question"—what should have been done—and instead focused on the consequences of what was actually written. I tried to include the same basic ingredients in *Side Effects and Complications*, and treated the implementation of the ACA as an opportunity to learn about the economy and applied economic theory, operating under the assumption that the ACA would inevitably go into effect without significant modification of the law (as interpreted by the Obama administration as of early 2014, with exceptions noted in the book). As it turns out, I reached conclusions analogous to Keynes's: that full execution of the document (the treaty in his case, the ACA in mine) would create significant economic side effects, and that advocates of the document were not fully aware of, or forthright about, the costs created.[2]

After Keynes, many detailed economic analyses of public policies and the national economy—Friedman and Schwartz (1963), Costa (1998), Cole and Ohanian (2004), and Goldin and Katz (2008) are good examples—have been executed after the policy of interest is in place for a number of years and thereby with the benefits of hindsight and ample time for reflection, debate, and synthesis. The historical approach is valuable and should be continued, but it sometimes gives the impression that policy consequences are inherently unknowable until after the fact, if ever. With its reliance on hindsight, the historical approach arguably fails to profit from one of the major strengths of economic theory, which is to identify common elements of economic events on the basis of incentives instead of outcomes. I deliberately completed this book before mid-2014, and therefore before the release of any of the data needed to execute a historical evaluation of the ACA, in order that we may have a detailed and comprehensive analysis of the law's effects on the economy that cannot rely on hindsight.

To the economic theorist, few events are fundamentally new; rather, they tend to be new collections of familiar economic forces. Thus plenty of data were available to assess likely consequences of the ACA even before the law went into effect. The law itself is data on the types and magnitudes of incentives that would be created when (and if) it is enforced. A wealth of historical episodes provides quantitative information about how employers, employees, and consumers react to employment taxes, insurance costs, and other economic forces unleashed by the new law. This book presents and refers to much of that data, and it organizes them with some of the basic models in economics such as the theory of substitution effects, Adam Smith's theory of equalizing differences, and the neoclassical growth model.

Quantitative forecasting with economic theory also offers a kind of discipline against excessive simplification or exaggeration of the main effects because they will likely be punished with obvious contradictions by future events. Forecasting also has a way of honing one's attention on what really is unknown—for example, the degree to which people and businesses will comply with the new law—and the possible effects of the unknowns on the outcomes of interest (Tetlock 2006, p. 217). In the years ahead, studies will be released that have more data than I have, more complex models built on those data, and new ideas for sifting through the old data. New studies will undoubtedly teach us about the consequences of the ACA and about economic theory itself, but we may never know how many of their successes rely on hindsight and the freedom from future events that might contradict their conclusions.

Forecasting is frequently attacked as imprudent or immodest. It is well known that price changes on the stock market are difficult, if not impossible, to predict (Malkiel 1973). This result is sometimes taken a step further to suggest that changes in gross domestic product and other aggregate indicators of economic performance cannot be predicted (Campbell and Mankiw's 1987 results might be interpreted this way) and that it is foolish to try. Yet even the harshest critics of expert predictions of policy consequences admit some economic policy hypotheses are reliable: for example, that communist planning delivers terribly low living standards compared to market alternatives (Huemer 2012, p. 16). What, then, should be said about a law that takes the economy 80 percent of the way to communism? Or 20 percent? Or 2 percent? The real issue, I think, is the size of a policy impulse relative to the many other changes that would be occurring in the economy even without the policy—the smaller and more uncertain is the policy impulse relative to the other changes, the more difficult it is to predict how the economy will be different after the law is in effect than it was before—which is why the first half of this book deals exclusively with measuring the size of the new incentives contained in the ACA. The size is great enough that I would be shirking my responsibility if I concluded that anything is possible.

Short-term forecasts can readily consider some of the forces that are unrelated to the ACA, and thereby cut down on forecast errors due to the omission of non-ACA factors. Population growth and inflation are two of them, which I handle by offering predictions for hours worked per person, employees per person, and inflation-adjusted national income per person. I consider the aging of the population by making age adjustments to the hours and employment data. I also assume that technological progress or something like it tends to put inflation-adjusted national income per person on an upward trend, and that the ACA and other factors cause deviations around the trend. Also important are non-ACA tax changes that are coincident with the ACA, especially the December 2013 expiration of extended unemployment benefits, which are considered in the same way the ACA tax changes are. These strategies are needed for predictions relating to a single economic variable, such as national income, but other predictions just refer to relationships among variables: the ACA's impact on weekly employment rates is greater than its impact on the average weekly hours worked by those employed, the ACA reduces some measures of productivity more than others, and so on. For the "relationships" predictions, inflation, population growth, technological advancements, and other factors may hardly matter, in which case I do not need estimates of their magnitude.

The purpose of the predictions in the second half of this book is not only to learn about the ACA, but also to learn about economic theory and policy analysis themselves, so that analysis of future policies can be improved. In this regard, the ultimately false predictions are just as important as the "correct" ones. This book lays out clear criteria for readers in the future, who will have the advantage of additional data, to use to determine which of the predictions turned out to be incorrect in the sense that reliable measures of the relevant economic outcomes will fall outside of the predicted range. In some scenarios, predictions fail because of unanticipated events unrelated to the health reform, such as a new and costly war. Or the ACA may be significantly amended without ever being executed in its current form, and without being executed in an alternative form that is examined in this book. But the more interesting failures will be economic effects of the law that are not adequately treated here, or improper quantification of the economic effects that are treated. For the reasons cited above, these lessons for economic theory and policy analysis would be harder to obtain without being able to look back at a detailed and comprehensive policy analysis that did not rely on hindsight.

Chapter 6 begins to formulate the predictions by adapting a model from the labor economics literature to offer predictions for the magnitude, direction, and incidence of the long-run impacts on weekly work schedules of the ACA's various taxes. Here the focus is on the impact of the ACA, which is a first step deliberately ignoring population aging, technological progress, and other non-ACA factors that would affect the economy regardless of whether the law had passed (those are added in later chapters). The model features, among other things, a couple of sharp incentives for employers and employees to limit weekly work hours to 29 or fewer. Nevertheless, it is possible that the ACA may increase, or hardly change, the average number of hours worked per employee, although the law also tempts employers and employees to change their methods for reporting hours and incomes even if they do not change their actual work habits.

A more visible impact of the law will be to reduce the fraction of the population that is employed during a given week. Although the model in chapter 6 accounts for many occupations and types of taxes, its quantitative conclusion for aggregate work hours can be closely approximated by mere multiplication of the total amount of taxation (documented in chapters 3 through 5) and a "reward coefficient" that summarizes the sensitivity of labor market behavior to tax rates. This part of chapter 6 contains the book's clearest demonstration that, without my findings as to the size and scope of the new taxes, my conclusions about the ACA's aggregate employment and hours effects would hardly be different from others in the literature. The literature uniformly fails to mention or quantify the large new implicit employee taxes (my chapter 4), fails to adequately quantify the new implicit income taxes (my chapter 5), and usually fails to consider the special tax treatment and anticompetitive effects of the employer penalty (my chapter 3).

C. Adam Smith's Theory of Equalizing Differences

Because the ACA does not tax all workers and sectors uniformly, its effects extend well beyond the employment rate and the average length of the workweek. Chapters 7 and 8 quantify and interpret the ACA's deviations from uniform taxation from the perspective of the theory of equalizing differences. The theory is a workhorse in labor economics today and dates back to the beginning of economics, when Adam Smith (1776/1904, chapter I.10.1, no relation to the aforementioned Mike and Laura Smith) explained how the free flow of workers among occupations and sectors can spread "disadvantages" located in one part of the economy—the ACA's employer penalty is an obvious disadvantage of that sort—across the entire economy. Indeed, Adam Smith's theory is the foundation of the health-economics concept of a "value of a statistical life," which is a critical part of cost-benefit analysis in the health-care field (Viscusi and Aldy 2003). The two chapters begin with an illustration of the profound effects of equalizing differences on everyday life, and then they obtain quantitative results with basic arithmetic (adding and multiplying pairs of numbers) that represents the theory as applied to the ACA. Chapter 7 focuses on insurance coverage and relative wages, whereas chapter 8 examines productivity (that is, the aggregate value of production per hour worked and related measures) building on recent research on "misallocations" of labor across sectors, regions, and firms.

Chapter 7 concludes that the ACA is likely to achieve the goal of significantly expanding the fraction of the population with health insurance, and it may do so to a surprisingly large extent, because it puts so many people in a position of having to pay more to be uninsured than insured. Workers having no direct contact with the ACA's penalties and subsidies will nonetheless experience the law's provisions, often in the form of lower wages, because they compete and produce with workers who do. Chapter 8 shows that the ACA will reduce the demand for both low- and high-skill labor because it reduces productivity and imposes penalties. The results in chapters 7 and 8 are sharply different from those obtained by other authors on the basis of "health insurance simulation models" because the simulation models fail to consider the theory of equalizing differences or otherwise put the employer-employee relationship in a market context.

Chapters 6 through 8 show why there is a paradox of affordability. The ACA makes health care more affordable for segments of the population, but in doing so it makes health care less affordable for the nation as a whole. The ACA will have the nation working fewer hours, and working those hours less productively, so that its nonhealth spending will be twice diminished: once to pay for more health care and a second time because the economy is smaller and less productive.

D. Economic Dynamics and Conclusions

It's one thing to estimate how much the ACA will eventually (say, within three or four years) depress employment rates, but it's another thing to say how those effects will unfold from month to month. The dynamics depend on several additional and unknown (to me) factors, such as the rate at which employers and employees will learn about the new incentives they face and the rate at which they process updates to the rules made by regulators who are themselves updating their understanding of the law's effects. Employees will form opinions as to the desirability of the new individual insurance plans, whose characteristics will change during the early years of the ACA. Chapter 9 therefore forms predictions for the labor market and the entire economy for a three- or four-year horizon following the beginning of the ACA's exchange subsidies by adding my estimates of the impact of the ACA to estimates of other factors creating economic change. The chapter also discusses possible scenarios for marginal tax rates, especially changes to the ACA itself through legislation or possible announcements by the federal government as to its enforcement of ACA provisions.

The federal government and other advocates of the Affordable Care Act have dismissed concerns that the coming labor market contraction would be significant, or even noticeable, by pointing to Massachusetts's recent experience with a reform also designed to expand insurance coverage. Chapter 10 looks at the Massachusetts experience and comes to some surprising conclusions.

Chapter 11 summarizes the main tax findings, impact estimates, and economic projections. It also suggests areas for future research, perhaps the foremost of which would be to quantify the ACA's incentives for human capital accumulation, including schooling, job training, health capital, and occupational choice. The end of the book also presents a list of the abbreviations.

2 | Too Good to Be True:
The Health Reform's Hidden Taxes

Western European governments have long provided health care to all of their citizens, regardless of age or income. In contrast, the U.S. government has covered its poor, elderly, and disabled, leaving the remaining majority of the population to privately finance their health care.

It's not an accident that, by offering less coverage, America had a health insurance payroll tax rate—1.45 percent of payroll owed by each employer and employee—that was less than in essentially all of the major Western European countries. Germany's government, for example, taxes employers and employees each about 7 or 8 percent of payroll to finance its various universal public health programs. As shown in the appendix to this chapter, the average health insurance payroll tax rate in Western Europe has been more than twice as much as the U.S. rate.[1]

The contrast between pre-ACA America and Western Europe is consistent with the commonsense idea that universal health coverage has a cost in the form of taxation of labor market activity. This is not to say that one system is better than the other. The point is that benefits appear to come with costs: more coverage requires higher tax rates. If the United States were to follow governments in Western Europe and cover all of its citizens, one might guess that the payroll tax rate would have to be roughly four or five percentage points higher than it would be without universal coverage.

Yet the ACA was advertised as expanding coverage with hardly any new taxes on middle-class workers. President Obama promised he would not burden the middle class with any new taxes (Hicks 2012). Media coverage now acknowledges that the ACA increases taxes but still insists that the middle-class tax burdens coming from the ACA are relatively minor, on the order of $10 billion per year in an economy larger than $17 trillion (Kessler 2013).[2] As the Department of Health and Human Services (the department that administers federal health programs) put it, "the health care law will improve the affordability and accessibility of health care without significantly affecting the labor market" (Contorno 2013).

Is it possible that, in writing the ACA, America discovered a radical new way of financing public health coverage expansions without significantly burdening its labor market with taxes? Have the decades of high Western European payroll tax rates been unnecessary for their governments to provide medical coverage for their nonelderly citizens? Unfortunately, the answers are both no. The ACA contains a variety of hidden taxes—provisions that politicians and journalists do not call taxes but nonetheless are the economic equivalent—that in combination have a lot in common with the payroll taxes Europeans use to help pay for their public medical programs. This book brings the hidden taxes out into the open, quantifies them, and forecasts their likely consequences.

For the most part, the ACA's hidden taxes are economically equivalent to either employment taxes or income taxes. Hidden employment taxes require people with jobs to pay more to, or to receive less from, the U.S. Treasury *because they have a job*. Employment taxes are economically distinct from income taxes: two families having the same yearly income can nonetheless pay unequal employment taxes if they worked a different fraction of the year. The foremost economic consequence of hidden employment taxes is less employment, with the size of the effect depending on the amount of the employment tax, the fraction of jobs subject to the tax, and the economic value created by those jobs. Other consequences of employment taxes include less income, spending, and production because the work that people do on their jobs is the single biggest reason for the economy generating production and incomes and for families being able to spend.

The ACA's hidden income taxes require people with high incomes to pay more to, or to receive less from, the U.S. Treasury than people with low incomes do. Regardless of whether more taxes are collected from high-income families, more "means-tested" subsidies are paid to low-income families, or both, an essential consequence is the same: less income. The size of the effect depends on the rate at which incomes are taxed and the fraction of the nation's income subject to the tax.

Other consequences of income taxes include less work and production because they are activities that generate incomes and are therefore less rewarding the greater is the income tax rate.

The field of economics describes the work disincentives created by means-tested and employment-tested subsidies as "implicit" taxes, rather than "hidden" taxes.[3] But beginning in 2008 I began to notice that federal policy makers were creating large implicit income and employment taxes without being forthright about those taxes, and that outside-the-government economists commenting on the income- and employment-creating effects of those policies were also silent on the issue.[4] The neglect of implicit employment and income taxes became especially acute when several quantitative analyses, executed by distinguished and well-trained economists, of the employment effects of the ACA failed to account for any implicit taxes: see the White House Council of Economic Advisers (Council of Economic Advisers 2009b), Congressional Budget Office (2010), Cutler et al. (2011), Gruber (2012), and Blumberg, Holahan, and Buettgens (2014).[5] Others, such as the White House's "comprehensive analysis of the economic impacts of health care reform," briefly mention implicit income taxes (Council of Economic Advisers 2009a, p. 36) but fail to mention the ACA's implicit employment tax, which turns out to be more important. Remarkably, I am not aware of any document between 2009 and 2013 discussing the implicit employment taxes in the ACA or in its 2009 federal predecessor program assisting unemployed people with their health insurance premiums, with the exception of an article published by law professor and former U.S. Treasury official David Gamage.[6] Thus the ACA's implicit taxes really have been out of view.

There is a big economic difference between a tax—hidden or otherwise—and a voluntary contribution for health insurance, for the same reason there is a big difference between socialism and capitalism. A worker who voluntarily allocates part of his or her paycheck for health insurance, or who voluntarily accepts and retains a job where health coverage is automatically part of his compensation, gets what he pays for. If he declines to make premium payments, he loses his coverage. If he chooses a plan (or job) with low premiums rather than high, he gets low health benefits rather than high. Even though countries with national health insurance may finance their program with payroll taxes, the citizens who pay more payroll tax do not get better benefits than citizens who pay less. In effect, the tax approach has every person working for other people's benefits rather than his own. Changing from a voluntary contribution approach to a tax approach has consequences for the labor market because it reduces the rewards to employment and earning income. This is not to say one approach is necessarily better than the other, just that they differ significantly and the differences have to be examined in order to understand the economic consequences of the health reform.

The rest of this chapter lists the various taxlike provisions in the ACA as well as related tax provisions that predated the law. The list is in descending order of importance in terms of labor market impacts; the bulk of my results can be understood on the basis of the health insurance marketplaces (section A) and employer mandate (section B) alone. Each provision is described, and its main qualitative features are related to employment and income taxation. Readers already knowledgeable of the ACA's main provisions can skip ahead to the next chapter, which begins the quantitative economic analysis of the law's major provisions.

A. Health Insurance Marketplaces

In order to help the uninsured get health insurance coverage, the ACA created what it calls "health insurance exchanges," where individuals can shop for health insurance coverage for themselves and family members and in many cases get federal assistance with the health insurance expenses.[7] An exchange is not a physical location; rather, this refers to the collection of health insurance policies offered to each state's residents by private insurance companies subject to state and federal regulations regarding standardization of policy benefits, provisions, and pricing.[8] Many, but not all, individuals shop on the exchanges by visiting an Internet site that gathers customer information and quotes prices.

In some ways, the health plans on the exchanges offer more benefits than individual health insurance plans did in the past. Sellers on the exchange are also prohibited from using an applicant's medical history to determine whether the person can participate in the plan or how much the person would pay to participate.[9] As long as they cover the federally specified medical services, sellers on the exchange have some discretion as to the identity of the health-care providers that they include in a plan's network, which refers to the collection of providers whose services are reimbursable under the plan. However, it is expected that state and federal governments will increasingly regulate exchange plans in order to discourage sellers from narrowing their provider networks.[10]

The exchange plans are categorized by "metal," which indicates the typical fraction of medical expenditures that are covered by the plan, as opposed to being paid out of pocket by the patient. A bronze plan pays 60 percent, with the other 40 percent paid, on average, out of pocket.[11] Silver, gold, and platinum plans pay 70 percent, 80 percent, and 90 percent, respectively (U.S. Department of Health and Human Services 2014d). Higher metal plans charge higher premiums. Silver plans are the most popular (U.S. Department of Health and Human Services 2014b) and also serve as pricing benchmarks.

The ACA includes a so-called Grassley amendment requiring congressmen and their staffs to get their employer-provided health insurance on the exchanges.[12] This amendment may create some extra political pressure to regulate the features of exchange plans so that they are not too undesirable to upper-middle-class people, who have traditionally participated in expensive employer plans.

Anyone lawfully present and living in the United States, but not incarcerated, can purchase health insurance on the exchanges (U.S. Department of Health and Human Services 2014a), as long as they pay full price with after-tax dollars.[13] However, most persons getting insurance through the exchanges are receiving financial assistance (U.S. Department of Health and Human Services 2014b), which is restricted to specific populations. As we shall see, the financial assistance rules mask many of the ACA's taxes.

1. PREMIUM TAX CREDITS

The exchange plans are expensive in comparison to other things families buy. The Kaiser Family Foundation estimates that a 2014 silver family plan for an average couple, both age 40, with two children costs $9,700 in premiums and another $4,157 in out-of-pocket costs every year, before tax credits and means-tested discounts. High insurance premiums are one of the major reasons people were uninsured prior to the ACA (Henry J. Kaiser Family Foundation 2013), which is why the ACA includes premium assistance tax credits to help families pay for their exchange coverage.

Exchange plan participants are eligible for premium tax credits only if they (1) are not eligible for affordable coverage, and not enrolled in any coverage, through their employer or an immediate family member's employer;[14] (2) have purchased coverage on the exchanges; (3) are not eligible for government-sponsored coverage (especially Medicare, Medicaid, and Children's Health Insurance Program or CHIP); (4) are citizens of, or lawfully in, the United States; (5) have family calendar year income between 100 and 400 percent of the poverty line; and (6) are either unmarried or filing a federal tax return jointly with spouse.[15] The amount of the premium tax credit is the excess, if any, between the full premium for the second cheapest silver plan and an ACA-specified percentage of their calendar year income.[16] The premium tax credits appear on the family's individual tax return for the year in which they satisfied criteria (5) and (6) and are prorated to the months of the year in which they satisfy criteria (1) through (4).[17]

When enrolling for the year, exchange plan participants have the option to receive an estimate of their premium tax credits in advance and have them delivered immediately to the insurer, in which case the participant pays only the difference between the full premium and the advanced credits. The premium tax credit estimates are determined at enrollment on the basis of family and income information available at the time, especially the federal income tax return for the calendar year prior to enrollment (that is, two calendar years prior to the coverage year). The advance credits are reconciled when filing the federal tax return for the coverage year, at which time the taxpayer may owe the IRS for some or all of the excess advance credits.

The excess advance credit repayments are limited by a means-tested cap. In effect, a family that received advanced premium credits throughout the year but violated one of criteria (1) through (4) for part of the year could still receive the credit for essentially the entire year because they are not required to pay back much of the excess, especially if family income turns out to be less than 200 percent of the federal poverty line.[18] For the same reason, a family that received the advance credits because its income was expected to be above the poverty line, but whose calendar income ultimately proved to be below it, could nonetheless receive the advance premium credits and keep most of them.

2. COST-SHARING SUBSIDIES

As noted above, the expected out-of-pocket costs on a silver plan are significant. This is part of the design of the law: health plan participants who are paying out of pocket have an incentive to seek out less costly care. However, families below 400 percent of the poverty line are asked to pay less than the full out-of-pocket costs for silver plans. One of the ACA's cost-sharing programs reduces the plan's out-of-pocket spending caps as a function of family income. The second, and quantitatively more important, program allows families expected to be below 250 percent of the poverty line to in effect get a gold or platinum plan for the price of a silver plan.[19]

Eligibility for cost-sharing assistance is based on criteria (1) through (6) noted above, except that the data used for eligibility are the same data as used on enrollment to determine eligibility for advance premium credits,[20] which typically will be the tax return from two calendar years prior to the coverage year. Neither cost-sharing subsidy is reconciled at the end of the coverage year.[21]

3. EXCHANGE SUBSIDIES ARE EMPLOYMENT-TESTED

Hereafter, I collectively refer to premium tax credits and cost-sharing subsidies as "exchange subsidies." Chapter 3 explains why the most significant hidden tax in the ACA comes from criterion (1) for exchange subsidy eligibility, because, much like eligibility for unemployment benefits, this criterion is linked with employment status. A person who is not employed cannot be barred by criterion (1) from receiving exchange subsidies.

Conversely, criterion (1) bars a majority of nonelderly household heads and spouses from receiving exchange subsidies, and it thereby saves the U.S. Treasury hundreds of billions of dollars every year. Tens of millions of working heads and spouses choose to pay this hidden tax by continuing in a job that offers affordable coverage.

For the people receiving health coverage on their job, the ACA's exchange subsidies are like a new form of unemployment benefits: no subsidy is received as long as they are employed, but as soon as they are laid off from that job the exchange subsidies become available. If it weren't for the ACA, being laid off would mean paying full price for their coverage, or going without. The exchange subsidies are actually more generous than traditional unemployment benefits because even people who quit their job can get the exchange subsidies and potentially continue to receive the subsidies for decades afterward.

Because the employment tax hidden in the exchange subsidies does not apply to all jobs, the exchange subsidies also affect the composition of employment in the direction of shifting employment toward jobs that do not offer coverage. Part of the hidden compositional tax is offset by the individual and employer mandates (introduced below), but the compositional dimension of the ACA's hidden taxes is given a lot of attention in this book.

The amount of exchange subsidies varies by family income and composition, but it can be large. At the high end, take a 50-year-old couple with three children. According to the Kaiser Family Foundation, their full annual silver plan costs would be $19,837. If their income were, say, 145 percent of the poverty line, and they satisfied the other criteria (1) through (6), then their annual exchange subsidies would be more than $17,100.[22] Because the subsidies themselves are not subject to state or federal taxes, the subsidies would be more valuable than a 50 percent increase in family income.[23]

The health insurance exchanges are vehicles for other hidden taxes, such as insurer risk-mitigation provisions. Discussion of the additional hidden taxes is delayed until the end of this chapter because they are less significant from a labor market perspective.

B. The Employer Mandate

Because of criterion (1)—that exchange subsidies are available only to persons who are not eligible for affordable employer coverage—the ACA requires that large employers either provide affordable, qualified coverage or pay a penalty. The law defines a large employer to be one that had at least 50 full-time-equivalent (FTE) employees in the calendar year previous to the year in which it failed to provide coverage. Part-time employees count toward full-time-equivalents in proportion to their hours worked.[24]

The penalty for failing to provide any coverage is levied monthly at a rate of $167 per full-time employee, indexed for health cost inflation after 2014. Part-time employees, defined to be anyone working fewer than 30 hours per week, are exempt from this penalty, as are the first 30 full-time employees. Employers with zero employees receiving exchange subsidies are also exempt. Although employees are tabulated separately for each month for the purposes of determining an employer's liability, henceforth I express the penalty rate on a more familiar annualized basis: $2,000 per full-time employee plus health cost inflation.

The employer penalty is a tax on employment. It is also an employment-composition tax because many jobs are not subject to the penalty.[25] The penalty is not an entirely hidden tax: employers are already complaining about it (Graham 2014), and budget forecasters have quantified the government revenue that may be obtained from the penalty (Congressional Budget Office 2012c). But three aspects of the penalty are frequently ignored, even though they also contribute to the size of the employment tax created by the ACA. First, unlike employee wages and benefits, the penalty is not deductible for business income tax purposes; the salary equivalent of a $2,000 penalty is about $3,046.[26]

Second, the exemption of small firms creates a number of employers who do not pay a penalty but nonetheless face an employment tax because they would be heavily penalized for hiring one more full-time worker. For example, an employer with 49 full-time employees and no part-time employees would pay no penalty by falling short of the law's large employer threshold, whereas an employer with 50 full-time employees and no part-time employees would pay $40,000 in penalties per year. In effect, the fiftieth employee-year costs $40,000 more with the ACA than it would without it. As long as the employer restrains hiring to remain below the threshold of 50, the $40,000 hiring disincentive does not appear as government revenue even though it affects the labor market.

Third, the employer penalty puts new administrative burdens on nonpenalized employers because they must prove they are exempt. Penalized employers also have to prove they calculated their penalty correctly, including proper classification of part-time employees and new hires. The administrative burdens on employers are large enough that the Obama administration twice delayed the implementation of the employer penalty, and with its second delay it noted the disproportionate burden put on smaller employers (U.S. Department of Treasury 2014). This is why it is a mistake to assume that the employer penalty will not reduce the demand for labor among employers not paying it.

As of the time of my writing, the federal government has not collected any penalties on employers for failing to offer coverage. This book therefore examines the consequences of at least two versions of the ACA: one with a fully enforced employer penalty and another without any employer penalty.

Employers that do offer health coverage to their employees can still be penalized as a result of the ACA. For every employee for whom the employer's coverage is not affordable and who receives exchange subsidies,[27] the employer owes $3,000 (plus health cost inflation after 2014) per year.[28] The $3,000 penalty is another tax on employment created by the ACA, but so far I have only briefly examined its effects on the composition of employment (chapter 7) and do not yet have an estimate of its effects on the total amount of employment.

A second possible penalty on employers that offer coverage is the longstanding excise tax on employer health plans that are not compliant with federal rules. The amount of the penalty is $100 per day per person affected if the federal government determines that the employer intended to violate the rules.[29] The excise tax is not new, but avoiding it is more complicated because of the ACA's new restrictions on employer health plan characteristics. I doubt that many employers will pay the excise tax, but employers are spending resources on consultants, attorneys, and accountants, and distorting their benefit offerings in order to make sure they are not liable for the excise tax (Troy and Wilson 2014). The compliance costs created by the ACA are another hidden tax on employment, but I have not yet been able to quantify their economic significance separate from the ACA's monetary employer penalties.

C. The Individual Mandate

The ACA requires individuals to get coverage, pay a penalty, or receive a hardship exemption. The penalty is administered as part of the federal personal income tax return, and its amount is the maximum of a $695 per uninsured household member (uninsured children count half and the total uninsured is capped at three), indexed to inflation, or 2.5 percent of household income.[30]

As with the employer penalty, the individual mandate penalty is not entirely hidden, but its exemptions serve as additional hidden taxes on income and employment. Families below the income threshold applicable in their state are not liable for the individual penalty, which means the individual mandate penalty is a new tax on earning above the threshold. For example, in many states the threshold is 133 percent of the poverty line, which means that a childless, able-bodied, and uninsured couple would pay $1,390 more tax for crossing the threshold than they would without the ACA.[31]

Being laid off from a job may also be classified as a hardship and therefore an exempting event. In this case, the ACA provides a new kind of assistance when an uninsured person experiences unemployment: relief from the individual mandate penalty. Like unemployment insurance itself, tax assistance for the unemployed amounts to a hidden tax on employment.

Although the ACA precludes the Internal Revenue Service from criminally prosecuting taxpayers who refuse to pay the individual mandate, it is a mistake to assume that people will not pay it or will otherwise fail to respond to its incentives. After all, banks and other private-sector creditors cannot criminally prosecute debtors, yet they still manage to collect from most of their borrowers. The IRS can withhold the individual mandate penalty from tax refunds and add penalties and interest. They may also establish a statutory lien against the delinquent taxpayer's property so that, should the property be sold, sales proceeds can go toward paying the IRS.[32]

D. Medicaid Expansions

Medicaid is a longstanding health insurance program for the poor, and it is essentially free for its participants. Income eligibility limits are set by states; in 2012 they averaged 84 percent of the poverty line for working parents and somewhat less for jobless parents.[33] Many states also impose asset limits (that is, families with more than a few thousand dollars in assets cannot participate even if they have no income), especially for adult participants. Beginning in 2014, the ACA expands Medicaid participation by raising (in participating states) the income threshold for adult eligibility to 133 percent of the poverty line and reducing barriers to participation.

The new income thresholds for Medicaid create a complicated system of subsidies for families near but above the poverty line because exchange subsidies are supposed to be withheld from persons who are eligible for their state's Medicaid program even though they may have a calendar year income above the poverty line and thereby satisfying the income criteria for exchange coverage.[34] To make matters more complicated, the exchange subsidies and Medicaid use different income concepts. A family's income satisfies Medicaid eligibility criteria if it falls below the threshold for just part of the year (in principle, participation would be limited to that part of the year), whereas, as noted above, exchange subsidies are based on the entire calendar year's income. A family could have calendar year income below the poverty line but for parts of the year have income above its state Medicaid threshold and for that part of the year fail to be eligible for either Medicaid or exchange subsidies. Or it could have calendar year income above the poverty line and above its state's Medicaid threshold but have income during part of the year below the latter and therefore be eligible for Medicaid during part of the year and for exchange subsidies for the rest of the year.

Unless noted otherwise, the analysis in this book assumes that Medicaid eligibility does not prevent receipt of exchange subsidies. This simplifies the analysis and, for several reasons, may be a pretty good approximation to actual practice, especially for purposes of aggregate analysis. First of all, the vast majority of people in families satisfying the income-eligibility criteria for exchange subsidies are not Medicaid eligible. Second, many of the states are not raising their Medicaid income threshold. Third, the ACA has no mechanism for measuring the dynamics of family income within the calendar year and thereby identifying the parts of the year in which exchange subsidies should be withheld from a participating family. Fourth, Medicaid-eligible participants have a three-month period (or more) during which they can continue exchange coverage while they prepare a Medicaid application (recall endnote 17). Fifth, recall that the cost-sharing subsidies and advance premium credits are based on reasonable expectations at the time of enrollment of what family income will be during the coverage year. The cost-sharing subsidies cannot be recovered if coverage year income ultimately proves to be outside the eligible income range. At most, $600 of the premium assistance could be recovered if family income ultimately proved to be below the state's Medicaid threshold.[35]

My assumption about the overlap between Medicaid and exchange subsidies could be significant for the purposes of studying specific groups with a large fraction of its members having incomes between 100 and 133 percent of the poverty line. I also note in chapter 7 how this assumption affects interpretation of my results for the impact of the ACA on the composition of insurance coverage.

The ACA also reduces barriers to participation among persons already eligible. The website www.healthcare.gov is intended to quickly show people whether they are eligible for Medicaid and facilitate their enrollment; healthcare.gov will not be asset-testing applicants, and states will be encouraged to waive asset tests too.

E. Insurer Risk-Mitigation Provisions

Three provisions of the ACA subsidize sellers on the exchanges, and the subsidies result in lower prices for exchange participants. The provisions are a transitional reinsurance program, transitional risk corridors, and a permanent risk-adjustment program. To some degree the programs tax employer plans in order to subsidize exchange plans.[36]

By redistributing funds from employer plan participants to exchange plan participants, the risk-mitigation programs are, like the premium tax credits, a hidden employment tax on people whose participation in employer versus exchange plans is linked to their employment status. Unlike the premium tax credits, the employment tax hidden in the risk-mitigation programs does not vary with family income.

The amount of the hidden tax is likely small, except perhaps in the first year or two of the exchange plans. The exchange plans' prices for coverage year 2014 appear to be less than the prices of comparable employer plans,[37] in part because the federal government was encouraging insurers (e.g., with promises of compensation for losses) to price low as the exchanges were first coming on line. For this reason, the exchange subsidies are, perhaps temporarily, not limited to the means-tested premium tax credits and cost-sharing subsidies.

The ACA also included a temporary program that subsidized employer health plans on the basis of claims by their early retirees. The program spent about $5 billion until it ran out of funds at the end of 2011 (Centers for Medicare and Medicaid Services 2012). While it lasted, the program may have encouraged early retirement.

F. Medicare Tax Hikes

Before the ACA, the Medicare tax was entirely a payroll tax of 1.45 percent from every employer and employee. The ACA raised the rate on earned income above $200,000 per year ($250,000 for married couples) by 0.9 percentage points (U.S. Internal Revenue Service 2013c). The ACA also created a 3.8 percent Medicare tax on investment income (dividends, interest, and capital gains) earned by individuals, estates, and trusts with annual income (earned plus unearned) above essentially the same thresholds.[38] The investment income subject to the tax is after corporate taxes (i.e., corporations are not subject to the tax but their shareholders likely are) and after the taxpayer pays other allowed investment expenses.

The marginal tax rate on earnings created by these two provisions is zero for the roughly 98 percent of workers with income below the threshold, although the size of this group will fall over time because the thresholds are not indexed to inflation. For the remaining workers, the marginal tax rate is 0.9 percent, 3.8 percent, or 4.7 percent,[39] which means the Medicare rate increase averages (across workers) less than 0.1 percentage points. As shown in the following chapters, this increase is an order—maybe two orders—of magnitude less than the increases associated with the ACA's other hidden taxes.

Although the vast majority of workers will not pay the new Medicare taxes, their productivity and wages may be affected because the new taxes discourage capital accumulation. This and other productivity effects of the ACA are examined in chapter 8.

G. The Cadillac Tax

The ACA creates an excise tax on high-cost—aka "Cadillac"—employer health plans, defined to be plans with premiums (employer and employee combined) exceeding certain thresholds. The tax is scheduled to take effect in 2018, and the amount is 40 percent of the difference between plan premiums and the legislated thresholds. Cadillac tax payments are not deductible for business income tax purposes. In other words, this is a tax on employer plans that are deemed to be too expensive, and it is intended to discourage employers from providing coverage that is too broad and too generous.

Because the Cadillac tax is a tax on employer plans, it is a tax on the types of employment associated with those plans. It therefore reduces total employment and changes the composition of employment, to a degree that depends on the amount of the tax and the fraction of workers whose plans are subject to it.

If the tax had been imposed immediately on passage of the law, it would have directly affected 5 percent or fewer of employer health plans and directly affected the compensation of an even lesser percentage of workers.[40] The percentage of plans that owe the tax will likely remain in single digits into the 2020s (Egan 2013). The CBO projects that it will collect about $11 billion per year in 2020, or less than 0.1 percent of aggregate employee compensation (Congressional Budget Office 2013). For this reason alone, the aggregate employment effects of the Cadillac tax will be one or two orders of magnitude less than the rest of the provisions examined in this book, at least for the next decade or so.

Moreover, it was not an accident that the Cadillac tax was delayed more than any other provision of the law. The Cadillac tax upsets powerful interest groups without promising much revenue (Piotrowski 2013). If Congress were to repeal it or the administration neglect to fully enforce it, the Cadillac tax provision would still have served an important political purpose: helping supporters point to a part of the ACA that may reduce excessive health spending without actually requiring persons engaged in such spending to change their behavior or supply additional funds to the Treasury. In this scenario, the Cadillac tax may be entirely a political phenomenon with no economic consequences aside from its contribution to the law's initial political successes.

H. The Medical Device Tax

The ACA creates a 2.3 percent tax on the sales of certain medical devices (U.S. Internal Revenue Service 2013a). As a sales tax, it distorts labor supply by reducing the purchasing power of wages and salaries. As a sales tax on selected items, it affects productivity by distorting the composition of goods and services sold.

However, the overwhelming majority of the items purchased by consumers are not subject to the medical device tax, and the rate of the tax is not all that high as sales taxes go. For these reasons, the CBO expects the tax to obtain about one-quarter of the revenue that would be obtained by the Cadillac tax (if enforced), which puts its aggregate importance two orders of magnitude less than the provisions examined in the rest of this book.

I. Uncompensated Care

The uninsured sometimes receive uncompensated care from health providers, and the amount of uncompensated care is likely based on the patient's income. To the extent that the ACA reduces reliance on uncompensated care (Goolsbee 2011, oral testimony at 77:45), it may reduce the implicit income tax associated with it. In other words, parts of the ACA help reduce longstanding hidden taxes. This tax is quantified in chapter 5.

J. Health Insurance "Waste"

Much health spending in the United States is said to be wasteful (Emanuel and Fuchs 2008). Baicker and Chandra (2006) point to medical malpractice payments, some of which they interpret as hidden taxes paid by employers and employees via their health plans.[41] Using data by state for the years 1996–2002, they find that medical malpractice payments increase health insurance premiums, reduce employment, and lower employee cash compensation. These results suggest that a national health reform that reduced malpractice payments might increase employment by reducing the hidden tax created by those payments.

However, the ACA does not legislate changes to malpractice payments. It merely states that "health care reform presents an opportunity to address issues related to medical malpractice and medical liability insurance." These words alone cannot create jobs or reduce health insurance premiums.[42]

Cutting health insurance premiums can reduce employment if the premium cuts occur by eliminating the kinds of health spending that employees value,[43] even if this spending were excessive from a social point of view, but employees value the excess because it helps them avoid income and payroll taxes. Taxes on employers that induce them to cut the least valuable health spending—like the Cadillac tax—will not create jobs, despite their effect on health insurance premiums, because the taxes add to the burden on employers. Excise taxes on employer health plans have many of the same characteristics of the malpractice payments studied by Baicker and Chandra (see also the Cadillac tax section above).

Cutting medical spending among persons who do not obtain health insurance through an employer could increase employment by reducing both the prices charged by health providers and the attractiveness of health options available to nonworkers. The ACA does attempt to cut Medicare spending, but as noted above it enhances health options for nonelderly people and increases the number of people with health insurance.

David Cutler and Neeraj Sood (2010) claimed that "modernization aspects" of the ACA would cut wasteful health spending by employer plans and by this mechanism "boost employment by 250,000 to 400,000 per year" over the next decade. Almost 300 economists endorsed Cutler and Sood's estimate and warned Congress that repealing the ACA would result in the loss of all of these jobs (Cutler et al. 2011).

TABLE 2.1. Possible savings on employee health costs as a share of employee compensation

Private industries, 2011

Item	Amount	Units
Employer and employee premium payments	708	Billions of pre-tax dollars
Employer and employee premium payments	496	Billions of after-tax dollars
ESI employee out-of-pocket costs	145	Billions of after-tax dollars
Premiums and out-of-pocket costs combined	641	Billions of after-tax dollars
Compensation of employees	6,553	Billions of pre-tax dollars
Cost savings assumed to be offered by the ACA	32	Billions of after-tax dollars
Cost savings assumed to be offered by the ACA	0.49%	Percentage of compensation

Notes: Premium payments from CDC Table 119. Tax savings are assumed to be 30% of premium payments. Out-of-pocket costs for ESI plans are derived from premium payments assuming that the actuarial value of ESI plans average 83%. Cost savings are assumed to be 5% of premiums and out-of-pocket costs, which is Cutler and Sood's (2010) forecast of the savings that would be achieved by the ACA during its first five or six years.

The modernization aspects cited include reduced administrative costs, better coordination of care, and reductions in unused (but still costly) health-care capacity.

Aside from an incomplete analysis of the employer penalty, the Cutler and Sood study did not attempt to combine the ACA's modernization effects with the effects of the various hidden taxes noted above.[44] In other words, Cutler and Sood's modernization effects are at best an extra tax effect, akin to reducing medical malpractice payments, that should be added to the many tax effects listed above and examined throughout this book. Moreover, I suspect that Cutler and Sood have overestimated the modernization piece because, as mentioned above, the ACA also creates new administrative costs for employers, which is in part why the employer penalty has been delayed and why employer participation in the ACA's small business tax credit programs is so low.[45]

For the sake of argument, let's take Cutler and Sood's estimates at face value: that the ACA will reduce employer health costs by 5 percent within five or six years of the passage of the law. Table 2.1 puts those cost savings in a labor market perspective. The first row of the table is the total amount of premiums paid in the private sector for employer-provided health insurance, in billions of dollars for the most recent year available (2011). The second row is the net cost of those premiums, accounting for the fact that they generate payroll and personal income tax savings for employees.[46] The third row is an estimate of out-of-pocket costs incurred by participants in health insurance plans sponsored by private sector employers.[47] The next row combines the two above to find that out-of-pocket and premium costs together, net of tax savings, totaled $641 billion.

If employees could have saved 5 percent of their health expenses— that's how much Cutler and Sood say the ACA will be reducing health expenses by 2015—they would have been saved $32 billion. In order to view this amount from the perspective of the entire labor market, I divide it by total labor compensation in private industries in 2011 and find that it is less than 0.5 percent.[48] (This kind of comparison is done throughout the book for assessing the aggregate significance of the ACA's provisions.)

In the extreme case that none of the $32 billion of health spending would be perceived by employees as reduced health benefits or as re- duced convenience *and* that the ACA was not creating any health sav- ings for nonelderly people who are not covered by employer-sponsored health insurance, the ACA's health costs savings represented by the $32 billion would have many of the effects of cutting hidden labor in- come taxes by about 0.5 percentage points.[49] For the many reasons cited above, a more reasonable tax equivalent of the ACA's moderni- zation provisions is less than 0.5 percentage points, so chapter 9 as- sumes that they are equivalent to an earnings tax cut of 0.3 percentage points. Because the remainder of the ACA contains taxes in the other direction that are collectively at least an order of magnitude greater, I ultimately conclude that the claim that the ACA would create jobs at a rate of "250,000 to 400,000 annually over the next decade" (Cutler et al. 2011) is wholly inaccurate because it focuses on and exaggerates the ACA's modernization provisions without adequate attention to its many other provisions.

K. Other Taxes

The ACA contains other provisions, ranging from small business tax credits to a tax on indoor tanning services, that have the economic characteristics of taxes. The aggregate economic significance of these provisions is even less than the smaller of the provisions noted above.

Of these, the ACA's small business tax credits are potentially the most interesting. They subsidize employers, but they also discourage employers from hiring because the credit is withdrawn if employment exceeds the threshold. The credits also encourage employers to keep wages low because some of the credits are withdrawn as employee pay rises. All of these distortions reduce productivity. Judging from employer participation so far, one might guess that the administrative burdens of the tax credit programs are high. It would be surprising if the small business tax credits amounted to more than $1 billion a year.

L. Cuts to Medicare and Medicaid Spending

The ACA also includes cuts to Medicare and Medicaid spending that help pay for the ACA (Congressional Budget Office 2012c). Under the ACA, the Medicare program continues to furnish the same benefits but reduces the rate of growth of the program's payments to providers (Mercer 2014), especially physicians and hospitals. Because most of the scheduled cuts are in the distant future, and the Office of the Actuary at the Centers for Medicare and Medicaid Services expects "that Congress would find it necessary to legislatively override or otherwise modify the reductions in the future to ensure that Medicare beneficiaries continue to have access to health care services," the scheduled Medicare and Medicaid spending cuts are not included in my analysis except to the extent that they reduce health insurance costs for nonpoor nonelderly people (Center for Medicare and Medicaid Services, Office of the Actuary 2011, p. 1).

In theory, the amount and composition of government purchases may have a long-term "income effect" on aggregate employment and work hours that offsets the substitution effect of the taxes levied to finance them. However, this possibility is not particularly applicable to the ACA. For one, the government spending in the ACA is primarily transfers, which have less aggregate income effect because the transfers increase income for the recipients but decrease income for taxpayers.[50] Moreover, by (purportedly) cutting Medicare and Medicaid spending rather than increasing it, the law's aggregate income effect may well be in the direction of less work, which would only reinforce the substitution effects emphasized in this book.

If the federal medical spending cuts in the ACA are insufficient to fund the exchange subsidies (either because the cuts are ultimately less than expected, or the exchange subsidies more than expected), additional taxes will someday be needed. This book does not estimate the economic impact of those additional taxes.

M. Conclusions

Even a brief perusal of the ACA, with an eye toward incentives, begins to reveal how the law's financing of expanded coverage is not as different from Western European financing as it would first appear. In Western Europe, practically all citizens are entitled to health assistance, but those who work and earn more pay extra for that assistance in the form of higher taxes, especially health insurance payroll taxes. Under the ACA, those who work and earn more usually receive less assistance, if any.

With that said, the ACA is more complex than a payroll tax. In percentage terms, some of the ACA's highest implicit tax rates fall on low-income households. The ACA also has tax effects in multiple directions and effects that vary according to family situation. As a result, quantitative analysis is needed even to determine the direction of some of the law's effects, and to understand how the ACA's financing is different from a payroll tax. This chapter explains why a number of the ACA's taxes—like the Cadillac tax, the medical device tax, the tanning services tax, and the small business tax credits—might affect aggregate employment or productivity but are not large enough for the effects to be noticeable in aggregate data.

A number of subsidies are attached to the new health insurance marketplaces. The exchange subsidies contain hidden and potentially large taxes on income and, especially, employment because subsidies are not available to most workers as a consequence of their employment situation. The well-known employer penalty is also an employment tax and is larger than it first appears. The ACA's lesser-known employer penalties further add to the hidden employment tax created by the employer mandate. The individual mandate has characteristics of employment and income taxes. The ACA's additions to Medicare taxes are additions to both the rate of earnings and capital income

TABLE 2.2. Approaches to quantitative labor market modeling in this book

ACA provision	SD/NGM model	Workweeks model	Skills and sectors model
Employer shared responsibility penalty	x	x	x
Income taxes implicit in the exchange subsidies	x	x	x
Employment taxes implicit in the exchange subsidies	x	x	x
Reconciliation of advance premium credits	x	x	
Individual mandate relief	x		x
Implicit taxation of unemployment benefits	x	x	
Move off implicit uncompensated care tax	x	x	
HI subsidies stop at the poverty line	x		
Medicaid expansions for the poor	x		
Two Medicare surtaxes	x		
Health cost containment	x		

Note: SD/NGM is the supply and demand/neoclassical growth model.

taxation, but most workers will primarily experience the capital income tax component through its negative effect on capital accumulation and worker productivity (chapter 9).

Although the ACA probably eases some longstanding but hidden income taxes, the Western European comparison already provides an educated guess as to the general direction of the combined effects of these taxes: less employment and less income. The next step is to carefully quantify the magnitude of the ACA's various taxes from the perspective of decisions about employment, income, and the composition of activity. Chapters 3, 5, and 7 take that step.

Table 2.2 offers an overview of how this book quantifies the ACA's taxes and their economic effects. Each row is an ACA provision related to labor supply or labor demand; many of them were introduced above, and others are introduced in subsequent chapters. Each column refers to an economic model used in the book to quantify the combined economic effects of the ACA provisions. Moving from left to right, the models allow for increasingly detailed (less aggregated) predictions by type of worker and type of job. The most aggregate model is the "supply and demand" or "neoclassical growth model" (chapter 9), which has just two or three labor market outcomes that it can track: aggregate work hours per capita and two measures of wages. But it has something to say about dynamics and how the labor taxes affect consumption, savings, and capital accumulation. Another advantage of the aggregate model is that it can readily consider all of the ACA provisions I've examined.

The second model is a workweeks model (chapter 6) that makes predictions for the decomposition of aggregate hours between weekly employment and hours per week, and for the cross-sectional distribution of those variables. The third model (chapters 7 and 8) differentiates workers by skill and employers by sector. Of the three models, this is the only one with much of interest to say about productivity, sectors, or the extent of insurance coverage. But it deals with only the four largest of the dozen components of the ACA.

Appendix 2.1: International Comparisons of Health Insurance Payroll Tax Rates

In order to examine the degree to which workers in the major Western European countries pay different rates of payroll tax for health insurance than American workers do, I used the Social Security Administration's standardized description (2010, and previous issues) of the financing of public health insurance programs. Because all of the countries also use payroll taxes to pay for (expensive) old age pension programs, I eliminated countries that do not earmark part of their payroll tax for medical benefits, sickness benefits, or maternity benefits.[51] A number of countries have a health payroll tax that is separate from the payroll tax for old age pensions, but still shared between medical benefits and cash benefits that are paid to persons with qualifying health conditions. Arguably the cash benefits should be considered too, because those receiving the cash assistance use it to help pay for medical expenses. However, to be conservative as to the magnitude of Western European health payroll tax rates, I take the medical part of the payroll tax rate to be 0.81 times the combined rate for medical and cash-sickness benefits; 0.81 is the average share among Belgium, Greece, and Luxembourg, which earmark a specific component of the combined payroll tax for medical benefits as opposed to cash-sickness benefits.

Countries also differ in terms of the amount and types of payroll tax they levy on employers rather than employees. The overall burden of payroll taxes cannot be measured according to the sum of the employer and employee rates because the employer payroll tax is excluded from the base for the employee payroll tax (Barro and Sahasakul 1986). I have therefore converted each country's employee and employer payroll taxes into an employee-equivalent rate that would have the same burden if there were no employer payroll tax rates. The formula for the medical benefit component τ_{eq} of the employee-equivalent payroll tax rate is:

(2.1)
$$\tau_{eq} = \frac{1 - \tau_{other}}{1 + t_{other}} - \frac{1 - \tau_{other} - \tau_{med}}{1 + t_{other} + t_{med}}$$

where t and τ denote actual employer and employee rates, respectively, and subscripts denote the earmarking (medical benefits versus all other programs). I also doubled Finland's medical payroll tax rate because Social Security Administration (2010) indicates that the general revenue pays for half of the medical benefits.[52] Note that τ_{eq} would simply be the employee medical payroll tax rate if there were no employer payroll taxes (i.e., all of the t's were zero). The U.S. employee equivalent rate is 2.54 percent, reflecting the employer and employee Medicare tax rates (both 1.45 percent before conversion to employee-equivalent) and their interaction with the other payroll tax rates.

Table 2.3 shows the results. The eight Western European countries have an average rate of 6.8, and every one of them has a higher rate

TABLE 2.3. Payroll taxes earmarked for medical benefits in the U.S. and Western Europe, 2010

Country	Medical benefits payroll tax rate, employee equivalent
U.S. (before the ACA)	2.5
Austria	4.2
Luxembourg	4.4
Greece	4.5
Belgium	5.1
Finland	5.3
France	6.4
Germany	9.0
Netherlands	15.2
Western Europe average	6.8

Note: In addition, Switzerland has an individual mandate with premiums capped at 8 percent of income.

than the United States did before the ACA. Switzerland, which was not included among the eight, requires individuals to buy their own insurance but caps the premium at 8 percent of their income (premium amounts above the cap are paid by the government). In effect, the Swiss are paying for their health coverage with an 8 percent income tax up to a cap equal to the full price of health insurance, plus whatever taxes are needed to pay for the premium subsidies.

3 | Some Unpleasant Penalty Arithmetic

Most of the taxation hidden in the ACA relates to its exchange subsidies or employer penalties. In order to measure the total amount of hidden taxation, this chapter begins by quantifying the economic significance of the employer penalty. Chapter 4 measures the larger but more complicated taxes hidden in the exchange subsidies.

People and businesses will adjust their behavior in response to the ACA's hidden taxes, but analysis of the behavioral responses is deliberately deferred until chapters 6 through 10. The purpose here and in chapter 4 is to first assess the magnitude of the hidden taxes holding behavior constant, so that later chapters can use that magnitude to predict the law's likely impacts on work schedules, wages, output, and so on.

Much of the measurement of the total full-time employment tax associated with the employer penalty for not offering coverage—both its visible and its hidden parts—is just a matter of simple multiplication and division. The last part of the chapter uses a household survey to estimate the number and types of workers who will be exposed to this tax, especially in its most prohibitive forms. The results begin to show how much the employer penalty interferes with the operation of the labor market.[1]

A. Penalties Are More Expensive Than They First Appear

The (annualized) amount of the penalty on employers for failing to provide any coverage is $2,000 per full-time employee, indexed for health cost inflation after 2014. As noted in chapter 2, the penalty amount is not deductible for the purposes of calculating the employer's taxable business income.[2] Table 3.1 shows how this makes the penalty more expensive to an employer. Each row of the table tracks an employer expense. The first column looks at an employer paying a $2,000 employer penalty, with no change in employee salaries. Two zeros appear at the bottom of the penalty column because the penalty payment does not affect the employer's payroll or business income tax.

TABLE 3.1. The salary equivalent of the employer penalty

A $2,000 ACA penalty costs no less than raising salaries by $3,046

	Scenario:		
Expense items	Penalty imposed	Salary raised	
ACA penalty	2,000	0	
Salaries	0	3,046	
Payroll tax	0	233	7.65% rate
Business income taxes	0	−1,279	39% rate
Net result for employer expenses including taxes:	$2,000	$2,000	

The second column looks at an employer who is, hypothetically, forced to raise salaries by $3,046. Because the employer owes payroll tax on salaries, but not on employer penalties, the second column shows that the employer payroll tax liability increases by $233, which is 7.65 percent of the salary increase. Both salaries and employer payroll taxes are deductible from business income for the purpose of determining business income tax, which at a 39 percent business income tax rate saves $1,279 in business income taxes.[3] Altogether, the $3,046 salary increase costs the same as a $2,000 employer penalty. In other words, from an employer's point of view, a $3,046 salary increase is no more expensive than a $2,000 ACA penalty.

B. Penalties Will Grow Faster Than Salaries

By law, the employer penalty is indexed to health cost inflation. Specifically, in every year after 2014, the annualized employer penalty per full-time employee must exceed $2,000 by a percentage equal to the "premium adjustment percentage," which the ACA describes as "the percentage (if any) by which the average per capita premium for health insurance coverage in the United States for the preceding calendar year (as estimated by the Secretary no later than October 1 of such preceding calendar year) exceeds such average per capita premium for 2013 (as determined by the Secretary)."[4] The "Secretary" refers to the secretary of the Department of Health and Human Services. In other words, in order for the employer penalties to be set for years 2015 and beyond, the ACA directs the secretary to measure average per capita premiums for health insurance coverage and from her measurements calculate a premium adjustment percentage. When it comes to the premium adjustment percentage applicable to 2015 employer penalties, the ACA says that the secretary must compare 2014 premiums to 2013 premiums because 2014 is the calendar year preceding 2015.

Even without measurements, basic economics gives us some idea of what probably happened to the average per capita premium for health insurance coverage after 2013: it increased sharply because 2014 was the year when the ACA began to require health plans to provide a wider range of benefits. Early data confirmed this prediction: the ehealth .com price index was about 40 percent greater during the first quarter of 2014 than it was for calendar year 2013. If the premium adjustment percentage were set to 40 percent on the basis of the ehealth.com data, the $2,000 employer penalty would increase to more than $2,700 in one year! However, according to my reading of the secretary's final rule in the March 11, 2014 Federal Register, the secretary will use her discretion to determine and update methodologies in order to prevent any sharp premium change after 2013 from resulting in a large premium adjustment percentage for any year subsequent to 2014.[5] She has already determined that the premium adjustment percentage applicable to 2015 employer penalties is the remarkably precise 4.213431463.

The labor market significance of the employer penalty depends on its magnitude relative to hourly employer costs, which increased about 2 percent over the past year.[6] In other words, the first year of indexing of the employer penalty to health inflation has increased it about 2.2 percent more than employer costs because 2.2 is the 4.2 premium adjustment percentage minus 2.0 percent employer cost growth. I assume that future premium adjustment percentages will coincide with hourly employer cost inflation plus 1.6 percentage points, which is the historical average gap between premium inflation and hourly employer cost inflation. As a result of these assumptions, I estimate that the salary equivalent of the employer penalty (for the purpose of comparing to 2014 salaries) will be $3,113 in 2015, $3,163 in 2016, and $3,370 in 2020. Notice that I am using the secretary's 2015 premium adjustment percentage for my estimates and, from the above, assume that the premium adjustment percentages for 2016 and beyond will never reflect the sharp jump in premiums that occurred after 2013 as the ACA began to require plans to provide a wider range of benefits.

These dollar amounts, and all of the other dollar amounts in this book, are in 2014 dollars (the occasional exception is explicitly noted), even though most of the economic consequences of interest will occur in 2015 and beyond.[7] I take this approach because, as of the time of writing, I do not know the rates of wage and price inflation after 2014. Moreover, these two inflation rates are hardly relevant for my purposes because economic consequences typically depend on the various ratios of dollar amounts, such as the ratio of employer penalty to wages or the ratio of income to the poverty line.[8] For example, my estimates imply that a 2014 employer whose employee's wages follow the national average over the next two years will experience the employer penalty in 2016 as if it were an increase in salaries equal to $3,163 plus the national average rate of wage growth.

C. Penalties Will Apply to Relatively Low-Wage Workers

It is also helpful to compare the dollar amount of the employer penalty to the hourly compensation of the employees of firms that might pay it. Dividing the two is an estimate of the number of hours per week that a worker's efforts are, in effect, paying for the ACA's employer penalty rather than obtaining income for the worker. Figure 3.1 shows the results for hourly compensation ranging from the federal minimum wage of $7.25 per hour to $23 per hour. The weekly work-hour equivalents of the employer penalty are measured on the left-hand axis. Figure 3.1 has a red vertical dotted line at the minimum wage. The intersection of the minimum wage line with the black curve shows that a minimum-wage worker has to work more than eight hours per week for 52 weeks in 2015 just to earn the amount of income that would pay for the $3,113 penalty an employer would owe in that year for having a worker on the full-time payroll.[9] The intersection with the red curve shows that a minimum-wage worker would have to work almost 10 hours per week to generate income equivalent to the 2025 employer penalty.

Most workers earn more than the minimum wage. The black vertical dashed line is drawn in figure 3.1 at the median hourly wage among workers whose usual work schedule is at least 30 hours per week and who are not likely to work for an employer offering coverage: about

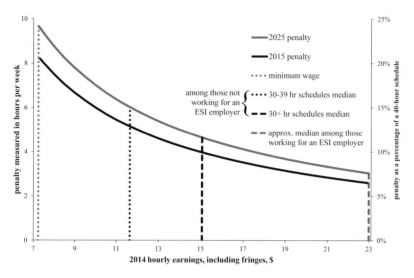

FIGURE 3.1. The work hours equivalent of the employer penalty. After 2015, the penalty is assumed to grow 1.6 percent per year in excess of wages.

$15.[10] At that wage, it takes four hours of work per week, 52 weeks per year, to obtain income equivalent to the $3,113 employer penalty in 2015. To put it another way, half of the full-time workers at penalized employers earn less than $15 per hour and would each have to work at least four hours per week for free in order to compensate his employer for the penalty owed because of his employment. The point here is not that the employer penalty is the employee's "fault"; it's just to gauge the magnitude of the employer penalty from the perspective of the parts of the labor market where the penalties will accrue.

Note that workers likely to work for penalized employers earn less than workers at employers offering coverage.[11] The median worker in the latter group has hourly earnings of about $21, not including employer-paid health insurance premiums. This worker's hourly earnings including employer premiums is therefore about $23, which is displayed as the red vertical dashed line at the right edge of figure 3.1. The gap between the two dashed lines in figure 3.1 illustrates how the full-time workers not offered coverage have less earnings potential than those offered coverage, which makes the $3,113 employer penalty more significant to the former group.

As explained further in chapter 4, behavioral responses to the penalty may be most noticeable among workers who would otherwise have work schedules between 30 and 39 hours per week, because for them reducing weekly hours to 29 (and thereby saving their employer a penalty) is a relatively small adjustment. The median hourly wage among persons (1) working for employers not offering coverage and (2) with schedules in that range is less than $12. The black dotted vertical line in figure 3.1 shows that a worker earning this median wage needs 5.1 hours per week to obtain the income equivalent to the 2015 penalty.

In order to help readers compare the significance of the employer penalty to the more familiar payroll taxes, the right-hand axis expresses the hours equivalent of the penalty as a percentage of 40 hours. This can be interpreted as the amount of the penalty as a fraction of full-time earnings at the hourly rate measured on the horizontal axis. The 2025 penalty is, for example, a lot like a 24 percent tax on the earnings of a minimum-wage worker and a 15 percent tax on the earnings of the median worker without employer-sponsored insurance coverage (hereafter, ESI) and a 30–39-hour schedule. The penalty is on top of all of the other taxes that employers and employees have to pay.

D. The Disturbing Distribution of Marginal Penalties

Large employers not offering coverage and having more than 30 full-time employees in 2016 will, as a consequence of the employer penalty, owe the salary equivalent of an additional $3,163 per year for every full-time employee they add to their payroll, and save an additional $3,163 per year for every full-time employee they remove from their payroll. But the status of being a large employer itself depends on the number of employees. If the employer has only full-time employees, then the salary equivalent of her penalty is $63,261 if she has 50 employees but only zero if she has 49 employees. In other words, that 50th employee costs her $63,261 plus the employee's normal salary and benefits![12]

Employers at the large-employer threshold have a different penalty associated with reducing full-time employment than with increasing it. For example, a 50-employee firm (all full time) that eliminates a full-time employee saves the salary equivalent of $63,261 (that is, 20 penalties) but adds only $3,163 (just one penalty) by adding an employee. In this case, I refer to the marginal penalty cost of full-time employment

TABLE 3.2. The distribution of marginal penalty amounts among employees not offered coverage

Coverage year 2016. Dollar amounts in 2014 $.

Number of full-time employees	Penalties triggered by the marginal employee			Possible frequency distributions		
	Number	Amount		w/o ACA	w/ ACA	Average
<49	0	0		0.650	0.650	0.650
49	10	$31,630		0.033	0.094	0.063
50	10.5	$33,212		0.022	0	0.011
51+	1	$3,163		0.296	0.256	0.276
Employee-weighted average $ amount:				$2,684	$3,783	$3,233

Notes: Marginal penalties are the average of the penalties incurred from adding one employee and the penalties saved by subtracting one employee. The table assumes zero part-time employees and ignores the "look back" for determining large-employer status. The possible frequencies are employee-weighted and are for purposes of illustration.

to be the average of the two, which is $33,212 (10.5 penalties). By my definition, the marginal penalty cost of full-time employment is zero for employers that have 48 or fewer full-time employees (and no part-time employees), $31,630 for employers with 49 full-time employees (and no part-time employees), $33,212 for employers with 50 full-time employees (and no part-time employees), and $3,163 for employers with more than 50 full-time employees. These four possibilities are tabulated in the left half of table 3.2. The number of penalties triggered by the marginal employee is shown in the second column, and the dollar amount of the penalty triggered is shown in the third column.

For my purposes, it suffices to illustrate some of the possibilities, as I do in the right half of table 3.2. The fourth column is a rough guess as to the size distribution (among employers not offering coverage) without the ACA. Note that, without the ACA, my illustration has almost two-thirds of employees (and an even greater fraction of employers) with fewer than 49 employees and therefore zero marginal penalty. Nevertheless, a few employees work for firms just at the threshold where the marginal penalty is equivalent to more than $30,000 in salary. As a result, the average marginal penalty is, in salary terms, $2,684, when the four penalty possibilities are weighted by the employer size distribution without the ACA.

The average marginal penalty is likely even greater if the four penalty possibilities are weighted by the employer-size distribution with the ACA, because a few employers that would have 51-plus employees will deliberately reduce their employment in order to stay below the large-employer threshold and thereby put their marginal penalty amount at $31,360. The (salary equivalent of the) average marginal penalty amount using both frequency distributions is $3,233, which is similar to the $3,163 marginal penalty among employees working for firms with at least 51 employees. For this reason, this book assumes that all firms not offering coverage have the same average marginal penalty equal to $3,163, an assumption I interpret as an approximation to the actual and more complicated distribution of marginal penalty amounts.

Another way to reach the same conclusion is to examine the competitive pressures created by a marginal penalty structure like the one shown in table 3.2. The employers with a $3,163 marginal penalty can, in the labor market, outbid the employers with $30,000-plus marginal penalties because the former employers can expand indefinitely without further increasing their penalty rate. But the $0 marginal penalty employers cannot so easily outbid the $3,163 marginal penalty employers, because too much success at hiring will push the former group into large-employer status and thereby quite large penalty payments. This suggests, but does not prove, that the labor market equilibrium structure of wages will tend to reflect the $3,163 marginal penalty rather than either $0 or $30,000-plus. A full analysis of the consequences of the employer penalty requires both good data on the size distribution of employers and a more detailed understanding of the ability of the marketplace to adjust that distribution in response to incentives. I have neither, but I highly recommend the work by Trevor S. Gallen looking at the ACA and the size distribution of employers (Gallen 2013).

Table 3.2 pertains only to employees working for employers that do not offer coverage to their full-time employees. By all estimates, these employees are a minority of total employment. The CBO estimates that, in 2008, they were 27 percent of all workers (Congressional Budget Office 2007). Using Census Bureau data, Janicki (2013) estimates 29 percent for 2010. Using the Medical Expenditure Panel

Survey (MEPS), Crimmel (2012) estimates 15 percent for 2011. The simple average of these three is 24 percent,[13] which I take as my estimate of the percentage of workers before the ACA who were working for an employer that did not offer coverage.

Whatever the historical percentage, it is likely that at least a few employers will drop coverage because of the ACA or because of ongoing health cost trends. I therefore assume that 26 percent of workers are represented in table 3.2.

This is not to say that 26 percent of employees will generate a penalty for their employer. Many of the 26 percent will avoid a penalty by working part-time schedules. But for simplicity, I do assume that (1) 26 percent of employees generate a penalty for their employer only if they work 30-plus hours and (2) the penalty is uniform across employees (the $3,163 amount noted above).[14] As noted in the context of table 3.2, this overstates the marginal penalty faced by some workers and understates the penalty faced by others. For all of these reasons, the 26 percent estimate does not tell us the amount of revenue that the federal government may obtain from the penalty, but it does reveal the penalty's economic significance.

E. For Millions, Full-Time Work Will Pay Less Than Part-Time Work (Penalty Edition)

Part-time employees, defined to be anyone working fewer than 30 hours per week, are exempt from the employer penalty. Reducing employment (see above) or offering coverage (see chapter 6) are two alternatives for reducing or eliminating the penalty, but there's a third alternative: reducing the work schedules of full-time employees to 29 hours or fewer.

Take the minimum wage employee noted in figure 3.1, for whom the employer penalty is equivalent to more than eight hours of work per week. If the employee's weekly schedule without the penalty would be, say, 35 hours, then cutting hours to 29 costs the employee six hours for which he or she could be earning a wage but saves the employer a penalty equivalent to eight hours. To put it another way, the employer penalty taxes more than 100 percent of the work done by this minimum-wage employee beyond the twenty-ninth hour every week: the worker would earn less during hours 30 through 35 than the $61 weekly pen-alty that would be created by working those hours.[15]

Table 3.3 shows the same arithmetic for various other work sched-ules. If a penalized employer has a 30-hour work schedule, but for the ACA—and there are workers with 30-hour work schedules—clearly the employer should consider cutting the schedule to 29 in order to save the $61, unless the average employee were expected to produce more than $61 of value during that hour. On the basis of their hourly pay, a minimum-wage worker, or even a $50-per-hour worker, would not sat-isfy this criterion. Table 3.3 also shows that cutting 31-hour schedules would save $30 per hour cut, and cutting 32-hour schedules would save $20 per hour cut.

This ignores the work expenses such as commuting or child-care costs that an employee might save with a shorter work schedule. The next column of table 3.3 shows how the results are different with work expenses equal to $20 for every eight hours worked. In this case, even a 41-hour work schedule would, at minimum wage, be worth cutting down to 29 because the schedule cut would both avoid the penalty and reduce weekly work expenses.

Two criteria therefore tell us when the privilege of working a full-time schedule will earn this employee less than it will cost her em-ployer in penalties: (1) employer not offering ESI, and (2) average hourly wages (net of work expenses) less than the amount shown in table 3.3 corresponding to usual weekly hours.[16] Chapter 7 answers the question of whether, in this "100 percent tax" situation, the employer avoids the penalty by paying the worker to accept a 29-hour schedule, or the employee, in effect, is forced to accept a 29-hour schedule be-cause she cannot sensibly compensate her employer for the penalty triggered by her full-time work. The purpose of the remainder of this chapter is just to estimate the number of full-time workers for whom a 29-hour schedule could be a win-win proposition as compared to their usual schedule before the ACA, as it is for the minimum-wage worker on a 35-hour schedule for an employer subject to penalties.

The remaining columns of table 3.3 estimate the number of workers whose usual work schedules in 2011 were at least 30 hours per week and who satisfy criteria (1) and (2) above, with average hourly wage mea-sured for calendar year 2011 and converted to 2014 dollars, under two

TABLE 3.3. Penalized employees who would make more by working less

Calendar year 2016. Dollar amounts in 2014 dollars.

Weekly work hours but for the penalty	Weekly penalty and work expenses, per hour worked past 29		Number of penalized workers with hourly earnings at or below:	
	Penalty only	Penalty + work expense	Penalty only	Penalty + work expense
30	$61	$63	1,862,296	1,863,952
31	$30	$33	7,898	8,889
32	$20	$23	489,338	519,837
33	$15	$18	40,343	43,696
34	$12	$15	40,558	51,568
35	$10	$13	1,026,073	1,416,052
36	$9	$11	124,108	186,999
37	$8	$10	34,477	69,395
38	less than $7.25	$9	0	118,661
39		$9	0	15,757
40		$8	0	2,564,832
41		$8	0	3,074
42		less than $7.25	0	0
Total workers:			3,625,091	6,862,711
Aggregate weekly hours taxed 100+ percent:			11,011,276	43,709,880

Notes: The penalty is expressed as a salary equivalent. Work expenses are assumed to be $20 per 8 hours. Numbers of workers are national projections from the March 2012 CPS, and scaled for population growth through 2016 by a factor of 1.01^4. I assume that no workers have hourly earnings below $7.25.

TABLE 3.4. Propensity that the penalty fully erases the reward to full-time work

among persons working sometime during a calendar year			
Age	Men	Women	Both
Less than 25	0.091	0.102	0.096
25–34	0.043	0.062	0.052
35–44	0.026	0.050	0.037
45–54	0.021	0.041	0.031
55–64	0.019	0.033	0.026
65+	0.028	0.040	0.033
All ages	0.036	0.055	0.045

Notes: The reward to work is net of work expenses. The alternative to full-time work is assumed to be a 29-hour work schedule.

alternative assumptions about work expenses. The estimates from the March 2012 Current Population Survey (hereafter, CPS) are prepared in three steps. First, every employee in the CPS is assigned a probability of working for an employer that does not offer coverage (details given in appendix 3.1) so that it averages 26 percent in the entire sample of workers. Second, the probability is multiplied by the CPS health insurance weight in order to project 2012 national totals and then scaled by a factor of 1.01^4 to project 2016 national totals. Third, the resulting person count is summed across observations satisfying criteria (1) and (2) and reported in the right half of table 3.3.

Assuming that employees' hourly pay is equal to the hourly value that they create, the sum of the indicators is the number of workers in 2016 whose weekly hours could be cut to 29 without reducing the weekly value they create net of the employer penalty and work expenses. The sum ranges from 3.6 to 6.9 million, depending on the assumed work expenses.[17] If we count the number of hours subject to the 100 percent tax, rather than the number of workers, the total is up to 43.7 million hours per week.[18]

Table 3.4 displays the likelihood that workers of various characteristics experience the 100 percent tax in the form of the employer penalty. Female workers are more likely than male workers to experience the 100 percent tax because their weekly work schedules tend to be closer to 29 hours. The likelihood declines with age among nonelderly workers because average hourly earnings increase with age.

It is easy to see why the number of people facing a 100 percent tax in the form of the employer penalty is in the millions, rather than the hundreds of thousands, or even less. According to the CPS, there were about 5 million workers in 2011 with usual hours of exactly 30. If roughly 26 percent (the population average) of them work for an employer that did not offer coverage to full-time workers, then 1.3 of the 5 million will avoid an employer penalty by cutting hours to 29. If roughly 90 percent of workers earn less than $61 per hour, workers with 30-hour schedules alone contribute over a million workers to the totals shown in table 3.3.[19] The more exact amount shown at the top of the table accounts for the fact that the wage distribution among, and the types of jobs held by, 30-hour workers are different for the general population.

The results in tables 3.3 and 3.4 are affected by inaccuracies, if any, in the CPS measure of the usual weekly work schedule. For example, if a significant fraction of the workers reporting exactly 30 hours per week are really working 32 hours per week, then the tables may exaggerate the number of people whose hours beyond 30 will be taxed 100 percent by the employer penalty. On the other hand, if a significant fraction of the workers reporting exactly 40 hours per week (that's about half of the sample!) are really working 35 hours per week, then the tables may underestimate the number of people whose hours beyond 30 will be taxed 100 percent by the employer penalty. If the overall level of hours is overestimated by the CPS usual weekly hours measure, then I will have underestimated hourly wages and thereby exaggerated the number of people whose hours beyond 30 will be taxed 100 percent by the employer penalty.[20]

F. Conclusions

The employer penalty is significant in comparison to the wages of the workers whose employers will be penalized for having them on the payroll. First of all, the employer penalty is not deductible for the purposes of calculating the employer's taxable business income. As a result, a $2,000 employer penalty is more costly than $3,000 in additional employee salary. Second, the ACA indexes the employer penalty to health costs, which by all estimates will grow faster than wages; the employer penalty only becomes more important over time. Third, to judge from their market wages, essentially half of workers at firms not offering coverage would have to work, for free, at least four hours per week for 52 weeks per year—that is, at least 10 percent of a full-time full-year schedule—in order to produce enough to compensate their employer for the penalty.

Fourth, another full-time employment tax hidden in the employer penalty is the threat of paying multiple penalties for the one employee who puts the employer over the ACA's threshold defining large employers. Because of this hidden tax, the actual employer penalty and its complicated size provisions can (for the purposes of economic analysis) be more tractably approximated by ignoring the small-employer exemption and treating the employer penalty as a single $2,000-per-year tax on all full-time employees at firms not offering coverage (that is, about 26 percent of all full-time employees), plus the aforementioned adjustments for health cost inflation and employer business taxes. I take this approach for the rest of the book.

Finally, somewhere between 3.6 and 6.9 million workers will have all of their work hours beyond 29 per week effectively taxed at 100 percent or more by the penalty. In other words, the weekly amount of the employer penalty exceeds what these employees earn for all of the hours they work beyond 29 per week. This situation is especially common among female workers and among workers under 25 years old.

As will be shown in chapter 5, this chapter estimates magnitudes of the hidden taxes that are important for understanding the consequences of the ACA for employment rates, work schedules, and the structure of wages. Another way of looking at the size of the employer penalty is in terms of the incentives it creates for employers to offer (or refrain from dropping) health insurance coverage, for workers to change employers, and for customers to change the composition of their expenditures. This exercise requires estimates of the exchange subsidy amounts too, so it is deferred until chapter 7.

No chapter in this book quantifies the economic significance of the ACA's penalty on employers who *do* offer coverage. I also do not quantify the amount the ACA adds to employee-administration costs or to the threat of the longstanding excise tax on noncompliant employer plans. Arguably the employer penalties created and enhanced by the

ACA are even more significant than this chapter estimates and will result in even greater behavioral changes than are estimated in chapters 6 through 9.

Appendix 3.1: The CPS Samples Used in This Book, with Some Sensitivity Analysis

Unless noted otherwise, the microdata used in the book are from the March 2012 Current Population Survey (hereafter, CPS). In this chapter, I use the 93,477 persons in the sample who report positive weeks and positive wage income for calendar year 2011. For each of them, I also use the CPS variables on their usual weekly work hours in 2011, their amounts and types of income, their source of health insurance in March 2012, the size of their employer in March 2012 (fewer than 100 or 100+ employees), their age, their relationship to the head of the household, and the health insurance weight assigned to them to project national totals.

Of the 93,477 sampled workers, 67,246 are nonpoor, nonelderly heads of households or spouses, including unmarried partners of household heads as heads of their own one-person household. The chapters that follow look at incentives for nonpoor, nonelderly household heads and spouses, so they use just these persons and their families. Foster children are analyzed as children. Any other person not related to a household head or spouse is excluded from my sample.

1. HOURS AND EARNINGS

Average hourly earnings are calculated as the ratio of wage income to annual hours worked in calendar year 2011, with annual hours worked calculated as the product of weeks worked and usual weekly work hours. Average hourly earnings are converted from 2011 dollars to 2014 dollars using an inflation factor of 1.058593146, censored below at the 2014 federal minimum wage of $7.25, and omitted for unincorporated self-employed workers. These are the average hourly earnings estimates used in table 3.3 to compare, among persons without health insurance coverage from their jobs, with the weekly penalty amount. These are also the estimates used to calculate median hourly earnings in various samples, as noted in the main text.

2. POSSIBLE SOURCES OF HEALTH INSURANCE

For workers not enrolled in health insurance through their employer, the CPS does not indicate whether their employer offers coverage to its full-time employees. I therefore assign each employee in the CPS a probability of working for an employer that does not offer coverage. For nonelderly household heads and spouses working with usual work schedules of at least 35 hours per week, this probability is initially set to either zero or one depending on whether they are covered through their job or not, respectively. Among samples of the elderly, dependents, or part-time workers, this would be a poor indicator of type of employer because the elderly are typically insured by Medicare, dependents are typically insured by a family member's policy, and part-time workers are typically not offered coverage even while their full-time coworkers are. For the elderly, dependents, and any worker working fewer than 30-five hours per week, I assign a probability that their full-time coworkers are not offered ESI as the fitted value of a probit equation with dependent variable equal to the non-ESI-employer indicator noted above, estimated in the sample of non-elderly household heads and spouses working at least 35 hours per week.[21] All of the workers in the CPS sample have their probability rescaled by the same factor (0.62) so that the sample-average probability is 26 percent, which is my estimate (see the main text) of the fraction of workers under the ACA who will work for an employer that offers coverage to its full-time coworkers.

As a result of this algorithm, any nonelderly household head or spouse in the sample who is actually covered through an employer is ultimately assigned a zero probability of working for an employer that does not offer coverage and thereby excluded from table 3.3. Any nonelderly household head or spouse in the sample who is actually not covered through an employer, and working at least 35 hours per week, is ultimately assigned a probability of 0.62. The elderly, dependents, and any worker working fewer than 35 hours per week is ultimately assigned probabilities between these two extremes.

An important function of the assigned probability is to determine how hourly wages (among those working at least 30 hours per week) are different for persons working for an employer that does not offer coverage. As noted in the main text, the median of that sample is $15.06 (2014 dollars). An alternative would be to look at the distribution of wages among the sample of those working at least 30 hours per week and actually not covered by their employer, regardless of whether the employer is likely to be offering it. The hourly wage median of that sample is $14.76.

3. THE PENALTY'S HOUR EQUIVALENT

This chapter estimates a single weekly-hours equivalent of the 2016 employer penalty as a ratio to a single estimate ($3,163/52, in 2014 dollars) of the weekly salary equivalent of the employer penalty to the aforementioned $15.06 median hourly wage. In this way, the employer penalty is taken to be equivalent to 4.0 hours per week for the typical worker not offered health insurance coverage. Mulligan (forthcoming) has an alternative approach that estimates the penalty's hour equivalent separately worker by worker, among the sample of CPS respondents deemed to be at employers not offering coverage. In doing so, the paper accounts for different business tax rates among employers. It also assumes that CPS respondents employed full time by the federal government are offered health insurance coverage. It estimates that the average hour equivalent of the employer penalty is somewhere in the range 3.9 to 4.3, depending on what is assumed about the quality of hourly wage measurements in the CPS. This is another way of concluding that the employer penalty is typically about four hours per week for workers not offered health insurance coverage.

Appendix 3.2: Assumptions about Inflation

The rate of health cost inflation in excess of wages is important. To the extent that health cost inflation is incorporated into the premium adjustment percentage, its excess over wage inflation determines the magnitude of the employer penalty relative to wages. The economic consequences of the employer penalty will not grow even with a high rate of health cost inflation, as long as wage inflation keeps up with it.[22] The same excess inflation determines the economic significance of the implicit FTET (chapter 4) and the implicit income tax conditional on 1–4 FPL (chapter 5), even if health cost inflation is not fully incorporated into the premium adjustment percentage because the exchange subsidies that create the two implicit taxes are the difference between actual health costs and affordability caps.

The difference between wage inflation and price inflation determines the economic significance of the FPL because the FPL is indexed to the Consumer Price Index (CPI). If wages grow faster than the CPI, then more and more workers will find themselves in families with income in excess of four times FPL and thereby automatically ineligible for exchange subsidies. Because the employer penalty does not discriminate among workers on the basis of their family income relative to FPL, the economic significance of the employer penalty is hardly affected by wage growth that outpaces CPI inflation.

The poverty line used for determining exchange subsidies is for the year of enrollment, which is the year before the coverage year. A high rate of inflation would create a kind of bracket creep in which the poverty line does not keep up with consumer prices and nominal wages, and it might reduce the number of people eligible for exchange subsidies below the numbers I estimate in chapters 4 and 5. Of particular importance for my estimates is the inflation rate between 2015 and 2016, because I assume that the poverty lines in 2015 and 2016 will be essentially the same.

4 | Some Unpleasant Subsidy Arithmetic

This chapter unveils the tax from the ACA that is simultaneously its largest and its most hidden: the full-time employment tax implicit in the rules for the ACA's exchange subsidies.[1] The full-time employment tax (hereafter, FTET) is the largest, but not the only, tax created by the exchange subsidies, which makes the subsidies somewhat more complicated than the employer penalties are. I therefore begin by applying some of chapter 3's lessons for employer penalties, estimating the number of workers who will face the implicit FTET, and assessing its magnitude. Consideration of additional exchange subsidy features is deferred until chapter 5.

Figure 4.1 illustrates some of the economic relationships between the ACA's employer penalties and the exchange subsidies by measuring how they depend on the monthly employment situation of nonelderly household heads and spouses. A full-time worker for an "ESI" employer—that is, an employer that conforms to the employer mandate by offering employer-sponsored insurance coverage to its full-time employees—is ineligible for exchange subsidies. Every other kind of worker and nonworker is potentially eligible, which is why the pink subsidy bars appear only next to the top two employment situations in figure 4.1.[2] As noted in the preceding chapter, the employer penalty applies to persons who work full time for a non-ESI employer (i.e., one that does not offer coverage), but not to any other kind of employee, which is why a black penalty bar appears only next to the top employment situation. Each employment situation's red star indicates the net subsidy, that is, the length of the subsidy bar (if any) minus the length of the penalty bar (if any).

The non-ESI full-time situation has a net-subsidy star close to zero ($623 per year, to be exact) because its penalty and subsidy bars are approximately equal. The ESI full-time situation has a net-subsidy star at exactly zero because neither subsidies nor penalties apply. But we cannot conclude that full-time employment is unaffected because the alternatives to full-time employment—namely, part-time employment

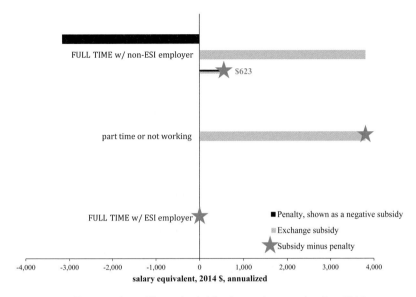

FIGURE 4.1. Patterns of penalties and subsidies by employment situation, 2016.

or not working—receive a significant net subsidy. Figure 4.1's middle employment situation is the only one where the subsidy can be received without an offsetting penalty. By subsidizing without penalties all employment and nonemployment situations except full-time work, the ACA is creating a large hidden full-time employment tax.[3]

Measuring the size and prevalence of the hidden FTET requires measures of both penalties and subsidies. Chapter 3 measures the penalties, so the purpose of this chapter is to measure the exchange subsidies. Figure 4.1 shows how measurement of the subsidy bars involves quantifying the amount of the subsidy, if any, that an ESI employer's full-time workers forgo as a consequence of their employment status.

To put it another way, withholding a subsidy on the basis of employment status is essentially the same as charging a penalty. Suppose that the ACA had not disqualified the full-time employees at ESI employers from receiving subsidies like those received by persons covered on the exchanges, and paid for this expansion (relative to the actual ACA) by forcing ESI employers to reimburse the Treasury for the subsidies received by their full-time employees. In this case, the net-subsidy stars would be exactly the same as they are in figure 4.1; the difference would be that the bottom employment category would have a pink subsidy bar too, with a black penalty bar of exactly the same length pointing in the other direction. But this approach would not do as well at hiding the ACA's full-time employment tax because millions more people would be working for penalized employers. One of the conclusions of this book is that FTETs need to be measured regardless of how well hidden they may be.

Section A of this chapter begins by looking at the number of people employed full time by ESI employers and decomposing it into reasons for being ineligible for exchange subsidies, with special attention to the ACA's "family glitch." Section A finds that about 20 million workers are ineligible solely because of their employment status. Because the ACA's premium assistance (a major part of the exchange subsidies) is the difference between the cost of an exchange plan and ACA-specified spending caps for each household, section B discusses the cost of exchange plans and the value that households might (or might not) perceive in them, including the fact that exchange subsidies are not taxable by the personal income tax or any other safety net program. Sections C through F measure the amount and economic significance of the implicit FTET.

A. At Least 20 Million Workers per Year, and Their Families, Will Be Excluded from ACA Subsidies Solely Because of Their Employment Situation

Table 4.1 presents estimates of the number and composition of nonelderly household heads and spouses in 2016 who would work for an employer offering coverage, assuming for the moment that neither employers nor employees adjust the overall level of employment or its distribution between full- and part-time work, on the basis of the Current Population Survey (CPS).[4] The total number is 87 million, of which 47 million would be ineligible for exchange subsidies regardless of their employment situation because they are from a family with income outside the interval in which subsidies are available: 100–400 percent of the federal poverty line (hereafter, FPL).[5] Take, for example, heads and spouses from families of four who are working for ESI employers and living in the contiguous United States. Those with family incomes between $23,850 and $95,400 measured in 2014 dol-

TABLE 4.1. ESI employees: reasons for ineligibility

Millions of nonelderly household heads and spouses only, projected to 2016
Holds full- and part-time employment rates constant at 2011 values

	Worker counts are in millions		
	Full-time schedule	Part-time schedule	All schedules
All working nonelderly household heads and spouses	80.9	33.2	114.1
Working for an ESI employer	63.8	22.8	86.6
(−) family is outside 1–4 FPL	35.0	11.9	46.9
(−) spouse works full time for an ESI employer	4.5	2.3	6.8
Full-time employment by itself renders the worker (and family) ineligible for exchange subsidies	**24.2**	**8.7**	**32.9**
Addendum: actually covered by their employer in 2012	20.0	4.9	

Notes: An ESI employer is one offering coverage to its full-time employees. An ESI employee is anyone working for an ESI employer. National populations are based on the March 2012 CPS, excluding persons not working or without wage income in 2011. The CPS health insurance weights were multiplied by 1.01^4 in order to project to 2016. If part-time workers with ESI continue to be offered it under the ACA, then their eligibility for exchange subsidies does not depend on full-time status. A full-time schedule is 35+ hours per week. FPL refers to the federal poverty line.

lars would not be among the 47 million subtracted on the table's third row, whereas those with family incomes outside the interval would be among those subtracted.[6]

Exchange subsidies are not available to those who can obtain employer coverage through a spouse.[7] The ACA's exchange subsidies are not a hidden tax on such a person's employment status because, owing to this so-called family glitch, the entire family is ineligible for the subsidies even if the person gives up ESI by leaving employment or moving to part time. Table 4.1 therefore subtracts all 6.8 million married persons who (1) work for ESI employers, (2) live in a family between 100 and 400 percent of FPL, and (3) have a spouse working full time for an ESI employer.

Twenty-four million full-time workers and 9 million part-time workers remain. For these 33 million workers, the entire family's eligibility for exchange subsidies hinges on their employment status. In any month when they are off the payroll, or working part time, they can get coverage on the ACA's exchanges and the subsidies that go with it. In any month when they are working full time for their employer, they are ineligible for exchange subsidies, regardless of how low their family income may be.[8]

The exchange subsidies are attached to insurance coverage and are therefore not received by the uninsured. In principle, a person could choose to be uninsured, in which case receipt of exchange subsidies is not dependent on employment status. There are a couple of reasons to expect this situation to be relatively rare. First, table 4.1's addendum shows that more than 80 percent of the CPS sample members used to project the 24 million full-time workers shown in the bottom line actually had coverage through their employer in March 2012. Second, in 2014 the ACA began to penalize persons without health insurance coverage, and by 2016 those penalties will be significant.

As in chapter 3, the approach of this chapter is to first assess the magnitude of the ACA's various taxes, holding behavior constant, so that later chapters can use these magnitudes to predict the law's likely impacts on work schedules, wages, output, and so on. This is one reason the estimates in this chapter (e.g., table 4.1) of the number of workers in various employment situations should not be interpreted as best forecasts; those are coming in later chapters that incorporate behavioral adjustments. Nevertheless, table 4.1's 33-million-worker bottom line—about a fifth of the workforce—is the first and simplest demonstration of perhaps the most important result in this book. Although the ACA is more than four years old, nobody has presented measures of the significance of its implicit full-time employment tax. I am aware of only one instance prior to February 2014 where anyone publicly acknowledged even the existence of this tax.[9]

B. Exchange Plans: Costs and Perceived Values

Recall that the ACA's exchange subsidies are primarily cost-sharing subsidies and premium assistance. The cost-sharing subsidies are essentially a proportion of medical expenses covered by the plan.[10] A family's premium assistance is the difference, if any, between (1) the full premium on the second cheapest silver plan, which is based on the average covered medical expenses among plan participants, and (2) the amount of premiums that the family can afford, as defined by the ACA. Item (2) is discussed extensively in chapter 5; for now we need only to note that the 2014 affordable amount for families in between 100 percent and 400 percent of the federal poverty line is independent of premiums or medical expenses. Thus, the amount of the premium assistance increases more than proportionally with premiums and medical expenses, and the cost-sharing subsidies increase proportionally.[11]

Measuring the amount of the exchange subsidies therefore requires measurements of premiums or medical expenses. Because the subsidies are being measured for the purpose of understanding employee and employer choices that affect source of coverage, we need to know not only what the exchange subsidies cost the federal government, but also how the subsidies are valued by workers at a margin between one employment status and another.

A proper valuation of the exchange subsidies needs to recognize, among other things, how health insurance has traditionally been delivered. Most private health insurance plans among the nonelderly have been obtained through employers, with a large majority of the benefits financed with health insurance premiums. The premiums are shared between employer and employee, but either way the income that goes to pay the premiums does not count as income for the purposes of determining payroll and personal income taxes. The ACA does little to change this. ESI premiums therefore continue to serve two economic purposes: financing health coverage and avoiding taxes. The two purposes are not always harmonious, and one consequence may have been for ESI plans to offer too much health coverage in order to avoid additional taxation. By design, premiums paid for exchange plans do not receive the same tax treatment: the income that families earn to pay for exchange plan premiums is part of the income to be taxed by the payroll and federal income tax. I follow the convention of referring to these tax situations as paying for premiums "with after-tax dollars" (exchange plans) or "with pretax dollars" (employer plans).

Employees often continue to participate in their former employer's plan after they leave employment. Employer health plans for early retirees are an example. Since the 1980s, federal and state laws give employees who are leaving ESI jobs the option of continuing their health coverage for up to 18 months (U.S. Department of Labor 2013). The former employees reimburse their former employer for the full cost of the coverage with after-tax dollars, plus a small administration fee. The continuation coverage is usually referred to as "COBRA coverage"; the acronym is for one of the statutes regulating such coverage.

1. THE EXCHANGE FEATURES DISCOUNT AND EXCHANGE SUBSIDY TAKE-UP

Measuring premiums and medical expenses is complicated by the fact that exchange plans are different from employer plans. Exchange plans have higher deductibles than the average employer plan (before cost-sharing subsidies), and many states' exchange plans limit participants to narrower provider networks than employer plans do (Hancock 2013). In theory, ACA regulations and participant cost sharing (with after-tax dollars) may be encouraging more economical health spending on the exchanges, and the narrower provider networks may merely reflect improved value for the premium dollar. But it is also possible that ACA regulations reduce the value of health spending on the exchanges, especially as perceived by persons who would otherwise have employer coverage. For example, sellers may distort their offerings—perhaps with narrow provider networks—in order to discourage more expensive participants from joining their plan. The ACA may also disproportionately require exchange plans to offer benefit options that participants value at less than what they cost. It is also possible that those familiar with employer coverage fail to appreciate the advantages of exchange plans simply because the latter are less familiar, or because exchange plans are stigmatized as a form of "welfare."

For the purposes of measuring the amount of the FTET implicit in the exchange subsidies, all of these possibilities can be summarized in terms of the discount (hereafter, the "exchange features discount"), if any, that a marginal nonemployed person or part-time employed person would need so as to purchase exchange coverage during periods of not being offered coverage by an employer, rather than going uninsured or using after-tax income to continue coverage through the former employer (e.g., via the COBRA rules). The exchange features discount could be zero, especially among people taking advantage of COBRA before the ACA, because (in theory) the exchange plans are a

TABLE 4.2. Health insurance coverage among the unemployed

Nonelderly household heads and spouses who were unemployed in March 2012

Coverage status	All family incomes		2011 family income in 1–4 FPL	
	Millions	Percentage	Millions	Percentage
Uninsured	1.57	41%	0.82	41%
Former employer	1.32	34%	0.75	38%
Individual market	0.22	6%	0.11	5%
Medicaid	0.75	19%	0.32	16%
Covered through family member	0.93		0.46	
National total unemployed	4.78		2.46	
Total, excluding coverage through family	3.85	100%	2.00	100%
Addendum: Unemployed persons sampled	2,996		1,617	

Note: National totals are projected from the March 2012 Current Population Survey using the health insurance weight. Percentages exclude "covered through family member" from their denominators. FPL is the federal poverty line.

better use of after-tax dollars than employer plans are, or because the exchange plans offer a wider range of choices than COBRA does. In this zero-discount case, people not offered coverage through an employer would be willing to pay full price for an exchange plan. On the other hand, the exchange features discount could be greater than the ACA's subsidies in which case people leaving an ESI job for nonemployment or part-time work without coverage would not purchase an exchange plan, even if it is subsidized. The exchange features discount is therefore also a way to represent the degree of "take-up" of subsidized exchange plans.

Table 4.2 shows the March 2012 health insurance status among nonelderly household heads and spouses who were unemployed during the CPS reference week. It was common for the unemployed to have private insurance even when not obtaining it through a family member (usually, a spouse). Table 4.2 includes unemployed persons who did not have coverage on their prior job; presumably the 38 percent in the final column would be even greater—perhaps more than 50 percent—if such persons could be eliminated from the sample. In theory, unemployed persons who would normally get their coverage through their former employer may, for the reasons mentioned above, be revealing willingness to pay full price for exchange coverage (that is, revealing that their exchange features discount is zero). On the other hand, the persistence of their employer coverage may only indicate that they are attached to employer coverage and would need a considerable discount in order to choose exchange coverage instead.

The fact that many of the unemployed did not purchase any insurance suggests they were not particularly interested in spending their own money on health insurance. The ACA's individual mandate may change that, but otherwise the unemployed uninsured seem to be revealing that many of them have positive exchange features discounts and would not purchase exchange plans without a subsidy. Overall, the results suggest that the exchange features discount is often economically significant and that take-up of exchange plans among the unemployed will be well less than 100 percent.

The amount of the FTET implicit in the exchange subsidies is the difference, if any, between (1) the full price (premium and cost sharing) of exchange coverage discounted for exchange features and (2) the subsidized premium and cost sharing. In the case of the exchange features discount being zero, this difference is just the dollar amount of the subsidy. To put it another way, the exchange subsidies in the zero-discount case are just giving nonemployed and part-time employed people cash for buying an insurance product they would have purchased anyway.

It is possible that someone would be willing to buy exchange coverage at a market rate without subsidy, and indeed even be willing to pay more than full price for the coverage, during a period in which the person is not offered coverage through an employer. To the extent that this is true on average for the entire workforce or on average for any of the specific groups I examine in this book, however, I do not consider this an addition to the FTET beyond the amount of the subsidy; instead I consider it a separate and additional effect of enhancing the market for individual coverage.[12]

2. ESTIMATING EXCHANGE PREMIUMS FOR 2015 AND BEYOND

As of the time of writing, one approach to measuring the full price of exchange plans during the time period of interest (especially 2015 and beyond) is to measure them in 2014 and augment them for normal health cost inflation. One could measure the 2014 premiums using

TABLE 4.3. Estimates of 2014 family plan premiums
for the purposes of projecting to 2015 and beyond

	70% AV	83% AV	Ratio to KFF1	
KFF2 calculator	$10,100	$11,976	0.84	Quoted as 70% AV
KFF1 calculator	$12,024	$14,257	1.00	Quoted as 70% AV
Average private sector ESI plan	$13,923	$16,508	1.16	Quoted as 83% AV for 2012, and adjusted 6.7% to 2014
Addendum: KFF1 calculator projected to 2016 (2014 $)	$12,487			

Notes: AV denotes the actuarial average percentage of medical expenses that are covered by the plan. KFF calculators assume two nonsmoking adults each aged 43 plus two children. In the March 2012 CPS, the average nonelderly married household head or spouse with at least one child and covered by his (or her) employer had an average age and family size of 43 and 4.0, respectively.

the latest version of the Henry J. Kaiser Family Foundation's premium calculator (hereafter, KFF2 calculator) as a function of family size and composition, and then inflate them by 1.6 percent per year beyond wage growth. However, the exchange plans' premiums for coverage year 2014 appear to be less than the prices of comparable employer plans, in part because of their unique features (see above) but also because the federal government was encouraging insurers (e.g., with promises of compensation for losses) to price low as the exchanges were first coming on line.[13] Many observers expect exchange plan premiums to jump approximately 10 percent between 2014 and 2015.[14]

The KFF2 calculator estimates that the 2014 silver plan premiums for a family of four consisting of two 43-year-old nonsmoking adults and two children would total $10,100 in the average state without subsidies. Because a silver plan reimburses 70 percent of expected covered expenses, the premium translates to $11,976 per year for a plan that reimburses 83 percent of expenses, as the average ESI plan does (Gabel et al. 2012). These family plan results are shown in the top row of table 4.3.

Another approach is to measure the costs of comparable employer plans. The MEPS administered by the Department of Health and Human Services indicates that the 2012 average family plan premium for private sector employer plans was $15,473.[15] Assuming a cumulative health cost inflation of 6.7 percent between 2012 and 2014, this translates to a $16,508 premium for 2014, as shown in the third row of table 4.3.[16] This is comparable to the $11,976 in the top row because the average age and family size of a married nonelderly household head or spouse with coverage on the job and at least one child are 43 and 4.0, respectively. The comparable-employer-plan approach is more accurate to the degree that exchange plans will become more like employer plans over time.[17]

The first edition of the Kaiser premium calculator (hereafter the KFF1 calculator), created in mid-2013 before the ACA's exchanges opened, had exchange premium estimates that were in between those shown in the top and bottom rows of table 4.3.[18] For example, the KFF1 calculator predicted that a 43-year-old couple with two children would pay $12,024 per year in 2014 without subsidies for a silver plan, which reimburses 70 percent of expected expenses. This translates to $14,257 per year for a plan that reimburses 83 percent of expenses.

The KFF1 calculator is an earlier edition that relied on older data and probably is inferior to the KFF2 calculator as a predictor of actual exchange plan premiums in 2014.[19] However, as noted above, exchange plan premiums in 2015 and beyond are expected to be significantly greater than 2014 premiums. I therefore use the KFF1 calculator, plus 1.6 percent per year growth in excess of wages (except in the first year, where it is 2.2 percent as discussed in chapter 3), for my benchmark estimates of exchange plan premiums in 2015 and beyond, and I use the KFF2 calculator and employer plan average premiums as part of my sensitivity analysis. For example, to calculate the premium assistance for coverage year 2016 for a family with such characteristics, I take the difference between the $12,487 amount shown at the bottom of table 4.3 and the premium cap assigned to them by the ACA. To calculate the effective amount of the FTET created by the premium assistance, I adjust the $12,487 for the exchange features discount (if any) and then subtract the premium cap.

C. The Size of the Hidden Employment Tax by Family Type

For each of the 20,730 March 2012 CPS observations used to estimate the bottom line in table 4.1, I calculated a family premium for a silver plan on the exchanges with the KFF1 calculator and family adjusted gross income (hereafter, AGI) as the worker's personal income for 2011 plus spouse personal income (if any) minus an estimate of what (if anything) the worker paid in ESI premiums. Family AGI tells me the premium cap applicable to that family. The combination of family AGI and the family premium tells me the value of the cost-sharing subsidy. The worker's FTET is the cost-sharing subsidy plus the discounted premium minus the premium cap (or zero, if the premium cap is greater).

Table 4.4 shows the results. The overall average annualized subsidy forgone while working full time is $7,016, as shown in the table's "entire sample" row. Assuming a 25 percent exchange features discount (as I do in much of the book), the average implicit FTET is $4,723. Both of these averages are after-tax dollars and include zeros for households for whom full-price premiums are deemed affordable by the ACA. The $4,723 average also includes zeros for households (about 10 percent of the households included in the average) that have to pay more than 75 percent of the full premium. In effect, I assume they do not value the subsidy that they forgo when they work full time for an ESI employer, perhaps because they would not participate in an exchange plan during times of nonemployment.[20]

Table 4.4 also shows the results separately by demographic groups, listed in order of aggregate weeks worked in 2011. The top group is married households with dependents in which one spouse works full time with ESI and the other spouse either does not work full time or works for an employer that does not offer coverage. Their average annualized subsidy forgone is shown in the right column and is about $10,000 after income and payroll taxes because of the number of family members whose exchange subsidy hinges on the job situation of the one family member who is working full time with ESI.

According to table 4.1's fourth row, almost 7 million married workers do not face an FTET (and are thereby excluded from table 4.4) solely because their household has two earners, each with access to family coverage on the job. Table 4.1 is based on 2012 data, and therefore on the patterns of employer coverage that prevailed then. Because the ACA does not require employers to cover employee spouses, it is possible that employers begin to exclude spouses from their plans and thereby reduce the number of workers in table 4.1's fourth row to be subtracted

TABLE 4.4. Implicit FTET amounts by demographic group

Millions of nonelderly household heads and spouses only, projected to 2016
Holds full- and part-time employment rates constant at 2011 values

Marital status	Employment and coverage status	Dependents	Percentage of all work-weeks subject to implicit FTET	Average annualized	
				Subsidy forgone	Exch. features discount of 25%
Married	FT ESI w/o access through spouse	Spouse & dependents	27.1%	$10,259	$6,803
Unmarried	FT ESI	One person household	25.7%	$2,424	$1,491
Unmarried	FT ESI	Dependents	14.8%	$7,487	$5,299
Married	PT no-ESI, but FT coworkers have ESI	All	11.4%	$10,374	$7,137
Unmarried	PT no-ESI, but FT coworkers have ESI	One person household	8.2%	$3,490	$2,417
Married	FT ESI w/o access through spouse	Spouse, no dependents	7.5%	$8,392	$5,459
Unmarried	PT no-ESI, but FT coworkers have ESI	Dependents	4.4%	$7,950	$5,826
Married	FT ESI w/o access through spouse	Spouse on Medicare	1.0%	$6,225	$3,829
Entire sample			100.0%	**$7,016**	**$4,723**
Entire sample, excluding PT workers covered in 2012			85.7%	$6,999	$4,710
Married sample members only			47.0%	$9,905	$6,608
Unmarried sample members only			53.0%	$4,457	$3,054

Notes: FTET denotes the full-time employment tax. FT denotes full-time worker. ESI denotes employer-sponsored health insurance. Dollar amounts are in 2014 dollars after income and payroll taxes and are NOT salary equivalents. The "Exch. features discount of 25%" is the subsidy forgone minus the minimum of 25% of the full premium or the premium subsidy. Subsidy averages include zeros for households with full-price premium below the ACA-determined affordability cap.

from the population of ESI workers. If so, the table's bottom line underestimates the number of workers who will face the implicit FTET. At the same time, table 4.4 would overestimate the average amount of the implicit FTET because, with spouses excluded from employer plans, a number of ESI workers forgoing an exchange subsidy would be forgoing a subsidy for only themselves, and not the rest of their family.

The next two groups forgoing exchange subsidies are single-parent households and one-person households in which the head is working full time with ESI. According to the Kaiser premium calculator, annual silver plan premiums for a one-person household are about $4,000, which means the likely exchange subsidies are relatively small.[21] However, adding dependents to the household adds significantly to the exchange subsidies forgone: about $7,000 annually for the average unmarried household with dependents and with income in the eligible range. The top three groups together contain about two-thirds of the persons (weighted by weeks worked) expected to face an implicit full-time employment tax under the ACA.

I suspect it will be increasingly rare for employers to offer coverage to part-time employees, because the offer will usually prevent them from getting an exchange subsidy. An alternative view is that the few employers who offered coverage to part-time employees in 2012 will continue to do so, in which case the exchange subsidies are an implicit employment tax on all of their employees (full- and part-time), rather than a full-time employment tax, because by working any amount of hours they are eligible for employer coverage and thereby denied exchange subsidies. The third-to-last row of table 4.4 shows the results of excluding CPS respondents who were working fewer than 35 hours per week but nonetheless were insured through their employer, and it suggests that my results are not particularly sensitive to which of these two views is adopted.

Tables 4.5 and 4.6 show the subsidy amounts by family income and family size. Weighted by weeks worked in 2011, the workers subject to the implicit FTET are pretty evenly split between the three income brackets. The amount of the FTET declines sharply with family income; chapters 7 and 8 show how this pattern will affect the labor productivity and incidence of employment under the ACA. As shown in table 4.6, the amount of the FTET increases with family size, with amounts facing workers in families of five or more that are many times larger than those facing workers from one-person families.

Tables 4.4, 4.5, and 4.6 display the average subsidies for premiums and cost sharing. Unlike wages and salaries, the subsidies are not taxable by payroll or personal income taxes. For example, a household with a 25 percent marginal tax rate has to earn another $1,333 in order to make up for the loss of $1,000 of its subsidies because it would pay $333 worth of tax on the additional $1,333 it earned. Table 4.7 shows

TABLE 4.5. Implicit FTET amounts by income bracket

Families of nonelderly household heads and spouses only, projected to 2016
Holds full- and part-time employment rates constant at 2011 values

Income bracket	Percentage of all workweeks subject to implicit FTET	Average annualized	
		Subsidy forgone	Exch. features discount of 25%
100%–200% FPL	32.2%	$11,537	$9,052
200%–300% FPL	37.3%	$5,831	$3,544
300%–400% FPL	30.4%	$3,683	$1,587
Entire sample	100.0%	$7,016	$4,723

Notes: FTET denotes the full-time employment tax. Dollar amounts are in 2014 dollars after income and payroll taxes and are *not* salary equivalents. The "Exch. features discount of 25%" is the subsidy forgone minus the minimum of 25% of the full premium or the premium subsidy. Subsidy averages include zeros for households with full-price premium below the ACA-determined affordability cap.

TABLE 4.6. Implicit FTET amounts by family size

Families of nonelderly household heads and spouses only, projected to 2016
Holds full- and part-time employment rates constant at 2011 values

Nonelderly family members	Percentage of all workweeks subject to implicit FTET	Average annualized	
		Subsidy forgone	Exch. features discount of 25%
1	34.5%	$2,746	$1,747
2	20.8%	$7,242	$4,869
3	16.1%	$8,490	$5,739
4	16.8%	$9,770	$6,503
5+	11.8%	$13,158	$9,240
Entire sample	100.0%	$7,016	$4,723

Notes: FTET denotes the full-time employment tax. Dollar amounts are in 2014 dollars after income and payroll taxes and are *not* salary equivalents. The "Exch. features discount of 25%" is the subsidy forgone minus the minimum of 25% of the full premium or the premium subsidy. Subsidy averages include zeros for households with full-price premium below the ACA-determined affordability cap.

how after-tax dollars can be converted into salary equivalents. The rows of the table are for subsidy amounts in after-tax dollars (from table 4.5's final column), and the table entries are salary equivalents. The columns of the table show different assumed marginal tax rates.

Many families below 400 percent of the poverty line but above about 220 percent of it would have a marginal income tax bracket of about 25 percent: 7.65 percent for employee payroll taxes, 15 percent for federal individual income taxes, and roughly 3 percent for state individual income taxes.[22] The federal rate would commonly be between

21 and 36 percent (instead of 15) for families between roughly 100 and 220 percent of the poverty line as the federal earned income tax credit is phased out (Congressional Budget Office 2012b), putting the combined rate over 30 percent and perhaps higher than 45 percent. Additional rates are possible if the household is participating in transfer programs such as housing allowances. Chapter 5 shows that the ACA itself adds to the non-ACA marginal tax rates and thereby the salary equivalent of every after-tax dollar. Throughout the book, I assume a combined 25 percent marginal income tax rate for non-ACA programs, but I also show results in table 4.7 and elsewhere for a 35 percent non-ACA marginal rate.

The overall average full-time employment tax is $4,723, including the 25 percent discount for exchange features. The middle row of table 4.7 shows that the salary equivalent of this average FTET is $6,297 at a 25 percent marginal tax rate and $7,266 at a 35 percent marginal tax rate, at least twice as large as the employer penalty examined in chapter 3. The salary equivalent of the FTET can easily exceed $10,000 per year for households between 100 and 200 percent of the federal poverty line.

TABLE 4.7. The annual salary equivalent of the 2016 FTET
as a function of the base combined marginal tax rate.
Amounts in 2014 dollars and net of exchange-features discount.

Subsidy in after-tax dollars	Assumed marginal tax rate			Notes
	25%	30%	35%	
$1,587	$2,116	$2,267	$2,442	Average among 300%–400% FPL
$3,544	$4,725	$5,063	$5,452	Average among 200%–300% FPL
$4,723	**$6,297**	**$6,747**	**$7,266**	**Average among 100%–400% FPL**
$9,052	$12,069	$12,931	$13,926	Average among 100%–200% FPL
$10,000	$13,333	$14,286	$15,385	For illustration
Addendum: Salary equivalent of the 2016 employer penalty		$3,163		

Notes: The marginal tax rate represents employee payroll tax, personal income tax (state and local), and phaseouts of non-ACA benefits and credits, but *not* employer payroll tax or any health program. Average subsidies are from table 4.5 and are net of a 25 percent exchange-features discount.

D. The Size of the Employment Tax Measured in Hours per Week

It is also helpful to compare the dollar amount of the implicit FTET to the hourly compensation of the employees who might pay it. Dividing the two is an estimate of the number of hours per week that a worker's efforts are, in effect, paying extra for health care compared to what the worker would pay if not working full time. Figure 4.2 shows the results for compensation ranging from $10 to $45 per hour.[23] The weekly work-hour equivalents of the implicit FTET are measured on the vertical axis, as weekly (nontaxable) subsidy amounts divided by after-tax hourly compensation using a 30 percent marginal earnings tax rate intended to represent both ACA and non-ACA income taxation at the margin. The dollar amount of the FTET is measured in the same two ways as in tables 4.4 through 4.6: as the entire subsidy (pink series) and net of a premium discount for the various features of exchange plans as compared to employer plans (red series). For example, a value of eight hours per week measured from the pink series means that the average weekly exchange subsidy forgone by ESI workers is equal to the amount they earn, after taxes, in eight hours of work.

The series in figure 4.2 slope down because low-wage workers take more hours to earn a given dollar amount than high-wage workers do. Because this is the same sort of result shown in figure 3.1 for the employer penalty, I also include an employer penalty series in figure 4.2 even though workers facing the implicit FTET are not subject to the employer penalty. Moreover, unlike the employer penalty, the implicit FTET is not the same dollar amount for all workers: it depends on the size and composition of the worker's family. The FTET series in figure 4.2 are therefore based on the average dollar amounts conditional on hourly compensation.[24]

Figure 4.2 has a red vertical dashed line at the $22 per hour median hourly compensation among workers with ESI, a work schedule of at least 30 hours per week, and facing the implicit FTET. The average subsidy at $22 per hour is equivalent to about eight hours per week. Including the exchange features discount, the average value forgone by working full time for an employer offering coverage is more than 5.5 hours per week.

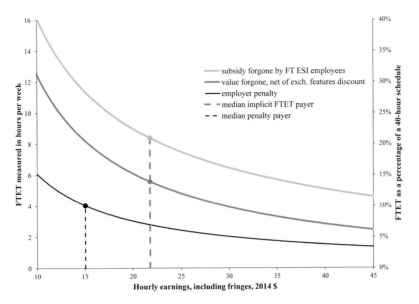

FIGURE 4.2. The 2016 implicit FTET measured in hours per week.

The salary equivalent dollar amount of the implicit FTET exceeds the salary equivalent of the employer penalty ($3,163 in 2016), which is why the black penalty series is the lowest of the three in figure 4.2. In principle, the hour equivalent of the employer penalty could be greater than the hour equivalent of the implicit FTET because workers facing the penalty earn less than workers facing the implicit FTET. However, the dashed black line in figure 4.2, reproduced from figure 3.1, shows that, measured as hour equivalents, the median employer penalty among the workers likely to face it, 4.0 hours per week, is less than the implicit FTET among most of the workers likely to face it.

In order to help readers compare the significance of the implicit FTET with the more familiar payroll taxes, the right-hand axis expresses the hour equivalents as shares of a 40-hour schedule. This can be interpreted as the amount of the implicit FTET as a fraction of full-time earnings at the hourly rate measured on the horizontal axis. The 2016 implicit FTET (net of the exchange features discount) is, for example, a lot like a 21 percent tax on the earnings of a $15 per hour worker and a 14 percent tax on the earnings of a $22 per hour worker.

E. Make More by Working Less: An Example

As an example of the extreme incentives that will be created by the implicit full-time employment tax, consider a hypothetical person comparing a part-time position to a full-time position in 2016. The full-time position, shown in the left column of table 4.8, requires 40 hours of work and $100 of employment expenses (such as commuting or child care) per week, for 50 weeks per year. The part-time position requires 29 hours of work and $75 of employment expenses per week. Each position costs the employer $26 per hour worked, including employer payroll taxes and employer contributions for health insurance (if any).[25]

Only the full-time position includes affordable health insurance, which means a full-time employee would not be eligible to receive assistance from the ACA for premiums or for out-of-pocket health expenses. The employer pays 78 percent of the premiums for the family insurance plan and withholds the remaining premiums of $3,146 from the paychecks of participating full-time employees (they also pay out-of-pocket costs, which are discussed separately below). A full-time employee's income subject to tax is $35,021, which excludes employer payroll taxes (7.65 percent of the $35,021), employer health insurance contributions, and employee premiums withheld.[26]

Part-time employees get less total compensation—$37,700—because they work fewer hours. The part-time employees are not eligible for ESI and the tax exclusions that go with it, which makes their income subject to tax ($35,021) equal to their total compensation minus employer payroll taxes. It is a coincidence that income subject to tax is the same for full-time and part-time employees; more on this below.

The part-time employees are eligible for subsidized health plans from the ACA's exchanges because they are not offered affordable health insurance by their employer. I assume that the second-cheapest silver plan has the same expected covered medical expenses as the employer plan, namely, $17,300 per year including out-of-pocket payments for the covered expenses that are not reimbursed by the plan because of deductibles, copayments, and so on. By definition, a silver plan's full premium finances 70 percent of expenses and is therefore

TABLE 4.8. The ACA's implicit tax on full-time work: an example

Positions offered in 2016 by employers offering health insurance only to full-time employees. All dollar amounts are annualized 2014 dollars unless noted otherwise. Subsidies are calculated for a family of four with one earner.

Job attributes	Full-time position	Part-time position		
	ESI	ACA exchange		
Health insurance source	ESI	ACA exchange		
Employee costs				
Weekly hours worked	40	29	(1)	
Weekly work expense	$100	$75	(2)	
Employer costs				
Hourly cost	$26	$26	(3)	
Annual cost	52,000	37,700	(4)	= 50*(3)*(1)
Employer payroll taxes	2,679	2,679	(5)	= [(4) − (6) −(7)]*0.0765/1.0765
Health insurance premiums				
Employer	11,154	0	(6)	= 78% of total premium (ESI only)
Employee, excluded from tax base	3,146	0	(7)	= 22% of total premium (ESI only)
Employee, included in tax base	0	1,379	(8)	= 3.9% of (12)
ACA	0	10,731	(9)	= 70% of total health expenses − (8)
Out-of-pocket health expenses				
Employee	3,000	1,038	(10)	= 17% (6%) of total ESI (exch.) expenses
ACA	0	4,152	(11)	= (3/7)*[(8) + (9)] − (10)
Employee income subject to tax				
Total	$35,021	$35,021	(12)	= (4) − (5) − (6) − (7)
Ratio to federal poverty line	1.47	1.47	(13)	= (12)/23850
After health & work expenses, annual	$27,021	$28,854	(14)	= (12) − (8) − (10) − 50*(2)

Notes: Both types of employees work 50 weeks per year (see rows (4) and (14)). The ACA exchange plan is assumed to be a silver plan (70 percent actuarial value). Neither employee type is subject to the employer penalty.

$12,110 per year.[27] However, because the employee has a family income subject to tax of 147 percent of the federal poverty line (the employee is the sole earner in a family of four), the ACA caps premiums for the second-cheapest silver plan at 3.9 percent of their income subject to tax, or $1,379 per year. The other $10,731 is paid by the U.S. Treasury to the insurer as an advance premium tax credit.

By design, the silver health plans have lower premiums and greater out-of-pocket costs (deductibles, copayments, etc.) than the typical employer plan. That design feature is visible in table 4.8 because exchange plan out-of-pocket costs total $5,190 rather than the $3,000 of out-of-pocket health expenses associated with ESI.[28] However, because the employee's family is at 147 percent of the poverty line, the employee gets an 80 percent discount on the out-of-pocket expenses, with the remainder paid by the U.S. Treasury to the insurer as a cost-sharing subsidy.[29]

After health and work expenses, the part-time employee makes $28,854 per year, which exceeds the full-time income ($27,021) after health and work expenses! Table 4.8 does not show the employee payroll and personal income taxes, but those would be the same for the full-time and part-time employee because the amount of the income subject to the two taxes is, in this example, independent of full-time status. Thus, the part-time employee makes more after taxes, health expenses, and work expenses.

None of table 4.8's results reflects the employer penalty because the comparison shown is for positions at employers that are offering affordable coverage to their full-time employees. However, as explained in chapter 3, the employer penalty has many of the same economic characteristics as forgone exchange subsidies, and vice versa.

The hypothetical worker examined in table 4.8 can, under the ACA, have more income by working fewer hours. Table 4.8 does not show that this worker will have more income with the ACA than without it (he may), because both columns assume that the ACA is in place. Among other things, the ACA may affect the hourly employer cost shown in table 4.8's third row.[30] The purpose of table 4.8 and the rest of this chapter is to look at situations under the ACA in which a decision to work less does not reduce disposable income.

Table 4.8 contains two results about the ACA and part-time work. The first result is that moving from full-time employment to part-time employment can trigger generous new assistance with health premiums and out-of-pocket expenses that can offset much of the income lost from reduced work hours. Workers and employers should not be expected to uniformly continue making the same work-schedule decisions under the ACA that they did before the ACA, when the assistance was not available. This result does not depend on table 4.8's quantitative details such as the hourly wage rate or the assumed health costs, as long as (1) the employer is not offering affordable coverage to part-time workers, (2) the worker is from a family between 100 and 400 percent of the poverty line, and (3) the worker cannot be covered through a spouse's employer.

Table 4.8's example is a bit simplified in that part-time employees have the same income subject to tax and the same hourly employer cost as full-time employees.[31] Nevertheless, it contains a second and more dramatic result: that the ACA puts some workers in the position where a part-time schedule gives them more disposable income than a full-time schedule would. The dramatic result primarily derives from the size of the combined subsidy in rows 9 and 11 as compared to the earnings lost from cutting hours (row 4).

F. For Millions, Full-Time Work Will Pay Less Than Part-Time Work (Subsidy Edition)

Withholding exchange subsidies can, in effect, tax more than 100 percent of the work done beyond the twenty-ninth hour every week: the employee featured in table 4.8 would earn less after taxes during hours 30 to 40 than the $298 weekly subsidy forgone by working those hours. This happens even though part of the employee's earnings beyond the twenty-ninth hour include the significant tax savings from the fact that the payroll and personal income taxes do not tax the income the employee and the employer pay for ESI premiums (see the sixth and seventh rows of table 4.8). Most of the 20 to 30 million workers facing the ACA's implicit FTET are unlike the worker shown in table 4.8 in that their full-time employment still offers somewhat more disposable income than part-time employment would, but the purpose of this section is to estimate how many people are put in an implicit "100+ percent tax" situation, like the one shown in the table.

Measuring the frequency of 100 percent implicit FTETs requires two kinds of data: the distribution (among workers) of family situations and the distribution of earnings among workers in a given family situation, assuming that they work their normal full-time schedule. Family situation is the combination of household size, spousal and asset income, age of the family members, and the number of hours per week the worker normally spends at work. For example, one family situation represents all 40-hour workers age 30 with a spouse the same age, two children, but no spousal or asset income. For any family situation, the ACA and one of the KFF calculators are sufficient to calculate a critical compensation amount that equates full-time disposable income to part-time disposable income. With the critical compensation amount in hand, estimating the fraction of workers in the family situation that is subject to a 100 percent tax is simply a matter of estimating the fraction of workers having full-time compensation less than the critical value.

This section is the most complicated in the book thus far because of the number of variables that go into a scenario like that of table 4.8. Some readers may want to jump ahead to the concluding section of this chapter, especially if they do not need to know the methods used to estimate the frequency of 100 percent implicit FTETs.

1. THE INCENTIVE TO WORK FULL TIME AS A FUNCTION OF FAMILY SITUATION

Three features of the family situation affect the reward to full-time work under the ACA: expected (in the actuarial sense) annual medical expenditures for the family, hereafter denoted M;[32] the length h of the full-time work schedule; and the amount O of spousal and asset income in a worker's family. Larger families and families with older adults are expected to have greater medical expenses. Because silver plan premiums are set to cover 70 percent of expected medical expenditures, I take M to be the silver plan premium (without subsidies, as estimated by the KFF1 calculator) divided by 0.7. In order to represent incentives for calendar year 2016, the 2014 values from the KFF1 calculator are scaled by the aforementioned assumed 2014–16 health cost growth relative to wages. For example, the situation noted above of the family of four and parents age 30 has a silver plan premium of \$10,684 plus assumed health cost growth beyond 2014. Both M and O are expressed as a ratio to the federal poverty line.[33] The family-of-four situation noted above has $O = 0$ by definition and $M = 0.66$.

For each family situation defined by $\{h,M,O\}$ with $h > 29$, I compare two employment situations: situation (FT), in which the work schedule is h hours per week; and situation (PT) with a 29-hour work schedule. Exchange subsidies are available in situation (PT) but not in situation (FT). I calculate the hypothetical amount E of pretax compensation, if any, that would generate the same disposable incomes in both situations (FT) and (PT). That amount satisfies

$$
\begin{aligned}
0 \equiv (1-t)\left(1-\frac{29}{h}\right) E - A &+ \left[0.83t - 0.3\delta\left(O + \frac{29}{h}E\right)\right]M \\
&- max\left\{0, 0.7M - \pi\left(O + \frac{29}{h}E\right)\left(O + \frac{29}{h}E\right)\right\}
\end{aligned}
$$

(4.1)

where t denotes the marginal personal income tax rate (not including the phaseout of ACA subsidies), $h > 29$ denotes weekly work hours in 2011, and A denotes the extra work expenses associated with working h hours rather than 29, also expressed as a ratio to the federal poverty line. $O + \frac{29}{h}E$ is household AGI, relative to the poverty line, if the worker earning E for h hours of work would work 29 hours instead. $\delta(\cdot)$ and $\pi(\cdot)$ are the schedules specified by the ACA determining the discount on out-of-pocket costs and the cap on the share of AGI to be spent on premiums paid to the health insurance exchanges.[34]

The first two terms in equation (4.1) are the income after taxes and work expenses, respectively, created by working h hours rather than 29, holding tax exclusions constant. The first term in square brackets denotes the tax savings from the exclusion of ESI premiums, equal to $0.83M$, that are available when obtaining coverage through the employer but not available when obtaining coverage on the exchanges.[35] The second term in square brackets is the savings on out-of-pocket costs available only when obtaining subsidized coverage on the exchanges. The max term denotes the premium tax credits received so that premium payments do not exceed the ACA's cap.[36]

For anyone who has worked full time for an employer offering ESI, the actual compensation in situation (FT) (including the amount of employer-paid premiums for health insurance, and expressed as a ratio to the federal poverty line) can be compared with the critical value E, if one exists, from equation (4.1) and corresponding to his family situation. If E does not exist or is less than actual compensation, then working h hours results in more disposable income than working 29 hours because the worker is earning enough per hour beyond 29 to offset the various taxes and forgone subsidies that come with working full time. Otherwise, working h hours results in no more disposable income than working 29 hours does, and the ACA's subsidies present the worker with a 100+ percent tax situation like the one illustrated in table 4.8.

The family-of-four situation noted above has a critical compensation value of $E = 209$ percent of the federal poverty line.[37] Anyone working in that family situation with actual compensation (including the value of employer health insurance) less than the critical value would have less disposable income in a full-time position than with a 29-hour schedule. Because there are millions of families with incomes between 100 and 209 percent of the poverty line, readers should not be surprised that millions of workers will find that part-time work pays more than full-time work.

2. ONE HUNDRED PERCENT FTET FREQUENCIES MEASURED FROM THE SURVEY DATA

In order to use these results to measure the national frequency of persons facing 100 percent implicit FTETs, I take the members of table 4.4's CPS sample who had coverage through their employer in March 2012. I measure the normal (that is, but for the ACA's implicit FTET) weekly work schedule h as usual weekly work hours as reported in the March 2012 CPS, and I discard sample members with $h < 30$.[38] I measure spousal and asset income as the difference O between the CPS variable for family income and the CPS variable for the worker's wage and salary income, expressed as a ratio to the federal poverty line. The CPS also indicates the number and age of family members, which is what the KFF1 calculator needs to calculate M.[39] These three variables $\{h,M,O\}$ by themselves are enough to calculate the critical compensation-to-poverty ratio E.

For every sample member, I measure 2011 full-time compensation, including the amount of employer-paid ESI premiums, as a ratio to the federal poverty line and compare it to the critical ratio E. Those with compensation less than the critical value are, on the basis of their CPS health insurance weight, projected to represent the national population in 2016 and shown in table 4.9. Depending on whether additional work expenses are considered to be an expense of working full time, 2.6 to 3.8 million household heads and spouses would, under the ACA, have more disposable income working 29 hours than working their usual full-time schedule. If we count the number of hours subject to the 100 percent tax, rather than the number of workers, the total is up to 39 million hours per week.[40]

Because the ACA presents about 20 million full-time heads and spouses with an implicit FTET of some magnitude, by subtraction I conclude that the implicit FTET is usually less than 100 percent. Nevertheless, 3 million workers is a lot on the scale of overall part-time employment.

Table 4.9 shows that somewhat more than half of the workers subject to the 100 percent FTET report 40-hour work schedules, but this is the result of the fact that (reported) 40-hour schedules are generally common among workers with ESI. Among the few workers facing an implicit FTET and reporting, say, a schedule with 30 to 32 hours, the majority face an FTET rate in excess of 100 percent because they would lose relatively little wage income by cutting their schedule just an hour or two.

Only household heads and spouses in which at least one of them is under 65 years old are represented in table 4.9. Table 4.10 displays the likelihood of various subdemographics of nonelderly heads and spouses to experience an FTET rate of at least 100 percent. Unmarried people are more likely than married people to face the 100-plus rate because the former do not have a spouse with opportunities for family coverage. Unmarried women are more likely to do so than unmarried

TABLE 4.9. ESI employees who would make more by working less by work schedule, calendar year 2016.

Weekly work hours but for the implicit FTET	Number of ESI workers that would have more disposable income with a 29-hour schedule:	
	Ignoring work expense	Including work expense
30	175,019	181,054
31	1,865	1,865
32	136,280	142,510
33	10,485	10,898
34	7,418	9,329
35	257,991	311,634
36	91,242	118,694
37	36,657	58,887
38	82,028	112,981
39	5,721	9,066
40	1,713,374	2,652,045
More than 40	109,520	231,042
Total:	2,627,601	3,840,005
Aggregate weekly hours taxed 100+ percent:	24,738,654	38,671,497

Notes: Work expenses are assumed to be $20 per 8 hours.

The workers in the table are not subject to the employer penalty. Numbers of workers are national projections from the March 2012 CPS, and scaled for population growth through 2016 by a factor of 1.01^4. I assume that no workers have hourly earnings below $7.25. The table excludes workers with 2011 work schedules of less than 30 hours per week.

TABLE 4.10. Propensity that the implicit FTET fully erases the reward to full-time work among nonpoor nonelderly heads and spouses working at least 30 hours and in households less than 400 percent FPL

	Overall				
Age	Unmarried		Married		All
	Men	Women	Men	Women	
Less than 25	0.025	0.034	0.049	0.020	0.031
25–34	0.038	0.071	0.052	0.034	0.050
35–44	0.061	0.111	0.058	0.043	0.066
45–54	0.068	0.127	0.082	0.078	0.090
55–64	0.124	0.232	0.120	0.169	0.162
All ages	0.059	0.116	0.073	0.070	0.080
Among those covered by their employer and facing an implicit FTET of some magnitude					
Less than 25	0.061	0.092	0.143	0.114	0.088
25–34	0.068	0.116	0.122	0.136	0.105
35–44	0.110	0.166	0.117	0.147	0.134
45–54	0.109	0.184	0.164	0.219	0.169
55–64	0.186	0.305	0.236	0.348	0.271
All ages	0.103	0.181	0.152	0.215	0.159

Note: The alternative to full-time work is assumed to be a 29-hour work schedule.

men because the former are more likely to be working 30 to 39 hours even without the ACA. Married men are about equally likely as married women to face the 100-plus rate because men are more likely to be in a position offering ESI (e.g., married women may not be employed full time), but women are more likely to be working 30 to 39 hours.

G. Conclusions

At least 20 million workers, and probably as many as 30 million, will have their eligibility for the ACA's generous new exchange subsidies hinge on their employment situation. During months when they are either working part time (fewer than 30 hours per week) or not working at all, they are eligible. During months when they are working full time, they are ineligible. For these workers, full-time work thereby carries with it a large new tax: giving up exchange subsidies. Both the exchange subsidies and the employer penalty act as full-time employment taxes—FTETs for short—and are central to the economics in this book.

Full-time workers can avoid the exchange subsidy instance of the FTET by working for an employer that does not offer coverage, but then they run into the employer penalty instance of the FTET. This is the lesson from figure 4.1 that begins this chapter. Full-time employees at employers offering coverage are neither subsidized nor penalized, which is why the figure's bottom red star is at zero. Full-time employees at employers not offering coverage experience both, and on average they nearly cancel, as shown by figure 4.1's top red star.[41] The net subsidy is not exactly zero, but figure 4.1 suggests it is much closer to zero than either the full penalty or the full subsidy, which is why an important combined effect of the two FTETs is to push full-time employees into figure 4.1's middle category: either part-time schedules or not working.[42] Figure 4.1 is only a small first step toward measuring incentives for workers to switch employers and employers to change their coverage offerings—chapters 5, 7, and 8 offer additional results for that purpose—but it does show how it can be useful to look at the ACA from the perspective of FTETs.

The longstanding exclusion of ESI premiums from payroll and personal income taxes is itself an instance of an FTET, with a negative sign. That is, full-time workers can use the exclusion to avoid taxes, but nonworkers and uncovered part-time employees cannot. The exclusion is relevant for understanding coverage decisions under the ACA (see chapter 7), for measuring the combined total of ACA and non-ACA incentives (see sections D and E above), or for comparing actual full-time work incentives with the incentives that would be present in a hypothetical world without taxes. But the hypothetical no-tax world is not of interest in this book. My purpose is to compare the labor market with the ACA to how the labor market would have evolved without the ACA, and to calculate the impact of the ACA as the difference between the two. In both of those cases, ESI premiums are excluded from payroll and personal income taxation and thereby are hardly relevant for understanding the impact of the ACA on the incentives to work full time. Because the ACA is not creating or eliminating the ESI tax exclusion, the tax exclusion is not a significant part of the ACA's contribution to overall incentives to work full time.[43]

In other words, a new FTET levied on ESI employees will affect behavior on average, even if the new tax is not enough to offset the tax advantages of ESI, because there were employees before the ACA who were on the margin between ESI and other types of coverage (including no coverage). Even a small subsidy to the other types of coverage would move a few employees off ESI, because even without the subsidy the value of the tax advantage is offset (from the point of view of the employees on the margin) by other costs of ESI or other benefits of other coverage. The empirical studies reviewed in Congressional Budget Office (2007) confirm that marginal changes in the relative price of ESI affect behavior even when ESI remains a net tax advantage.

Among the 20 or 30 million workers whose exchange-subsidy eligibility hinges on their employment situation, the salary equivalent of their average subsidy forgone is more than $9,000 per year. Because exchange plans have different characteristics from employer health plans, I estimate that the average effective FTET among them is about $6,000 or $7,000 per year. To put it another way, a typical one of the 20 to 30 million workers who will face the implicit FTET would, if she discontinued full-time employment status, make her family eligible

TABLE 4.11. Aggregate weekly hours taxed 100% in 2016 by the ACA in millions, compared with national aggregate hours

	Treatment of work expense	
	Ignored	Included
Hours 100% taxed by the employer penalty	11.0	43.7
Hours 100% taxed by the exchange subsidies	24.7	38.7
Total hours 100% taxed	35.7	82.4
Total as a percentage of national aggregate hours	0.6%	1.5%

Note: National aggregate hours are from the March 2012 CPS and are projected to 2016 assuming 1% population growth per year. See also tables 3.3 and 4.9.

for subsidies that are worth an amount equal to what could be earned in five or six hours of work per week for 52 weeks per year.

Large subsidies like these create prevalent and especially perverse incentives. In 2016, 3 or 4 million workers will have no short-term financial reward to working full time because a full-time schedule will not add enough income to offset the exchange subsidies forgone. These are in addition to the 5 million workers or so who have their reward to full-time work erased by the ACA's employer penalties. Table 4.11 compares the hours subject to confiscatory taxes to all of the hours worked in the economy. The first row is the number of weekly hours worked beyond 29 by a worker who, in 2016, would make more by cutting his usual full-time schedule to 29 hours and thereby relieving his employer from the ACA's employer penalty (see table 3.3). The second row is the number of weekly hours worked beyond 29 by a worker who, in 2016, would make more by cutting the usual full-time schedule to 29 hours and thereby becoming eligible for exchange subsidies (see table 4.9). The columns show results from two alternative estimates of work expenses. For example, each worker with a usual weekly schedule of 40 hours and facing a 100 percent FTET contributes 11 hours to one of the two rows in the table, depending on the source of the FTET (penalty or subsidy). The third row is the sum of the two above, and the final row expresses the total as a percentage of national aggregate hours. The hours taxed 100 percent by the ACA will be up to 1.5 percent of total hours in the economy, and this does not even begin to count the hours that are taxed somewhat less than 100 percent.

It is not difficult to imagine that hours taxed so heavily might disappear from the market economy. An economic model capable of reaching conclusions about the consequences of the ACA's various taxes is beyond the scope of this chapter, but table 4.11 is our first hint that the ACA might be depressing aggregate work hours by at least a couple of percent.

Although the exchange subsidies are primarily an FTET, they also contain large new implicit income taxes. Moreover, the structure of the implicit income taxes is related to the patterns of FTETs across families, and it is therefore important for understanding both the types of families whose behavior will be changed by the exchange subsidies and how employers will be induced to change their use of labor. Chapter 5 introduces the mechanics of the implicit income taxes and presents additional measures of their economic significance.

Appendix 4.1: Using the ARRA's COBRA Subsidy to Forecast Participation in the ACA's Premium Assistance

Since the 1980s, federal and state laws have given employees leaving ESI jobs the option of continuing their health coverage for up to 18 months (U.S. Department of Labor 2013). Family ESI coverage can also be continued. The former employees reimburse their former employer for the full cost of the coverage with after-tax dollars, plus a small administration fee. The continuation coverage is usually referred to as COBRA coverage.

Under the March 2009 American Recovery and Reinvestment Act (hereafter ARRA), 65 percent of the employee cost of COBRA coverage was paid by the federal government to the former employer on behalf of the former employee if the person was involuntarily terminated after September 1, 2008, and was not eligible for another group health plan or for Medicare. Subsidy recipients were required to pay 35 percent of the coverage. On filing personal taxes for the year in which the subsidy was received, the subsidy was clawed back for filers whose AGI exceeded $125,000 ($250,000 if married and filing jointly).

The ARRA subsidy has a lot in common with the exchange subsidies created by the ACA. Both subsidies become available to an ESI employee only on leaving the payroll, and then only if they have no other group plan option such as spousal coverage. The ARRA subsidy was more restrictive in that it excluded voluntary terminations such as quits or retirements, and it did not subsidize out-of-pocket health expenses. Both subsidies were paid directly to the insurer (the employer in the case of ESI and an insurance company in the case of the exchange subsidy).[44] In both cases, the subsidized household was paying some of the health insurance premiums with their own after-tax dollars. Both programs could have imperfect take-up among the unemployed because, among other things, people might be unaware of the program, or they might choose to forgo health insurance. Under the ACA, however, former ESI employees will have to change health plans—leave their former employer plan and join an exchange plan—in order to obtain the subsidy.[45] The ARRA COBRA subsidy was enacted as a temporary subsidy and was in fact terminated after less than two years. The ACA subsidies were enacted permanently, although of course a future Congress could modify or terminate them.

At the time of my writing, data are sparse on the ARRA COBRA subsidy, but there is enough to get a rough idea of the program's take-up rate, the fraction of ESI employees who can obtain coverage through a spouse, and perhaps also the willingness of the Treasury Department to verify whether a program participant has access to coverage through a spouse. In order to estimate the fraction of ESI job terminations among nonelderly household heads and spouses in families satisfying the ACA's income criteria that will result in exchange subsidies, including the fact that some eligible families will elect not to participate, I estimate the fraction of nonelderly ESI employees involuntarily terminated during 2009 who received COBRA subsidies as household head or spouse. To measure the numerator, I have the U.S. Treasury's report that 1.05 million households received the COBRA subsidy during the fourth quarter of 2009, although Treasury noted additional 2009 subsidy claims would be received after the report went to press (U.S. Department of Treasury 2010).

Ideally the denominator would be the number of nonelderly household heads and spouses who were involuntarily terminated from ESI jobs after September 1, 2008, and were still unemployed as of the fourth quarter of 2009, which is approximately a 12-month window of terminations. I use the March 2010 CPS to make an approximation to the denominator to a slightly different window of terminations: calendar year 2009.

Using the nonelderly household heads and spouses employed at the time of the March 2010 CPS interview and working at least one week in 2009, I estimate the probability of having ESI at the time of the interview as a linear function of a cubic in age, and a full set of interactions among gender, marital status, presence of children, and (most important) full-time work status in 2009. I project the probability to the unemployed in the sample who worked at least one week in 2009 and were unemployed at least one week in 2009, and predict that 58 percent of those 3.8 million would be in ESI jobs if they were working.

Mulligan (2012b) estimated that 68 percent of nonelderly household heads and spouses receive unemployment benefits (hereafter, UI) during at least part of their unemployment spell. Because UI also has involuntary termination as an eligibility criterion, I use the 68 percent again as an estimate of the fraction of unemployed household heads and spouses who were terminated involuntarily.

Table 4.2 shows that 19 percent of unemployed nonelderly household heads and spouses in March 2012 actually were insured through a family member, and presumably more could have been insured that way but declined the option. The data used for table 4.1 suggest that 25 percent of full-time ESI workers also have a spouse working full time for an ESI employer, so I assume that 75 percent of the unemployed cannot obtain coverage through a spouse.

Finally, some of those unemployed at the end of 2009 returned to work or left the labor force before the March CPS interview. I therefore rescale by a factor of 1.44, which is the ratio of the number of nonelderly household heads and spouses in December 2009 unemployed from one to 49 weeks to the number of nonelderly household heads and spouses in March 2010 unemployed 14 to 62 weeks.

Assuming that UI eligibility and ESI eligibility are uncorrelated, the denominator of my subsidy incidence rate estimate would be 1.63 million = 1.44*0.75*0.68*0.58*3.8 million. The corresponding subsidy take-up rate estimate is 64 percent. This take-up rate could be more or less than the exchange subsidy take-up rate among persons leaving ESI jobs. On one hand, unemployed people exercising their COBRA option were staying with an insurance plan that was familiar, whereas a person leaving a former employer's coverage for an exchange plan will be trying something new. On the other hand, employer plans are expensive and unemployment may be a good time to consider a cheaper plan: the exchanges offer that option (e.g., apply the premium assistance to a bronze plan). The individual mandate increases the demand for coverage, and the mandate did not begin until after the ARRA expired.

The exchange subsidy take-up rate among persons leaving ESI jobs is not relevant for any of the exhibits in the chapter, but it is needed in chapter 5. In those cases I use the 64 percent estimate.

Appendix 4.2: Additional Sensitivity Analysis

Figure 4.2 shows that, at the median hourly compensation, it takes 5.6 hours of work per week to earn the amount equal to the average exchange subsidy forgone by a household head or spouse who works full time for an ESI employer. When calculated separately by marital status using table 4.4, the average subsidy net of an exchange-features discount is about $6,600 for those married and $3,100 for those unmarried. Expressed as an hour equivalent, the weekly amounts are 7.3 for those married and 4.3 for those unmarried. Note that these amounts are conditional on facing an implicit full-time employment tax, which is more common among unmarried household heads.

Mulligan (forthcoming) has an alternative approach that estimates the exchange subsidies' hour equivalent separately worker by worker, among the sample of CPS respondents deemed to be eligible for a positive exchange subsidy if only their employer had not offered them coverage. In doing so, the paper assumes that CPS respondents employed full time by the federal government are offered health insurance coverage. It estimates that the average hour equivalent of the exchange subsidies (net of an exchange-features discount) is somewhere in the range 6.8 to 7.5, depending on what is assumed about the quality of hourly wage measurements in the CPS. The paper also notes that the median hour equivalent in the same sample is only 4.7 hours per week and discusses the influence of households with more than two adults on estimates of the average. Although most of this book takes the hourly equivalent to be 5.5 or 5.6 hours per week, based on Mulligan (forthcoming) and the other factors noted above, the book also presents various sensitivity analyses that consider hourly equivalents as high as 7.2 and as low as 4.1.

5 | Exchange Subsidies and Their Implicit Income Taxes

Chapter 4 shows how exchange subsidies are linked to employment status, and it uses the average dollar amount of the exchange subsidies to measure the contribution of the subsidies to the incentives to change employment status. The exchange subsidies are also linked to family income and thereby act as a new implicit income tax in addition to their role as a full-time employment tax. The purpose of this chapter is to measure the size of the implicit income tax and estimate the number of people who will face it.

Section A introduces an income-based formula that determines the amount and types of the exchange subsidies received by eligible families. Sections B and C show that the new implicit income tax rates commonly add more than twenty percentage points to the usual income and payroll taxes, and will be faced by more than 10 million workers in 2016. Section D shows how, as a result, there will be workers who can earn more unemployed than employed. Sections E, F, and G look at additional income-based formulas related to the exchange subsidies and incentives to work, including an examination of the disincentives associated with uncompensated care received by people without insurance coverage. The chapter concludes with a summary of the main measurement results from this and the previous two chapters that is used in chapters 6–10 to estimate the ACA's economic consequences.

A. The Sliding Scale for Exchange Subsidies

Every family's size and composition determines its opportunities for exchange subsidies. As in chapter 4, let $0.7M$ denote a family's premium for the second-cheapest silver plan on the basis of its size and composition (before subsidies), M denote the associated expected medical expenditures (in the actuarial sense, including loadings), and $0.3M$ denote average out-of-pocket expenses for participants in the silver plan, with all three quantities expressed as a ratio to the FPL.[1] The annualized exchange subsidies are, as a ratio to FPL:

(5.1) $$S(M, Y) = max\{0, 0.7M - \pi(Y)Y\} + \delta(Y)\,0.3M$$

where Y denotes the combined AGI ("family income") of the household head and spouse, expressed as a ratio to FPL. AGI is the amount that head and spouse show on their federal personal tax return as their wage and asset income for the calendar year.[2] $\pi()$ and $\delta()$ are the schedules specified by the ACA determining the cap on the share of AGI to be spent on premiums and the discount on out-of-pocket costs, respectively. Because the full premium is $0.7M$ and the ACA says that a family with AGI equal to Y does not have to spend more than $\pi(Y)Y$, the subsidy is $0.7M - \pi(Y)Y$ unless the full premium is already less than the spending cap.

Table 5.1 displays the parameters that describe the schedules $\pi()$ and $\delta()$. Each row is a household income interval relative to FPL beginning at the income amount indicated in the first column. The second column shows the premium charge for a family with income at the bottom end of the interval, expressed as a percentage of household income.[3] The premium percentage increases smoothly within the interval, and as it crosses the next income threshold, with the exceptions (noted in the last column) of (1) the 1–1.33 interval where the percentage is constant at 2 percent and jumps discretely to 3 percent and (2) the 4+ interval where there is no premium cap (the premium jumps from 9.5 percent of income to the full premium). For example, a family with AGI equal to twice the poverty line ($Y = 2$) has its 2014 family premium capped at 6.3 percent of income. In terms of equation (5.1), this means $\pi(2) = 0.063$ for calendar year 2014. A family with AGI equal to 225 percent of the poverty line ($Y = 2.25$) has its 2014 premium capped at 7.175 percent of income because 2.25 is halfway between 2 and 2.5 and 7.175 is halfway between 6.3 and 8.05. Each premium cap is greater in years 2015 and beyond according to the degree to which health insurance premiums increase more than national income.[4]

Plan participants pay their designated premium, and then their health-care providers are reimbursed amounts that are expected to be

TABLE 5.1. Sliding scale exchange subsidies
as a function of household income for the calendar year

Income as a ratio to FPL	Percentage of income owed as premium	Discount on out-of-pocket cost (jumps when crossing thresholds)	Notes on interval
1	2%	80%	Premium percentage is constant on this interval, jumping at 1.33
1.33	3%	80%	
1.5	4%	57%	
2	6.3%	10%	
2.5	8.05%	0%	
3	9.5%	0%	Premium percentage is constant on this interval
4	9.5%	0%	
4+	Full premium	0%	Premium jumps here because the premium cap is eliminated

Notes: (a) The first column indicates the bottom threshold of the income interval.

(b) Exchange participants pay a premium that is the minimum of the full premium and the applicable percentage from the second column. The premium assistance is the amount, if any, that the premium is less than the full premium.

(c) Income percentages change linearly between income thresholds unless otherwise noted.

(d) FPL = federal poverty line.

(e) Income percentages for 2015–18, and any year thereafter in which the exchange subsides are less than 0.504% of GDP, are indexed to the excess of health cost inflation over income growth.

less than (typically 70 percent of) total covered medical expenses, with the remaining costs "shared with" (that is, charged to) plan participants as various out-of-pocket costs such as deductibles, co-payments, coinsurance rates, and so on. The third column of the table shows the "cost-sharing" discount families receive as a function of their household income. This discount is a step function of income, jumping down to 57 from 80 percent at 1.5 FPL, to 10 percent at 2 FPL, and then down to zero at 2.5 FPL. For example, people at 1.4 FPL on a silver plan can expect (in the actuarial sense) to have their premiums cover 70 percent of medical expenses. Of the remaining 30 percent, six percentage points would be paid by the participant and the remaining 24 percentage points paid by taxpayers in the form of a cost-sharing subsidy for the plan participant.

The exchange subsidies shown in equation (5.1) are a function of AGI Y and expected family medical expenses M. Family medical

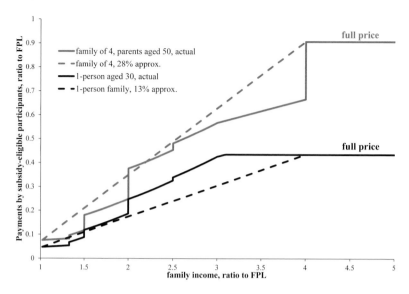

FIGURE 5.1. 2016 health payments as a function of household income and policy type.

expenses net of the subsidies are therefore the difference between M and the subsidies shown in equation (5.1), which is itself a function of Y and M. Figure 5.1's solid lines graph the payment function for two selected values of M: the black line corresponds to the relatively low value of M associated with a one-person household age 30, and the red line corresponds with a higher level associated with a couple age 50 with two children. Values of M associated with families in between these two in terms of size or member age would make a subsidy schedule between figure 5.1's solid lines. The horizontal axis measures family income (Y) and the vertical axis measures the payments. Both schedules reach a plateau indicating the full health payments without subsidies. For a high M family like the one shown in red, the plateau is reached at 400 percent FPL because at that point the family ceases being eligible for subsidies. For a low M family like the one shown in black, the plateau is reached at lower incomes because the full premium itself is considered affordable for families at, say, 350 percent FPL.[5]

Although the premium caps $\pi(Y)$ are the same for the two types of families, health payments can differ because larger and older families have more total out-of-pocket expenses. The out-of-pocket expenses are greatest for the families with income near 400 percent FPL, which is why the gap between the black and the red schedules are greatest in that range.

B. The Sliding Scale Contains a Large Implicit Income Tax

Each of figure 5.1's solid schedules refers to a single health plan. The points along a schedule reflect differing payments for the same plan. For example, a family of four will pay twice as much if its income is 240 percent FPL than it will if its income is 180 percent FPL, but the health benefits are exactly the same. To put it another way: by earning more, a family pays more for the same benefits. The extra payments are economically equivalent to an income tax, because tax payments and the extra health payments are not resulting in any extra goods or services for the family that pays them. To acknowledge this equivalence, the field of economics refers to schedules like the two shown in figure 5.1 as "implicit income tax" schedules (Congressional Budget Office 2010). The slope of the schedule is the marginal income tax rate.

For any family enrolled in an exchange plan for the entire calendar year, the slope of any one of the solid schedules is the rate that the ACA taxes their income for the year, in addition to other taxes paid by the family such as payroll tax and normal federal individual income taxes. A slope of, say, 0.2 means that an additional dollar earned by the family results in 20 cents in additional health payments for the same plan, which makes the implicit income tax rate 20 percent at that point on the schedule. The value of the implicit tax rate is especially sensitive to the exact position on the schedule because the schedule has a number of discrete "notches" or "cliffs" in it. In order to emphasize results that are not especially sensitive to notches and cliffs, I approximate the slopes of the sliding scales by averaging the various slopes, weighting by the width of the income interval over which they apply. Geometrically, the weighted average slope is equal to the slope of the straight dashed lines shown in figure 5.1. I used the weighted average slopes only for looking at the implicit income tax; my estimates of the implicit FTET in chapter 4 and elsewhere in the book use the solid schedules showing the precise health payments specified by the ACA.

The weighted average slope is equal to

$$(5.2) \qquad \tau(M) \equiv \frac{0.7M - \pi(1) + \delta(1)0.3M}{3} \approx 0.3M$$

where $\delta(1)$ is 0.8 (recall table 5.1) and the denominator is the width of the income interval over which the maximum subsidy is phased out. $\pi(1)$ is 0.02 in 2014 and indexed to the excess health cost inflation over income growth thereafter, which is why the weighted average slope is approximately 30 percent of the ratio of medical expenses to the poverty line.[6] A family of four therefore has a greater slope than a one-person family, as illustrated by the comparison of the two dashed lines in figure 5.1.

Also note that the marriage of two exchange plan participants increases the work disincentive for both of them by increasing M for both bride and groom. As the groom earns a dollar before marriage, he loses some of his subsidies but none of hers. As he earns a dollar after marriage, both of them lose subsidies from his earnings. The situation is symmetric for the bride. In terms of the arithmetic of equation (5.2), an unmarried person has a marginal income tax rate of about 0.3 times his or her personal M (including dependents, if any), whereas a married person has a marginal income tax rate of about 0.3 times the couple's M, which is the sum of bride's and groom's personal M's.

The income taxes implicit in the exchange subsidies are most relevant for nonelderly household heads and spouses who receive the exchange subsidies even when they are working because the amount of work they do determines where they are on the health payment schedule applicable to their family. In other words, these are typically heads and spouses whose employers do not offer coverage and who choose to get coverage from the exchanges rather than going uninsured or enrolling in Medicaid. Figure 5.2 displays my estimates of the likely distribution of the weighted-average slope (equation 5.2) among nonelderly household heads and spouses between 100 and 400 percent of the poverty line, based on the members of the CPS sample I used in chapters 3 and 4 who do not work for an ESI employer and do not have a spouse working for an ESI employer. The average and median slopes are 21 and 20 percent, respectively. Half of the sample is between

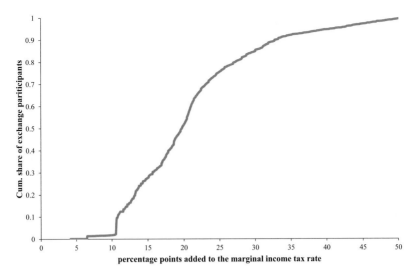

FIGURE 5.2. The distribution of the ACA's implicit income tax rates among subsidy-eligible heads and spouses on exchanges throughout 2016. Cliffs are smoothed and premium reconciliation is excluded.

14 percent and 25 percent. The ACA's implicit income tax rates can exceed 40 percent for a couple approaching age 65 or for a couple with a dependent adult who is less than age 65.

C. The Number of Workers Facing the New Income Tax

The workers described in figure 5.2 will, by definition, be subsidy eligible and insured on the exchanges throughout calendar year 2016, and thereby face a new implicit income tax created by the ACA. It follows that they are not facing the ACA's implicit FTET, usually because they are never working for an ESI employer during the year. That is, none of the workers described in figure 5.2 are among the 20 to 30 million workers tabulated in table 4.1. However, some of the workers who will face the ACA's implicit FTET and included in table 4.1 will have parts of the calendar year in which they are not working full time for an ESI employer. To the degree they are covered on the exchanges during those parts of the year, the ACA also presents them with an implicit tax on their income from the entire calendar year because calendar year income is used to determine what they pay for coverage during the parts of the year in which they are covered on the exchanges. The rate of implicit taxation is the rate (equation 5.2) times the fraction of the year for which they participate.[7]

The Congressional Budget Office estimates that, after a phase-in period of a couple of years, exchange plan enrollment will reach about 25 million people.[8] On the basis of CPS data, I assume that about half of them—13 million, or about 9 percent of the workforce in that year if it continues to grow at the rate of population growth—are household heads and spouses who work sometime during the calendar year, and the rest of the 25 million are either dependents or people who do not work.[9] I assume 64 percent of ESI workers get exchange coverage when they are subsidy eligible (see appendix 4.1), which means 6 million part-time workers and almost 1 million people out of work who normally work full time are already represented in table 4.1 and about 7 million are not. The remaining 7 million, or about 4 percent of the workforce, are working for an employer that does not offer affordable coverage.

Table 5.2 summarizes the results on the number of workers affected by (first two columns), and the magnitudes of (remaining columns), the taxes examined so far in this book. The top part of the table represents the 26 percent of the workforce working for employers not offering coverage. Five percentage points of the 26 are heads and spouses insured on exchanges (the 6 million noted above) and are represented in the second row of table 5.2. The 6 million exchange participants who are part-time workers for ESI employers are represented in table 5.2's sixth row. As noted above, the exchange subsidies add about 21.1 percentage points to the marginal tax rate on earnings (and other income sources) by heads and spouses insured on the exchanges, which is why table 5.2 has 21.1 percent entered in the fourth column for those two rows. Table 5.2 has 0.4 percent entered in the fourth column for those employed full time by employers offering coverage because their income counts against the exchange subsidies they receive during the parts of the year (if any) in which they are not employed.

The heads and spouses insured and subsidized on the exchanges also face a full-time employment tax, in addition to the implicit income tax from the exchange subsidies. The amount of the applicable

TABLE 5.2. ACA-incentive scenarios

Calendar year 2016. Categories are mutually exclusive.

Type of worker	Employment shares	Marginal earnings tax rates					FTET measured in hrs/wk
		Base	Exchange subsidies	Premium reconc.	Uncomp. care	Combined	
Works for employer not offering affordable coverage	0.26						
Head or spouse insured on exchanges, and subsidized	0.05	25%	21.1%	2.2%	−2.4%	45.9%	4.0
All others	0.21	25%	0	0	0	25.0%	4.0
Works for employer offering affordable coverage	0.74						
Full-time status alone blocks eligibility for exchange subsidies	0.17	25%	0.4%	0.0%	0	25.5%	5.5
Head or spouse insured on exchanges, working part time	0.04	25%	21.1%	2.2%	−2.4%	45.9%	5.5
All others	0.54	25%	0	0	0	25.0%	0
All workers (employment-weighted average)	**1.00**	**25%**	**1.9%**	**0.2%**	**−0.2%**	**26.9%**	**2.2**
Addendum: all working heads & spouses insured on exchanges	0.09	25%	21.1%	2.2%	−2.4%	45.9%	4.7
Addendum: all ESI workers facing the implicit FTET	0.20	25%	4.3%	0.4%	−0.4%	29.3%	5.5

Notes: FTET denotes full-time employment tax, either explicit or implicit, and is net of a 25 percent exchange features discount, when applicable. The "part time" row of the second panel also includes full-time employees who are transitionally insured on the exchanges. The employment shares indicate the shares of workers who have an FTET in their budget constraint, even those who make choices that avoid any payment. The uncompensated care column refers to the ACA's impact on uncompensated care; a baseline amount of uncompensated care is reflected in the base marginal earnings tax rate.

FTET, if any, is shown in table 5.2's final column. For those working for employers not offering affordable coverage, full-time work triggers a penalty for the employer, or the threat of a penalty, which chapter 3 showed to be an amount that is typically the earnings generated by 4.0 hours of work per week. The remaining working and subsidized heads and spouses on the exchange must be working for an employer that does offer affordable coverage and, with a very few exceptions, thereby working part time or else they would not be eligible for subsidies. These part-time workers face, but do not actually pay, an implicit FTET, which means that moving to full-time work by itself will render them ineligible for subsidies. A typical amount of FTET that they face is, as shown in chapter 4, an amount equal to the earnings generated by 5.5 hours per week.[10] Readers interested in the household budget constraint arithmetic represented in table 5.2 should pause here to take a look at appendix 5.1.

D. Under the ACA, Unemployment Will Sometimes Pay as Much as Work Does

It is well known that, in some circumstances, families before the ACA could face combined marginal income tax rates close to 50 percent for personal income and payroll taxes, not to mention the implicit taxes associated with the loss of unemployment benefits and means-tested subsidies.[11] For example, even without the ACA, a family between 100 and 200 percent of the poverty line might be in a 10–15 percent normal federal personal income tax bracket, plus another 21 percentage points from the phase-out of its federal earned income tax credit (hereafter, EITC), plus 7.65 percentage points for employee payroll taxes, plus another five points or so for state income taxes.

High marginal tax rate situations are amplified by the rates shown in figure 5.2 to the degree that high marginal tax rate families get health insurance on the exchanges. Table 5.3 illustrates the extreme possibilities by comparing two calendar year scenarios. The first column of the table is a scenario in which the sole earner is employed for 10 months and unemployed the other two. I assume that unemployment benefits replace half of the normal paycheck, so the first scenario

TABLE 5.3. The ACA can erase the reward to work for exchange plan participants

An example of how unemployment can be almost "free" under the ACA

	Scenario for the calendar year		Difference =
	10 months employed	Employed all year	consequence of working 12 months rather than 10
Income sources			
Employment	10 paychecks	12 paychecks	2 paychecks
UI (only replaces half)	1 paycheck	0 paychecks	−1 paycheck
All income sources	11 paychecks	12 paychecks	1 paycheck
Incremental work-related expense amounts			
Individual Income Tax (IIT)			
Normal federal tax @ 10% * 1 paycheck			0.100 paychecks
EITC phase out @ 21.06% * 1 paycheck			0.211 paychecks
Exchange subsidy phase out @ 28% * 1 paycheck			0.280 paychecks
State IIT @ 5% * 1 paycheck			0.050 paychecks
Employee payroll @ 7.65% * 2 paychecks			0.153 paychecks
Work expense 10% * 2 months			0.200 paychecks
All expense categories			0.994 paychecks
Incremental income sources net of work-related expenses			**0.006 paychecks for 2.000 months work**

Notes: A "paycheck" is an amount of money equal to one month's salary from work. UI denotes unemployment insurance benefits. EITC denotes earned income tax credits. To simply illustrate the economics of a 50 percent UI replacement rate, UI is assumed to fully replace employment income for half of the time unemployed rather than replacing half of the income all of the time. UI is taxable by the IIT, but not by the payroll tax.

yields 11 months' total pay for the year, before expenses, as shown in the top panel of the table. The second scenario yields 12 months' total pay before expenses, all of it from the employer. The final column of the table is the difference between the two scenarios, namely, one month additional total pay from working the two extra months.

The next panel shows the various expenses incurred as a consequence of working 12 months rather than 10. Only one month of additional personal income tax is owed by working 12 months rather than 10 because, as noted above, the extra two months of work generates only one additional month of personal income. The individual income taxes are of four types: normal federal tax at 10 percent, phaseout of the EITC at 21.06 percent, phaseout of exchange subsidies at 28 percent, and state income tax at 5 percent. Payroll taxes and work expenses accrue only for both of the months. Altogether, working the eleventh and twelfth months adds practically as much to expenses as to income, about one month's pay. In other words, the short-term financial reward to working the two extra months is essentially zero—0.006 paychecks to be exact.

Table 5.3 cannot be "blamed" on notches or cliffs in the exchange subsidy schedules because, as shown by the red dashed line in figure 5.1, the 28 percent rate is based on a linear approximation to those schedules that eliminates all notches and cliffs. In some ways, table 5.3 underestimates the incentives for exchange plan participants to remain unemployed because it assumes that the alternative to unemployment is employment at a normal rate of pay, rather than a lower rate of pay (Mulligan 2012a). Nevertheless, the marginal income tax rate from the ACA's exchange subsidies varies across families; 28 percent is just an example. Many workers will not experience table 5.3's prohibitive disincentives because they do not experience the phaseout of the earned income tax credit or do not experience the new income tax implicit in the ACA's exchange subsidies. As of the time of writing, I have not calculated the number of workers for whom the ACA's implicit income tax makes their combined marginal tax rate exceed 100 percent, but for sure the number is significantly greater than zero because none of the expense situations shown in the table are especially rare or mutually incompatible.

E. Yet Another Means Test: The Reconciliation of Advanced Premium Tax Credits

The means-tested discounts a family receives during the calendar year (hereafter, "coverage year") will often derive from the income they reported on historical tax returns (usually the return from the second year prior), and its subsidies must be reconciled with the family's actual income at the conclusion of the coverage year.[12] In principle, the subsidies could be fully reconciled by having subsidy excesses debited, or shortfalls credited, on the family's personal income tax return, in which case there would be no additional earning disincentive from the reconciliation process itself. At the other extreme, reconciliation could be zero, in which case the earning disincentives noted above would apply to earnings in the year before last rather than earnings in the coverage year, but the reconciliation itself would not create additional disincentives.

The reconciliation process prescribed by the ACA is a hybrid of these two scenarios, and in so doing it adds to the implicit income tax. In particular, premium credits are fully reconciled for any family to be credited on its tax return. Cost-sharing subsidies are not reconciled. Families who received excess premium credits during the coverage year are limited on the amount they must repay, with the limits determined by family income during the coverage year. Appendixes 5.1 and 5.2 show how, on average among workers covered on the exchanges throughout the year, the means-tested reconciliation of excess credits adds an additional 2.2 percentage points to the marginal taxation of income reported on applicable tax returns for the coverage year. The 2.2 percentage points are therefore recorded in table 5.2's fifth column in the rows representing heads and spouses insured on the exchanges throughout the year.[13] The 2.2 percentage points are added to the 21.1 percentage points calculated in section B above.

F. Two Longstanding Disincentives Eased by the ACA's Exchange Subsidies

Unemployment insurance (UI) is a major safety net program, and the benefits paid by the UI program are implicitly taxed by the ACA (and any other income tax) because UI benefits are part of the household income that determines a household's assistance with health insurance premiums and out-of-pocket costs. In particular, persons laid off from a non-ESI job before the ACA would find their UI benefits taxed at normal marginal personal income tax rates, but under the ACA those marginal rates jump about 21 percentage points for recipients of exchange subsidies thanks to the ACA's "sliding scale" premium assistance. Table 5.3's example shows that the ACA still subsidizes unemployment, but in effect it transforms part of the longstanding assistance for the unemployed from cash benefits to tax credits.

The uninsured sometimes receive uncompensated care from health providers, and uncompensated care is likely means-tested. To the extent that the ACA reduces reliance on uncompensated care (Goolsbee 2011, oral testimony at 77:45), it may reduce the implicit income tax associated with it. I am not aware of a calculation of the nationwide average marginal tax rate from uncompensated care, but it can be estimated by assuming that its value is a linear function of household labor income, and by noting that (1) the uninsured paid, in 2008, an aggregate of $30 billion in health expenses (another $56 billion was uncompensated care for those patients) and (2) aggregate labor income among the uninsured was $510 billion.[14] This puts the average marginal labor income tax rate (including in the average those among the uninsured who do not use any health care) from uncompensated care at 5.9 percent.

Assuming that 40 percent of the heads and spouses insured on the exchanges would have been uninsured without the ACA, this makes the ACA's average impact (among heads and spouses insured on the exchanges) on the implicit marginal tax rate associated with uncompensated care equal to −2.4 percentage points. The combined income tax rate effect of the exchange subsidy phaseout and moving people off uncompensated care is still overwhelmingly in the direction of higher rates because the ACA does not merely move people from one implicit income tax to another. The large majority of people insured on the exchanges who would not, but for the ACA, have received uncompensated care during the calendar year are being faced with an implicit income tax from health care for the first time.[15] In addition, uncompensated care does not cover the range of services that silver plans do.

G. Conclusions

The ACA implicitly taxes incomes in a number of ways, in both positive and negative directions. Table 5.2 estimates that more than 10 million nonelderly household heads and spouses—about 9 percent of the workforce—will face the new income taxes in 2016, and among them marginal income tax rates will be about 20 percentage points higher than they would be without the ACA. Even without their cliffs or notches, the new income tax rates will be enough to completely erase the reward to work for some people, meaning more unemployment will give them more disposable income.

The implicit income tax rates in this chapter (not to be confused with implicit taxes on full-time employment) are limited to those faced by workers in households between 100 and 400 percent of the poverty |line. The ACA income-eligibility limits create both incentives and disincentives for poor workers to earn income. Some of the poor have been traditionally eligible for Medicaid as long as their income was below the program's income limit, and this opportunity encouraged them to keep their incomes low enough for eligibility (Yelowitz 1995). The ACA blunts their disincentive by giving them opportunities for health subsidies even when their income is above the poverty line. On the other hand, the ACA exempts the poor from the individual mandate, and the exemption is a new implicit tax on earning income above the poverty line (see chapter 2). Moreover, the disincentives associated with Medicaid's income limit are relevant for more workers now that the ACA is expanding eligibility for the program. The ACA also creates work disincentives for people above 400 percent of the poverty line to the extent that their work decisions might put their family income below the 400 percent FPL threshold.[16]

Economists were aware of the new implicit income tax created by the ACA's income-based payment schedules like those shown in figure 5.1.[17] But it was thought that the new implicit income tax was the largest new tax in the ACA, and even then affecting less than 10 percent of the workforce (Congressional Budget Office 2010, p. 48). My results contradict this assessment: as long as workers continue to be insured through employers, the most prevalent implicit tax in the ACA will be the implicit full-time employment tax featured in chapter 4. The bottom half of table 5.2 estimates that 20 percent of the workforce will face the implicit FTET in 2016.[18] Whereas the implicit *income* tax is measured by the slope of the payment schedules shown in figure 5.1, the implicit *FTET* is about the distance between the payment schedule and the full price for premiums and cost sharing. In effect, people avoid the FTET by leaving a full-time position and thereby jumping from the full-price payment amount onto figure 5.1's payment schedule indicating their family's subsidized payment.

The economic consequences of the health reform depend on the size and types of its taxes. The estimates from this and the previous chapters, summarized in table 5.2, are therefore critical to quantitatively modeling the effects of the ACA on the labor market and the rest of the economy. Chapters 6 through 9 show how such an analysis can be built on the tax estimates.

Appendix 5.1: The Household Budget Constraint Created by the ACA

So far this book has measured the ACA's new taxes without showing how they might affect economic performance. The household budget constraint is the first tool for examining the behavioral consequences of taxes because the budget constraint shows how taxes might affect household incentives and opportunities. This appendix briefly introduces a household budget constraint in order to clarify what incentives are being measured in table 5.2. Subsequent chapters revisit household budget constraints and their place in the wider economy.

Let $s_i \geq 0$ denote the annualized exchange subsidy received by the family of full-time worker i when the family is eligible, and worker i is either head or spouse of the family. $s_i(y_i) = FPL_i S(M_i, y_i/FPL_i)$ is the difference shown in equation (5.1), if any, between the full price of the family's health care and the health expenditure caps shown in figure 5.1, scaled up by the FPL for worker i's family so that the subsidy amount is in dollars.[19] y denotes income reported on the personal income tax return, including spousal income (if any). As long as reported family income is between 100 and 400 percent of FPL and worker i cannot be covered through a spouse's employer, worker i's family disposable income c_i is, net of taxes, subsidies, and health expenses:[20]

$$(5.3) \quad c_i = y_i + \chi_i n_i h_i w_i + [(1 - ESI_i n_i) s_i(y_i) - (1 - ESI_i) U_i(y_i)] - T_i(y_i, n_i)$$

$$(5.4) \qquad y_i = n_i h_i w_i + (1 - n_i) UB_i + o_i - (1 - ESI_i) n_i pZ$$

where, for the moment, I ignore the dynamics of earning and reporting incomes for the purposes of determining subsidies. n_i is the fraction of the year person i was on a payroll, h_i is weekly work hours, and w_i is the hourly wage rate excluding untaxed fringes (times 52 because n is a fraction of the year). $\chi_i w_i n_i h_i$ denotes nontaxable compensation from work. pZ is the salary equivalent of the employer penalty, and p is its hours equivalent.[21] UB denotes a taxable unemployment insurance benefit, which is zero for someone ineligible for benefits during their nonwork time. ESI_i is an indicator for being offered ESI when at work. o_i denotes other sources of reported income such as spousal earnings and asset income. U_i denotes uncompensated care forgone owing to ACA health insurance coverage and equals zero for persons who would be privately insured but for the ACA. T_i denotes non-ACA taxes, subsidies, and health expenses, including uncompensated care when applicable. T_i depends on income, but the marginal tax rates created by this dependence have been examined extensively in previous work (Mulligan 2012b); the purpose of table 5.2 is to look at the additional marginal tax rates created by the ACA itself. The term in square brackets is the effect of the ACA on insurance funding opportunities for people who cannot be covered through a spouse's job; it is the difference between the exchange subsidies received and the uncompensated care that would have been received but for the ACA.

The ACA has both income and employment taxes. Employment is the main way households generate income, but in order to see the two taxes separately I look at the disposable income effects of taxable income y holding constant employment:

$$(5.5) \qquad \left.\frac{\partial c_i}{\partial y_i}\right|_{dn_i=0} = 1 - t_i - \tau_i$$

$$(5.6) \qquad \tau_i \equiv -[(1 - ESI_i n_i) s_i'(y_i) - (1 - ESI_i) U_i'(y_i)], \ t_i \equiv \frac{\partial T_i}{\partial y_i}$$

where τ and t summarize the ACA and non-ACA provisions, respectively, that levy taxes or withhold benefits on the basis of taxable income. My benchmark specification takes the non-ACA marginal tax rate t to be 25 percent for all workers. The marginal tax rate columns in the table are my estimates of the ACA terms in equation (5.6), with $-s' = 23.3$ percent (this is the exchange subsidy marginal tax rate, including premium reconciliation) and $-U' = 2.4$ percent.[22] The coefficients on these tax rates are one for workers on the exchanges, which is why their full amounts are entered in the second and sixth rows of the table. They have $t + \tau$ equal to 45.9 percent. For ESI workers who are ineligible for exchange subsidies only when they are working full time, the coefficient on the s' term is either $(1 - ESI_i n_i)$ or zero, depending on whether they would participate in the exchanges when not employed. As noted above, the weighted average of these coefficients is used to make the entries in table 5.2's fifth row, with $t + \tau$ equal to 25.5 percent.

Equation (5.7) shows the effect of weeks employed on disposable income:

$$(5.7) \quad \frac{\partial c_i}{\partial n_i} = (1 - t_i - \tau_i) \left\{ h_i w_i - UB_i - \left[(1 - ESI_i)p + ESI_i \frac{s_i(y_i)}{1 - t_i - \tau_i} \right] \right\} + \chi_i h_i w_i$$

Other than the marginal income tax rate term τ discussed above, the only ACA-related terms in equation (5.7) are in the square brackets. The p term is the employer penalty, which does not apply to ESI workers. The s term reflects the access to the schedule that comes with an ESI worker's time off the payroll. s is *not a slope* of the exchange subsidy schedule; it is the level. Both the p and s terms in equation (5.7) are salary equivalents, but the s term has a tax factor in its numerator because s is not considered part of personal taxable income. In effect, the employer penalty is deductible for the purposes of personal taxable income because the employer penalty reduces salaries. Both terms also serve as employment taxes—they are negative terms in equation (5.7) for the reward to employment—even though only one of them is called a "penalty."

The final column of table 5.2 reports the estimates of the magnitude of equation (5.7)'s square bracket term, expressed as a ratio to

$(1 + \chi_i)w_i$, in order to measure the FTET amounts in hours per week. The weekly-hours equivalent of the employer penalty, 4.0, is entered in the top panel of table 5.2 because the s term in the equation does not apply to people who work for employers that do not offer affordable coverage. The equivalent of the implicit FTET amount, 5.5 hours per week, is entered in the next panel because the penalty term does not apply to ESI workers. An exception is the large number of ESI workers who cannot become eligible for exchange subsidies even by changing their employment status, either because their family income is outside of the 1–4 FPL range or because they can be insured through a spouse's employer; zeros are entered in their row of table 5.2.

Recall that equations (5.3) through (5.7) describe the budget constraint for a full-time head or spouse who cannot be covered through a spouse's employer. If the worker can be covered through a spouse, or is a dependent, then the square bracket term is absent from equation (5.3) and the only possible effect of the ACA is through the employer penalty, which depends on whether the worker has a full-time schedule. Chapter 6 shows how the budget constraint (equation 5.3) can be generalized to take into account both full- and part-time schedules for heads or spouses who cannot be covered through a spouse's employer by multiplying equation (5.3)'s square bracket term and equation (5.4)'s penalty term by an indicator for a full-time schedule.

Appendix 5.2: Advance Premium Credits, Reconciliation, and the Timing of Implicit Income Taxes

In practice, the means-tested discounts that a family receives during the calendar year (coverage year j) will often derive from the income they reported on historical tax returns (usually the return from the second year prior, $j - 2$). Its cost-sharing subsidies are never reconciled, which means that cost-sharing rules create disincentives for earning in $j - 2$, or during whatever other accounting period is examined at the time of enrolling for year j coverage. The advance premium credits will be reconciled with its actual income at the conclusion of the coverage year.[23] In order to understand how reconciliation itself adds to marginal tax rates, assume that advance premium credits for year j are set on the basis of year $j - 2$ tax returns. Let $s(y)$ denote the premium credit schedule (equation 5.3) and $G(z,y)$ be the repayment schedule, where y denotes income and z the excess credit.[24] The total premium credit s_j for calendar year j, ignoring interest between the calendar year and the time of tax filing, is:

(5.8) $$s_j = s(y_{j-2}) - G(s(y_{j-2}) - s(y_j), y_j)$$

The ACA places a cap on the repayments of excess credits, which means the advanced credits are repaid in full (algebraically, $G(z,y) = z$) if and only if the full excess $s(y_{j-2}) - s(y_j)$ is less than the cap, which depends on y_j.[25]

Figure 5.3's solid step functions—one for individuals and another for families of three—display the actual reconciliation caps as a function of y_j, expressed as a ratio to the FPL. The step functions have notches or cliffs in which marginal tax rates are infinite over an infinitesimal income interval, but (as I did with the sliding scales shown in figure 5.1) I abstract from the notches and cliffs by approximating the step functions with dashed linear schedules whose slopes are equal to the weighted-average slope of the corresponding step function with the weights determined by the width of the income interval over which the slope applies. The weighted-average slopes are 4.1 percent and 4.8 percent for individuals and families of three, respectively, which I summarize as a 4.4 percent slope.

Notice from equation (5.8) that the year j subsidies potentially create disincentives to report income in both years $j - 2$ and j. To examine this more precisely, consider smooth approximations to s and G so that their derivatives are finite and add the derivatives of equation (5.8) with respect to y_j and y_{j-2}:

(5.9) $$\frac{\partial s_j}{\partial y_{j-2}} + \frac{\partial s_j}{\partial y_j} = s'(y_{j-2}) + G_z(s(y_{j-2}) - s(y_j), y_j)[s'(y_j) - s'(y_{j-2})]$$
$$- G_y(s(y_{j-2}) - s(y_j), y_j)$$

where G_z and G_y denote the first partial derivatives of the reconciliation function G. The top line of equation (5.9) is a weighted average of $s'(y_{j-2})$ and $s'(y_j)$, which means that G_y is an extra disincentive to the extent that it differs from zero. For households above 400 percent of the

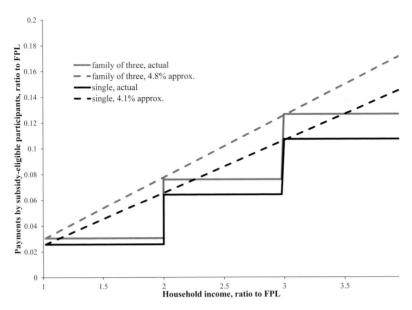

FIGURE 5.3. Reconciliation caps as a function of household income and policy type.

poverty line, households with $y_j < y_{j-2}$ and households with $s(y_{j-2})-s(y_j)$ less than the cap (that is, their income rose less than 5 percent or so between $j-2$ and j), G_y is zero because their premium credits are fully reconciled.[26] For the rest, G_y is approximately the slope shown in figure 4, which is 4.4 percent.

I assume that half of tax units receiving premium assistance for the entire calendar year have an income for the year that ultimately exceeds their income of two years before by 5 percent or more, which makes the average (among workers enrolled in the exchange for the entire year) marginal tax rate from the reconciliation of the premium tax equal to 2.2 percent (half of 4.4 percent). This is in addition to the marginal income tax rates from the cost-sharing subsidies, advance premium credits, the personal income tax, and so on.

Appendix 5.3: Sensitivity Analysis

Table 5.4 considers variations on the benchmark parameters: a larger non-ACA marginal income tax rate, no exchange-features discount, and getting premiums from the KFF2 calculator rather than the KFF1

TABLE 5.4. ACA-incentive scenarios: sensitivity analysis

Calendar year 2016. Categories are mutually exclusive.

Type of worker	Benchmark parameters		Add 10 %-pts to non-ACA MTR		No exchange features discount		KFF2 premium calculator	
	MTR	FTET (hrs/wk)	MTR	FTET (hrs/wk)	MTR	FTET (hrs/wk)	MTR	FTET (hrs/wk)
Works for employer not offering affordable coverage								
Head or spouse insured on exchanges, and subsidized	45.9%	4.0	55.9%	4.0	45.9%	4.0	45.9%	4.0
All others	25.0%	4.0	35.0%	4.0	25.0%	4.0	25.0%	4.0
Works for employer offering affordable coverage								
Full-time status alone blocks eligibility for exch. subs.	25.5%	5.5	35.5%	6.4	25.6%	8.2	25.3%	4.1
Head or spouse insured on exchanges, working PT	45.9%	5.5	55.9%	6.4	45.9%	8.2	45.9%	4.1
All others	25.0%	0	35.0%	0	25.0%	0	25.0%	0
All workers (employment-weighted average)	**26.9%**	**2.2**	**36.9%**	**2.4**	**26.9%**	**2.7**	**26.8%**	**1.9**
Addendum: all working heads & spouses insured on exch.	45.9%	4.7	55.9%	5.1	45.9%	5.9	45.9%	4.1
Addendum: all ESI workers facing the implicit FTET	29.3%	5.5	39.3%	6.4	29.4%	8.2	29.2%	4.1

Notes: MTR is the marginal tax rate on earnings, including subsidy phaseouts and non-ACA taxes. FTET is the full-time employment tax measured in hours per week. Benchmark details are shown in table 5.2.

calculator. Results for workers at employers not offering coverage are insensitive to these changes. The larger non-ACA income tax rate makes the exchange subsidies more valuable—their hour equivalent is 6.4 rather than 5.5—because the exchange subsidies are not subject to tax. It makes a big difference that I assume a 25 percent exchange features discount rather than zero, because in the latter case the FTET amount is 8.2 hours per week rather than 5.5. Recall that the KFF2 premium calculator has lower premiums; if they persist until 2016 then the amount of the FTET will be 4.1 rather than 5.5.

6 | Consequences for Employee Work Schedules

The ACA penalizes full-time work either by charging an employer penalty or by withholding eligibility for the new health insurance subsidies. The ACA also penalizes some families for earning income by phasing out the new subsidies with their income. Chapters 3, 4, and 5 quantify the magnitude of these taxes, estimate the number of people who will face them, and summarize the results in table 5.2. Those results account for the facts that a variety of longstanding tax and subsidy rules also create both incentives and disincentives for work and that many people will not participate in programs for which they are eligible.[1]

Section A of this chapter offers a summary of the two primary economic ingredients needed to estimate the effect of the ACA on the overall size of the labor market: the average amount of the ACA's tax changes and the sensitivity of labor market activity to tax rates. Section B introduces the household budget constraint, which is the primary economic tool for connecting the measurements in chapters 3, 4, and 5 to labor market outcomes. The budget constraint shows why some occupations will avoid the ACA's taxes by adopting part-time schedules, but that many more occupations will avoid them by working more hours per week. Section C points to the key behavioral magnitudes that are needed to project the market consequences of the new incentives, and it relates the magnitudes to historical studies of the labor market and work schedules. Section D displays the labor market projections, which differ from those in the literature because of the tax amounts I measure and not because of assumptions about the sensitivity of labor hours to each unit of taxation. Effects of income sheltering, income misreporting, and hours misreporting are discussed in section E. Section F concludes.

A. Why 3 Percent Less Work?

The ACA will likely reduce the amount of labor used in the economy because, as shown in the first half of this book, labor is what the ACA will be taxing. The law is creating a new set of subsidies that reduce work incentives as they are financed from taxpayers (e.g., employer-penalty payments) *and* as they are distributed to beneficiaries. The logic of supply and demand tells us that when we tax something we get less of it.[2] Because the size of the effect depends on the size of the tax, the bottom line from chapter 5's table 5.2 is critical: the ACA increases average full-time employment tax (FTET) rates by 2.2 hours per week and income tax rates by 1.9 percentage points.

In order to translate table 5.2 into a simple but rough estimate of the law's overall impact on the amount of work in the economy, let's assume for the moment that weekly work hours are a fixed characteristic of a worker, perhaps based on her occupation or family situation, so that the only real choice for workers is the number of weeks that they are at work.[3] In this case, the FTETs have no direct effect on part-time workers because those workers pay the same full-time employment tax amount regardless of how many weeks they work: zero. For full-time employees, who are about 83 percent of all employees, the FTETs are simply an employment tax because, by assumption, not working is the only way that such employees can avoid it.

The ACA's taxes vary across workers, which makes their economics different from the economics of uniformly taxing all workers. These economic differences are treated later in this chapter, and are the primary subject of chapters 7 and 8, but for the moment let us approximate the ACA's taxes as a single uniform tax that finances redistribution. Because the FTETs amount to 5.4 percent of a full-time schedule for full-time workers and zero for part-time workers (the remaining 17 percent of the workforce), the FTETs are, on average, of the same magnitude as a 4.5 percent employment tax on all employees, as derived in rows (1)–(3) of table 6.1.[4]

Row (4) is the average implicit income tax rate created by the ACA. As shown in chapter 5, this income tax is in addition to the full-time employment taxes. Altogether, the ACA taxes plus the non-ACA taxes

TABLE 6.1. The ACA's impact on aggregate hours: first-order considerations

The long-term impact of the ACA parameters for calendar year 2016

	Without the ACA	With the ACA	Row number and source	
Tax incentives for the average worker				
Fraction of workers who are full time, weeks weighted	0.83	0.83	(1)	March 2012 CPS. Full time = 35+ hours
Full-time employment tax as a % of full-time schedule	0	5.4%	(2)	Table 5.2 weighted-average FTET divided by 40
Employment tax as a percentage of full-time schedule	0	4.5%	(3)	= (1)*(2)
Implicit earnings tax rate	0	1.9%	(4)	Table 5.2
Non-ACA marginal earnings tax rate	25.0%	25.0%	(5)	Table 5.2
All tax rates combined	25.0%	31.3%	(6)	= (3) + (4) + (5)
Percentage of earnings kept at the margin	75.0%	68.7%	(7)	= 100% − (6)
ACA's impact on the percentage kept at the margin	−8.8%		(8)	= [row (7) ACA − non-ACA]/ [row (7) avg.]
Aggregate hours effect of tax incentives				
reward coefficient		0.36	(9)	Microeconometric literature on tax effects
ACA's impact on aggregate hours	−3.2%		(10)	= (8)*(9)
	first-order approximation			

Notes: The table presents a first-order approximation of the impact of the ACA, as parameterized in 2016, on aggregate work hours in the U.S. Its purpose is to just highlight the main economic determinants of that impact. The best impact calculations are later in this chapter and in the chapters that follow.

The employer penalty is 2.2 percentage points out of the 4.5 percentage points reported in row (3). The remaining 2.3 percentage points are from the implicit FTET.

of 25 percent add up to 31.3 percent. According to this calculation, the average 2016 worker under the ACA keeps 68.7 percent of what he earns at the margin, as compared to the 75.0 percent that he would have kept if the ACA had not been passed. This is a 6.3 *percentage point* reduction in the reward to work, which is 8.8 percent of the reward to work itself.[5]

The final estimation step is to approximate the direction and amount of the impact of an 8.8 percent reduction in the reward to work on the aggregate amount of work. Both everyday experience and extensive labor economics research has shown that, when labor taxes reduce the economic rewards that work generates for employers and employees, some of them respond to taxes by creating, retaining, and accepting fewer jobs. Obviously a great many people would *not* quit their job, shut down a business, or reduce work hours in response to a tax because the gains or "surplus" they get from working and producing far exceed the tax amount. But it's wrong to conclude that *all* people and businesses have a surplus from working that is large enough to withstand all of the ACA's taxes. Even without the ACA, well over 100 million Americans are not working, and many of them choose to be in that position. There are skilled stay-at-home mothers or fathers who can readily find a job but believe that the pay will not justify the personal sacrifices required. Others may turn down an out-of-town promotion in order to avoid relocating their family, and there are workers who eschew higher-paying but less-safe occupations. Working and earning require sacrifices, and people evaluate whether the net income earned is enough to justify the sacrifices. As the exchange subsidies emerge and include help for people not working, and as the employer penalties begin, the sacrifices that jobs require do not disappear. The commuting hassle is still there, the possibility for injury on the job is still there, and jobs still take time away from family, hobbies, sleep, and so on. But the exchange subsidies and employer penalties reduce the reward to working, because some of the money earned on the job is now available even when not working.

The logic of supply and demand therefore predicts that the ACA will reduce the average amount that people work by moving some of the low-surplus workers, some of the time, from working to not working. Recall Mike Smith, the California man introduced in chapter 1. According to National Public Radio (NPR), he had been working as a district manager but the job was "unfulfilling" and required too many hours that prevented him from practicing his guitar and spending time with extended family members. NPR's account suggests that Mike's "surplus" from working was low, so that he would be especially likely to stop working when the ACA began to subsidize coverage for early retirees. Consistent with the logic of supply and demand, Mike did in fact retire and receive those subsidies before he reached age 65.

As noted in chapter 1, anecdotes are for illustrating economic ideas and should not serve as the foundation for careful economic analysis. Before the Affordable Care Act was passed, much evidence, obtained from large representative samples, had accumulated as to the effects of labor taxes on the amount of labor used in the economy. This evidence ranges from income tax reforms to household experiments to country comparisons to the rollout of social programs with implicit taxes. Unemployment benefits are an example of an implicit employment tax, and one that has been well studied.[6] Unemployment benefits reduce labor supply both by discouraging unemployed people from returning to work (Krueger and Meyer 2002) and by encouraging layoffs (Topel and Welch 1980). Although economists continue to gather new data and reconcile the variation in results among historical studies, the evidence is also starting to show roughly the *amount* that labor is reduced with every unit by which taxes reduce the reward to work. From a slightly conservative reading of all this (that is, leaning in the direction of less responsiveness), I assume that aggregate hours worked fall, in the long run, about 0.36 percent for every 1 percent that taxes reduce the economy-wide average reward to working, including both the substitution effect and the aggregate income effect of the taxation.[7]

The 0.36 reward coefficient is entered in table 6.1's row (9). Multiplying it by the ACA's impact on the reward to work (row (8)), the reward coefficient is enough to give us an estimate of the ACA's percentage impact on aggregate work hours. That product is shown in the final row of table 6.1 and says that the ACA will reduce aggregate work hours 3.2 percent below what aggregate hours would be without the ACA.

Although the 3.2 percent estimate assumes uniform taxation, it does not imply that the responses to taxation are uniform. The 0.36 reward coefficient reflects the historical average response to taxes, which includes large responses by some people and small—often zero—responses by others. It is both a logical fallacy and inconsistent with the historical evidence to conclude from instances of zero response that the average response is also zero. Table 6.1 says that 3.2 percent of the work that would have been done without the ACA will not be done; the other 96.8 percent of work will continue even under the law. For many of the same reasons that the vast majority of people who work will continue to do so even during severe recessions, the vast majority of people who work will continue to work despite the ACA's disincentives. In other words, the economics of the ACA says that situations like Mike Smith's will be far outnumbered by situations in which people continue to work in spite of the ACA's taxes, but nonetheless instances of early retirements and additional unemployment will be prevalent enough to noticeably affect the national averages.

To be clear, table 6.1's estimate is derived with a number of short-cuts so that the result can (a) be understood with just simple arithmetic and (b) have its ingredients limited to just the essential economic forces. Table 6.1 assumes fixed weekly work hours, uniform taxation, and fixed worker productivity at the margin despite the reduced amount of labor supplied. The rest of the book relaxes these assumptions in order to obtain more accurate estimates, which turn out to be remarkably close to the 3.2 percent reduction in aggregate work hours shown in table 6.1.

Row (1)'s entry is important in the sense that the table's bottom line would be far different if it were, say, zero. However, because there is little doubt that a great many people will work full time even with the ACA, row (1) is not a primary reason that the ACA's impact might be different from 3.2 percent.[8]

Row (4) and especially row (2), taken from chapters 3–5 of this book, are both critical and very different from previous studies.[9] If rows (2) and (4) were set to zero, then the table's bottom line would be no effect on aggregate labor hours. For this reason, the first half of this book walks carefully through the prevalence and magnitude of all of the ACA's new taxes. Yet, in effect, previous studies set rows (2) and (4) to zero (or even to a negative number). Cutler and Sood (2010), for example, claimed "modernization aspects" of the ACA would cut wasteful health spending by employer plans and by this mechanism "boost employment by 250,000 to 400,000 per year" over the next decade. The fundamental differences between their result and mine are the taxes in rows (2)–(4) of table 6.1. As a result, my row (6) has +6.3 percentage points from the ACA whereas they have something like −0.1 percentage points for every year the ACA is in effect (recall table 2.1). Thus my complaint about the statements by Cutler, Sood, and their many endorsers is that they fail to acknowledge the size, scope, and direction of the ACA's new taxes.

In a separate paper (Mulligan forthcoming), I do not assume uniform taxation and look especially closely at the ACA's various taxes among low-skill workers. There I conclude that the average full-time employment tax is 6.5 percent of a full-time schedule, rather than the 5.4 percent shown in table 6.1's row (2). This adjustment by itself would change the table's bottom line from −3.2 percent fewer work hours to −3.7 percent.

Table 6.1's simple calculation assumes that the non-ACA marginal earnings tax rate is only 25 percent, including implicit taxes on earnings and employment. The rate would be greater for parts of the population, such as households receiving unemployment benefits or losing earned income tax credits as they earn more. If table 6.1's row (5) were set to 35 percent rather than 25, the bottom line would be −3.7 percent fewer work hours rather than −3.2 percent.

The bottom line is proportional to the assumed reward coefficient, which quantifies the sensitivity of labor hours to labor taxes. The history of taxation suggests that the reward coefficient is about 0.36. Nevertheless, it is possible that the reward coefficient most accurate for ACA analysis is different, perhaps because the law affects different groups or because taxpayers process information about the law differently. For example, Cutler and Sood (2010) assumed that employment is *more* sensitive to taxes than I do.[10] Thus, my findings are different from the literature because of the tax amounts I measure, not because I assume that labor hours are particularly sensitive to each unit of taxation.

Table 6.1 does not provide any information about the kinds of labor that will be cut back as a result of the ACA. The remainder of this chapter estimates the types of work schedule changes that will contribute most to a 3 percent contraction of the labor market and the types of workers whose schedules are most likely to change.

B. Distorting the Workweek

1. TRADE-OFFS BETWEEN HOURS AND EMPLOYMENT

Although table 6.1 combines all taxes into a summary tax rate, in fact earnings taxes, employment taxes, and full-time employment taxes create somewhat different incentives and therefore have somewhat different behavioral effects. An earnings tax, such as the payroll tax or the implicit tax from the income-based phaseout of exchange subsidies, does not depend on the source, timing, or sequencing of the earnings. One person may have low income due to working part time all year, while another may have low income due to working seasonally, for only part of the year. If the two have the same total earnings for the year, and are in the same tax bracket, then the two pay the same implicit and explicit earnings taxes.

By contrast, employment taxes and full-time employment taxes are not neutral as to the source of earnings during the calendar year. For a person who works part time all the year, the implicit full-time taxes would be zero for both employer and employee, whereas for a person working full time half of the year, full-time employment taxes would accrue for that half of the year even though his annual earnings might be the same as the full-year part-time worker. These two people are also different in terms of the employment taxes that they pay: the full-year part-time worker pays employment tax for the entire year, whereas the part-year full-time worker pays employment tax only for the parts of the year that he is employed.

As a first step to modeling the economy's distinct reactions to the ACA's various taxes, it helps to build a household budget constraint that includes part-time work, full-time work, the employer penalty, and exchange subsidies, as well as other factors that affect work schedules. Consider a large family that, in a given week, supplies n workers each working h hours per week. For the moment, assume all family members are identical in terms of the pecuniary costs and benefits of their work. Every person-week worked generates labor income subject to tax in the amount $wh - q - p(h)$, where $q > 0$ is a quasi-fixed cost of employment and $p(h)$ is the employer penalty. q is a cost that employers pay, aside from a penalty, for every worker they have. It includes scheduling costs, payroll costs, hiring and training costs, and perhaps management and coordination costs. Labor economics refers to q as a "quasi-fixed" cost because it does not vary with the number of hours worked, but it does vary with the number of workers on the payroll. The quasi-fixed cost is one reason an employer cannot simply replace one 40-hour worker with four 10-hour workers and get the same results. The employer running 10-hour weekly schedules will encounter additional administrative costs, more workers in need of training, and so on.

In reality, both the employer penalty $p(h)$ and the quasi-fixed cost q are paid by the employer. I assume for the moment, and later prove, that the employer simply passes those costs on to the employee, which is why a worker's income is the product of his marginal hourly wage w and work hours h minus these two costs.

The penalty is a function of the length h of the work schedule, namely, a step function:

(6.1) $$p(h)=I(h>P)pZ$$

where $I()$ is the indicator function that is one when the condition in parentheses (a full-time schedule) is satisfied, and zero otherwise. P is the hours limit for "part-time" employment, which refers to the positions exempt from the penalty at assessable employers on the basis of their work schedules. The ACA sets the limit at 29 hours per week (i.e., 30-hour workers are considered full time and thereby subject to penalty), with some caveats noted below, so the bulk of my analysis sets $P = 29$. The constant p (note lowercase) is the amount of the employer penalty measured in hours per week, as in chapter 3 and table 5.2, and Z is a parameter converting hours per week into units of the consumption good (more on Z below). In other words, equation (6.1) says that part-time employees pay zero penalty and that full-time employees pay pZ dollars (which takes them p hours to earn).

The household pays a tax at constant rate $t + \tau$ on its taxable labor income, where τ is the ACA component of the overall tax rate and t is the non-ACA component, especially employee payroll taxes and employee personal income taxes. The household also incurs a per-employee quasi-fixed cost a that by itself makes households prefer to work more hours per week and fewer weeks per year (or employees per household) because the quasi-fixed cost is a/h per hour worked, which is less for long work schedules, and na in total. A commuting cost is an important example. Employee tax and administrative savings from fringe benefits are also captured in a—they reduce a—to the extent that employees cannot receive these benefits during times when they are not employed.

The two quasi-fixed costs q and a serve the same basic economic purposes but different accounting purposes. In practice, q is subtracted from employee pay but a is not, which means empirical measures of taxable weekly earnings should be compared with $wh - q - p(h)$, and not $wh - q - a - p(h)$. Because income taxes are levied on the former and not the latter, a is effectively more expensive to the employee than q is because q helps reduce payroll and income taxes. An employment tax is represented by the quasi-fixed cost term q if that tax affects the amount of income subject to income tax, as unemployment benefits do (see appendix 6.1), and otherwise represented by a.

Finally, each employed family member pays a convex cost $f(h)$ of supplying hours, and the household receives a lump sum transfer g from the government. The household budget constraint is:

(6.2) $$c = g + \{(1-t-\tau)[wh - q - I(h > P)pZ] - a - f(h)\}n$$

where c is household consumption. With a caveat mentioned below, the term in square brackets is the contribution of a week's work to income subject to income tax (technically, adjusted gross income).[11]

The pZ term can be interpreted narrowly as the employer penalty, or as the salary-equivalent value of an exchange subsidy potentially forgone by people working for ESI employers. In the former case, the budget constraint (equation 6.2) is an embellishment of the $ESI = 0$ version of equation (5.3) in chapter 5 that accounts for both full- and part-time work and for additional quasi-fixed costs.[12] In the subsidy-forgone case, pZ is the value of the subsidy divided by the tax factor $(1 - t - \tau)$ because, unlike $wh - q$, the exchange subsidy is not taxable. However, the budget constraint represented by equation (6.2) does not recognize that an ESI employee's marginal income tax rate from the ACA depends (slightly; see appendix 6.1) on the number of weeks worked.

Although equation (6.2) may appear unfamiliar to many readers, it is closely related to the microeconomics of average and marginal production costs. Consider the question of how a work time should be supplied between weeks n and hours per week h, holding constant total annual work hours nh. The average hourly cost is the combination of the q, pZ, a, and f terms in equation (6.2), each expressed as a ratio to total hours nh. Figure 6.1's dashed red curve ("AC w/o ET") graphs that average hourly cost versus the length of the workweek, ignoring for the moment the penalty term $I(h > P)pZ$. If it were not for the convex cost $f(h)$, the average cost would simply be inversely proportional to

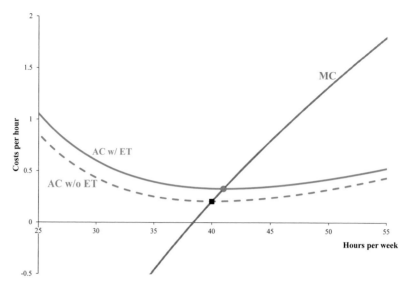

FIGURE 6.1. The hourly costs of working, with and without an employment tax (ET).

weekly hours as the quasi-fixed costs are amortized over more hours. The convex cost term $f(h)$ causes the average hourly cost to reach a minimum, which is shown in figure 6.1 as the place where average hourly cost crosses the marginal hourly cost $f'(h)$. Thus, figure 6.1 is a graphical version of the models Sherwin Rosen developed of the trade-off between an increasing marginal hours cost like $f'(h)$—shown in the figure as the "MC" curve—and avoidance of quasi-fixed employment costs.[13]

From the perspective of employers and employees, the optimum weekly schedule is at the minimum of the average hourly cost curve. Take, for example, an employment tax paid by employers. Because the employment tax amount is the same regardless of how many hours each worker is scheduled, the employment tax increases q and thereby shifts up the average hourly cost curve—especially for short schedules where the employment tax is amortized over fewer hours—without affecting the marginal hourly cost curve $f'(h)$. That shift is shown in figure 6.1 as the solid "AC w/ ET" curve. The optimal response to an employment tax is therefore to work fewer weeks—less tax that way— and more hours per week as shown in figure 6.1 as the difference between the square and the circle. From an employer's point of view, she has fewer employees in any given week, but her employees are, on average, each working more hours that week. This result does not say that the employment tax would be almost completely avoided by having just a few employees working very long hours because those long hours have high marginal cost. The point is that the optimal weekly work schedule is longer when employment is taxed than it is when employment is not taxed.

Figure 6.2 illustrates two alternative FTET scenarios that might be experienced by somebody working more than 30 hours per week. In one scenario (red), the full-time employment tax is small, and in the other case the tax is large (pink). In both scenarios, the average cost curve jumps at the threshold $P = 30$ hours per week because the tax only applies to work schedules that are at least that long. The average cost jump reflects the $I(h > P)pZ$ term in equation (6.2) and its size is the amount pZ of the weekly FTET divided by 30. Beyond the 30-hour threshold, the marginal cost of hours $f'(h)$ is the same as it would be without the FTET because the amount of the tax is the same for all full-time schedules regardless of how many weekly hours they have.

Assuming that the optimal schedule would be full time without taxes, an FTET of any size results in an average hourly cost curve with

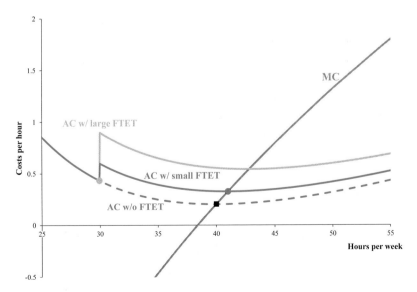

FIGURE 6.2. The hourly costs of working, with large and small full-time employment taxes (FTETs).

two local minima. One local minimum is the minimum-cost full-time schedule at the bottom of the "U" shape. The other local minimum is the average hourly cost of a 29-hour schedule.[14] For the small FTET, the lowest minimum is still a full-time schedule that is close to, but slightly longer than, the optimum without the FTET. The worker avoids some of the small FTET by working slightly fewer weeks.

For the large FTET, the minimum-cost full-time schedule is more costly per hour than a 29-hour schedule. Thus, the large FTET causes a reduction in weekly hours from full time to 29, as illustrated by the difference between the square and the pink circle in figure 6.2. At the same time, the large FTET may increase the number of weeks employed. Altogether, we see from figure 6.2 that FTETs can either increase or decrease the number of hours worked during the weeks that a person is employed, depending on the size of the FTET and other factors.

Either way, FTETs increase the average hourly cost of working. For workers that continue to work a full-time schedule, work costs more because of the penalty. For workers with weekly hours cut to 29, work costs more because the quasi-fixed costs of employment are amortized over fewer hours (equivalently, the weekly hours cut means that more quasi-fixed costs need to be paid in order to maintain total hours worked nh). With work costing more, expect less work. In other words, figure 6.2 is both showing us the effects of FTETs on the allocation of total hours between n and h, and the fundamental reason why FTETs depress total work hours nh.

2. OCCUPATIONS THAT WILL BEGET "TWENTY-NINERS"

The position and curvature of the cost schedules, and therefore the equilibrium weekly work hours, vary across workers due to occupational and personal factors. An outdoor job that benefits from daylight has cost schedules related to the time that the sun rises and sets, with the marginal cost schedule rising quickly once a worker attempts to work beyond sunset. Other workers differ in their quasi-fixed costs owing to, say, different distances between home and workplace. Table 6.2 shows the average weekly work hours from the March 2012 IPUMS-CPS for selected detailed occupations with unusually long or short weekly work schedules.[15]

Derrick operators, ship operators, and sailors are workers with a

TABLE 6.2. Selected occupations with weekly work hours above or below average

Occupation (private sector unless noted otherwise)	Average weekly hours
Long workweeks	
Derrick, rotary drill, and service unit operators, oil, gas, and mining	64
Ship and boat captains and operators	60
Physicians and surgeons	51
Sailors and marine oilers	51
Firefighters (public)	51
Short workweeks: working with young children	
Bus drivers	36
Preschool and kindergarten teachers	36
Bus drivers (public)	35
Other teachers and instructors	32
Teacher assistants	32
Child-care workers (public)	32
Child-care workers	31
Crossing guards (public)	17
Short workweeks: food service	
Bartenders	35
Food preparation workers	33
Dishwashers	33
Waiters and waitresses	32
Dining room and cafeteria attendants, bartender helpers, and misc. food preparation and serving related workers	30
Counter attendants, cafeteria, food concession, and coffee shop	27
Hosts and hostesses, restaurant, lounge, and coffee shop	24
Short workweeks: other	
Stock clerks and order fillers	36
Bookkeeping, accounting, and auditing clerks	36
Retail salespersons	35
Hairdressers, hairstylists, and cosmetologists	35
Janitors and building cleaners	35
Cashiers	30

Source: IPUMS-CPS for March 2012
Note: Occupations average about 40 hours per week.

long distance from home to workplace, so it is no surprise that they work long hours for the weeks that they are at work. Firefighters work especially long hours: often two or more 24-hour shifts per week (Mower 2012; Don McNea Fire School 2014; U.S. Bureau of Labor Statistics 2014b). In part, a firefighter's marginal cost schedule increases less rapidly because he can rest on the job in between fires and other emergencies.[16]

Occupations that work with children have schedules that are different than many other occupations. Table 6.2 shows that the weekly work hours tend to be few: in the 31–36 range with the exception of crossing guards who average 17 hours per week.

Note that March 2012 is before the ACA's primary taxes took effect. I therefore interpret each occupation's weekly hours in table 6.2 as indicating the number of hours achieving the minimum average hourly cost—the bottom of the u-shaped curve—without full-time employment taxes. In particular, several "short workweek" occupations shown in the table have a minimum average hourly cost achieved at 30–36 hours, as compared to minima near or above 40 hours for the large majority of occupations. Figure 6.3a shows the cost curves with and without the FTET for a short workweek occupation. Without the FTET, the minimum shown in the figure is 35 hours (e.g., bus drivers) whereas the minimum with the FTET is 29 hours. People working part time just below the 30-hour threshold for full-time work are sometimes known as "twenty-niners." The twenty-niner occupations may not reduce their employment, and may even increase it, because the twenty-niners will be working fewer hours per week than they were before the ACA.

Contrast figure 6.3a with figure 6.3b, where a full-time schedule still achieves the minimum average cost even with the FTET. Thus, one prediction is that "short workweek" occupations such as food service workers will adjust to the ACA's various taxes by reducing weekly hours to 29, whereas long workweek occupations such as firefighters will not.

It is interesting to note that schools and food service businesses are disproportionately reporting that the ACA induces them to limit employee work schedules to 28 or 29 hours. *Restaurant News* reported that David Barr, an owner of 22 Kentucky Fried Chicken locations, is "looking at employees who work between 30–33 hours per week and will likely be reducing their hours to below the 30-hour threshold" whereas he would not cut back the hours of those employees working closer to 40 hours per week (Dostal 2012). School District #1 from Sweetwater County, Wyoming, said in a press release that staff mem-

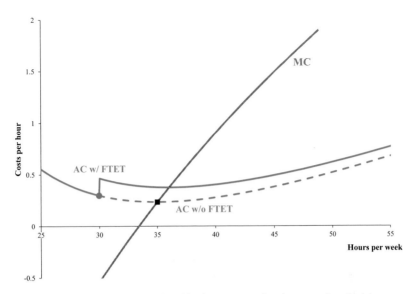

FIGURE 6.3A. The hourly costs of working in an occupation that normally schedules 35 hours per week.

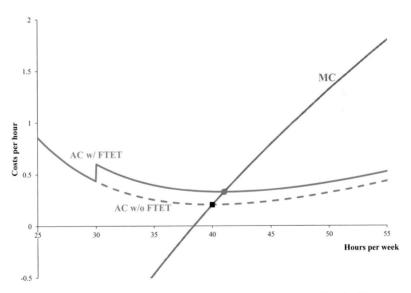

FIGURE 6.3B. The hourly costs of working in an occupation that normally schedules 40 hours per week.

bers with 30–34 hour schedules would be cut to 29 and that, in some of those cases, new opportunities would be available for more weeks of work per year (Sweetwater Now News Desk 2014). Hundreds of other examples have been compiled by Jed Graham of *Investors Business Daily* (Graham 2014). However, the basic economics used in this book is a theory of behavior—especially aggregate market behavior—and not a theory of press releases or other statements of motive or intention. The representatively sampled data necessary to carefully measure work-schedule changes may not be available until 2017. If actual behavior ultimately coincides with the reported employer intentions, then it would confirm some of the twenty-niner predictions in this book.

In summary, the Rosen model of scheduling costs predicts that FTETs have three alternative qualitative effects on work scheduling, with the applicable alternative depending on occupational factors, worker preferences, the amount of the FTET, and the hours threshold defining full-time work. In one case (figure 6.3b), the worker's optimal schedule is full time despite the FTETs, so that an FTET is just another quasi-fixed cost and thereby encourages substitution of hours for employment. In the twenty-niner case (figure 6.3a), persons working full time without the FTETs but near the margin are induced to work part time, but potentially at a higher employment rate, in order to avoid the tax. The third possibility is that the worker would have a part-time schedule even without the FTETs, so that the FTETs have no direct effect on weekly hours and employment rates.

3. INCOME-TAX EFFECTS

Recall that the cost-minimizing workweek reflects a tradeoff between quasi-fixed costs and marginal costs, with larger quasi-fixed costs encouraging longer workweeks. An income tax therefore reduces the cost-minimizing workweek, as long as some of the marginal costs are not income-tax deductible. In effect, income-taxed employees are less willing to incur the marginal costs of a long week because the income tax shifts some of the quasi-fixed costs from employees to the government. To put it another way, the income tax matters for the optimal workweek only according to its contribution to the quasi-fixed costs of working net of income taxes.

The magnitude of the income-tax effect on hours depends on the amount by which income taxation reduces after-tax quasi-fixed costs, which is the product of the ACA component of the marginal income tax rate and the magnitude of the income-reducing quasi-fixed costs (ACA related or not). The ACA's income-tax effect on weekly hours would therefore be economically significant only if the ACA were adding a number of percentage points to the marginal income tax rate.

Income taxes reduce aggregate hours because they reduce the reward to work. In principle, an income tax could increase employment as employees substitute employment for weekly hours, if aggregate hours were inelastic enough to taxes. However, as I explain below, the historical evidence does not support the view that aggregate hours fail to respond significantly to income taxes, which suggests that income taxes reduce both weekly employment and weekly work hours among employees.

C. A Quantitative Model of the Distribution of Weekly Employment and Work Hours

Regardless of the population frequency of the three types of responses to FTETs, the taxes reduce aggregate work hours, which are the product of the employment rate and the average weekly hours among those employed. The next step is to quantify the tax effects. The quantitative work requires measures of the amounts of the ACA's taxes, the structure of scheduling costs, and the effects of wages on the composition and aggregate amount of labor demand. These measures are introduced in order below.

1. THE MAGNITUDES OF THE ACA TAXES: FOUR SCENARIOS

The ACA has a number of transitional features that complicate assessment of its economic effects. The original 2010 legislation arranged for delayed implementation of its main features, including the health insurance exchanges and the employer penalty. Some of the language in the law was vague and thereby required a back and forth between regulators and the public before it was finally determined how the law would be enforced (Burkhauser, Lyons, and Simon 2011). In some instances, as with the employer penalty and the open enrollment period for exchange coverage, the administration responded to political pressures by delaying implementation beyond what was specified in the original law. It will also take time for the private sector to fully comprehend and adapt to the new economic environment created by the law. In this chapter, I attempt only to examine the consequences of the ACA as it will stand when it is essentially fully implemented, perhaps in the year 2016 or beyond. I therefore measure the size of the tax incentives from the perspective of employers and employees situated in the year 2016 and show how the results might be different if the employer penalty were delayed beyond that year, or indefinitely. All of these measures are made relative to a (presumably) hypothetical world in 2016 in which (1) the ACA does not exist and (2) the hypothetical non-ACA policies coincide with actual non-ACA policies.[17]

As explained in chapters 3–5, the ACA introduces three major disincentives: (1) the explicit penalty for non-ESI employers who employ full-time workers; (2) the implicit tax on full-time employment for those people who work at ESI employers and could get exchange subsidies if they worked part time or spent time off the payroll; and (3) the implicit tax on income for people who get ACA exchange subsidies (because the subsidy amounts are determined on the basis of family income, with more income resulting in less subsidy). For the purpose of labor market analysis, the important feature of an income tax is that it is a tax on earnings from working. In 2016, any given worker faces one of four possible combinations of the three disincentives, meaning that there are four different ACA "tax scenarios" for U.S. workers. Table 6.3 lays out these tax scenarios (rows) as they relate to each of the disincentives (columns). The four scenarios are:

No new incentives. None of the three ACA disincentives appear in the worker's budget constraint.

Non-ESI worker without subsidy. These are workers who are not receiving insurance from their employer, but either are ineligible for the exchange subsidies or are not heads of households or spouses and so do not have their subsidies determined by their own work hours or income. Their employer does suffer the penalty for employing them without offering affordable coverage (column 1), but the employees do not face the implicit full-time employment tax (column 2) or the implicit income tax (column 3).

Non-ESI worker with subsidy. These are workers who are not receiv-

TABLE 6.3. Tax scenarios created by the Affordable Care Act's disincentives

Scenario	Disincentives		
	Employer penalty	Implicit FTET	Implicit income tax
A: No new incentives	No	No	No
B: Non-ESI worker without subsidy	Yes	No	No
C: Non-ESI worker with subsidy	Yes	No	Yes
D: ESI worker with subsidy forgone by working full time	No	Yes	No*

*Unless employee spends part of the calendar year off the full-time payroll and is getting subsidies during that time.

ing insurance from their employer, and are receiving an ACA subsidy from the government. Their employer is suffering the penalty or the threat of a penalty (column 1), and the employees are faced with the implicit income tax (column 3), but the employees do not face the implicit full-time employment tax (column 2).

ESI worker with subsidy forgone by working full time. Such workers face the implicit full-time employment tax (column 2), because they could receive the subsidies if they changed to part time (or left employment altogether), or would lose their subsidies upon switching from part time to full time. Workers in this scenario meet all the other criteria for exchange subsidies (residency, income, tax filing status). Their employer is providing health insurance, and is therefore not penalized (column 1). Because the workers are not getting the subsidies, they do not face the full implicit income tax (column 3), although they may face a partial implicit income tax if they get the subsidies for a part of the calendar year in which they are not an ESI worker.

Although any one disincentive may appear in multiple scenarios, the amount of the disincentive typically varies from scenario to scenario. Table 6.4 is a summary of table 5.2 and shows tax amounts for each scenario, with earnings taxes shown in percentage points and full-time employment tax shown in hours per week. The first and most common tax scenario A is no (new) incentives: leaving employment or changing work hours has no effect on employer penalties owed and ACA subsidies received. In terms of equation (6.2), this case has $\tau = p = 0$ and will be experienced by 54 percent of potential workers (a "potential worker" is someone who would be working sometime during 2016 if the ACA did not become law). Each scenario has an overall marginal

TABLE 6.4. Benchmark ACA-incentive scenarios to be simulated

Includes both implicit and explicit taxes for calendar year 2016. Categories are mutually exclusive.

Scenario	Marginal earnings tax rates		Weekly penalty on full-time work (hours equiv.), p	Frequency
	Non-ACA, t	ACA, τ		
A: No new incentives	25%	0%	0	54%
B: Employer penalized, but employee not receiving exchange subsidies	25%	0%	4.0	21%
C: Employee receiving exchange subsidies, and employer penalized	25%	20.9%	4.0	5%
D: Worker at ESI employer without access to part-time own ESI or coverage through spouse	25%	4.3%	5.5	20%
Frequency-weighted average	**25%**	**1.9%**	**2.2**	

Notes: This table summarizes table 5.2. The marginal earnings tax rate includes pre-ACA payroll and personal income taxes at a 25% rate. "Receiving exchange subsidies" refers to heads or spouses of households receiving subsidies; dependents in such households are considered "not receiving" for the purpose of determining incentives. "Employer penalized" includes all employers not offering affordable coverage (see chapter 3). p is measured in hours per week.

earnings tax rate of t = 25 percent, which is my estimate of a typical combined rate from personal income taxes (state and federal) and employee payroll taxes that are unrelated to the ACA.

Scenario B applies to workers who do not receive subsidies and work for an employer not offering affordable coverage. For example, a penalty (or threat of a penalty) will be owed on a Medicare participant who works full time for an employer not offering health insurance to its full-time employees.[18] This person is prohibited from receiving exchange subsidies because of eligibility for Medicare. As shown in chapter 3, the typical employee subject to the employer penalty has to work 4.0 hours per week just to produce the value equal to the employer penalty and needs to work beyond that to produce any value for employer and employee. Table 6.4's second row therefore has τ = 0, t = 25 percent, and p = 4.0 hours per week. As estimated in chapter 5, 21 percent of potential workers experience scenario B.

Scenario C is for any worker who receives subsidies and works for an employer not offering affordable coverage. As a consequence of receiving the exchange subsidies, this worker faces an additional marginal tax rate on earnings of 20.9 percent. Because the employer does not offer affordable coverage, this worker will create a penalty liability for her employer if she works a full-time schedule. Scenario C therefore sets t = 25 percent, τ = 20.9 percent, and p = 4.0 hours per week. It is the least common of the four scenarios, experienced by only 5 percent of potential workers.

When the "penalty" p is interpreted to include the subsidies forgone by full-time ESI workers, the budget constraint (equation 6.2) also describes people whose employers offer affordable coverage to full-time employees, but not to their part-time employees. Because the exchange subsidies are not subject to income and payroll taxes whereas pZ is multiplied in equation (6.2) by the tax factor $(1 - t - \tau)$, pZ must be measured as the ratio of the exchange subsidies forgone to the tax factor. This is exactly the ratio calculated to prepare table 5.2's 5.5-hour estimate, which is why table 6.4's fourth tax scenario sets p = 5.5 hours per week. It has τ = 4.3 percent. Scenario D is experienced by 20 percent of potential workers.

Any one of the scenarios can be experienced by a full-time worker or a part-time worker. Because p is a full-time employment tax, employers are not penalized for part-time workers experiencing any scenario with $p > 0$, so long as those employees maintain work schedules that do not exceed the ACA-defined threshold P for part-time work.[19] The value of p only indicates the cost of setting work hours above the threshold, if employer and employee choose to do so.

My national labor market model assumes that the population experiences the tax scenarios according to the frequencies shown in table 6.4. For example, it assumes that 54 percent of potential workers face no new taxes as a consequence of the ACA. Twenty-one percent face a new FTET of 4.0 hours per week, and no new earnings tax, because their employer is penalized while they receive no subsidy.[20]

Because specific demographic groups, such as unmarried household heads, are more likely to experience some tax scenarios than others, my group-specific results are based on appendix 6.2's group-specific versions of table 6.4. The most interesting group-specific patterns are that (a) 74 percent of elderly workers experience no new disincentives, and never experience scenario D, and (b) 42 percent of unmarried household heads experience scenario D, but their FTET amount for that scenario is only 4.2 hours per week rather than the national average 5.5.

2. QUANTIFYING AVERAGE AND MARGINAL COST CURVES

As shown with figures 6.3a and 6.3b, the scheduling effects of FTETs depend on the position and shape of the cost curves, especially the marginal cost curves.[21] I assume that, conditional on tax scenario, all workers' cost curves have the same quantitative properties, except that the position of the marginal cost curve varies across workers according to the number of hours they worked in 2011.[22] Table 6.5 summarizes the distribution of 2011 weekly work hours by demographic group. Of particular interest are the people working 30–34 hours in 2011, because the bulk of the twenty-niners in 2016 will be people like them. Female workers are twice as likely to be in that category as men, which suggests that women will be disproportionately represented among the twenty-niners. Elderly workers are especially likely to be working part time even without the ACA, which is yet another factor distancing them from the law's new labor taxes.

The position of the marginal cost curve is not enough to determine a worker's response to taxes. The curve's slope also matters: the flatter it is, the more sensitive is the weekly schedule to taxes and the less convex is the average cost curve. Figure 6.4 is a version of figure 6.3b with the same FTET but a flatter marginal cost curve. The optimum hours without the FTET is the same in both figures—40 hours per week—but figure 6.4 shows a greater hours increase in response to the FTET—up

TABLE 6.5. The distribution of 2011 usual weekly hours by demographic group

Usual weekly hours	All groups	Men	Women	Unmarried HH head	Married HH head or spouse	Nonelderly	Elderly
<26	0.114	0.076	0.157	0.056	0.079	0.107	0.291
26–29	0.006	0.003	0.009	0.004	0.005	0.006	0.011
30–34	0.052	0.035	0.071	0.045	0.040	0.051	0.065
35–39	0.075	0.053	0.101	0.085	0.064	0.075	0.090
40	0.520	0.531	0.506	0.559	0.529	0.525	0.394
41+	0.233	0.302	0.156	0.250	0.284	0.237	0.148
Total	1.000	1.000	1.000	1.000	1.000	1.000	1.000
Addendum: Group's share of those working 30–34 hrs/week	0.362	0.638	0.190	0.384	0.953	0.047	

Notes: The six hours categories above are summaries of the 85 categories used in the labor market model. Source is March 2012 CPS.

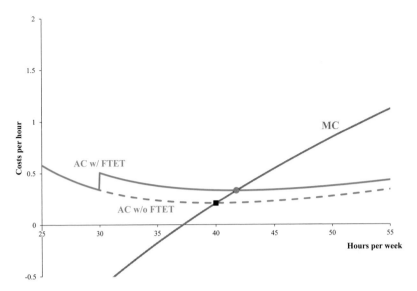

FIGURE 6.4. The hourly costs of working in an occupation with a flatter marginal cost curve.

to 42 hours per week rather than the 41 in figure 6.3b. This by itself suggests that, in response to a given FTET, a flatter marginal cost curve causes full-time employees to increase their weekly hours more than a steeper marginal cost curve would.

However, recall that FTETs can, and for some workers do, push weekly hours in the other direction by inducing them to forgo full-time employment and work 29 hours instead. With the flatter marginal cost curve, there are more twenty-niners because the average cost curve is less convex. For example, a 35-hour employee (without the FTET) would remain a full-time (30+ hours) worker if his marginal cost curve were steep, but would become a twenty-niner if the curve were flat enough. A flatter marginal cost curve is therefore associated with both larger positive impacts and larger negative impacts of FTETs on average weekly hours, but not necessarily a larger overall average impact (including both the positives and negatives).[23]

To put it another way, accurate predictions about the *distribution* of weekly work hours, such as the number of twenty-niners, require accurate estimates of the steepness of the marginal cost curve whereas accurate predictions about *average* employment and weekly work hours may not. This book therefore devotes little space to estimating the slope of the marginal cost curve and instead experiments with alternative plausible slopes as part of it sensitivity analysis.[24]

If the ACA had no effect on the marginal income tax rate (as distinct from full-time employment taxes), then the law's effect on the workweek would hardly depend on the magnitude q/Z of the quasi-fixed cost of working, expressed in hours per week. Although 95 percent of workers will have much the same marginal income tax rate with the ACA as they would without it (table 6.4), for completeness I estimate q/Z from the relationship between hours and weekly earnings. Following Hirsch (2005) and others who have interpreted the low hourly pay from part-time work as evidence of a quasi-fixed employment cost, I assume that the causal effect on average hourly earnings of switching from part-time work to full-time work is about 10 percent, which implies that q/Z is about four hours per week.[25]

With a four-hour quasi-fixed cost, adding 20.9 percentage points to the marginal income tax rate, as in scenario C, reduces quasi-fixed costs net of taxes by about 0.9 hours per week. Adding 1.9 percentage points, as in the frequency-weighted average, reduces quasi-fixed costs net of taxes by about 0.08 hours per week, which is more than an order of magnitude less than the average full-time employment tax from the ACA. Thus, to a close approximation, my quantitative results for the nation's cross-section distribution of weekly work hours can be understood without regard for income-tax effects. Income-tax effects specific to scenario C would be economically more significant, but still less than scenario C's full-time employment tax of 4.0 hours per week.

3. MORE ON THE SOURCES OF TWENTY-NINERS

Table 6.2's occupations were selected because, before the ACA, they had weekly schedules that were especially long (top panel) and especially close to 30 hours (the remaining panels). These are the two extremes where full-time work and twenty-niners, respectively, are especially likely under the ACA. The FTET effects in intermediate cases depend on the various factors discussed above: the size of the FTET measured in hours per week and the position of the costs curves. Figure 6.5 helps assess the intermediate cases by calculating the "Rubicon" number of non-ACA hours beyond which the adjustment to part-time

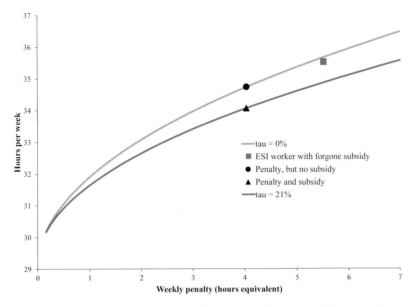

FIGURE 6.5. Weekly hours of the marginal "twenty-niner" but for the ACA as a function of the tax parameters.

work is too costly (as measured by cost curves such as those shown in figure 6.2) to justify the savings in full-time employment taxes. I call that number of hours the "marginal twenty-niner" because a person who would work those hours but for the ACA is on the margin between working 29 hours and avoiding the FTET and working his optimal number of full-time hours.

The figure displays two schedules: one for each of two alternative amounts τ ("tau") that the ACA might add to the marginal earnings tax rate.[26] The figure also shows the nontrivial tax scenarios B, C, and D from table 6.3 as a circle, triangle, and square, respectively. Figure 6.5's horizontal axis measures the penalty in hours per week. Its vertical axis measures the "Rubicon" value for weekly hours but for the ACA. For example, the circle located at (4.0,34.7) indicates that persons working more than 34.7 hours but for the ACA would prefer to pay the 4.0-hour penalty and work full time (by the ACA definition of 30 or more) rather than cutting hours to 29. Persons working less but for the ACA would work part time under the ACA, and in many cases do so by working just below the 30-hour threshold.

The greater the number of hours shown in figure 6.5, the greater the percentage of workers who will work just below the threshold (i.e., work as twenty-niners) under the ACA. This result is illustrated in the figure because each of the schedules slopes up. For the workers at ESI employers who satisfy the other income and family criteria for exchange subsidies, the critical value is shown as a square. The height of the square is 35.5, which means that some of the "twenty-niners" would be working 35 hours per week (when they are working) but for the ACA.

Chapters 3 and 4 compare the amounts that workers earn in the hours beyond 29 to the salary equivalent of the employer penalty (or, as applicable, the forgone exchange subsidy). The salary equivalent is greater for millions of workers, which means that, holding constant weeks worked, they could have both more disposable income and more leisure time by cutting their schedule to 29 hours. At first glance, it would seem that knowledgeable workers in the "100 percent tax" situation should and will cut their hours. The 100 percent tax can be represented by a straight line in figure 6.5 (not shown) going through (0,29) and having a slope equal to one: workers above (below) the straight line have a penalty less (greater, respectively) than what they earn in hours 29 and beyond. The fact that the two curves in figure 6.5 approximate, but do not coincide with, the aforementioned straight line means the 100 percent tax is not a litmus test for who will cut hours in the model, although it is a handy approximation to the incidence of those cuts.

For example, figure 6.5 says that someone who would be working 30 hours per week but for the ACA becomes a twenty-niner even if the full-time-work penalty is less than one hour per week because the critical values in the figure are above 30 at a one-hour penalty. In other words, she reduces hours to 29 even though doing so reduces her weekly compensation because she enjoys leisure time and can make up for some of the lost weekly hours by working more weeks. On the other hand, penalties as large as, say, 10 hours per week (not shown in figure 6.5) have a critical value of less than 39, which means a person who would be working 39 hours per week but for the ACA does not cut hours to 29 despite the cut's increasing her weekly compensation because she prefers to avoid some of the penalty by working fewer weeks per year rather than adjusting her schedule so dramatically.

4. AGGREGATE HOURS SUPPLY AND DEMAND

Figures 6.1 through 6.5 hold fixed aggregate hours $N = nh$ and examine how it is composed of weekly employment n and weekly hours h. Aggregate hours depend on aggregate labor supply and aggregate labor demand. The supply of labor is modeled with "representative families," each of which has many adult members representing the various occupations. Each family experiences one of the tax scenarios from table 6.4, with the prevalence of each scenario in the model population of families coinciding with the frequencies shown in the table. The responses of specific family members depend on their occupation, with some of them having full-time schedules despite FTETs, others working as twenty-niners, and the remaining members with part-time schedules that are not constrained by the 30-hour threshold. FTETs reduce aggregate hours for the first two groups because they increase the average hourly cost of working. FTETs by themselves may slightly increase aggregate hours for the last group, due to an income effect.[27]

The size of the aggregate-hours reductions depends on the "Frisch wage elasticity of aggregate hours." The Frisch elasticity is closely related to the reward coefficient featured in table 6.1. The Frisch wage elasticity is set to about 0.6 (recall endnote 7) in order to represent the size of the responses of aggregate hours to historical tax changes and other disincentives.

Because it erodes incentives to work, the ACA reduces the supply of aggregate hours in an amount commensurate with the Frisch wage elasticity. In the short run, the reduced supply of labor increases wage rates and employer costs, and reduces profits, because the same stock of capital competes for fewer workers. But the low profit rates begin a process of low investment that eventually brings the capital stock back into line with the supply of labor. For simplicity, the model used in this chapter abstracts from the length of time that it takes for capital to adjust, and finds that overall wage and profit rates (inclusive of taxes) are independent of labor supply. In other words, on average and in the long run, the various taxes on labor reduce the reward to working rather than increasing employers' labor costs per hour. These should be interpreted as long-run results that also abstract from most of the productivity effects examined in chapter 8.

I do not assume that wage rates or hourly employer costs are fixed for specific occupations. Rather, relative wages increase in the occupations experiencing the greater reductions in labor supply. The elasticity of output substitution between the different occupations is assumed to be two based on Montgomery and Cosgrove's study (1993) of the degree of substitution between full-time and part-time positions (see Mulligan 2014c for the full mathematical general equilibrium model). I also show results for an alternative substitution elasticity of four.[28]

D. Predictions for Work Schedules and Employment under the ACA

1. THE WORKWEEK BECOMES MORE UNEQUAL

This section shows the quantitative results, beginning with the impact of the ACA on the length of the workweek. Figure 6.6 shows the overall hours distribution with (red) and without (black) the ACA, excluding people who are not working during the week.[29] The horizontal axis measures the fraction of persons at work who have a schedule no longer than the hours indicated on the vertical axis. A flat segment of the hours distribution indicates a significant number of people working the same hours, with the width of the segment proportional to the number of people. For example, the black distribution has an especially wide segment at 40 hours per week because about half of workers reported exactly a 40-hour schedule before the ACA. Another example: both distributions have a flat segment at 20 hours per week because about 4 percent of workers did (will) report a schedule of exactly 20 hours.

For the same reason that flat segments of the distribution indicate hours equality, upward-sloping segments indicate hours *inequality*. The crossing of the black non-ACA distribution from below by the red ACA distribution illustrates that the ACA increases hours inequality. The ACA makes both 29-hour schedules and 41-plus-hour schedules more common; 30–35 hour schedules are less common, as are 40-hour schedules.

Because occupations have different schedules to begin with and adjust their employment rates differently to the ACA, the law is affecting the occupational composition of the workforce and thereby the overall average weekly hours. This is known as the "composition effect." For

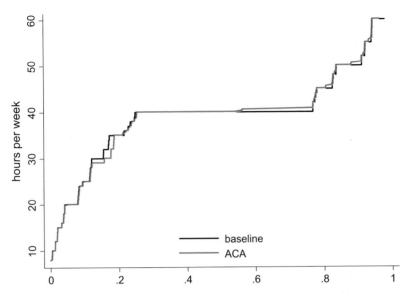

FIGURE 6.6. The ACA's impact on the weekly hours CDF among the employed.

Note: ACA is the weighted average of all tax scenarios.

the sake of illustrating the composition effect, suppose that half of the population works 22 hours per week and the other half works 40 hours per week. Also assume, for simplicity, that without the ACA both types of workers would work the full year, so that average work hours per employee in the whole workforce in any given week would be 31. With the ACA, the 40-hour workers may cut in half the number of weeks that they are on the payroll. Therefore, with the ACA, in any given week two-thirds of persons on payrolls would be 22-hour workers and one-third would be 40-hour workers. This would make the average work hours per employee in the whole workforce 28.[30] In this example, average hours per employee would be lower under the ACA entirely because of the composition effect.[31] The point here is that changes in average weekly hours per worker depend not only on changes in the weekly work schedules of individual workers, but also on the correlation between work schedules and changes in the propensity to be employed in any given week.

Table 6.6 displays quantitative estimates of the ACA's long-term impact on various summary indicators of labor market performance.

TABLE 6.6. The ACA's impact on various summary labor statistics

Impacts by tax scenario[a]

Tax scenario	Logs		Weekly hrs per employee		Percentage of employees working:	
	Weekly emp. rate	Aggregate hours	VW	IW	26–29 hrs/wk	1–34 hrs/wk
B: Penalty only	−0.045	−0.039	0.006	0.010	5.7	1.1
C: Subsidy phaseout and penalty	−0.189	−0.180	0.009	0.003	5.7	−0.2
D: Subsidy forgone due to ESI	−0.075	−0.076	−0.001	0.006	10.9	6.3
All (including no tax change)	**−0.033**	**−0.031**	**0.002**	**0.004**	**3.6**	**1.4**

Impacts by demographic group[a]

Demographic Group	Logs		Weekly hrs per employee		Percentage of employees working:	
	Weekly emp. rate	Aggregate hours	VW	IW	26–29 hrs/wk	1–34 hrs/wk
Female	−0.031	−0.031	0.000	0.009	4.7	1.8
Male	−0.034	−0.031	0.003	0.011	2.6	1.1
Elderly	−0.009	−0.009	0.000	0.008	1.8	0.4
Unmarried head[b]	−0.031	−0.030	0.001	0.003	3.6	1.5
Married head or spouse[b]	−0.035	−0.033	0.002	0.004	3.9	1.7
All (including dependents and elderly)	−0.033	−0.031	0.002	0.004	3.6	1.4

[a] Every table entry is a *difference* between the ACA outcome and the no-ACA outcome, and expressed in percentage points in the final two columns. VW impact (in logs) is the difference between the impacts for log aggregate hours and log employment rate. IW impact is the log change in weekly hours averaged across worker types (before logging) using non-ACA employment shares as weights.

[b] Excludes poor and elderly workers. Marital-status groups are the only demographic groups with custom estimates of the hour equivalents of the FTETs (the other groups are assigned the values from table 6.2).

The top panel has a breakdown by tax scenario (listed in the same order as in table 6.4), and the bottom panel a breakdown by demographic group. The bottom row of each panel shows the total for all scenarios or groups combined. The middle two columns of the table summarize the weekly-hours distributions shown in figure 6.6. The first VW (variable-weight) measure may be the most familiar because it just divides aggregate hours by the number of employees. As noted above, this measure could be affected by the ACA even if every employee kept the same hours per week because employment rate impacts could be correlated with the length of the workweek. The IW (initial-weight) measure averages occupation-specific weekly-hours changes, using non-ACA employment rates as weights. By construction, the IW measure shows an impact only if an impact is nonzero for at least one occupation. The IW measure is different from the VW measure to the extent that the ACA affects the composition of occupations among those employed during a given week.

Overall, both measures show essentially zero impact on weekly hours per employee because some occupations reduce their weekly hours (conditional on employment; recall figure 6.3a), and other occupations increase them (figure 6.3b). However, the two measures are somewhat different at a scenario level because, due to full-time employment taxes, tax scenarios B and D have employment rates falling more for high-hour workers whereas the other ("C: subsidy phase-out and penalty") has employment rates falling more for low-hour workers.

The final two columns in table 6.6 quantify the bump in the hours distribution shown in figure 6.6: 3.6 percentage points more of the workforce will work 26 to 29 hours per week—the twenty-niners—than would without the ACA.[32] The final column shows that the percentage of workers under the ACA who are part time by the BLS definition (34 or fewer hours per week) is within 1.5 points of the percentage without the ACA. This is another indicator that the frequency of twenty-niners can go up without increasing as much the fraction of workers working part time by the BLS definition.

The CPS reports that an extraordinary fraction—about half—of workers work exactly 40 hours per week. The CPS is arguably the best data I have for this purpose.[33] But if that data is faulty and that fraction is exaggerated, it presents two possible problems for making and interpreting predictions about the distribution of weekly work hours. First, if past CPS respondents who were working above or below 40 hours a week (say, 38 or 41 hours a week) have been rounding their answers on the Current Population Survey to exactly 40 hours a week, the ACA's incentives tied to work hours may make those respondents more aware of the exact number of hours that they are working. This may make them more likely to report those exact numbers on the Current Population Survey. So the ACA may change reporting patterns in the CPS even if it doesn't change the actual behavior that the CPS is supposed to measure. Second, the historical CPS data may understate the number of persons working 30–39 hours per week (by tending to report them as working 40 hours per week) and thereby it may have understated the number of persons who will be induced by the ACA to cut their hours to 29 or fewer.

2. EMPLOYMENT AND HOURS PER CAPITA

Table 6.6 reports results from a model that is far more sophisticated than table 6.1's simple arithmetic because, among other things, the former features three economically distinct types of taxes (rather than summarizing all three as an earnings tax) and explicitly models a wide array of occupations. Nevertheless, the two approaches closely agree on the aggregate hours impact (−3.1 and −3.2 percent, respectively) because they begin with the same tax measurements and use the same reward coefficient.

Given that the ACA has little effect on average weekly hours per employee, it follows that the ACA also reduces weekly employment rates by about 3 percent (the table's first column). The effects on employment rates and aggregate hours are economically significant under the two most common scenarios—"penalty only" and "subsidy forgone due to ESI"—but nonetheless far less than under the remaining (and least common) scenario.

3. RESULTS BY DEMOGRAPHIC GROUP

The bottom panel of table 6.6 shows results for demographic groups formed by changing the scenario and worker-type weights to match the group of interest, rather than for the population as a whole. Women (without regard to marital status) are especially likely to cut their hours to the ACA's hours threshold, because they are disproportionately likely to otherwise work 30 to 34 hours (recall table 6.5) and they can therefore move to 29 hours with comparatively little cost.[34] The elderly, defined to be persons in households in which the youngest person is at least 65 years old, have the impacts closest to zero because they cannot receive exchange subsidies regardless of how much they earn or work. The elderly may work at employers that are assessed the employer penalty, in which case they experience the "penalty only" tax scenario.

Unmarried heads are more likely to have their exchange subsidy-eligibility hinge on their ESI status, because by definition they do not have a spouse who could get them ESI coverage. They also have somewhat lower hourly compensation. However, the amount of the exchange subsidy at stake for married heads and spouses is more than twice as large as it is for unmarried heads (recall chapter 4's table 4.4) because of the size of the family to be insured. The first two factors create greater ACA impacts for the unmarried, whereas the last factor creates greater impacts for the married. The final two rows of table 6.6 show that the ultimate result is essentially the same ACA impacts on married and unmarried household heads and spouses.[35]

4. SENSITIVITY ANALYSIS

In a way, the ACA full-time threshold of 30 hours per week strikes a balance between groups of workers reducing weekly hours and groups increasing them, resulting in entries for table 6.6's middle two columns that are essentially zero. For this reason, the willingness of employers and employees to adjust work schedules does not matter much for determining the employment and hours effects. If adjustments are more costly than I assume, then the size of the downward hours adjustments would be smaller than I assume—there would be fewer twenty-niners—but the size of the upward adjustments would be less too, so the net weekly-hours results would not be much different than what is shown in table 6.6. Nonzero adjustments would occur in both directions, though, and by assumption the work schedule adjustments are costly, so the ACA still significantly reduces the reward to employment even when employers or employees find work schedule adjustments to be costly. By the same reasoning, the results should not be much different if work schedule adjustments are less costly than I have assumed, except that the number of twenty-niners will be greater.

Table 6.7 confirms this intuition. The top row of the table displays the results under my benchmark assumptions, namely, the results shown in the bottom row of table 6.6. The next two rows show the results under two alternative assumptions about the employee costs of schedule adjustments. The following "high employer substitution" row shows results under the assumption that employers are easily (that is, with minimal loss of productivity) able to substitute part-time positions for full-time positions.[36] Notice that the employment rate, aggregate hours, and average weekly-hours columns are hardly different in rows (2) through (4) from what they are under the benchmark. What varies more is the number of workers who become twenty-niners under the ACA, and the number of workers who work part time under the BLS definition.

The next two rows of the table look at 34-hour and 35-hour thresholds for full-time work, rather than the 30-hour threshold that is in the law. Nobody becomes a twenty-niner under the 34- and 35-hour thresholds, because a 29-hour schedule has no special advantage. However, with a 34-hour threshold 4 percent of the workforce changes their work schedule from 34-plus hours to fewer than 34 hours (typically, they change to exactly 33 hours). Moreover, the middle columns of the table show that the 35-hour threshold no longer attains the balance between groups of workers reducing weekly hours and groups increasing them. The former groups dominate, and average weekly hours fall more than 3 percent. With the 35-hour threshold, even workers who would otherwise be working 40 hours may find it worthwhile to cut their schedule by six hours in order to avoid the 5.5-hour quasi-fixed cost. It is even possible that aggregate employment rates increase.[37] Thresholds greater than 30 hours result in less net government revenue (not shown in the table) than the actual 30-hour threshold, because the higher threshold encourages more workers to avoid the penalty or obtain the exchange subsidies.

Because the exchange plans through which households receive subsidies are not identical to employer plans, one might infer that households value the subsidies less than they cost the government. Recall from chapter 4 that my benchmark assumption is that households

TABLE 6.7. Sensitivity analysis

ACA impacts under alternative assumptions[a]

Assumption		Logs		Weekly hrs per employee		Percentage of employees working:	
		Weekly emp. rate	Aggregate hours	VW	IW	26–29 hrs/wk	1–34 hrs/wk
(1)	**Benchmark**	**-0.033**	**-0.031**	**0.002**	**0.004**	**3.6**	**1.4**
(2)	Schedule adjustments are more costly	-0.033	-0.032	0.002	0.002	2.5	0.3
(3)	Schedule adjustments are less costly	-0.032	-0.031	0.001	0.004	5.2	3.0
(4)	High employer subst. between FT & PT	-0.033	-0.031	0.002	0.004	3.6	1.5
(5)	34-hour threshold rather than 30	-0.031	-0.030	0.001	0.003	0.0	4.1
(6)	35-hour threshold rather than 30	0.018	-0.020	-0.038	-0.033	0.0	27.2
(7)	Lower subsidy valuation rate	-0.032	-0.029	0.003	0.004	2.6	0.4
(8)	"ESI dump" affects 10 million more workers	-0.034	-0.035	0.002	0.003	3.4	1.2
(9)	ACA lacks employer penalty	-0.023	-0.023	0.000	0.001	1.7	0.9
(10)	Lower employer quasi-fixed cost	-0.032	-0.030	0.002	0.004	3.6	1.4
(11)	Half employee quasi-fixed cost	-0.029	-0.028	0.001	0.004	3.6	1.5
(12)	Higher employer quasi-fixed cost	-0.035	-0.034	0.001	0.003	3.6	1.5
(13)	Double employee quasi-fixed cost	-0.042	-0.040	0.002	0.004	3.5	1.4
(14)	Add 10 points to non-ACA tax rate	-0.038	-0.036	0.001	0.003	3.5	1.4
(15)	Subtract 10 points from non-ACA tax rate	-0.028	-0.027	0.000	0.002	4.7	2.5
(16)	Reward coefficient = 1/2	-0.045	-0.043	0.002	0.004	3.6	1.5

[a] Every table entry is a *difference* between the ACA outcome and the no-ACA outcome, and expressed in percentage points in the final two columns. VW impact (in logs) is the difference between the impacts for log aggregate hours and log employment rate. IW impact is the log change in weekly hours averaged across worker types (before logging) using non-ACA employment shares as weights.

discount exchange plans at 25 percent of their full cost, owing to their unique plan features.[38] Table 6.7's row (7) shows the result if instead the remaining net subsidy is discounted an additional 25 percent, that is, using a 4.1-hour equivalent of the implicit full-time employment tax rather than 5.5 hours. Row (7) also gives a good indication of what the impact estimates would be if I have overestimated exchange plan premiums for 2016.

As noted in chapter 4, other reasonable approaches might yield somewhat greater estimates of the average hour equivalent of exchange subsidies (net of the aforementioned 25 percent discount) and employer penalties. For example, going in the opposite direction of table 6.7's row (7) by using a subsidy value of 6.5 hours per week rather than the benchmark 5.5 hours, the ACA's impact on aggregate hours would be −3.2 percent rather than the benchmark result of −3.1 percent. A −3.2 percent aggregate hours impact is also obtained by deviating from the benchmark 4.0-hour penalty with a 4.4-hour penalty. Neither of these two sensitivity analyses is shown in table 6.7.

For the purposes of setting the frequencies of table 6.4's tax scenarios, I may have overestimated the degree to which the employer penalty will prevent ESI employers from dropping their coverage. Row (8) therefore shows the results of changing the scenario weights to reflect 10 million more people (including dependents) on the exchanges and correspondingly fewer workers in the implicit FTET scenario. This adjustment decreases the prevalence of twenty-niners because the implicit FTET is typically greater than the employer penalty (recall figure 4.2), but it reduces aggregate hours because the workers on the exchanges face a greater marginal earnings tax rate than ESI workers do.

As I discuss further in chapter 9, it is also possible that the employer penalty is weakly enforced, cleverly avoided, or never implemented.[39] Row (9) therefore takes the setup from row (8)—with more workers on exchanges and fewer workers at ESI employers—and eliminates the employer penalty. By comparison with row (1), row (9) suggests that the employer penalty is responsible for only about a quarter of the employment and hours reductions, in part because it helps keep employees away from the exchanges and their high marginal income tax rates.[40] The same comparison from table 6.7 also suggests that the employer penalty is responsible for more than half of the twenty-niners, but part of the reason the employer penalty creates twenty-niners is that it makes it difficult for full-time workers at ESI employers to obtain the exchange subsidies without reducing their hours.

The next four rows show alternative values for the quasi-fixed costs on both the employer and the employee sides. Increasing either quasi-fixed cost matters more for the ACA employment and aggregate hours impact estimates than decreasing the quasi-fixed costs because quasi-fixed costs cut heavily into the surplus of workers with low weekly hours. In effect, increasing quasi-fixed costs while holding constant the utility parameter η makes the employment rate of low-hour workers especially sensitive to income and employment taxes. The ACA's impact on the prevalence of twenty-niners is insensitive to non-ACA quasi-fixed costs.[41]

Although quasi-fixed costs determine the responsiveness of aggregate hours to incentives, the value t of the non-ACA marginal earnings tax rate determines the effect of ACA tax parameters on incentives. The greater the rate t, the greater is the proportional effect of ACA tax parameters on the after-tax earnings share, and it is proportional changes in the after-tax share that drive aggregate hours. Rows (14) and (15) confirm this idea, showing that the ACA's aggregate hours impact is greater when t is set higher than 25 percent and less when t is set lower than 25 percent.

The final row shows that the negative employment and aggregate hours impacts exceed 4 percent when the reward coefficient is adjusted to be 0.5 for the median worker rather than the value of 0.36 it has with the benchmark parameters.[42] However, the reward coefficient has little to do with the model's predictions for the prevalence of twenty-niners.

E. Window Dressing, Misreporting, and Other Strategies for Avoiding the New Taxes

This chapter focuses on the ACA's consequences for work schedules, but some of the same disincentives have other effects as well. People and businesses may shelter incomes, misreport incomes, or work entirely off the books, in order to maintain eligibility for income-tested benefits. They may also misreport hours worked (or manipulate their measurement) so that the employer avoids a penalty or the employee remains eligible for exchange subsidies.

There are both criminal and civil penalties for providing false information to the marketplaces.[43] On the other hand, the U.S. Government Accountability Office was able to obtain subsidized health insurance coverage for 11 of 12 fictitious persons (Bagdoyan 2014, p. 5). A handful of undercover videos purport to show federally-funded navigators advising applicants to lie about their income in order to receive larger subsidies (Farenthold 2013).

Misreporting hours and incomes is not necessarily an alternative to genuine adjustments of hours and incomes, especially if misreporting has limits and the ACA's income or employment taxes are still experienced by workers who misreport. Take, for example, two non-ESI workers each from families earning 450 percent of the poverty line. One of them reports truthfully, and the other hides $20,000 of income. Only the second worker can receive exchange subsidies and, as a result, is the only one who has the marginal income tax rate elevated by the ACA (because earning more income means paying more for health care). Because of the misreporting, the second worker ends up with a greater incentive to reduce income by working less than the first worker does. This is not to say that, by leaving misreporting out of the model, this chapter necessarily underestimates the genuine employment effects of the ACA.[44] To a first approximation, misreporting is another factor reducing reported incomes and hours, in addition to genuine behavioral effects.

Now consider the possibility of misreporting work hours or manipulating their measurement. If there were unlimited opportunities to misreport hours, then any one of the 33 million ESI workers shown in table 4.1 could get exchange subsidies if he wanted, regardless of how much he was really working. In the same way, tens of millions of full-time non-ESI employees could spare their employer from a penalty (or the threat of a penalty) merely by reporting 29 hours per week even while they are truly working full time.[45] However, I do not expect hours misreporting to be so rampant and am not aware of any economist predicting that it will be. Thus I assume misreporting will occur but be limited enough that a great many workers will admit they really do work full time and thereby face an FTET in the sense that avoiding a penalty or receiving a subsidy requires reducing their actual work hours, or not working at all.

This chapter's model can describe behavior in an economy in which hours are misreported to a limited degree. Suppose that every worker has an opportunity to hide two hours from her usual schedule, perhaps by "punching out" during lunch and coffee breaks or doing some (unreported for ACA purposes) work at home. In effect, P becomes 31 hours per week because anyone with that schedule is free to represent herself as a twenty-niner, whereas someone working 32 hours per week appears to be working at least 30 hours. Similarly, the effective P is 32 or 33 if hours misreporting can be as large as three or four hours per week, respectively. In effect, sensitivity analysis with respect to the part-time threshold can be interpreted as sensitivity analysis with respect to the limit on hours misreporting. Table 6.8 shows the results, with the only difference between table 6.8 and the threshold-sensitivity analysis shown in table 6.7 being that the former measures all persons working between 30 hours and P hours as twenty-niners.

Table 6.8 shows that the ACA's impacts on the employment rate and true aggregate hours are not sensitive to the possibility of hours misreporting as long as misreporting is limited to four hours per week. Not surprisingly, a result of misreporting is that the ACA reduces reported hours more than true hours, but the impact on reported aggregate hours is still within 0.005 log points of the impact on true aggregate hours, so long as the misreports are limited to four hours per week. The main effect of misreporting is to increase the ACA's impact on the percentage of workers who report themselves to be twenty-niners. All of these results follow from the fact that a 29-hour schedule is a full 11 hours away from (what appears to be) most workers' actual work hours before the ACA, so that reaching the ACA's threshold for part-time work requires significant behavioral change even if it is not the full 11 hours.

If workers can misreport more than four hours per week, then an 11-hour combination of misreporting and true hours reductions can be worth it to avoid the FTETs. A large fraction of the workforce would reduce their reported and actual weekly hours and may well increase their weekly employment rate (see the bottom row of table 6.8). But even when the combination of the ACA and misreporting increases the

TABLE 6.8. Hour misreporting and the real effects of the ACA

ACA impacts[a]

Assumption	Logs						Percentage of employees reporting:	
	Weekly emp. rate	Aggregate hours		Weekly hrs per employee				
		True	Reported	True	Reported		26–29 hrs/wk	1–34 hrs/wk
Benchmark (accurate reporting)	**−0.033**	**−0.031**	**−0.031**	**0.002**	**0.002**		**3.6**	**1.4**
Misreport up to one hour/week	−0.031	−0.031	−0.032	0.000	−0.001		7.0	2.9
Misreport up to two hours/week	−0.030	−0.030	−0.033	0.000	−0.002		7.4	3.3
Misreport up to three hours/week	−0.030	−0.030	−0.034	0.000	−0.004		8.9	4.0
Misreport up to four hours/week	−0.031	−0.030	−0.034	0.001	−0.004		9.0	4.1
Misreport up to five hours/week	0.018	−0.020	−0.058	−0.038	−0.076		32.7	27.2

[a] Every table entry is a *difference* between the ACA outcome and the no-ACA outcome, and expressed in percentage points in the final two columns. Each log weekly hours impact is the difference between the impacts for log aggregate hours and log employment rate.

weekly employment rate, the ACA still significantly reduces true aggregate hours and reduces reported aggregate hours even more than that. The large gap between true and reported hours would also manifest itself in this case as a sharp increase in productivity per measured hour worked: the bottom row of table 6.8 suggests about 4 percent because the impact on reported hours is about four percentage points more negative than the impact on actual hours.

Full-time workers could also react to the ACA by splitting their work time between two employers and being considered part-time employees of each. CNNMoney reported on employers who are helping coordinate this kind of activity, as with some of the owners of Fatburger fast-food restaurants who "began 'job sharing' with other businesses, teaming up to share a higher number of employees all working fewer hours. Someone could work 25 hours at one Fatburger, 25 at another one with a different franchise owner, and still not be a full-time worker under Obamacare rules" (Pagliery 2013). As it is, the model in this chapter already says that n increases for many of the worker types who move from full time to part time. The increase would reflect multiple-job holders if the model variable n were interpreted as job-weeks rather than person-weeks worked, with each worker contributing to job-weeks according to the number of jobs held during the week.[46] In this case, n should be measured from the U.S. Labor Department's employer survey rather than its household survey, because the latter does not distinguish between multiple-job holders and single-job holders for the purpose of measuring employment during the reference week.

Burkhauser, Lyons, and Simon (2011) explain how low-income ESI workers may gain access to exchange subsidies if their employers rearrange the financing of ESI premiums so that the employer plan is considered unaffordable for low-income employees. This kind of window dressing may produce gains for both employer and employee, but it nonetheless reduces incentives to work because it is an example of shifting employees from ESI to exchange coverage as examined in row (8) of table 6.7. The window dressing somewhat reduces the amount of the full-time employment tax, but it increases the worker's marginal income tax rate because it permits getting federal assistance with premiums and cost sharing. The net result is even less employment than in the benchmark specification.

In summary, misreporting and other tax-avoidance strategies may be complements to, rather than substitutes for, the genuine adjustments of employment and incomes that are the focus of the second half of this book.

F. Conclusions

The Affordable Care Act has multiple and economically distinct types of taxes that will affect work schedules. A contribution of this chapter is to estimate the long-term impact of the new taxes on employment and the distribution of weekly work hours, done separately by demographic group, by adapting and calibrating a model familiar from the labor economics literature. Not surprisingly, the model predicts that a large majority of the workforce works full time despite the new full-time employment tax. For them, the full-time employment tax is just an employment tax and thereby induces them to work fewer weeks and slightly longer weekly schedules than they would without the ACA. A smaller part of the workforce makes a larger absolute change in their weekly work hours—in the direction of a shorter workweek—to avoid the full-time employment taxes. The law may also disproportionately reduce the employment rate among persons who normally work short schedules, and thereby increase average work hours per employee by changing the composition of the workforce. Perhaps contrary to the conventional wisdom, I predict an overall impact on average hours per employee that is essentially zero.

In a way, the near-zero average weekly work hours effect reflects a balance, created by the law's 30-hour threshold, between groups reducing their weekly hours and others increasing their hours. But the near-zero average effect does not mean the ACA fails to distort work schedules and their efficiency; it's just that the work schedule effects may not be detectable with aggregate data, even if they are disaggregated according to the 35-hour definition of full-time work that has been used by the Bureau of Labor Statistics over the years.

A conventional wisdom says that employment rates increase to "compensate" for work hours lost from taxes on full-time schedules. Under this view, more people working 29 hours rather than, say, 35, would mean that employers simply have to hire more or keep workers on the payroll longer in order to accomplish the tasks necessary to conduct their business. The conventional wisdom fails in two ways. As noted above, full-time employment taxes can be avoided by reducing employment and increasing hours per employee. My conservative estimates suggest that this case will be far more prevalent than the twenty-niner situation: the ACA will reduce the nationwide weekly employment rate by 3 percent below what it would have been without the ACA.[47] As shown in table 6.1, the 3 percent estimate is primarily a consequence of two previous results: the size and prevalence of the new taxes as measured in chapters 3, 4, and 5, and the microeconometric literature on the effects of taxes on total hours worked.

Moreover, even if full-time employment taxes were avoided by reducing weekly work hours, there would not be a commensurate increase in the employment rate because weekly hours would not be reduced for normal business or personal reasons, but rather to avoid penalties and implicit taxes. The penalties and implicit taxes make the business of an employer more expensive, or being an employee less rewarding, even in those cases when people avoid the new tax by adjusting their employment conditions rather than writing a check to the federal treasury. Some employers may go out of business, or never start their businesses in the first place, because of the extra cost of the tax (or the costs of adjustments needed to avoid the tax) or because of the additional costs (e.g., higher wages) needed to attract workers to positions that render them ineligible for exchange subsidies. The net result is that the labor market will involve fewer total hours, and that higher employment rates, if any, will not be enough to compensate for the reduced hours per week. This economic reasoning has been confirmed by empirical studies of previous public policies that raised the relative employer cost of weekly work hours, and failed to create a commensurate increase in employment because the average hour worked by employees had been made more expensive or less productive.[48]

The ACA reduces the incentive for out-of-work people to accept jobs at the same time that it subsidizes layoffs, quits, and retirements. Before the ACA, people found health insurance to be less expensive when employed than it was when not working, and health insurance expenses were one reason unemployed people have been eager to get back to working in a position with coverage (Gruber and Madrian

2004). But the ACA permanently reverses the calculus by giving people who do not work more opportunities for subsidized coverage than employed people will have. Employers and employees used to find layoffs, quits, and (before age 65) retirements to be financially costly because, among other things, many people want to have health insurance coverage even after their job ends.

For example, a survey of employers shows how layoffs traditionally created a liability for them because "they provided some amount of free or reduced cost [continuing] coverage for laid-off workers," but federal assistance can free employers from this expense by allowing them to reduce or drop their benefits for laid-off workers.[49] Employers have already realized that the ACA's exchange subsidies make early retirements less expensive than they would be without the ACA. One of them is the city of Chicago, which "plans to start reducing health insurance coverage [in 2014] for more than 30,000 retired city workers and begin shifting them to President Barack Obama's new federal system" (Dardick 2013).

The ACA's labor market effects vary by demographic group. Work behavior among the elderly is hardly affected by the law because the longstanding Medicare program renders the elderly ineligible for the new exchange subsidies and the implicit income and full-time employment taxes that go with the subsidies. Women are about twice as likely as men to have their weekly work hours pushed below 30 as a consequence of the law.

This chapter probably underestimates the low-skill employment effects of the ACA by assuming that wages can fully adjust in the long run to reflect supply and demand in the low-skill labor market. A somewhat different analysis is needed to the extent that legislated minimum wages get in the way of these adjustments, as they might for the types of workers who currently earn near the minimum wage. The employer penalty is about $1.50 per hour worked by full-time workers at non-ESI employers, and the model in this chapter predicts that this cost is reflected in the structure of wages. Chapter 7 explains why the ACA puts other pressures on wages, such as depressing the wages of part-time workers and creating wage differentials between sectors, which means that no group of low-wage workers necessarily has to see its wage fall by $1.50. Nevertheless, some low-wage workers will see the demand for their labor depressed by the penalty and thereby see minimum-wage laws interfere with the operation of their labor market more than the laws would without the ACA.[50]

My estimates suggest that 3 or 4 percent of the workforce will work as twenty-niners (that is, work a schedule below the legislated 30-hour threshold) solely to avoid implicit and explicit full-time employment taxes included in the ACA. The twenty-niner estimates have an especially wide confidence interval because they depend on preference and cost parameters that have not received much attention in the micro-econometric literature and on unknown details of enforcement of, and compliance with, the ACA. This chapter may also underestimate the number of twenty-niners by ignoring much of the heterogeneity in hourly compensation, which puts up to 7 percent of the workforce in a situation in which a 29-hour schedule pays (net of taxes and subsidies) more than their normal full-time schedule (see chapters 3 and 4).

The model in this chapter is consistent with the hypothesis that, in the long run, full-time employment taxes come out of worker pay rather than out of employer profits. But it goes further, to say that FTETs are subtracted from worker pay even without any explicit adjustments by labor or capital. Chapter 7 presents a conceptually more elaborate model of wages in which the wage reductions from FTETs are shared by some of the workers who do not experience them directly, which means the 3 percent reduction in aggregate hours will be spread more widely across demographic groups and tax scenarios than is suggested in table 6.6. All else the same, the number of twenty-niners created by the ACA is less according to chapter 7's model than it is here.

The bulk of this chapter assumes that real work schedule changes are the only ways to avoid the ACA's new explicit and implicit taxes. But the chapter also briefly discusses and analyzes the possibilities for employers and employees to misreport incomes and hours worked. Misreporting and other strategies are consistent with my quantitative conclusions for aggregate work hours, and likely also the conclusions for employment rates. It is possible, although unlikely if the law is diligently enforced, that work hours will be commonly and massively underreported, in which case the ACA could significantly reduce true and reported aggregate hours, and sharply increase the reported number of twenty-niners, but could increase the employment rate.

Appendix 6.1: Derivation of the Household Budget Constraint

HEADS AND SPOUSES NOT OFFERED ESI COVERAGE DURING ANY PART OF THE CALENDAR YEAR

Worker i's family disposable income c_i is, net of taxes, subsidies, and health expenses:

$$(6.3) \qquad c_i = y_i - an_i + (s_0 - \beta y_i) - ty_i$$

$$(6.4) \qquad y_i = n_i h_i w_i + (1 - n_i) UB_i + o_i - n_i I(h_i > P) pZ$$

where y_i denotes income reported on the personal income tax return, including spousal income (if any). a denotes quasi-fixed costs paid by the household. The term in equation (6.3)'s parentheses is the exchange subsidy, which is approximated as a linear function of income y, or zero if the household is not eligible. The ty term is the non-ACA income and payroll taxes. n_i is the fraction of the year person i was on a payroll, h_i is weekly work hours, and w_i is the hourly wage rate. UB denotes a taxable unemployment insurance benefit. o_i denotes other sources of reported income such as spousal earnings and asset income. pZ is the salary equivalent of the employer penalty, and p is its hour equivalent. The nI term reflects the fact that the penalty applies only when worker i is on a payroll as a full-time worker.

Equations (6.3) and (6.4) are the same as (5.3) and (5.4) from chapter 5, except that chapter 5's equations do not account for the possibility of part-time work and are not explicit about the linear approximation to the subsidy schedule. Substituting (6.4) into (6.3); defining $q = UB$, $\tau = \beta$, and $g \equiv s_o + (1 - t - \tau)(UB + o)$; and inserting the work-schedule term $f(h)n$ yields equation (6.2) from the main text.[51]

HEADS OR SPOUSES OFFERED ESI COVERAGE WHEN WORKING FULL TIME

In this case, the exchange subsidy is received only when worker i is not at work full time (and has a family member enrolled in exchange coverage). The budget constraint is:

(6.5) $c_i = y_i - an_i - f(h_i)n + (s_0 - \beta y_i)[1 - I(h_i > P)n_i] - ty_i$

With three definitions, the budget constraint becomes

$$c = g_i(y_i, I(h_i > P)n_i) + (1 - t - \tau_i)y_i$$
$$- \{(1 - t - \tau_i)I(h_i > P)p_i Z + a + f(h_i)\}n$$

(6.6)

$$\tau_i \equiv [1 - I(h_i^* > P)n_i]\beta, \; p_i Z \equiv \frac{s_0 - \beta y_i^*}{1 - t - \tau_i},$$

$$g_i(y_i, I(h_i > P)n_i) \equiv s_0 + \tau y_i - \beta y_i - (y_i^* - y_i)\beta I(h_i > P)n_i$$

where asterisks indicate values before the ACA. The budget constraint
(6.6) is different from (6.2) only in that the g term in (6.6) is not a constant. It is constant to a first-order approximation, though, because the
two first partial derivatives of the g function are zero in the neighborhood of the values of income, hours, and weeks that occurred before
the ACA. In other words, equation (6.6) is a more complicated version
of the budget constraint in which the marginal income tax rate varies
with the number of weeks worked and with full-time status, whereas
equation (6.2), which I use in the model, treats the marginal income
tax rate as a constant.

Appendix 6.2: Additional Statistics by Tax-Scenario and Demographic Group

Figure 6.6 shows the weekly-hours cumulative distribution function
(hereafter, CDF) for the "entire economy," that is, 54 percent no new
incentives, 21 percent penalty-only scenario, and so on (see table 6.4).
Figure 6.7 shows the CDFs for the two more common scenarios.

Table 6.9 shows the frequency weights used for all the tax scenarios.
The first column is copied from table 6.1, and the other columns show
the scenario weights used for specific demographic groups. I assume that
men and women have the same scenario weights. The elderly cannot receive exchange subsidies regardless of work status, so all of their weight
is on the first two scenarios (I assume the elderly are as likely to work
for a penalized employer as is the general population). Unmarried and

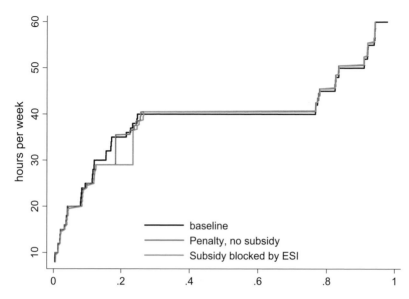

FIGURE 6.7. The ACA's impact on weekly hours CDFs among the employed, two more common tax scenarios.

Note: Only 2 of 3 ACA tax scenarios are shown.

TABLE 6.9. Tax-scenario weights by demographic group

Tax scenario	Full population	Men	Women	Elderly	Household heads & spouses Unmarried	Married
A: No new incentives	54%	54%	54%	74%	32%	55%
B: Employer penalized, but employee not receiving exchange subsidies	21%	21%	21%	26%	20%	20%
C: Employee receiving exchange subsidies, and employer penalized	5%	5%	5%	0%	6%	6%
D: Worker at ESI employer without access to part-time own ESI or coverage through spouse	20%	20%	20%	0%	42%	19%
Total	100%	100%	100%	100%	100%	100%

Notes: "Receiving exchange subsidies" refers to heads or spouses of households receiving subsidies; dependents in such households are considered "not receiving" for the purpose of determining incentives. Household head and spouse categories exclude poor and elderly workers.

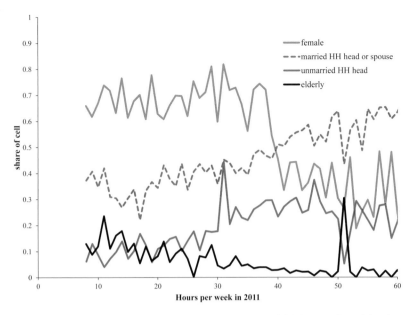

FIGURE 6.8. Demographic group representation among no-ACA-hours cells weighted by weeks worked.

Note: 51-hour cell has only 13 observations.

married household heads are different in terms of the weights shown in the bottom row (and also in the top row, because the top row is a residual) for the reasons noted in the main text (see especially table 6.7).

Figure 6.8 shows the demographic composition of people working a specific number of weekly hours in 2011, as measured in the March 2012 CPS. For example, 5 percent of the 32-hours-per-week workers were elderly, 72 percent were female, 44 percent were married heads or spouses, and 20 percent were unmarried heads (these categories are not mutually exclusive).

Simulations by gender and age all assume the same hour equivalents shown in table 6.4. For simulations (among household heads) by marital status, I assume that the weekly-hour equivalent of the employer penalty is 3.5 and 4.5 for married and unmarried, respectively, since unmarried heads have relatively low hourly compensation. The forgone exchange subsidy is assumed to be equivalent to 7.2 (4.2) hours of work for married (unmarried) household heads and spouses, respectively (see also appendix 4.2, but note that the marginal income tax rate assumed there is slightly greater).

7 | Adam Smith's Equalizing Differences: More Hidden Taxes and More Health Coverage

The Affordable Care Act's effects extend well beyond the employment rate and the length of the workweek. The purpose of this chapter is to examine the law's incentives for workers to change the sectors where they work and the type of coverage they get (if any) and to examine the law's incentives for employers to adjust the amount and composition of their employee compensation. The theory and arithmetic of equalizing differences is essential to this analysis because it shows how workers having no direct contact with the ACA's penalties and subsidies nonetheless experience the law's provisions because they compete and produce with workers who do. The first results given in the chapter are for the wage effects of the law separately for "low-skill" and "high-skill" workers. The last part of the chapter demonstrates the strength of the law's incentives to expand health insurance coverage and how its employer penalty is essential for determining the source of coverage.

A. The Theory of Equalizing Differences

Both the employer penalty and the exchange subsidies affect the structure of wages, by which I mean the average level of wages and wage patterns across types of workers. The theory of equalizing differences is the best way to understand the ACA's impact on the structure of wages, so this chapter begins with a simple, everyday illustration of the theory in action.[1] I then apply the theory to consider the employer penalty in isolation—as if it were the only tax in the ACA—and afterward analyze the exchange subsidies.

1. INTRODUCTION: A TALE OF TWO OCCUPATIONS

Even after adjusting for inflation, workers today earn far more than they did decades ago. The primary reasons for this are the changes in

Dan albone with his 1902 Prototype
"Ivel" Agricultural Motor

FIGURE 7.1. Antique and modern farm tractors.
Sources: Figure 7.1a is credited to *North Bedfordshire Gazette*, January 23, 1903. Figure 7.1b is licensed from Leonid Ikan/Shutterstock and was cropped and converted to black and white.

workers and their work environments that have made them vastly more productive. Workers today typically have more and better machinery to accomplish their tasks. Take the farmer. An early twentieth-century farm tractor is shown on the top (figure 7.1a), and a modern tractor is shown on the bottom (figure 7.1b).

Today 100 bushels of corn can be produced with fewer than three labor hours and less than one acre of land (U.S. Department of Agriculture, National Institute of Food and Agriculture 2014). In 1945, it took 14 labor hours and two acres of land to produce the same 100 bushels because farmers then did not have the farm equipment and education that is available today. Even more farmwork was required to produce the same results at the beginning of the twentieth century. It's no puzzle that farmers can earn more today than they did years ago.

But wage growth is not limited to occupations where technology has progressed, capital has accumulated, or education is essential. Barbers today cut hair almost exactly the way they did in the first half of the twentieth century. The barbershop photographed in figure 7.2a is circa 1920, and the equipment looks about the same as it does now (figure 7.2b): scissors, chairs, and a sink. Yet barbers now are paid much more than the barbers from the era of the earlier photograph.[2]

The fact that both farmers and barbers shared wage growth but not technology and other sources of productivity growth would seem to defy productivity explanations for wage growth, but this impression ignores the theory of equalizing differences. Because men's desired quantity (not styles!) of haircuts have been pretty constant over the years, men must pay barbers enough to induce people to pursue the occupation and not some other profession for which productivity has been significantly advanced by capital accumulation, modern technology, and advanced education. Through the market mechanism, wage growth for barbers is a consequence of productivity growth in other occupations.

2. THE EMPLOYER PENALTY, SECTORAL SHIFTS, AND HIDDEN TAXES

As shown in chapter 3, the ACA's employer penalty is significant. At first glance, the penalty would seem to be just the problem of workers employed at penalized employers, with their workers receiving less weekly pay or losing their jobs altogether. And perhaps many of them go unharmed by the penalty because those "who can no longer be employed at those firms will find jobs with a different employer" (Moffitt 2015). But claims like these suffer from the same error as concluding that the pay of barbers is unaffected by technological changes outside

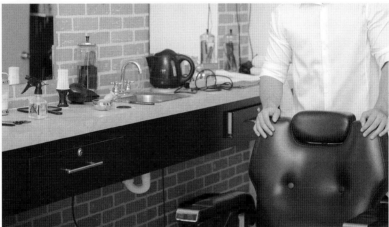

FIGURE 7.2. Antique and modern barbershops.
Sources: Figure 7.2a is credited to Richardson (Texas) Historical and Genealogical Society (circa 1920). Figure 7.2b is licensed from Antonio Diaz/Shutterstock and was cropped and converted to black and white.

their profession. As workers leave penalized employers and compete for jobs at employers that offer coverage, their departures drive down wages at ESI employers and mitigate some of the penalty's effect on wages at non-ESI employers.

Figure 7.3a illustrates. The overall height of the bars indicates compensation per employee in each of two sectors (no-ESI and ESI) without the ACA, adjusted for any sectoral differences in nonpecuniary job attributes.[3] The two heights are equal to indicate the competition between the two sectors for employees, so that employees cannot get a better deal by leaving their sector. Now the ACA penalty comes along and takes part of the pay of the no-ESI (i.e., penalized) sector, as indicated by the red "penalty" part of the no-ESI bar.[4] Employees leave the penalized sector to take advantage of the higher ESI-sector pay. The more employees who seek work in the ESI sector, the less ESI employers are willing to pay for them.[5] At the same time, the more employees who leave the penalized sector, the more penalized employers are willing to pay the employees who remain. Just as barbers were partially compensated for the technological progress that occurred outside their occupation, non-ESI employees will be partially compensated for the penalty-free opportunities existing outside their sector.

The labor market equilibrium in the presence of the penalty also equalizes compensation between sectors, as shown in figure 7.3b. The figure includes a dashed outline of the ESI bar to indicate its height without the penalty (see figure 7.3a) and thereby the amount by which the penalty depresses pay among ESI employees. This amount can be interpreted as a hidden tax on ESI employees: the employer penalty reduces their pay even though their employers do not pay it! In effect, penalized employees escape part of their penalty by passing it on to ESI employees. Ultimately employees in both sectors pay the same amount, which is the degree to which the two gray bars in figure 7.3b are less tall than the bars in figure 7.3a. Here is how the father of economics, Adam Smith, would put it:

> The whole of the advantages and disadvantages of the different employments of labour and stock must, in the same neighbourhood, be either perfectly equal or continually tending to equality. If in the same neighbourhood, there was any employment evidently either more or less advantageous than the rest, so many people would crowd into it in the one case, and so many would desert it in the other [think "employer penalty"], that its advantages would soon return to the level of other employments. (Smith 1776/1904, chapter I.10.1)

The gross wage gap for ESI employees shown in figure 7.3b as the red box is known as a "compensating" or "equalizing" difference because it equalizes wages net of the other advantages of ESI employ-

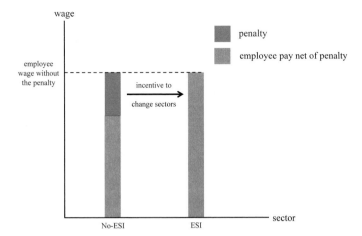

FIGURE 7.3A. Sector-specific penalties create compensating differences. Without a wage reduction in the ESI sector, the penalty encourages employees to change sectors in the direction of the arrow.

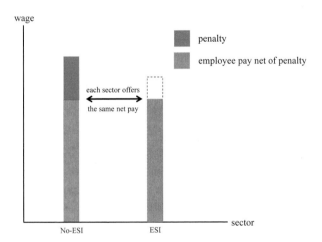

FIGURE 7.3B. Sector-specific penalties create compensating differences. The penalty must depress ESI-sector wages as shown in the figure in order for the no-ESI sector to retain employees. The arrow indicates that employees are willing to move in either direction.

ment (in this case, the advantage is tax avoidance), exactly as Adam Smith observed.[6]

The workers in figure 7.3 just move from one sector to another and do not leave work entirely. If some of them did leave work entirely, then wages might rise in both sectors as workers became somewhat more scarce. For this reason, the sectoral shifts shown in figures 7.3a and 7.3b describe the effect of a sector-specific penalty on overall labor demand—even the demand for workers who work in untaxed sectors—and not necessarily the effect on overall wages. The overall wage impact and the labor demand impact would coincide if the total supply of labor were held fixed.

Figure 7.3 is a more elaborate model of the penalty's effects on wages than the model shown in chapter 6. Both models are consistent with the long-term hypothesis that the employer penalty comes out of worker pay rather than employer profits, but chapter 6 had the penalty subtracted from worker pay even without any explicit adjustments by labor or capital. Figure 7.3 shows how the employer penalty causes penalized sectors to contract and other sectors to expand, which in the short run may reduce profits in the penalized sectors and increase profits in the others. Figure 7.3 also shows how some of the wage reductions from the penalty will be experienced by ESI workers, which also suggests that some of the effects of the penalty on aggregate work hours featured in chapter 6 will be experienced by ESI workers rather than non-ESI workers.

B. The Magnitude of the Wage Effects of the Employer Penalty

The effect of the employer penalty on employee pay increases with the size of the penalty itself, but it also depends on the size of the no-ESI sector. The larger the no-ESI sector, the more that ESI wages will have to fall to absorb workers leaving the sector and thereby the more the employer penalty is a hidden tax on ESI employees. A helpful estimate of the amount that the penalty depresses overall wages is the product of the penalty and the no-ESI share of the labor market. Table 7.1 shows my estimates by worker's family income. On average, workers from families with income no greater than triple the poverty line spend 22 percent of the year working full time (by the ACA definition) for an employer that does not offer coverage to any employees. In other words, the size of the no-ESI sector is about 22 percent of all employment by such workers; $683 per year is 22 percent of the full penalty and therefore an estimate of the average effect of the penalty on annual wages of workers from such families. Before the ACA, their av-

TABLE 7.1. The 2016 employer penalty and economy-wide labor demand: first-order estimates

Amounts are in 2014 dollars. Penalty impact on earnings holds aggregate labor supply fixed.

	Type of worker		
	Family income <= 3*FPL	Family income > 3*FPL	All
Penalty amount, annual salary equivalent	$3,163	$3,163	$3,163
Share of the year that an average worker is both with a non-ESI employer and working at least 30 hours	0.22	0.16	0.18
Average annual earnings per worker			
Without ACA or penalty	$21,254	$63,461	$47,160
With penalty (but not the rest of the ACA)	$20,571	$62,951	$46,583
Penalty impact, dollars per year	−$683	−$510	−$577
Penalty impact, log points	**−0.033**	**−0.008**	**−0.012**

Notes: FPL refers to the federal poverty line. Earnings do not include fringe benefits and include zeros for weeks not employed and are estimated from the March 2012 CPS. The magnitude of the penalty impact estimate is the product of the first two rows of the table.

erage annual wages were $21,254. Subtracting the $683 is therefore a rough estimate of what their average annual wages will be with a penalty, holding labor supply fixed. For all workers, the penalty impact averages $577 per year.

Measured in log points, the penalty's impact on log wages is about −0.033 (to a close approximation, log points are percentages divided by 100; this is an impact of about 3.3 percent) for workers from low-income families and −0.008 (a reduction of about 0.8 percent) for workers from high-income families, holding fixed the total amount of labor supplied by each type of family. These are just rough estimates because they include only the first-order determinants of impact rather than being derived from an explicit quantitative equilibrium model of competition for workers between sectors. Among other things, the first-order approach treats the earnings changes as a zero-sum game and thereby misses the effects of taxes on average productivity (more on this below). However, the productivity effects of the employer penalty may be small, because Mulligan and Gallen (2013) estimate log earnings impacts (with labor supply fixed) with a full quantitative equilibrium model and find −0.026 and −0.010 for workers from low- and high-income families, respectively.[7]

C. The Wage Effects of the Exchange Subsidies

The exchange subsidies are also sector-specific: full-time workers in the ESI sector cannot get them. However, the theory of equalizing differences says that exchange subsidies may increase the wages of such workers, precisely because they do not receive exchange subsidies. In a way, the exchange subsidies by themselves turn figure 7.3's arrow in the other direction as employers that offer coverage find it harder to compete for employees than it would be without the ACA because the ACA gives workers nonemployer coverage options. ESI employers will have to increase compensation to retain workers, and non-ESI workers will be able to reduce it, so ESI workers who get higher wages but no subsidy are no longer attracted to non-ESI employment that may involve subsidies but lower wages.

The depressing effect of sector-specific subsidies on wages and productivity in those sectors has already been seen with the unemployment insurance (UI) program. As explained by Ferris and Plourde (1982), "UI is not uniform in its effective incidence across industries [and] will itself reallocate labour and other resources among industries." They find that Newfoundland's inshore fishing industry was a seasonal activity particularly favored by the UI program for a period of time, and during that time had more fisherman and (the authors suspect) less productive fisherman. Another seasonal occupation is lifeguarding on the New Jersey shore where, until recently, qualifying lifeguards were permitted to collect unemployment benefits during the offseason. Bill Hefney, who was the mayor of North Wildwood, New Jersey (one of the beach towns on the Atlantic shore), explained how the UI program supplemented seasonal workers' incomes and thereby enabled the town to have more seasonal workers at a lesser hourly rate: "If we couldn't get these people to help we wouldn't be able to give the quality of life services we give. They might not be able to take a seasonal job at $10 per hour" (Nurin 2012). Georgia State Representative Mark Hamilton explained how school bus companies "pay a little bit less but supplement that by helping you [bus drivers] get your unemployment" (King 2014). The lesson here is that we should expect ACA subsidies by themselves to reallocate labor toward activities

TABLE 7.2. The 2016 exchange subsidies and economy-wide labor demand: first-order estimates

Amounts are in 2014 dollars. Earning impacts hold fixed aggregate labor supply and total factor productivity.

	Type of worker		
	Family income <= 3*FPL	Family income > 3*FPL	All
Subsidy value, annual salary equivalent	$8,620	$2,244	$6,679
Share of the year that an average worker is receiving exchange subsidies	0.16	0.04	0.09
Average annual earnings per worker plus value of subsidy received			
Without ACA or subsidy	$21,254	$63,461	$47,160
With subsidy (but not the rest of the ACA)	$22,665	$63,557	$47,749
Subsidy impact, dollars per year	$1,411	$96	$589
Subsidy impact, log points	**0.064**	**0.002**	**0.012**
Addendum:			
Subsidy & penalty impact on earnings + subs., $/yr	$728	−$413	$13
Subsidy & penalty impact, log points	**0.034**	**−0.007**	**0.000**
Share of workers in category	0.37	0.63	1.00

Notes: FPL refers to the federal poverty line. Earnings do not include fringe benefits and include zeros for weeks not employed and are estimated from the March 2012 CPS. The penalty impact is from table 7.1. Subsidy values are from table 4.5 and reflect 25 percent exchange-features discount. The subsidy impact estimate is the product of the first two rows of the table.

where workers can receive subsidies and thereby depress wages and productivity in those activities.

The size of the effect of the subsidies on the sum of wages and subsidies, and therefore the size of the effect on wages at ESI employers, depends on the amount of the subsidy and fraction of the workforce that receives it. If subsidy eligibility were restricted to a small group, then most ESI employees would not be attracted to non-ESI employment because the latter employment would typically not be sufficient to get them a subsidy. Moreover, a relatively small wage increase by ESI employers would, in the narrow-eligibility case, attract a large number of employees from employers that do not offer coverage because many of them are not receiving subsidies anyway. The first two rows of table 7.2 therefore report estimates of the average value of the subsidy to an eligible worker (on the basis of table 4.5) and the fraction of work being done by employees who are receiving exchange subsidies. The overall fraction of 0.09 is from table 5.2 and represents about 13 million workers who are expected to be receiving exchange subsidies in 2016. I disaggregated the 13 million by low- and high-income families using the percentages shown in table 4.5 and expressed the result as a fraction of all workers in low- or high-income families.

Each income group's product of the fraction and the subsidy amount is a rough estimate of the economy-wide impact of the subsidies on its earnings plus subsidies, holding the penalty constant. The low-income group's earnings plus subsidies are increased about $1,400 per year, which means their earnings at ESI employers increase by that amount. The high-income group's earnings plus subsidies are affected much less because fewer of them are eligible for subsidies (e.g., zero families above four times the poverty line are eligible) and the subsidies among the eligible are less. The overall average impact of the subsidies is, by table 7.2's rough estimates, to add $589 to annual earnings plus subsidies.

The bottom part of table 7.2 combines the penalty and subsidy impacts from tables 7.1 and 7.2. The penalty and subsidy together increase the low-income group's earnings plus subsidies by $728 per year. In log points, the combined impact for the low-income group is 0.034 (about 3.4 percent) on earnings plus subsidies. Among other things, this means ESI employers will tend to pay low-skill workers more as a consequence of the ACA, despite those employers' not paying a penalty. The combined impact for the high-income group is in the opposite direction: −0.007, which is −0.7 percent.

Although not shown explicitly in table 7.2, the ACA's impact on the wages of workers who receive subsidies is, regardless of family income, sharply negative because of the employer penalty and because workers will compete for positions that are consistent with subsidy eligibility. This is another way of seeing chapter 6's conclusions that the exchange subsidies reduce the reward to working: a nonworker who wants to keep the subsidy has to get into a job that is low paying precisely because it is subsidy eligible. The ACA reduces the reward to work even in cases where it increases wages because the subsidies are more available and more generous when not working.

Table 7.2's estimates are also just rough ones because they include only the first-order determinants of impact rather than being derived from an explicit quantitative equilibrium model of competition for workers between sectors. One problem with the first-order approach is that it treats the sectoral productivity changes as a zero-sum game and thereby misses the effects of taxes on average productivity. As shown in chapter 8, the combination of subsidies and penalties shifts low- and high-skill labor in opposite directions and thereby reduces aggregate productivity. As a result, Mulligan and Gallen (2013) estimate combined earnings impacts (with labor supply fixed) with such a model and find 0.04 and −0.02 for workers from low- and high-income families, respectively.[8]

D. The Coverage Effects of the Individual Mandate and the Exchange Subsidies

Before the ACA, employers were the primary source of insurance for nonelderly workers and their families. Table 7.3 lists the sources of worker coverage in 2012 and shows that it was far more common for a worker to be uninsured than to buy coverage in the individual market. Absent its subsidies and penalties, the ACA probably would further exaggerate this pattern because it requires health insurance plans to offer more benefits and thereby be more costly. However, the ACA's exchange subsidies and individual mandate penalty work together to significantly expand insurance coverage because in many cases the ACA makes being uninsured more expensive than being insured. The penalty amount is the maximum of $695 per uninsured household member (uninsured children count half, and the total of uninsured is capped at three), indexed to inflation, and 2.5 percent of household income.[9] Any family facing a penalty that exceeds the premium they would pay (net of subsidies) for a bronze plan is effectively able to enroll in a bronze plan for free, because the act of purchasing the plan prevents them from paying a penalty.[10] Only defiance, excessive enrollment effort, or lack of knowledge would prevent people in this situation from signing up for an insurance plan.[11]

Table 7.4 tabulates the population of the 2012 nonpoor nonelderly uninsured according to their family's bronze plan premium (net of subsidies) minus the amount of their individual mandate penalty.[12] This difference is expressed as a percentage of the unsubsidized bronze

TABLE 7.3. Health insurance coverage among the employed

Nonelderly household heads and spouses who were employed in March 2012

	All family incomes		2011 family income in 1–4 FPL	
	Millions	Percentage	Millions	Percentage
Uninsured	13.69	17%	8.95	22%
Employer	59.31	72%	26.33	66%
Individual market	4.71	6%	2.18	5%
Medicaid	4.22	5%	2.33	6%
Covered through family member	17.74		6.63	
National total employed	99.67		46.41	
Total, excluding coverage through family	81.93	100%	39.78	100%

Note: National totals are projected from the March 2012 Current Population Survey using the health insurance weight. Percentages exclude "covered through family member" from their denominators. FPL is the federal poverty line.

TABLE 7.4. The effective price of health insurance

as experienced by the nonpoor who would, in 2016, be uninsured without the ACA

Effective price of a bronze plan for the entire family	Percentage of but-for uninsured	Become insured, as a percentage of but-for uninsured	
		Low estimate	High estimate
Free or better	31%	31%	31%
1%–25% of full price	12%	5%	11%
26%–50% of full price	6%	1%	4%
51%–75% of full price	6%	1%	2%
76%–100% of full price	5%	0%	1%
Not applicable (poor or elderly)	41%	0%	0%
Total	100%	38%	47%

Note: "But-for uninsured" refers to those who would be uninsured without the ACA. "Become insured" does not include the but-for uninsured who get coverage from an employer, a parent's plan, or a public program. The estimates may (improperly) include undocumented immigrants. No adjustment has been made for the uninsured who can get afford-able coverage through an employer or Medicaid.

premium. For example, a percentage equal to 50 means that signing up for a bronze plan has a net cost—subsidized premium minus individual mandate penalty avoided—that is half of the full premium. Assuming that the percentages will be the same among the population in 2016 who would be uninsured but for the ACA, we see that, in table 7.4, 31 percent of those who would be uninsured without the ACA have a negative percentage, and therefore their family would spend less on a bronze plan than on penalties for being uninsured. In fact, about half of the uninsured who are not poor or elderly will find that a bronze plan for the family is cheaper than paying the penalty for being uninsured. This finding alone suggests that the ACA will sharply reduce the number of people without health insurance.

The right half of table 7.4 displays estimates of the effects of the ACA on insurance coverage among the uninsured who will not find bronze plans to be free. Most of them still face a very low effective price, but the degree to which their coverage decisions respond to the exchange subsidies and individual mandate depends on the sensitivity of their insurance demand to the price of insurance.[13] I use a range of econometric estimates from the literature.[14]

Table 7.4 assumes that bronze plan participants who would have been uninsured pay a premium (before subsidies) that is in proportion to silver plan premiums. However, insurers may figure out a way to create a bronze plan that healthy people want to join (to avoid the individual penalty) but do not intend to use. Because plan participants would rarely use it, this particular bronze plan could be especially cheap and thus be attractive to more of the healthy uninsured than table 7.4 suggests. This possibility highlights the fact that some of the people who will be officially classified as insured under the ACA will be *de facto* uninsured because their plan participation is just a formality to comply with the individual mandate, and they do not intend to seek health-care services under the plan.

Some of the nonpoor who were uninsured in 2012 were eligible for Medicaid but had not enrolled in the program. Others were not eligible for Medicaid but would be under 2014 rules because their state raised the income threshold. Neither type of persons would be eligible for exchange subsidies but could comply with the individual mandate by enrolling in Medicaid without paying anything. This is one reason table 7.4 underestimates the fraction of persons who would have been uninsured but will have free or heavily discounted coverage available as a consequence of the ACA.

E. The Employer Mandate, Sources of Coverage, and the Break-Even Myth

Table 7.4 shows how the ACA frequently makes a bronze plan more attractive than being uninsured, but it does not rule out the possibility that, as a consequence of the ACA, another exchange plan or an employer plan is even more attractive than the bronze plan. Employer plans offer the potential to avoid payroll taxes, income taxes, and employer penalties, but not any of the new subsidies created by the ACA. Exchange plans offer subsidies and different plan features, and they may relieve employers of some of the burdens of administering health insurance. I have quantified some of the net advantages of employer plans by calculating an ESI advantage factor for each full-time working household head in the March 2012 CPS according to ratio (7.1):

$$(7.1) \qquad \frac{0.83 m_i t + (1-t)\, pZ - s_i}{0.7 m_i}$$

where, as in the earlier chapters of this book, $0.7 m_i$ and $0.83 m_i$ refer to the dollar amounts of family i's premiums for a silver plan and an employer plan, respectively. pZ is the salary equivalent of the employer penalty, and s_i denotes the subsidies that family i would receive if it participated in the exchange plan and could not get coverage through an employer.[15] The first term in the ratio's numerator is the tax savings from the exclusion of employer plan premiums from income and payroll taxes, which are levied at a combined marginal rate t. Avoiding the employer penalty increases taxable income by pZ and thereby increases after-tax income by $(1 - t)pZ$. The numerator of the ratio is therefore the net advantage of ESI over exchange coverage, before any adjustment for the perceived value of exchange plan features or for ESI administrative costs.[16] The ratio itself expresses the net advantage as a share of the silver plan premium.

At first glance, it would appear that an employer's decision to offer health insurance to her full-time employees (hereafter, "coverage decision") is simply a break-even test: determining whether the average of the numerator among her employees is positive or negative. According to the employer's break-even test, if the average were positive, then the employer would break even or do better by offering coverage to her employees. At the same time, the test gives an illusion of conflict in the workplace between positive-ratio employees who want coverage and the tax advantages that go with it and negative-ratio employees who prefer that coverage not be offered so they can be eligible for large subsidies. Although ratio (7.1) is useful for understanding the incentives of various groups to have one kind of coverage or another, the employer's break-even test by itself cannot predict which or how many employers offer coverage to their employees. First of all, the numerator of (7.1) is positive without the ACA—pZ and s are there only because of the law—yet a large number of employers did not offer coverage. This fact alone shows us that the ratio omits other costs and benefits of ESI. In addition, empirical studies from before the ACA have shown that t increases the propensity of employers to offer coverage, which shows that the first term in the ratio's numerator is among the important benefits of ESI, but not the only one.

A second problem with the simple employer break-even test is that it needs to be conducted in a market context so as to account for Adam Smith's equalizing differences. Although the ratio includes the employer penalty, it fails to include the market "penalty" or equalizing difference that will emerge in the labor market as a consequence of the ACA's changes in the incentives for individual employees to have coverage through their employer. As a result of the equalizing difference, a profit-maximizing coverage decision will, in effect, consider the distribution of coverage preferences among workers outside the firm and the distribution of coverage decisions among competing employers. For example, even if her break-even test (properly augmented for the other costs and benefits noted in the previous paragraph) fails, an employer may want to consider offering coverage if few of her competitors are offering coverage, because the offer would give her an advantage in attracting and retaining employees who prefer ESI. Even if employers do not change their coverage offerings, employees and customers will move between ESI and non-ESI employers as a result of the taxes created by the ACA. The equalizing differences also explain why negative- and positive-ratio coworkers will not be in conflict: an ESI employer will have to compensate its negative-ratio employees for blocking their subsidy eligibility or else those employees will leave for an employer that does not offer coverage. Unfortunately, many of the simulation studies of the ACA and health insurance coverage have failed to consider Smith's equalizing differences or otherwise put the employer-employee relationship in a market context.[17]

To put it another way, even if the numerator of ratio (7.1) fully captured the net advantage of ESI coverage over exchange coverage, it would not necessarily be the loss suffered by an ESI worker when his employer drops coverage because the worker can move to another employer that continues to offer ESI. Moreover, changing employers may not even be necessary to avoid the loss because the employer dropping coverage may choose to compensate employees that lose from her coverage decision in order to retain them as employees. As shown below, the magnitude of these effects, and therefore the degree to which the numerator of (7.1) exaggerates the loss from a single employer's decision to drop coverage depends on the propensity of other employers to continue to offer coverage. In an economy dominated by ESI employers, a single employer's decision to drop coverage would create large benefits for his low-income employees who do not want to be offered coverage without creating large costs for his high-income employees because the latter employees have many alternative sources of ESI and the tax benefits that go with it. This is what I mean by putting the employer-employee relationship in a market context.

Authors of the aforementioned simulation studies might claim that theirs is a labor market analysis because the studies include an "elasticity" or regression coefficient estimated from data that reflect historical market adjustments. Such a claim misses the point of market analysis, which is that market outcomes depend on supply and demand. Supply and demand are not shifted in the same way by the ACA as they were in the past. Before the ACA, employees losing coverage when their employer stopped offering could not sign up for an exchange plan that was good enough for their congressman and his family. Another difference is that the ACA puts a number of employees in the position of being harmed by their employer's offer of coverage, and a market analysis does not simply add the harms of some employees to the gains of their coworkers. And the so-called elasticities do not even begin to capture the coverage changes that happen as firms expand, contract, and change the composition of their workforce. All of these omissions go in the direction of underestimating the coverage-composition effects of the employer penalty.

The most accurate way to project the effects of the ACA on forms of coverage is with a labor market equilibrium model of equalizing differences that is consistent with the historical data, of which Gallen and Mulligan (2013) is an example. As a shortcut to a detailed equalizing-difference calculation, this chapter examines two distributions of the

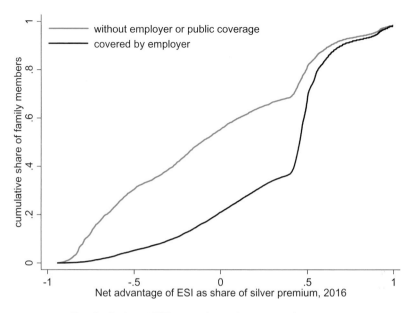

FIGURE 7.4. The distribution of ESI's money's worth among workers.

ESI advantage ratio among workers (not employers) with the reminder that zero is not necessarily the critical value for a worker's ratio that determines the type of coverage the worker gets. For a marginal income tax rate of $t = 0.25$, figure 7.4 shows the results separately for workers without employer coverage or public coverage and for workers who are covered by their employer.[18] Thirty-one percent of those without employer or public coverage, and 63 percent of those with employer coverage, have an advantage ratio above 0.4. Because the advantage ratio is always less than 0.3 without the ACA, this suggests that the ACA gives a significant share of the uninsured a substantial incentive to get employer coverage rather than exchange coverage and gives a majority of those with ESI a substantial incentive to keep it.

A relatively small fraction (about one-fifth) of families with ESI have negative advantage ratios, but they are as numerous as they are because ESI is the most common form of coverage. A majority of those without employer or public coverage have a negative ESI-advantage ratio. This suggests that a majority of the nonpoor who become insured because of the ACA will do so by enrolling in an exchange plan, rather than an employer plan.

The top half of table 7.5 uses the shares from figure 7.4 to make rough estimates of the effects of the ACA on coverage for the nonpoor and nonelderly. Using the March 2012 CPS projected to 2016 on the basis of population growth, I estimate that 192 million nonelderly persons will live in nonpoor households headed by a person who would be working full time were it not for the effects of the ACA. Of them, 150 million would be covered by ESI were it not for the ACA, 16 million would be covered on the individual market, and 27 million would be uninsured. Table 7.5 shows a −19 million impact on the number of uninsured because table 7.4 suggests that almost three-quarters of the nonpoor nonelderly uninsured will become insured because of the ACA. Of the estimated 19 million gaining coverage, 31 percent are assumed to take ESI coverage because of their high ESI-advantage ratios noted above.[19] Those who would have been on the individual market without the ACA are assumed to be on the individual market with the ACA unless their ESI-advantage ratio is above 0.4. Those who would have ESI without the ACA are assumed to keep it unless their ESI-advantage ratio is negative.[20] As a result, ESI loses 31 million participants it would have had (see the table's third column) but gains 11 million from among the uninsured and those who would have been insured on the individual market, for a net impact of −21 million.

Table 7.5 estimates are rough because they are not based on an explicit equilibrium model and because there is no single critical value for the ESI-advantage ratio that indicates a family's coverage status under the ACA. The final column shows the impact estimates from Gallen and Mulligan (2013) for the nonpoor nonelderly population; this is based on the study's multisector multiskill general equilibrium model of the labor market and employer benefit offerings. The Gallen-Mulligan estimates are fairly similar to those estimated in table 7.5.[21]

The top half of table 7.5 may also exaggerate the amount of ESI coverage under the ACA because it does not consider the ACA's impact on ESI coverage through its reduction in the number of persons working full time (see chapter 6) and through the coverage decisions on the part of small employers that are not liable for an employer penalty.[22] The bottom half of table 7.5 repeats the calculations from the top half but uses shares from a version of figure 7.4 that sets the employer penalty to zero. Without an employer penalty, none of the workers without

TABLE 7.5. 2016 Insurance coverage: first-order estimates among nonelderly persons in nonpoor households with heads working full time.

Table entries are millions of persons.

ACA includes employer penalty

	w/o ACA			Row totals are totals w/ ACA	ACA impact[a]	
	Uninsured	Individual market	ESI		This table	Gallen-Mulligan GE model
w/ ACA Uninsured	8	0	0	8	−19	−15
Individual market[b]	13	11	31	55	40	40
ESI	6	5	119	129	−21	−25
Column totals are totals w/o ACA	27	16	150	192		

ACA has no employer penalty

	w/o ACA			Row totals are totals w/ ACA	ACA impact[a] (w/o emp. penalty)
	Uninsured	Individual market	ESI		This table
w/ ACA, but no emp. penalty Uninsured	8	0	0	8	−19
Individual market[b]	19	16	49	84	68
ESI	0	0	101	101	−49
Column totals are totals w/o ACA	27	16	150	192	

[a]The impact on the number uninsured is an average of the low and high estimates in table 7.4.

[b]Individual market totals with the ACA include participation in exchange plans as well as any nonpoor persons enrolled in Medicaid as a consequence of the law.

employer or public coverage have an ESI-advantage ratio greater than 0.3, so I assume that none of those workers take ESI as a consequence of the ACA. More ESI workers have a negative ESI-advantage ratio, which is why the bottom half of table 7.5 has 49 million persons leaving ESI for the individual market.

As noted above, the individual mandate and the exchange subsidies are the primary ACA provisions that reduce the number of nonpoor people uninsured. The employer penalty primarily raises revenue both as a revenue provision and by limiting the number of people who leave ESI for larger subsidies awaiting them in the exchanges. A comparison of the top and bottom halves of table 7.5 is generally indicative of the coverage effects of the employer penalty, but it may overstate the penalty's propensity to maintain ESI coverage because of some of the aforementioned ways in which the labor market adjusts to avoid the penalty even when it is fully implemented.

A recent study by Blumberg, Holahan, and Buettgens (2014) that is based on the Urban Institute's Health Insurance Policy Simulation Model (HIPSM) claims the employer penalty by itself has essentially no effect on ESI coverage. Most of the discrepancy between their results and mine is that the HIPSM does not put the ACA and employer-employee relationships in a market context and thereby fails to consider Smith's equalizing differences. According to HIPSM, the employer penalty cannot cause an employee to seek ESI employment rather than non-ESI employment (without an identical employee making the exact opposite adjustment) or cause a large employer offering coverage to expand at the expense of a large employer not offering coverage. According to HIPSM, the employer penalty does not reduce the wage premium ESI employers have to pay in order to attract and retain low-skill employees who would get more subsidies by working for an employer that does not offer coverage. All the employers in the HIPSM model make an offer decision on the basis of the average preferences of their employees, who are the same number and types of people with and without the employer penalty. Contrary to the theory of equalizing differences, decisions about HIPSM-model employer coverage do not depend, even indirectly, on the preferences of people working for competing employers or on the types of coverage offered by competing employers (Urban Institute 2011). The HIPSM model offers some interesting insights because it contains, among other things, the kind of data shown in figure 7.4, but it is unreliable for policy analysis unless augmented with labor market equilibrium reasoning.

F. Conclusions

The Affordable Care Act is likely to achieve the goal of significantly expanding the fraction of the population with health insurance, and it may do so to a surprisingly large extent. The individual mandate and the exchange subsidies both make individual market health insurance cheaper—and many times, effectively free—for millions of the non-poor who would otherwise be uninsured. That's a powerful incentive for citizens to join the officially insured population.

However, we do not yet know how many of the transitions from uninsured to insured will be economically meaningful. Without the ACA, many of the poor and officially uninsured would be insured in practice in the sense that they could enroll in Medicaid when they wanted care, but the ACA encourages and probably streamlines the enrollment process from the point of view of persons who are eligible and healthy. In this way, some of the increase in health insurance by the official measures will just reflect a relabeling of the same kinds of activity that would occur without the law.

This chapter adds to the ongoing list of side effects of increasing insurance coverage with a law like the ACA. Before the ACA, non-ESI employers (that is, employers not offering coverage to their full-time employees) were at a competitive disadvantage and had to either pay extra for employees—an example of the "compensating difference" that Adam Smith wrote about—or be content with workers who didn't want employer health insurance. The ACA reduces or even reverses the competitive disadvantage experienced by non-ESI employers in the market for low-skill workers. One of the impacts of the ACA is therefore to move a significant number of low-skill workers and their families off employer-sponsored coverage onto the ACA's exchange plans. The ACA may reduce ESI participation by 20 million or more, even accounting for the employer mandate, which will encourage employers to offer coverage, and the individual mandate, which will encourage employees to participate in their employer's plan.

By itself, the employer mandate will depress wages (about 3 percent in the low-skill market), even among workers whose employer is not penalized. The employer penalty by itself does little to reduce the number insured, but it does affect the composition of coverage by imposing a cost on workers who try to switch from ESI coverage to subsidized exchange coverage. By affecting the composition of coverage, the employer penalty mitigates the amount that the ACA spends on subsidized exchange coverage in addition to bringing in some revenue. In other words, the employer penalty both obtains government revenue and reduces government spending.

It is worth comparing the 19 million nonpoor people (including dependents) who become insured because of the ACA with the number of nonpoor workers (plus their dependents) who have their work life significantly disrupted by the ACA. This chapter estimates that 36 million people who would be insured anyway (either on the individual market or through an employer) will change the source of their insurance to or from their employer, either as a consequence of ACA-induced changes by their employer's benefit offerings or as a consequence of ACA-induced job changes. In a given week, 4 or 5 million people will not be working as a consequence of the ACA, and they have another 5 million or so dependents. Another 5 million workers plus roughly 5 million dependents will work part-time schedules as a consequence of the ACA. So that's roughly 55 million people experiencing significant labor market disruption in a given week, not to mention those experiencing lesser changes in their wages or work schedules.

This chapter discusses effects of the ACA on relative wages while holding average productivity constant. The purpose of the next chapter is to examine a number of the effects of the ACA on labor productivity and thereby arrive at a more complete estimate of the ACA's wage effects.

Appendix 7.1: The Arithmetic of Equalizing Differences in the Zero-Sum Model

Let the economy consist of two sectors: a taxed "sector 1" and an untaxed "sector 0." The sectors pay wages w_1 and w_0, respectively. The equalizing differences model (figures 7.3a and 7.3b) says that the tax increases the sector 1 wage and reduces the sector 0 wage so that workers are still willing to work in both sectors despite the tax owed by workers in sector 1:

(7.2) $$\Delta w_1 - T = \Delta w_0$$

where Δw_1 and Δw_0 denote the impacts of the tax T on wages.

The zero-sum assumption says that the aggregate wage increase in sector 1 equals the aggregate wage reduction in sector 0:

(7.3) $$\alpha \Delta w_1 + (1-\alpha) \Delta w_0 = 0$$

where α is the share of workers in sector 1 without the tax. Solving the simultaneous linear system (7.2) and (7.3) yields the equilibrium impact of the tax on the reward to working in either sector:

(7.4) $$\Delta w_0 = \Delta w_1 - T = -\alpha T$$

which is exactly the calculation in tables 7.1 and 7.2.

In theory, the zero-sum assumption is a good approximation for small taxes. Otherwise, the wage losses in sector 0 exceed the wage increases in sector 1 because the tax harms productivity.[23] To put it another way, the impact of a sector-specific tax can be interpreted as the effect shown in (7.4) minus the loss in productivity examined in chapter 8.

8 | The ACA's Productivity Distortions

The Affordable Care Act has several effects on productivity (which refers to the value created in the economy per hour worked) and several effects on average wages. As noted in chapter 6, households and businesses sacrifice work time in order to avoid taxes and enhance subsidies that are tied to employment status. For the same reasons, they also sacrifice productivity in order to rearrange activities for less of a tax burden. These include excessive part-time work, segregation of low-skill and high-skill employees, constricting large employers in order to expand small ones, and failing to invest as much in business capital. Chapter 7 emphasizes how some of these rearrangements are related to gaps in wages among sectors, but they also affect the level of productivity and wages.

Section A begins with the cross-hauling of workers across employers distinguished by whether they offer health coverage to employees. Section B explains why the ACA has productivity effects in both directions, and it briefly shows results for sectors and occupations related to firm size and part-time work. Medicare tax hikes and their possible effects on capital accumulation and thereby productivity and wages are examined in section C. Section D notes quirks in the national income accounts related to the ACA. Section E concludes.

Throughout the chapter I refer to value added in the marketplace, which refers to the market value of the various types of production that occur in the economy net of interbusiness transactions (that is, when one business's production is part of the materials or services that another business uses to produce). Although the term *value added* is sometimes used synonymously with "production," the former depends not only on the physical quantities of items produced but also on the value of all of that production as measured by the price the final consumer pays. This distinction is important because one of the consequences of the ACA can be to increase the frequency of transactions with relatively little value at the expense of other transactions that would be more valuable.

I refer to the ratio of value added to hours worked as "productivity." Because chapter 6 examines the denominator of this ratio, its results together with productivity results are enough to tell us the ACA's impact on the numerator, especially when the numerator is aggregate value added or GDP. Either the numerator or the denominator, or both, can be subject to various adjustments such as measurement errors or (in the case of the numerator) the contribution of capital accumulation. In these cases, I refer to "adjusted productivity" and name the adjustments. I sometimes also follow the convention of referring to "total factor productivity" as a change in value added adjusted for the contributions of labor and capital to that change.[1]

A. Productivity Losses Associated with Labor Reallocation

1. CROSS-HAULING: AN EXAMPLE OF HOW TAXES CAN HARM PRODUCTIVITY

Cross-hauling is a term from the trucking industry. It refers to the presumed wasteful shipments of a single type of good in both directions on the same route at the same time. To use the trucking metaphor, it's understandable that policy makers might want to move workers on the road from uninsured to insured, and perhaps the individual and employer mandates are the fuel for their trips. But the exchange subsidies fuel trips in the opposite direction, because people already employed full time by firms offering coverage are automatically ineligible for the new assistance. As shown in chapter 7, some of those who were formerly uninsured will prefer employer coverage over exchange coverage, so they will be headed on the road in one direction. But there are millions of people who had employer coverage who are now heading in the opposite direction: looking to work for an employer that does not offer coverage because the exchange subsidies are more advantageous.[2]

From the productivity perspective, the situation is even worse than the cross-hauling metaphor suggests. First, the types of workers that the ACA causes to move toward ESI employers (high-skill) are different from the low-skill types it causes to move away from them.[3] As a result, the ACA's taxes are distorting the skill mix of each sector's workforce away from what maximizes productivity. Productivity would suffer less if the ACA encouraged employees to become insured in a skill-neutral way so that both types of employers could keep their optimal skill mix even if some of the employers grew and others contracted.[4] Second, although the trucking problem of cross-hauling is related to the "journey," the productivity losses from distorting employers' skill mix is ongoing and lasts far beyond any transition period as the ACA is implemented.

2. USING TAX SAVINGS TO ESTIMATE PRODUCTIVITY LOSSES

The ACA has enough taxes to affect labor market behavior in several dimensions. Moreover, changing behavior is not synonymous with reducing productivity, because some behavior changes do not affect productivity and others may increase it. The purpose of this section is, in the spirit of the cross-hauling example, to keep the total amount of labor constant and focus on how the ACA may reallocate labor among different sectors and activities. These reallocations have the potential of changing the value of production and thereby productivity in amounts that can be readily approximated from the results of previous chapters.

Figure 8.1 illustrates the methodology for the special case of reallocating low-skill labor between employers who would have offered coverage but for the ACA (hereafter, "ESI employers") and other types of employers. The downward-sloping curve is the demand for low-skill labor by ESI employers. For the purposes of drawing figure 8.1, I hold constant the allocation of high-skill labor among employers.[5] Movements down figure 8.1's demand curve therefore involve decreasing the skill mix of workers at ESI employers—more low-skill workers and the same number of high-skill workers—and increasing the skill mix of workers at non-ESI employers. The height of the demand curve at any one point is the contribution of an additional low-skill worker to total value added by ESI employers. It slopes down because the marginal productivity of low-skill workers for ESI employers declines with the number of low-skill workers they have.

Figure 8.1 also has an upward-sloping supply curve of low-skill labor to ESI employers. Recall that I am holding constant the total numbers of low- and high-skill workers in the economy in order to analyze

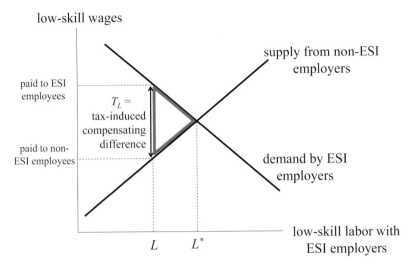

low-skill wages

supply from non-ESI
employers

paid to ESI
employees

$T_L =$
tax-induced
compensating
difference

paid to non-
ESI employees

demand by ESI
employers

L L^*

low-skill labor with
ESI employers

FIGURE 8.1. Sacrificing productivity to avoid new taxes, holding fixed the aggregate quantity of low-skill labor. The area outlined in red is the value added lost from allocating L rather than L^* to ESI employers.

productivity per hour worked. More low-skill workers for non-ESI employers is therefore represented by a movement down and to the left along the supply curve, because non-ESI employers obtain additional low-skill workers when ESI employers give them up. The height of the supply curve therefore reflects the value lost by non-ESI employers from an additional low-skill worker given up to ESI employers.

The difference between the height of the demand curve and the height of the supply curve is the value to be gained by moving a low-skill worker from the non-ESI sector to the ESI sector. L^* is therefore the aggregate value-maximizing allocation of low-skill labor to the ESI sector, because more low-skill labor than that would add less value to the ESI sector than it takes from the non-ESI sector and less low-skill labor would do the opposite. Deviations from L^*, such as the amount L shown in the figure, represent losses in aggregate productivity relative to what is feasible because less value is being produced than would be produced at L^*. The value lost is the area of the triangle outlined in red in the figure.

The ACA treats low-skill labor differently if it is with an ESI employer than with a non-ESI employer because only the former are automatically ineligible for exchange subsidies. In effect, low-skill labor faces a higher tax when it is working for an ESI employer than it does when working for a non-ESI employer. Market forces operate to maximize value produced net of taxes, which means that value produced will be sacrificed in order to reduce taxes (or enhance subsidies), if necessary. If T_L is the amount of excess tax imposed by the ACA on low-skill ESI labor as compared to low-skill non-ESI labor, then the market outcome under the ACA will be L. The loss in value produced will be $(L^* - L)T_L/2$ because the area of the triangle is the base times the height times one-half.

The $(L^* - L)$ workers shown in figure 8.1 as changing their behavior—switching sectors in this case—are all saving T_L in taxes by doing so. The loss in value is half of the tax savings because the behavioral changes that occur to achieve the savings have value losses ranging from zero to the full tax savings.[6] In some cases, essentially zero value is lost because the tax is new and there are a few workers who were already on the margin of making the change encouraged by the new tax. In other cases, the value loss is almost as much as the tax but occurs anyway because the tax savings is just enough to offset the loss from the decision maker's point of view.

The half-value loss result is for new taxes. If the new taxes are on top of old taxes (not shown in figure 8.1), then the behavioral changes associated with the new taxes will also be motivated by further avoiding old taxes. The total value lost as a consequence of adding new taxes to old taxes is, as above, half of the new taxes saved by changing behavior, plus all of the old taxes saved by the same behavioral change. For the purposes of this chapter, the primary "old tax" of interest is the exclusion of ESI premiums from income and payroll taxation (hereafter "ESI exclusion"), which may be reducing the productivity of labor regardless of the ACA by excessively encouraging the purchasing of health insurance through employers. To the extent that other incentives in the health reform move people from ESI to individual coverage, it may *increase* productivity above what it would be without the ACA.

3. SIX KINDS OF REALLOCATION: ESTIMATES

Table 8.1 shows six types of labor reallocation, listed vertically, and their possible effects on labor productivity. The columns of the table

TABLE 8.1. Productivity losses due to labor-composition distortions: first-order estimates

due to 2016 ACA tax parameters. Dollar amounts are 2014 dollars. Percentages are rounded to the nearest 0.1%.

Behavior distorted	Millions of persons	Tax savings from the behavioral change		Value created by the behavioral change
		Per person	% of labor income	% of labor income
Full-time work to part-time work	5	$3,600	0.2%	−0.1%
Longer full-time workweeks = less employment	1			−0.1%
ACA full-time employment tax		$3,600	0.1%	0.0%
Non-ACA unemployment insurance		$4,425	0.1%	−0.1%
ESI to individual market	31			0.0%
Exchange subsidies net of employer penalty		$2,841	1.2%	−0.6%
Non-ACA tax subsidy to ESI		−$1,416	−0.6%	0.6%
Individual market to ESI	5			−0.1%
Employer penalty net of exchange subsidies		$1,586	0.1%	−0.1%
Non-ACA tax subsidy to ESI		$1,374	0.1%	−0.1%
Uninsured to individual market	13	$3,276	0.6%	−0.3%
Uninsured to ESI	6			−0.3%
Individual penalty		$1,459	0.1%	−0.1%
Employer penalty		$1,586	0.1%	−0.1%
Non-ACA tax subsidy to ESI		$1,374	0.1%	−0.1%
Total = ACA's impact on value-added per hour worked				−0.9%
Total excluding coverage expansion				−0.6%

Notes: Number of persons moving to part-time work is the percentage from table 6.6 times total employment (142 million). The employment effect of longer weeks is explained in the main text. The other person counts are from table 7.5 and include dependents. Aggregate labor income in 2016 is assumed to be $10 trillion (2014 dollars) before taxes and 75% of that after taxes at the margin, only for the purpose of calculating the percentages. I assume that each $1 lost value added is associated with an average of $2 in savings on ACA taxes ("triangle"), but only $1 in savings on non-ACA taxes ("rectangle").

show millions of workers or persons reallocated, the taxes saved by each person reallocated, and the approximate value-added gain or loss from the reallocation. The first row shows the 5 million twenty-niners from chapter 6—that is, the number of workers with 29-hour work schedules who would have been full-time workers but for the ACA. These workers have reduced schedules because the 29-hour schedule gives them a subsidy or relieves their employer of a penalty, with an amount that averages $3,600 per twenty-niner per year after taxes.[7] Before taxes, that's about $24 billion per year in aggregate, or about

0.2 percent of what I project the nation's labor income will be in 2016 without any changes in the labor force.

"Only" 5 million workers become twenty-niners, while tens of millions more continue to work full time because the loss of value added from switching to part time would be too much to justify the tax savings. This is an indication that the 5 million also sacrificed some value added in the process of avoiding the full-time employment tax, but that the lost value was less than the amount of tax they avoided (otherwise they would not have avoided it). As noted above in terms of a triangle, the lost value is roughly half of the tax avoided. The final column of table 8.1's top row therefore divides the adjacent column by two to get an estimate of lost value of −0.1 percent of the nation's labor income. An important part of the lost productivity is the additional scheduling, coordination, management, and hiring costs associated with having more workers with shorter work schedules.

The −0.1 percent lost value shown in the top row of table 8.1 is based on estimates from chapter 6, but the loss is distinct from, and in addition to, the −3.1 percent impact on aggregate hours shown in the same chapter. The latter percentage is how much the ACA reduces aggregate work hours, whereas the former is the ACA's impact on the productivity of the work hours that remain under the ACA. Moreover, whereas some of the 3.1 percent "lost" aggregate work hours are still socially and privately valued as leisure or nonmarket time, the 0.1 percent lost value from table 8.1 is not creating any social value and is better described as a "loss" than the 3.1 percent. The −0.1 percent can also be interpreted as an impact on GDP per work hour of the ACA's shifting workers from full time to part time.[8]

The second part of table 8.1 shows the reduction in weekly employment among full-time workers that occurs because they work fewer weeks with slightly longer weekly schedules in order to reduce their forgone ACA subsidies and their employer's liability for penalties. Because their schedules are about 1 percent longer, the employment reduction I consider is only 1 percent of full-time employment, or about 1 million, in order to hold total work hours constant (this is the definition of productivity analysis). These 1 million persons save the same $3,600 annually in ACA taxes net of subsidies as shown in table 8.1's top row. In doing so, the lost value added is about half of the $3,600.

Some of the 1 million also receive unemployment benefits, which average $4,425 per year including zeros for persons not receiving the benefits. Because the unemployment benefit is a non-ACA tax on employment, avoidance of this tax reduces value dollar for dollar, as explained above in connection with figure 8.1.[9] The combination of the first two parts of table 8.1 is 0.2 percent less value created by workers.[10]

The third part of table 8.1 shows workers who leave ESI (taking their dependents with them—the 31 million includes dependents and is from table 7.5) for the individual market as a consequence of the ACA. In principle, these workers could be adding to productivity because the longstanding and implicit tax subsidy to ESI caused excessive usage of ESI. For example, too many workers (from a productivity perspective) may choose their employers for their health insurance and associated tax benefits. Too many workers may be "locked" into their ESI jobs, rather than leaving for another more productive job that does not include health coverage (Gruber and Madrian 2004). That's the −$1,416 amount shown in the second part of the table: $1,416 is the extra payroll and income taxes per insured family member that the employee will *pay* by giving up ESI.[11] In the aggregate, it is more than $44 billion per year, or about 0.6 percent of labor income in 2016.

If the ACA had only eliminated the tax exclusion of ESI premiums for the 31 million workers listed in the second part of the table, then productivity would increase 0.6 percent. But the 31 million workers and dependents are voluntarily leaving ESI to seek other tax advantages, namely, the exchange subsidies. Among these persons, the average exchange subsidies net of employer penalties (adjusted for payroll and personal income taxes) are $2,841. Relative to no ESI exclusion, this net subsidy of $2,841 reduces value added in an amount equal to about half of the $2,841 times the 31 million persons, or about 0.6 percent of total labor income. The combination of these two effects is approximately zero, which means that moving 31 million people from ESI to individual coverage reduces productivity (relative to a hypothetical economy with no ESI-related tax distortion) of about the same amount by which the ESI exclusion would be reducing productivity without the ACA. Thus, even though in theory it is possible that moving people from ESI to the individual market could enhance productivity by alleviating the tax distortion associated with the ESI exclusion, my estimates suggest that the same people are associated with too many new distortions for the net impact of their move to significantly enhance productivity.

Notice that my productivity impact estimates derive from the number of persons changing their behavior (table 8.1's first column) and the tax savings per person shown in the second column. Chapter 7 notes, and I repeat here, that the numbers of persons are just rough estimates, which makes my productivity estimates rough, not to mention that the "tax savings" approach to productivity estimation is itself an approximation. Future work can and should improve on both the quantitative estimates of behavioral change and their relationships with productivity, but table 8.1 shows orders of magnitude and reveals several of the economically important issues related to these productivity effects.

The fourth part of the table looks at changes in the other direction, another example of cross-hauling. Here the employer penalty is reinforcing the productivity losses from the longstanding ESI exclusion by pushing people from the individual market into ESI even though the tax exclusion by itself was not enough for them to justify employer coverage. The movement of these 5 million persons reduces productivity by about 0.1 percent.

The final two parts of the table record the 19 million nonpoor workers and their dependents whom I expect will gain coverage as a result of the ACA's subsidies and penalties. Chapter 7 suggests that 13 million of them will be insured on the individual market, thanks to the combination of avoiding the individual mandate and obtaining exchange subsidies. The combined average premium assistance received and mandate payment avoided is more than $3,000 per year per person insured.[12] Recall from chapter 7 that most of the 13 million are, in effect, getting the bronze plan for free, which means their cost of being insured absent the ACA's subsidies and penalties is somewhere between zero and the full price of the bronze plan. The last column of the table records the average of the two, which is 0.3 percent of labor income.

Another 6 million obtain ESI coverage in order to avoid the individual mandate penalty (averaging about $1,500 per year per uninsured) and to avoid the employer penalty (averaging about $1,586). They also save about $1,400 in income taxes per insured, which by itself must be less than the costs of being insured because without the ACA they were not participating in ESI and thereby were forgoing the tax savings. These costs may be costs of giving up their job with a non-ESI employer and finding a job with an ESI employer (likely an otherwise inferior job, which is why it takes penalties to put them in an ESI position), or costs for their employer to offer and administer a plan. The costs are somewhere in between the income tax savings and the sum of all three types of tax savings, which is why the last column of table 8.1 records 0.3 percent of labor income.[13]

Assuming for the moment that value is lost in the process of overcoming the barriers to being insured, the total productivity loss from the ACA provisions that reallocate labor in the economy is 0.9 percent, as shown at the bottom of table 8.1. Without counting the value losses associated with ACA-induced reductions in the aggregate quantities of labor and capital, the 0.9 percent value loss from labor reallocations is almost $100 billion per year, or about $5,000 annually per person who obtains health insurance as a consequence of the ACA (recall table 7.5). The $5,000 reallocation loss by itself makes the social cost of insuring the uninsured almost double what the private cost would be if the newly insured were paying full price for their health care.

Included in the 0.9 percent are the losses that occur as people give up things they value more in order to obtain insurance they value less, which is why the ACA uses penalties and subsidies to induce them to get it. But the purpose of the ACA is to expand coverage, so it is interesting to exclude any "costs" of moving people from being uninsured to being covered. Table 8.1's 0.6 percent productivity loss is such an estimate, obtained from excluding the fifth "Uninsured to individual market" panel and by excluding the individual penalty row of the table's last part. The employer penalty row in that panel is included, because it is changing the type of coverage and not creating coverage per se (recall chapter 7).

In principle, measures of national income and value added count every purchase in the marketplace according to what the consumer (or, in the case of an investment item, investor) paid. Consumer purchases that are expensive are presumed to be valuable because the consumer sacrificed a lot of money to get them. But there are exceptions, including Medicaid and other health assistance programs. When, say, a Medicaid participant visits a health provider, the goods and services provided are valued by the national accountants at what the Medicaid *program* pays, and not what the program participant pays or even what the program participant would pay if she had to pay with her own money. I presume that the same accounting practice will be followed for the ACA's exchange plans: health care obtained under the plan is presumed to be valuable regardless of whether the person receiving the care would have willingly paid her plan premiums. Thus, the official measures of output and value added may be essentially unchanged when she moves from uninsured to insured regardless of how much the plan participant actually values the coverage. This is another reason for focusing on the −0.6 percent as my best, but admittedly approximate, estimate of the measured productivity loss from the ACA provisions that reallocate labor in the economy.

Note that table 8.1 refers to value lost as a percentage of labor income, which is not the same as value lost as a percentage of *national* income because national income includes the income from capital. However, by making labor less productive, the ACA probably also makes capital less productive and thereby reduces the long-term amount of capital per worker. To a first approximation, labor reallocation has the same percentage effects on labor income per hour worked, capital income per hour worked, and therefore national income per hour worked (see appendix 8.1).[14] Negative 0.6 percent therefore represents both the long-term impact of ACA-induced labor reallocations on aggregate value added per hour worked and the share of labor income equivalent to the value added that is lost in the short run because of the same reallocations. In today's dollars, the long-term loss of value added is about $100 billion per year, which is solely as a consequence of the ACA's preventing labor from being allocated to its most efficient uses,[15] and it does not begin to count the value lost from the withdrawal of labor from the market economy.

B. The Quality and Measurement of Labor

Chapter 6 shows how the ACA reduces the quantity of labor 3 percent or more by reducing the average rewards to work. But the reward to work is most reduced among workers from relatively low-income families, that is, between the poverty line and roughly 300 percent of the poverty line. For example, table 7.2 shows that low-income families will be getting subsidies with dollar values that are almost triple what the nonpoor in general will get, not to mention the fact that every dollar is a larger fraction of the reward to work for a worker from a low-income family than for workers generally. Table 7.1 shows that workers from low-income families will have their log wages depressed by the employer penalty almost three times as much as the average. For all of these reasons, the ACA reduces the quantity of low-skill labor used in the marketplace much more than 3 percent.

With more low-skill labor withdrawing from the workforce than high-skill labor, the average skill in the workforce will increase. In order to someday compare empirical productivity measures to this chapter's predictions, either the measures must hold constant the quality of labor or the productivity predictions must include an offset for the tendency of the ACA to increase average skill in the workforce. Mulligan and Gallen (2013) estimate this tendency to be 1.5 percent, in the direction of higher average skill. The essence of their calculation is the impact of the ACA on the share of workers that are from low-income families—perhaps reducing it by 0.02 (recall table 7.2)—and the wage premium of high-skill workers over low-skill workers relative to the average wage. The more sensitive the low-skill labor supply is to the ACA's taxes, the greater is the composition effect in the direction of increasing the average skill of the workforce.[16]

Thus, even though the ACA's tendency to reallocate labor between occupations, sectors, and employers reduces productivity per hour worked, its tendency to disproportionately withdraw low-skill labor increases average labor quality more than enough to offset the reallocation effects on quality-unadjusted labor: the 1.5 percentage points from labor quality will be more than enough to offset −0.6 percentage points from labor reallocation. But remember that, of the two, only the −0.6 percentage points can be considered a gain or a loss (specifically, a loss). The 1.5 percentage points is an artifact of imperfect measurement of productivity (Jorgenson 2009) and is a symptom of the real loss, which is the failure to fully employ low-skill labor.

Also note that this holds constant the number of low-income families. The ACA redistributes income from high-skill families to low-skill families, and by this channel it may reduce the incentive for low-skill workers to become more skilled—accumulate human capital, as Gary Becker called it (1994)—especially through gaining work experience on the job. The human capital accumulation may take decades to become visible, but it could be just as important in the long run as any of the productivity effects quantified in this chapter. I am not aware of any study that quantifies the ACA's impact on incentives to accumulate human capital, let alone a study that reaches conclusions about the ACA's impact on human capital itself.

Not only do the ACA's full-time employment taxes (FTETs) encourage employers and employees to understate their work hours (recall chapter 6), but they also encourage those who have been overreporting or overestimating employment and work hours to stop their overreporting and overestimating. Take someone who normally works 28 hours per week on a four-day schedule and will continue to do so under the ACA but prior to the ACA was casually reporting 32 hours per week because that's four eight-hour days. Before the ACA there was little penalty or reward for accurate reporting of hours, but this employee may be subject to one of ACA's FTETs because of his lack of precision. The ACA induces him or his employer to track hours more carefully, so that the ACA's impact on his reported hours is negative 13 percent even though it has essentially zero effect on his production and actual work hours.[17] For similar reasons, employers may be more careful about exactly when they add or remove employees from their payroll, making sure to avoid leaving a person on a payroll even for a few days beyond the time when work for the employer ceases. These are all examples of reductions in the aggregate number of work hours reported without significant changes in actual work hours or production and therefore are examples of increases in measured productivity.

Table 6.8 (from chapter 6) shows how reporting behaviors can easily cause reported hours to fall 0.3 percent more than actual hours, and therefore increase measured productivity by 0.3 percent. The 0.3 percent would mask much of the real productivity losses estimated in table 8.1; however, as with the labor quality effects on productivity it is neither a gain nor an achievement of the ACA but merely an artifact of imperfect productivity measurement.

C. The Medicare Investment Income Tax and Capital per Worker

Before the ACA, the Medicare tax was entirely a payroll tax of 1.95 percent from every employer and employee. The ACA also created, among other things, a 3.8 percent Medicare tax on investment income (dividends, interest, and capital gains) earned by individuals, estates, and trusts with annual income (earned plus unearned) above about $200,000 per year. The new investment income tax is on top of longstanding taxes on investment income and thereby further encourages the sheltering of capital income in forms that are subject to less tax, such as housing. Tax sheltering reduces productivity for essentially the same reasons that labor misallocations reduce productivity (Engen and Skinner 1996). I am not aware of any estimates of the effects of the Medicare investment income tax on the amount of capital that will be reallocated, and therefore I cannot offer an estimate of productivity losses through these channels.[18]

The investment income tax will reduce the total quantity of capital, but its effect is small on the scale of the effects shown in table 8.1. The investment income tax is projected to collect about $15 billion per year (Americans for Tax Reform 2013), which is about 0.3 percent of total capital income in the economy.[19] Assuming that the non-ACA capital income tax rate is less than 40 percent (Mulligan 2004), the new tax is reducing the share of capital income (net of depreciation) kept by the owners of capital no more than 0.5 percent. Even with an infinitely elastic supply of capital, that would (in order to keep constant the net-of-tax return on capital) increase the marginal product of capital net of depreciation by no more than 0.5 percent and the gross marginal product by no more than 0.25 percent.[20] The long-term elasticity of labor productivity with respect to the gross marginal product of capital is about three-sevenths, which makes the impact (through the aggregate quantity of capital) of the new tax on labor productivity less than 0.1 percent.

D. National Accounting under the ACA

The ACA primarily redistributes income, which means it has few effects on the major value added, income, and expenditure aggregates in the national accounts apart from its effects on economic behavior such as discouraging work. For example, like federal unemployment benefits and other assistance programs, the ACA's premium assistance will be part of federal social benefits in the personal income accounts. The national income accounts, however, record incomes according to the people and means that earn it—employee wages, the profits of owners of corporations—and before the earners pay their direct taxes or otherwise help fund federal transfer programs. Federal social benefits are not separately added to national income in order to avoid double-counting transfer income; first when the income was earned by those financing federal spending and a second time when it was received by the social program beneficiaries.

One important exception is the national income treatment of the employer penalty. As explained in this book (especially chapter 6), the employer penalty has a lot of economic similarities with the employer payroll tax, which has long been treated in the national income accounts as part of employee compensation. But the Bureau of Economic Analysis has indicated that it will record private employer penalty payments as business transfer payments.[21] Table 8.2 illustrates how a single hypothetical business that operates as a C corporation would contribute to national value added and income with and without the ACA.[22] The hypothetical business has $15 million in revenue. Its value added is the same because it does not make any purchases from other businesses. The revenue is distributed to workers, owners, and the government as shown in the bottom half of the table. Without the ACA, employee salaries total $10 million. The employer owes 7.65 percent payroll tax on that amount, which is considered by national accountants to be part of employee compensation as a "contribution for social insurance." Altogether, employee compensation without the ACA is $10.765 million. The business pays sales tax, which is included in the $15 million of its revenue and is assumed to be 5 percent of what customers pay before sales tax. Employee compensation and sales tax payments are subtracted from revenue to get corporate profits for income tax purposes, which is about $3.52 million. The corporate tax rate (federal and state combined) is 39 percent, and payments are about $1.37 million, which leaves about $2.15 million of profit after taxes.

In order to focus on the accounting issues, revenue and employment

TABLE 8.2. National income accounting for the employer penalty: an example holding constant employer and employee behavior. The accounts below are for a hypothetical employer that is a C corporation that does not acquire inputs from other businesses and has 200 full-time employees.

	Without ACA	With ACA
Contributions to national value-added		
Revenue	$15,000,000	$15,000,000
Contributions to national income		
Compensation of employees		
Wages and salaries	$10,000,000	$9,390,861
Employer payroll tax	$765,000	$718,401
Indirect business taxes		
Sales tax	$714,286	$714,286
Business current transfer payments to government (penalty is recorded here)	$0	$340,000
Corporate profits	$3,520,714	$3,836,452
Taxes on corporate income	$1,373,079	$1,628,816
Profits after tax	$2,147,636	$2,207,636

Notes: For simplicity, the employer penalty shown in this table is not adjusted for health cost inflation. Business current transfer payments are employer penalty payments and are not deductible for the purpose of calculating taxes on corporate income (39 percent rate). The full cost of the employer penalty is assumed to be pass through to employees in the form of lower wages and salaries.

in table 8.2 are assumed to be the same with the ACA as they are without it. The salary equivalent of the $2,000 penalty, $3,046, is deducted from each of the 200 employees' pay, which makes ACA salaries total about $9.39 million. The employer owes payroll taxes of $718,401. Sales taxes are the same with the ACA, but the unique entry is for the employer penalties of $2,000 per employee with the exception of the first 30. Unlike the sales taxes and employee compensation, the penalties are not deductible for the purposes of calculating corporate income tax. Corporate income subject to tax is the $3.84 million plus the penalty payments, which puts the total corporate tax at about $1.63 million.

Perhaps the most surprising part is that the ACA can increase business profits after tax. This is the result of the 30-employee exemption from the employer penalty and my assumption that the proceeds of the exemption are not competed away in the labor market because small employers face prohibitive penalties if the exemption causes them to expand (recall chapter 3). Moreover, national accounting under the ACA puts some of the employer costs under business current transfer

payments and business income tax rather than employee compensation. Unless treated carefully by analysts, the combination of the economics and the accounting will give the false impression that the ACA
reduces employer costs.[23] Moreover, "correcting" or augmenting the
national accounts to measure true employer costs is not as simple as
adding employer penalty payments back into employee compensation.

On the expenditure side of the national accounts (not shown in
table 8.2), spending by the exchange plans on health goods and services will be counted as consumption expenditure. As noted above, the
health goods and services delivered by the plan are valued at what the
plan pays for them, without regard for what they might be worth to
the patient.

Another measurement challenge is not necessarily caused by the
ACA but coincident with it: the measurement of the number of people
insured. Throughout this book I use the ongoing measures created by
the U.S. Census Bureau, but the bureau is changing its methodology
this year at exactly the same time when the ACA began to enroll people
in the exchanges (U.S. Census Bureau 2014). Thus, insurance participation changes from 2013 to 2014 as measured by the Census Bureau
could indicate either genuine insurance status changes or just changes
in the bureau's measurement method.

E. Conclusions

Industries, firms, and regions will grow, decline, and change coverage
on the basis of their relative demand for skilled labor, their comparative advantage in delivering health insurance through the workplace,
and the ease with which they can convert full-time positions into
part-time ones. Those that would be hiring low-skill labor and offering employee coverage without the ACA will no longer have this competitive advantage in the labor market under the ACA because low-skill
employees will likely prefer subsidized coverage from the exchanges.
Their competitors in the labor market will grow by comparison, even
though they may be paying employer penalties (Gallen and Mulligan
2013).

The ACA will induce a segment of the population to move from
employer-sponsored coverage (ESI) to individual coverage, and my

analysis accounts for the fact that some of them will raise the nation's productivity by doing so because it was inefficient for them to have ESI in the first place. Perhaps this instance of productivity gain should be interpreted as the purported ACA-induced surge in entrepreneurship that has been advertised as a labor market benefit.[24] However, this benefit has to be put in the context of the subsidies involved: both the amount of the subsidies that were suppressing entrepreneurship in the first place, and the amount of the subsidies that are being used to get people to give up their ESI. Moreover, entrepreneurship is by no means the only margin on which the ACA operates; among other things, its employer penalty encourages part of the population to give up its individual coverage and get ESI instead![25] This chapter contains a more comprehensive productivity analysis than ACA advocates have offered so far.

Twenty-nine weekly hours per employees and 49 employees per business are not magic numbers in terms of creating value in the marketplace, but the new law's penalties and subsidies make them target business decisions. Economics says that businesses hitting one of these targets will typically sacrifice productivity by doing so. At the same time, they will, by comparison with other businesses, be the ones for whom the magic numbers are most advantageous or least disadvantageous. Business-specific factors put their decisions in the neighborhood of the law-created targets and the law itself pushes them the rest of the way. Unfortunately, this predicted pattern has, and will, invite journalists to shine a light on the business-specific factors, dismiss any role for the law itself, and thereby ignore the basic economic idea that the two types of factors reinforce each other (Lynch 2014).

A growing body of research is finding that productivity in economies is depressed by misallocations of resources across sectors, regions, and firms.[26] Restuccia and Rogerson (2008) show how, in theory, taxes and subsidies have the potential to significantly depress productivity if those policies fail to be uniform across firms, and they suggest that future research needs to carefully examine and quantify specific public policies causing misallocations. Hsieh and Klenow (2009) is a famous study suggesting that total factor productivity (that is, the amount of production adjusted for the contributions of the aggregate quantities of labor and capital) in manufacturing industries has been depressed 50 percent or so in both China and India because of misallocations of labor and capital across firms. Moreover, they suspect that many of the misallocations are unfortunate by-products of public policies that fail to be uniform across firms but have not conducted a detailed public finance analysis of such policies.

This chapter and the previous two offer quantitative analyses of specific public policies—namely, those contained in the ACA—that are affecting productivity in the United States by reallocating its labor. There are instances where the ACA enhances productivity by alleviating the longstanding tax distortion in favor of employer-provided insurance, but overall I find that ACA-induced misallocations will reduce both wages and GDP per quality-adjusted hour worked by about 0.6 percent in the long run and reduce total factor productivity by 0.4 percent. This does not include the ACA's effects on the total quantity of labor. The ACA's impact would be more negative if GDP accounting valued health care at what program beneficiaries are willing to pay for it rather than according to what the government pays.

As it is, the productivity loss is about $100 billion per year, which is a lot of unrealized value added but is still far less in percentage terms than Hsieh and Klenow's (2009) estimate for China and India. My approach tends to find smaller misallocation costs of the ACA because it assumes that the law cannot compound preexisting misallocations, except perhaps the excessive employment by ESI employers that appears to have been the result of the special and ongoing tax treatment of ESI. Another difference is that I limit my attention to the specific reallocations of labor examined in previous chapters as responses to taxes and subsidies. Undoubtedly there are other ACA-induced reallocations to examine, such as the allocation of employment by firm size, and reallocations associated with the ACA's many regulations. Still, so far it looks as if the ACA's impact on the aggregate quantities of labor and capital, and not misallocations, will be the primary way in which the ACA depresses GDP.

Table 8.3 summarizes the combined results from chapter 6 and this chapter. The top half of the table shows the ACA's impact on the factors of production: labor hours, labor quality (that is, the average skill among people who are working), the efficiency of labor allocations, and capital. As noted in chapter 6, the ACA will likely reduce

TABLE 8.3. The ACA's long-run impact on factors of production and incomes

Every table entry is a log difference between the ACA outcome and the no-ACA outcome

	Models			
		Sensitivity analysis		
	Benchmark	Hours misreport	Add 10 %-pts to non ACA MTR	More elastic labor supply
Factors of production				
Aggregate hours worked, actual	**−0.031**	−0.030	−0.036	−0.043
Labor quality	**0.015**	0.015	0.017	0.021
Efficiency of labor allocation	**−0.006**	−0.006	−0.006	−0.006
Capital	**−0.022**	−0.021	−0.025	−0.028
GDP and payments to labor				
Total	**−0.022**	−0.021	−0.025	−0.028
Per reported hours worked	**0.009**	0.011	0.012	0.015
Per reported unit of quality-adj labor	**−0.006**	−0.004	−0.006	−0.006
Addendum: log gap between actual and reported work hours, if any		0.002		

Notes: The sensitivity analysis is from tables 6.7 and 6.8. The misreporting model assumes that workers underreport their hours if and only if it helps them avoid an FTET, and that reported weekly hours are within two of actual hours. The ACA's impact on total factor productivity is −0.004: labor's share times the efficiency of the labor allocation. "More elastic labor supply" refers to a Frisch wage elasticity of aggregate hours of one, rather than 0.6.

work hours at least 3 percent below what it would have been without the ACA; my benchmark estimate is −0.031 log points (about −3.1 percent). Because the lost work hours are disproportionately experienced by low-skill workers, the ACA reduces skill-adjusted work hours about half as much: 0.016 log points (about 1.6 percent). The misallocation effects further reduce the productivity of labor for a given amount of capital. Altogether, the ACA reduces the amount of labor adjusted for quality and efficiency by about 0.022 log points (about 2.2 percent), the sum of the first three items in the table.

Both the misallocation effects and the withdrawal of work hours from the labor market reduce the productivity of capital and thereby reduce the amounts of capital and GDP, and payments to labor, by essentially the same 2.2 percent shown in the first row of the bottom half of table 8.3. The bottom half of the table also shows results for productivity and hourly wages. The ACA decreases measures of productivity and wages that adjust for labor quality and increases measures that are not adjusted.

Table 7.2 suggests that, holding constant the aggregate quantities of labor and aggregate productivity, wages at ESI employers might be increased about 3.4 percent for low-skill workers and decreased about 0.7 percent for high-skill workers. Table 8.1 suggests that, accounting for productivity (but still holding constant the aggregate amounts of low- and high-skill labor), these wage impacts would be about +2.8 percent and −1.3 percent, respectively. As low-skill workers disproportionately withdraw from the labor market, the wage impact would be somewhat more positive for low-skill workers and more negative for high-skill workers.

The last three columns of table 8.3 show how the results differ with deviations from my benchmark assumptions (recall tables 6.7 and 6.8 from chapter 6). All of them agree that the ACA's largest percentage impacts are on aggregate work hours and total GDP. They also agree that the direction of the impact on productivity and wages depends on whether the measures are adjusted for labor quality. Moreover, the labor quality impact is greater for the specifications in which more labor is withdrawn from the workforce by the ACA, because the labor withdrawals are disproportionately low-skill labor. The conclusions about capital and output hardly depend on the degree, if any, to which hours are misreported.

The literature on misallocations takes the factors of production as given in the aggregate and conducts the thought experiment of eliminating policies that prevent those factors from finding their most productive uses. But the example of the ACA's misallocation effects raises the question of whether the amount and composition of labor can be treated separately for public policy purposes, because the same economic forces in the ACA that cause misallocations are also withholding the supply of specific types of labor, and both of these can affect total factor productivity by some measures.

Table 8.3 brings us back to chapter 1's paradox of affordability. Making health care more affordable for a family means alleviating its needs to finance its health-care spending with longer work hours, working more productively, or spending less on nonhealth goods. The ACA makes health care more affordable for parts of the population, but table 8.3 shows why it makes health care less affordable for the nation as a whole. The ACA will have the nation working fewer hours, and working those hours less productively, so that its nonhealth spending will be twice diminished: first to pay for more health care and a second time because the economy is smaller and less productive as a consequence of the ACA.

Appendix 8.1: Labor Misallocations and Productivity in the Long Run

The purpose of this appendix is to present a model that illustrates the long-term relationship between various production measures. GDP in the model, y, is a Cobb-Douglas function of labor hours N and capital k:

$$(8.1) \qquad\qquad y=(ZN)^{\alpha}k^{1-\alpha}$$

where the parameter Z indicates the efficiency of labor. The purpose of tables 8.1 and 8.3 is to measure how much less, if any, Z will be with the ACA than it would be without it.

On the basis of equation (8.1), the marginal product of capital is equation (8.2):

$$(8.2) \qquad\qquad MPK = (1-\alpha)(ZN/k)^{\alpha}$$

I assume that the marginal product of capital in the long run is independent of the efficiency of labor because capital is infinitely elastically supplied. As shown above, the marginal product of capital depends on its ratio to efficiency-adjusted labor ZN, which means that the long-term capital stock falls by the same percentage as efficiency-adjusted labor does.

If we hold the quantity of labor N constant, then the ACA decreases Z, k, and y all by the same percentage in the long run. If, in addition, we account for the effect of the ACA on labor, then ZN, k, and y all fall by the same percentage in the long run, which is essentially the percentage reduction in Z plus the percentage reduction in N.

9 | Other Significant Causes of Economic Change, 2007–2017

The previous chapters have estimates of the long-term economic impacts of the ACA, which refer to differences between our "actual" economy with the ACA in place for several years and an otherwise similar "counterfactual" economy with no ACA. Assuming for the moment that the impact estimates incorporate all of the relevant ACA provisions, we see that they are not the same as predictions for the economic changes over time that will occur after the law is put in place. Rather, an economic change over this period is the sum of the ACA's impact and the counterfactual change that would have occurred without the ACA. For example, I estimate that a long-term impact of the ACA is to reduce hours worked per adult by somewhat more than 3 percent. If work hours per adult were to fall 1 percent without the ACA, perhaps owing to aging of the population, then I would predict that the work hours per adult eventually fall somewhat more than 4 percent after the implementation of the ACA. One of the purposes of this chapter is to quantify the likely counterfactual changes in labor, capital, and production that would have occurred if the ACA had never been passed so that the changes can be added to impact estimates to get predictions for changes over time. Readers who are just interested in my predictions for economic change, and not their building blocks, may want to jump ahead to section E, which summarizes the predictions in two tables.

The same kind of reasoning is needed to formulate predictions as to the economic changes that would occur after (and if) the ACA is repealed. If the ACA were in place for a sufficiently long time before repeal, then my prediction for a long-term economic change after repeal is the difference between the changes that would occur if the ACA remained in place and the impact of the ACA. For example, if hours worked per adult were going to fall 1 percent even without repeal, perhaps because of aging, then I predict that hours worked per adult would eventually increase somewhat more than 2 percent following the repeal: a decline of 1 percent from aging combined with an increase of somewhat more than 3 percent owing to the removal of the ACA's impact. (A similar national analysis would apply to repeal of the ACA's major provisions in specific regions of the country, but regional comparisons would also require additional attention to geographic equalizing differences akin to those discussed in chapter 7.)

The long-term impact estimates from previous chapters are technically incomplete because the ACA contains several additional taxes on labor (positive and negative) that were not included. Section A in this chapter examines those taxes and finds they collectively add about 0.2 percentage points to the average marginal earnings tax rate, compared to about six percentage points from provisions examined in chapter 6. Section A also includes an analysis of "employment lock," which may not technically be a tax but has a number of similarities to one.

Another complexity is that the ACA itself may change over time via modified legislation or by significant changes in how the original ACA is interpreted or enforced. Section B of this chapter discusses possible law changes and how the ACA's impacts would differ in those cases. Section C estimates counterfactual changes for labor per adult between 2012–13 and 2016–17.

Technically, "long run" means after infinite time; but with a few weak assumptions about dynamics, the impact in the long run can be related to the impact over a three- or four-year horizon. Section D discusses these assumptions as well as counterfactual changes for capital and production between 2012–13 and 2016–17.

The chapter's final section brings the results together in order to formulate the predictions for actual changes in labor, capital, and production between 2012–13 and 2016–17. The predictions involve comparisons for 24-month periods in order to reduce the influence of highly transitory events for evaluating predictions that are fundamentally long term. Moreover, the theories used in this book are not specific enough to say exactly what time interval is appropriate for measuring economic activity "before" the ACA's penalties and subsidies take effect.

A. Other Labor Tax Effects in the ACA

The model in chapter 6 captures the employer penalty, the income taxes implicit in the exchange subsidies and uncompensated care (including implicit taxes on unemployment income), and the full-time employment taxes implicit in the exchange subsidies. But the ACA also has two Medicare surtaxes, provisions to contain employer health costs and the labor market inefficiencies that the costs are said to create, an employment tax implicit in its rules for relief from the individual mandate, an income cliff for exchange subsidies at or near the poverty line, and Medicaid expansions. The purpose of this section is to quantify these additional ACA provisions individually and collectively. It turns out that each of them is small, and that their sum is smaller than most of the components because some of the provisions serve to increase tax rates on labor whereas others reduce them.

1. TWO MEDICARE SURTAXES

As explained in chapter 2, the marginal tax rate on earnings created by the two Medicare surtaxes is zero for the roughly 98 percent of workers with income below the threshold, although the size of this group will fall over time because the thresholds are not indexed to inflation. For the remaining workers, the marginal tax rate is 0.9 percent, 3.8 percent, or 4.7 percent, which means the Medicare rate increase averages (across workers) less than 0.1 percentage point. For the purposes of this chapter, I take the increase to be 0.04 percentage points, as shown in the top row of table 9.1 (the table shows only one decimal point).

2. HEALTH COST CONTAINMENT AS A TAX CUT

The ACA is expected to cut wasteful health spending by employer plans and by this mechanism increase employment (Cutler and Sood 2010). Chapter 2 takes cost savings estimates from the literature and translates them into tax effects and concludes that the cost savings are economically similar to an earnings tax rate cut of 0.3 percentage points, which should be added to the many tax effects cited in this book.

Chapter 2 also explains why the literature may have the wrong interpretation, and that the ACA's cost saving provisions themselves may *add* to employment taxation because much of the savings are sup-

TABLE 9.1. Other ACA taxes on earnings, including implicit taxes

excluding the provisions modeled in chapter 6

ACA provision	Addition to the average marginal tax rate on earnings
Two Medicare surtaxes	0.0%
Health cost containment	−0.3%
Individual mandate relief	0.2%
Exchange subsidies are bracketed by 100 and 400 percent FPL	−0.2%
Medicaid expansions for the poor: raise income-eligibility limits	0.1%
Medicaid expansions for the poor: reduce other barriers to participation	0.3%
Sum of the six provisions	0.2%

Notes: The Medicare surtaxes are not literally zero, but contribute 0.0 percentage points when rounded to the nearest tenth of a point. FPL refers to the federal poverty line. Also note that the ACA may have an "employment lock" effect that is akin to a tax effect but has not yet been quantified in those terms. Based on estimates from the literature (see the main text), I assume the ACA's employment lock impact on log employment over a two-year horizon is somewhere between 0 and 0.005, in addition to the impacts above and the impacts discussed elsewhere in this book.

posed to be achieved by threatening employers with additional excise taxes (namely, the Cadillac tax and other excise taxes on noncompliant employer plans). To put it simply, I am a little skeptical that threatening employers with new taxes is an effective way to mitigate, rather than aggravate, a longstanding and implicit employment tax when the channels by which the former mitigates the latter are rather indirect. Nevertheless, the second row of table 9.1 shows the estimate from the literature in order to be somewhat conservative as to the amount by which the ACA adds to taxes on labor.

3. INDIVIDUAL MANDATE RELIEF

Individuals who have access to affordable health insurance (either through their employer or through the marketplaces created by the ACA) but fail to participate are liable for the individual mandate penalty, unless they are experiencing hardship. When applicable, the amount of the individual mandate penalty is the maximum of a flat amount per uninsured household member and a percentage of household income (U.S. Internal Revenue Service 2013b). For the purpose of this chapter, I use the percentage that applies in 2016 and beyond: 2.5 percent. The hardship exemption acts as an implicit tax on work to the extent that not working allows a person to be classified as experiencing hardship. The text of the ACA is unclear as to the relation between employment and hardship for the purposes of granting the exemption. I assume that, conditional on not having insurance, the penalty is paid only when working or out of the labor force because unemployed persons will be eligible for a hardship exemption.

Tables 4.2 and 7.3 (from chapters 4 and 7, respectively) together show that 15 percent (15.3 million out of 104 million total) of nonelderly household heads and spouses in the labor force were uninsured in March 2012. Because nonelderly household heads and spouses do about three-quarters of the aggregate work in the economy, and 58 percent of the recent reductions in work hours have been through weekly unemployment rather than hours per week or time out of the labor force (Mulligan 2012b, table 3.5), I assume that 6 percent of reduced work time in the economy would trigger individual mandate relief. Table 9.1 records a 0.2 percentage point reduction in the average marginal earnings tax rate because that is 6 percent of the full mandate relief of 2.5 percent.

4. EXCHANGE SUBSIDIES STOP AT THE POVERTY LINE

Assuming for the moment that no one above the poverty line is eligible for Medicaid, we take the eligible calendar year income range for the ACA's exchange subsidies to be between 100 and 400 percent of the poverty line. Thus, holding Medicaid eligibility constant, the ACA introduces a subsidy for people above the poverty line without introducing a subsidy for those below the line.[1] This by itself increases the incentive (or, thanks to longstanding poverty programs, decreases the disincentive) for earning above the poverty line. In the same way, the ACA also creates a new disincentive to earn beyond 400 percent of the poverty line. One of the thresholds encourages work and the other discourages it; the relative size of the two incentives is an empirical question.

If employers and employees were primarily making marginal employment decisions—for example, when to start a new position or when to terminate one—of just a couple of weeks, then few of those decisions would push the worker and his or her family out of, or into, the eligible income range when income is measured on a calendar year basis. In this case, the threshold effects are especially small, from an aggregate point of view, regardless of which one dominates. Mulligan (2013a, table 2) finds that the threshold effects are more significant for longer-duration employment decisions and that the work-encouraging effect of the poverty line threshold is somewhat larger than the work-discouraging effect of the 400 percent threshold: an average net of about 0.2 percentage points of compensation.

5. MEDICAID EXPANSIONS FOR THE POOR

Medicaid is a longstanding health insurance program for the poor, essentially free for its participants. Income eligibility limits are set by states, and in 2012 they averaged 84 percent of the poverty line for working parents and somewhat less for jobless parents.[2] Many states also impose asset limits, especially for adult participants. The ACA expands Medicaid participation in three ways: raising the income threshold for adult eligibility (in some states), reducing barriers to participation, and eliminating some of the alternatives to Medicaid.

The ACA gives states the option, and funding if they exercise the option, of increasing the income threshold for adults to 133 percent of the poverty line, without an asset test. Holahan and Headen (2010) estimated that, if all states expanded, Medicaid participation would increase by 27.4 percent. Chapters 4 and 5 already examine ACA programs made available to people above 100 percent of the poverty line (defined on a calendar year basis), so this section avoids double-counting by focusing on Medicaid expansions for the poor population. Also note that Medicaid income limits are not necessarily examined on a calendar year basis, and a family could be in poverty for part of a year even while above poverty for the full calendar year.

Using the March 2011 CPS, Mulligan (2013a) found that, among the nonelderly heads and spouses who were working some time during 2010 and who are part of the population examined by Holahan and Headen, 14 percent were both below the poverty line and living in a state where Medicaid will be expanded (or the state was creating a substitute health premium assistance program for that population).[3] I therefore assume that, by increasing the income threshold in some states, the ACA increases by 3.5 percent (14 percent of 24.7 percent) the fraction of workers who can get assistance from, and would participate in, Medicaid during times of reduced earnings and thereby increase by

3.5 percent the contribution of the Medicaid program to the average marginal earnings tax rate. Before the ACA, the contribution was 4.3 percent,[4] which means the Medicaid-income-limit provision of the ACA adds 0.1 percentage points to the average marginal earnings tax rate.

In preparing their 24.7 percent estimate, Holahan and Headen looked only at the relative size of the population with incomes below the new threshold and above the old threshold. But the ACA also reduces barriers to participation among those already eligible. When it works, healthcare.gov is supposed to quickly show people whether they are eligible for Medicaid and facilitate their enrollment. Healthcare.gov will not be asset-testing applicants, and states will be encouraged to waive asset tests too.

Another barrier, so to speak, to Medicaid participation has been the availability of low-premium private health insurance coverage that lower-income families sometimes prefer to Medicaid. The ACA eliminates low-premium plans by requiring underwriters to provide a wide range of benefits, leaving Medicaid as sometimes the next best option (Hopkins 2013). Unlike private plans, Medicaid is income-tested, so this transition subjects a part of the population to a means test they otherwise would not experience.

Sonier, Boudreaux, and Blewett (2013) examine the Massachusetts health reform and estimated that it increased Medicaid participation by 36 percent among persons previously Medicaid eligible. However, they note that part of the 36 percent may be an increase in reported participation rather than actual participation. I also notice that the participation effect visible in their data seems to decline over time. Holahan and Headen (2010) look at the possibility of increased national Medicaid participation, holding eligibility constant, and guess that it could increase 12 percent as a consequence of the ACA. I take the 12 percent estimate and, to avoid double-counting people above the poverty line, scale it by the incidence of poverty (defined annually) among nonelderly heads and spouses working sometime during the calendar year and below 133 percent FPL, which is 62 percent. This Medicaid "barriers" effect of the ACA increases Medicaid's contribution to the average marginal earnings tax rate by 7 percent (0.12 times 0.62), which is the 0.3 percentage points recorded in table 9.1.

Overall, the six provisions above add about 0.2 percentage points to the average marginal tax rate on earnings, as compared to about 6.3 percentage points for the provisions examined in chapter 6 (recall table 6.1). For completeness, I include the 0.2 percentage points in the predictions below, but essentially all of my impact estimates come from the taxes considered in previous chapters.

6. "EMPLOYMENT LOCK"

The ACA also creates new opportunities for individuals to buy unsubsidized coverage apart from any employer.[5] These opportunities are said to "unlock" workers from their full-time jobs, for example, permitting near-elderly workers to retire before they become eligible for Medicare, without losing health coverage (Gruber and Madrian 2004). In this view, the opportunities for unsubsidized coverage have many of the qualitative characteristics of an implicit full-time employment tax because the appearance of the coverage opportunities creates a benefit for nonworkers and part-time workers, but not for the typical full-time worker who is already covered through employment. For the purpose of predicting the ACA's impacts on aggregate hours and the cross-sectional distribution of weekly hours, table 9.1 could show an additional factor reducing the supply of labor. However, the literature on employment lock has not quantified the effect in tax rate terms. Moreover, the 2006 health reform in Massachusetts (see especially chapter 10) also created new opportunities for individuals to buy unsubsidized coverage apart from an employer but was not followed by a visible shift in labor supply.[6] This might argue for treating the employment unlock effect of the ACA as approximately zero.

However, Garthwaite, Gross, and Notowidigdo (2014, hereafter, GGN) conclude, on the basis of changes in Medicaid eligibility rules in Tennessee, that the ACA might reduce nationwide employment by as much as 0.4 to 0.6 percent,[7] without beginning to count effects of (1) the employer penalty, (2) ACA taxes and subsidies experienced by families above 200 percent of the poverty line, and (3) ACA taxes and subsidies experienced by families below 200 percent of the poverty line who either have children or would not otherwise be insured by an employer.[8] One interpretation is that GGN confirm the central thesis of the second half of this book: that health reform's taxes on employment and incomes reduce aggregate employment and incomes and that even a relatively small portion of the ACA's taxes by itself may have a noticeable effect on employment. Another interpretation is that GGN have detected an income effect on labor supply (in the direction of working less) that may be offset elsewhere in the population among the taxpayers who have to pay for the subsidies going to people unlocked from their jobs. A third interpretation is that GGN have detected the effect of additional access to unsubsidized coverage apart from employment that, as noted above, is not included in my impact estimates. They describe their estimate as an upper bound, and my impact estimates should be adjusted only for the third effect. On the other hand, their study does not include all of the people who will be getting coverage from the ACA. I therefore consider an "employment unlock" effect ranging from 0 to 0.5 percent of aggregate employment and work hours, in the direction of less work. Because the 0.5 percent quantifies an employment rate impact over a two-year horizon rather than a tax rate, it is entered in table 9.1 only in the notes and below is added in after the tax effects have been converted to employment rate impacts.

B. Possible Reforms of the Reform

Because this is a book about the impact of the ACA and the evolution of the economy over the next couple of years, my purpose here is to discuss (arguably) likely changes to the ACA. To be clear, a "likely" change may or may not be a desirable change.[9] I consider the likely changes so that the book may still contain useful predictions in the event that changes are made to the ACA. I am admittedly not an expert on forecasting political outcomes or even on delineating possible political scenarios, but I take suggestions for likely modifications from the ACA itself, from health reforms at the state level, and from optimal tax theory.

1. SMOOTHING CLIFFS AND NOTCHES

The ACA's rules for subsidies and penalties contain several cliffs and notches where economically insignificant decisions can subject a worker or an employer to a comparatively massive implicit tax or penalty. For example, an employer not offering coverage who lets employees work

30 hours per week rather than 29 may find the one hour per week costs the business thousands of dollars in employer penalties. Or the head of a family of four who earns $95,500 rather than $95,300 for the year may find that that $200 of earnings cost the family a couple of thousand dollars in premium assistance because $95,500 is beyond 400 percent of the poverty line.

Notches and cliffs are generally viewed as economically inefficient, and the same view holds that a program's objectives can be achieved at less cost by smoothly phasing out benefits and smoothly phasing in taxes. Perhaps we also should expect future legislation to eliminate some of the ACA's notches and cliffs because they have been eliminated from, or mitigated in, tax and subsidy programs before (e.g., Social Security benefit rules).

Recall from chapter 5 that I have already assumed that, for some choices, households act as if the ACA's exchange subsidies are paid as a smooth function of household income, as if there were no income notches and cliffs. Analytical simplicity is one reason for my assumption. Another is that it may be difficult for coworkers to coordinate on notches and cliffs because coworkers may need to have a common work schedule for business purposes, whereas each employee's unique family situation puts the notches and cliffs at a unique spot in the schedule.[10] But if future legislation literally makes the subsidy schedules smooth rather than notched (as a function of income), then my assumption is even more accurate than it will be if the ACA remains unchanged.

I believe that the cliff at 30 hours per week, for the purpose of applying the employer mandate, will have noticeable effects on behavior, in part because the cliff is at the same number of hours for all coworkers. The model in chapter 6 takes the threshold literally, and some of its results depend on that approach. In particular, the hours-threshold approach to the penalty (it is in the ACA at the time of my writing) creates a large group of workers having an incentive to work somewhat *more* hours per week for fewer weeks. It also creates a smaller group of workers who work significantly fewer hours per week in order to stay under the threshold. The combination of these two effects is little impact on the average hours per employee but a widening of the cross-sectional distribution of hours. If the ACA were modified to make the employer penalty a smooth function of hours, perhaps as a proportion to total hours on the payroll (regardless of its decomposition between employees and hours per employee, as it was under the Massachusetts health reform), then the ACA's impact on average hours would be even closer to (i.e., exactly) zero. Both versions of the penalty significantly reduce weekly employment rates. Unlike the penalty written in the ACA now, the modified version of the employer penalty would have no impact (relative to no penalty) on the distribution of hours among workers subject to the penalty.

2. THE EMPLOYER PENALTY IS NEVER IMPLEMENTED

The ACA was passed in 2010, but the original legislation deferred the employer mandate until 2014. As 2014 approached, it was announced that enforcement would not begin until 2015. In early 2014, enforcement of the mandate on employers of fewer than 100 employees was delayed until 2016 (Pear 2012).

A similar timeline played out in Massachusetts in the years after the Michael Dukakis administration and continued for many years. In 1988, Governor Dukakis pushed through a law (not to be confused with the health law signed by Gov. Mitt Romney almost two decades later) that sought to achieve universal health insurance coverage in Massachusetts with a legislative package that included a $1,680 penalty per employee per year on employers who did not provide health coverage to their employees.

The Dukakis package passed by a narrow margin; to get it through the legislature, the law provided for a 45-month delay before the employer mandate took effect (McDonough 2000). Forty-four months after passage, the Massachusetts mandate was delayed three more years by a new law passed by the legislature over Gov. William Weld's veto. The employer mandate was delayed twice more. As the fourth date approached for carrying out the 1988 employer mandate, the legislature repealed it entirely. The employer mandate would return again in 2006 under Governor Romney, with its penalty set at one-tenth that of the Dukakis law; this mandate was also repealed.

These Massachusetts mandate events through 2005 are shown in figure 9.1's timeline.[11] Red shapes are dates of legislation and black

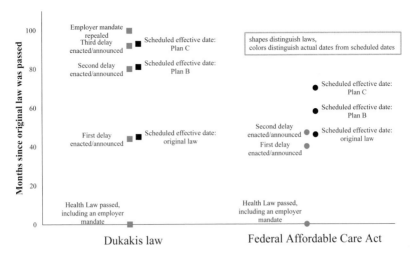

FIGURE 9.1. Comparing the Massachusetts and federal timelines for the employer mandate.

shapes are dates for putting the legislation into effect. The Massachusetts timeline is on the left, and that for the federal Affordable Care Act, which was passed in March 2010, on the right. (For both laws, month zero is when the law was passed.) The timeline for the ACA has a number of parallels with that of the Dukakis law. Both originally provided for an employer mandate delay: 45 months in Massachusetts and 46 months for the federal law.

In both cases, the employer mandate was delayed as the original effective date approached and businesses complained. The first federal delay was announced in the fortieth month subsequent to the original law; the first Massachusetts delay was enacted in the forty-fourth month. In both cases, a second delay was announced, but it did not happen in Massachusetts until the eightieth month. In February 2014, already in the forty-seventh month of the law, the federal government announced a second delay of the full employer mandate until January 2016 (which will be the seventieth month). So far, it looks as though a few employers will pay a reduced penalty as early as January 2015.

Both laws were passed when Democrats held the executive position and a majority in the legislature. In both cases, one-party rule ended soon after the health law was signed. In Massachusetts, the legislature

TABLE 9.2. ACA long-run impacts with and without various provisions

Indicator	ACA impact if it has:		ACA impact if exchange features are further discounted	Source
	Penalty	No penalty		
Aggregate hours per person, log	−0.031	−0.023	−0.029	
Weekly employment rate, log	−0.033	−0.023	−0.032	
Avg. weekly hours per employee, log	0.002	0.000	0.003	Table 6.7
Percentage of workers that are 29ers	3.6	1.7	2.6	
Percentage of nonpoor nonelderly who are uninsured	−10.0	−10.0		
Percentage of nonpoor nonelderly with employer coverage	−10.6	−25.3		Table 7.5
Ratio of low- to high-skill wages (ESI sector), log	0.040	0.063		Table 7.2

Notes: The first column is the benchmark specification. The final column discounts exchange plan values by 39 percent of their full premium, rather than the 25 percent discount assumed in the benchmark specification.

took the initiative to delay the employer mandate and carried out its decision as new laws. Federally, the Obama administration made the delays by notifying employers that the penalty would not be enforced, or enforced to a lesser degree than the original law specified.

The penalty amounts in the two laws are also similar. Adjusted for inflation, the Dukakis law's penalty (federal tax deductible) was equivalent to a $3,363 penalty in 2014. The federal law's penalty in 2014 would have effectively been $3,046 because it is not deductible from an employer's business taxes.

One hundred months after the Dukakis law was passed, its employer penalty was finally repealed. If the federal law were to follow the exact same timeline, it would be repealed in June 2018, in the second year of a new presidency. This is not to say that the federal employer mandate will necessarily be repealed or indefinitely delayed, but these seem like real possibilities. Throughout the book, I have therefore prepared long-term impact estimates with and without the employer penalty. Table 9.2 summarizes the results. The impact estimates for average weekly hours and the percentage of nonpoor nonelderly who are not insured do not really depend on the penalty part of the ACA. Without its employer penalty, the ACA would depress log aggregate work hours "only" 0.023, or about 2.3 percent, as compared to 0.031 with the penalty. The labor impact is still economically significant without a penalty, because without the penalty many workers move from employer coverage to the exchanges, where they are subject to an additional marginal tax rate on their income: 20 or more percentage points on top of the income taxes they usually pay. About half of the twenty-niners come from the penalty part of the ACA, as shown in the fourth row of 9.2. Without its employer penalty, the ACA does more to move people off employer coverage and more to increase the wages at ESI employers of low-skill workers relative to high-skill workers.

3. THE CADILLAC TAX IS NEVER IMPLEMENTED

The "Cadillac" excise tax on high-cost employer plans is one of the last ACA provisions scheduled to take effect, in 2018. Its eight-year delayed effective date suggests that the tax may be a politically vulnerable provision and therefore more likely to incur repeal or weak enforcement. In my judgment, the Cadillac tax does not have visible effects on any of the indicators in table 9.2. However, to be conservative table 9.1 included a tax impact of −0.3 percentage points for health cost containment, part of which is supposed to derive from the Cadillac tax. Without the Cadillac tax, perhaps the tax impact of health cost containment would be −0.2 percentage points because costs would be contained less. Even this adjustment would not have visible effects on any of the indicators in table 9.2.

4. EXCHANGE PLANS INCREASINGLY RESEMBLE MEDICAID

The ACA's exchange plans are not the same as employer-provided insurance, and plans like them were previously rare in the marketplace. Throughout the book I assume that consumers value the exchange plans at 25 percent less than what they cost, and that their valuation factors into their work decisions. It's possible that budget pressures or other factors induce lawmakers or regulators to take further steps to make exchange plans less attractive.

The "Romneycare" reform in Massachusetts in 2006 is a model in this regard because it ran its subsidized exchange plans, known as "Comm-Care" (see chapter 10), much like Medicaid, which is itself thought to offer coverage that is (perceived to be) far inferior to employer plans. CommCare was for adults only: parents who left ESI (or left the unsubsidized individual purchase market) for CommCare would have to put their children on Medicaid/CHIP, buy separate coverage for them, or leave them uninsured. CommCare did not have the same network of providers as unsubsidized plans did. People could not join CommCare until they had been six months without the opportunity for affordable insurance. If the ACA's exchange plans took on these features, or otherwise came to be perceived as far inferior (that is, worth significantly less than the exchange plans currently on the market, even after the discount that I have assumed), then the ACA's impact would be different.

The final column of table 9.2 reports the results. When the exchange features are 14 percentage points less valuable, aggregate labor hours fall 0.029 log points (about 2.9 percent) rather than 0.031.[12] The twenty-niners are also somewhat less. But this version of the ACA is still significantly depressing labor because of its employer penalty and because of its implicit income tax on workers getting coverage through the exchanges, regardless of how little they may like it.

Even though the federal government pays the bills, state insurance regulators have some influence on the characteristics of exchange plans because they have to approve plans (Hancock 2013). To the extent that early retirement from state government positions involves joining exchange plans (Dardick 2013), the state regulators may have a personal stake in the characteristics of exchange plans and would not want them to resemble Medicaid. Chapter 7 also notes there are market pressures for the exchange plans to include one or more bronze plans that participants do not use and are cheap because participants do not use them. It remains to be seen to what degree state regulators will resist those pressures; without any resistance, the ACA's impact on the number of people insured could be even greater.

A related issue is whether and when the ACA's nationwide cap on exchange subsidies takes effect (see chapter 5), or whether Congress takes other steps to make the premium assistance program less generous. Limits on exchange subsidies would reduce the ACA's long-term impact on the number of people with health insurance, although it could accelerate enrollment in the exchanges.[13] I would not be surprised if Congress tried to reduce official measures of government spending by introducing additional hidden taxes—that is, further withholding benefits on the basis of employment and income—and thereby increasing marginal labor tax rates beyond what I have estimated.

C. The Outlook for Labor Even without the ACA

The labor market would change even without the ACA. The purpose of this section is to quantify some of the non-ACA sources of change, especially recovery from the recent recession (and the implicit taxes that came with it) and the aging of the population. I also discuss a couple of scenarios for non-ACA labor market policy changes.

1. PARTIAL RECOVERY FROM THE RECESSION AND STIMULUS

By the end of 2013, work hours per adult were 7 percent below what they were before the 2008–9 recession began, largely because weekly employment per adult remained low.[14] Some of that was probably due to aging, which is quantified below, but most was from other factors. Economists disagree widely as to what caused the prolonged recession, but there is more agreement that some of the causes are temporary and that the labor market is "slowly healing" (Yellen 2014), which I take to mean that employment and other age-adjusted measures of labor market activity would be slowly rising even without the ACA. It follows that the age-adjusted measures of labor market activity would not fall 3 percent after the ACA even if the impact of the law were 3 percent in the direction of less work, because part of the ACA's negative impact would serve to offset recovery from the recession.

I agree that (adjusted for age) the labor market would largely recover, absent the ACA. Moreover, I think that the recovery is and will continue to be largely a tax effect, namely, the net reduction in marginal tax rates as the temporary components of various stimulus programs expired: a bonus on unemployment checks, health insurance assistance for the unemployed, enhanced food stamp benefits, and more (Mulligan 2012b). The most recent and significant of these was the expiration of the federal Emergency Unemployment Compensation

(hereafter, EUC) program that, until the end of 2013, paid unemployment benefits to the long-term unemployed. The EUC expiration itself
is a force increasing employment during 2014.

I use two methods of accounting for the 2008–9 recession for the
purpose of predicting labor market activity in 2016–17. One of them estimates a counterfactual change from 2012–13 (the years immediately
before the exchange subsidies began) through 2016–17 and adds an estimate of the impact of the ACA over a three-year horizon. The counterfactual change must include an estimate of the part of the recovery
from the recession that would occur during those years, especially the
expiration of the EUC program.

The second method estimates a counterfactual change from 2007,
the year immediately before the recession, through 2016–17 and, because the ACA subsidies did not begin until 2014, adds an estimate
of the impact of the ACA over a three-year horizon. For the second
method, the counterfactual change needs to consider the recession
only to the extent that, absent the ACA, the recession and stimulus
would have lingered nine years after they began. The recession was
associated with, and may have caused, some permanent increases in
state and local income and sales taxes. Parts of the stimulus are also
permanent (or at least unlikely to disappear before 2017): the expansions of food stamp (SNAP) eligibility and the "modernization" of the
unemployment insurance program that made it easier for the unemployed to claim benefits.

Table 9.3 quantifies these non-ACA causes of labor market change.
The first two columns of the table look at changes between 2012–13 and
2016–17. The final two columns look at changes over the longer period
2007 through 2016–17. The table's first row shows the safety net program expansions after 2007 that still persisted at the end of 2013, and I
expect to continue at least until 2017. Mulligan (2012b, chapter 3) measures the contribution of safety net programs to the average marginal
tax rate on employee compensation, and at http://marginaltaxrates.us
I have documented which of the programs still persist; the latter contribute 1.9 percentage points to the rate. The second row shows the
contribution of the expiration of the EUC program, based on the same
sources as the row above. Other safety net programs, and the payroll
tax rate, were changing during 2012 and 2013, so the 0.3 percentage

TABLE 9.3. Non-ACA causes of labor market change 2007–17: the tax effects

Change in the government percentage of marginal compensation, by type of tax effect.

Potential causes of change	Ending in 2016–17 and beginning in:				Source
	2012–13		2007		
	Low	High	Low	High	
UI program modernization & permanent SNAP expansions	0	0	1.9	0.9	Mulligan (2012) and marginaltaxrates.us
EUC expiration	−2.9	−2.9	0	0	
Payroll tax hike and other changes during 2012–13	0.3	0.3	NA		marginaltaxrates.us
Avg. marginal tax changes on Form 1040 (federal & state)	0.1	−0.1	−0.1	−0.3	NBER
Recession recovery: employer wedge diminishes	0	−1.2	NA		
Recession recovery: employee wedge diminishes	−0.5	−3.4	NA		
Recession still lingers in 2017: employer wedge	NA		1.8	0.6	Table 9.7
Recession still lingers in 2017: employee wedge	NA		0.6	0.0	
All non-ACA tax/distortion effects combined	**−3.0**	**−7.2**	**4.2**	**1.2**	
Addendum: ACA tax effects from table 9.1	0.2	0.2	0.2	0.2	

Notes: Population aging and "employment lock" are not in this table because they are not quantified as tax effects. The employee wedge is based on a 0.6 wage elasticity of labor supply. Because sales tax changes are include in consumer price inflation, they are part of the "employer wedge." Note that tax rates (this table) are not in the same units as employer and employee wedges (table 9.7).

points in the third row of table 9.3 shows the gap between the marginal tax rate at the end of 2013 and the average for the two calendar years combined.

The National Bureau of Economic Research (2012) calculates contributions of changes in federal and state personal income tax laws to average marginal tax rates on wage income, and they find a change of 0.3 percentage points of wages included in adjusted gross income, from 2007 to 2012–13. Converted to a percentage of employee compensation, it is 0.2 percentage points. As shown in table 9.3's fourth row, I assume that this rate may further change up or down 0.1 percentage points. For the entire period 2007 through 2016–17, that would make the cumulative change range from −0.1 to −0.3. Over both horizons, I show a range of possibilities. Any one row's range is intended to be narrower than, say, a 95 percent confidence interval because ultimately I will combine all of the "lows" into a single "low" and all of the "highs" into a single "high."[15] The right half of table 9.3 shows a fairly wide range for the tax effects of UI program modernization and food stamp expansions because the former has not been studied as much as other UI program parameters and because states may revert back to pre-ARRA program parameters now that the ARRA's modernization incentives have expired.[16]

As discussed in chapter 8, the wages paid to labor normally reflect the productivity of labor, with the two variables typically growing at the same rate over long horizons. During 2009, labor productivity grew about 3 percent relative to wages (Mulligan 2014b, figure 5). This "employer wedge" has persisted and even grown since then, and it may reflect some of the causes of the recession and slow labor market recovery. A small part (a tenth or less) might reflect changes in state and local sales tax rates, which I do not expect to be reversed before 2017.[17] Arguably the rest of the wedge would close as part of a full recovery, which means wages would grow about 3 percent relative to productivity along a full recovery. I doubt that a full recovery would be realized by 2016–17, so at the "high" end I assume a two-thirds recovery by that date, which means wages growing 2 percent relative to productivity. Because marginal labor income tax rates are about 45 percent (Mulligan 2014b), the tax rate equivalent of that part of the recovery would be a tax rate cut of 1.2 percentage points, as shown in the fifth row of table 9.3.

Some of the causes of the recession and lack of recovery are reflected in the fact that employment and work hours are low relative to employee wages, which I summarize as an "employee wedge." The measurement of both of these "wedges" is shown in appendix 9.2. Measured as a tax effect, the employee wedge has been declining about one percentage point per year since the end of 2009. Some—I would say most—of the decline is a consequence of marginal tax rate cuts between 2009 and 2012 and should not be expected to continue at the same rate. If it did continue at the same rate, that is a cumulative four percentage points (in the direction of less taxes); I assume a range of 0.5–3.4 percentage points, as shown in the sixth row of table 9.3.

For the purposes of comparing 2016–17 to 2007, which is the last year prior to the recession, the question is not how much the labor market can recover but rather how much of the recession still lingers after nine years. The final two columns of table 9.3 show the assumed ranges for employer and employee wedge changes from that perspective.

The total of the non-ACA tax effects between 2012–13 and 2016–17 is in the direction of less taxes and more work, primarily because of continued recovery from the recession and temporary assistance policies. My range for the total is −3.0 to −7.2 percentage points of that time period. The total of the non-ACA tax effects beginning in 2007 is in the direction of more taxes and less work, because the recession and assistance policy changes current after 2007 and some of that is expected to linger even in 2017. My range for the total tax effect over the longer time period is 1.2 to 4.2. All of these tax effects are percentage points (of employee compensation) added to the marginal labor income tax rate, on top of the implicit and explicit taxes already in place at the beginning of the period. For the purposes of comparison, the additional ACA tax effects from table 9.1 are shown as an addendum to table 9.3.

2. AGING OF THE BABY BOOM

In principle, employees per person can remain constant over time as retirees leave work and are replaced by workers coming out of school. However, a disproportionate fraction of our population was born in the years immediately following World War II, and there are more of these baby boomers in or near the normal retirement years than there are young people coming out of school. For a time, the aging of the baby boom tends to reduce employment and work hours per adult. In order to quantify this effect, I formed a measure of the age-adjusted adult population as the number of people age 16 and over, weighted by the average hours worked (including zeros for persons not working) by people that age in 2006 and 2007, and normalized so that the adjusted population coincides with the actual population in 2007-Q4, all estimated from the CPS Merged Outgoing Rotation Groups (CPS-MORG) microdata files.[18]

By design, the age-adjusted measure counts people in the prime working ages more than others. The measure falls over time relative to the unadjusted population as the baby boom begins moving into the normal retirement ages. My data ends with 2013, so I assume that the same average adjusted population growth rate (relative to the unadjusted rate) for 2005 through 2013 will persist through 2016–17.[19] As a result, I estimate that, relative to the actual population, the log of the age-adjusted adult population will be 0.015 less in 2016–17 than it was in 2012–13 and 0.039 less than it was in 2007. The relative population changes are estimates of how much aggregate work hours would, holding constant all other aforementioned determinants of work hours, change in the long run if the age distribution of the population remained static after 2016–17.

The U.S. population is also getting more educated, and educated people work more hours on average. Perhaps this is a reason to expect that, holding constant the population age distribution, hours per person would increase over time (Shimer 2014). Average education is changing too slowly to fully offset the aging effect, but it is changing enough to also consider an overall demographics effect that is closer to zero than the 0.015 and 0.039 noted above. I take two-thirds of those values as alternative demographic adjustments.[20]

3. SUMMARY OF THE NON-ACA CHANGES THAT ARE QUANTIFIED IN THIS BOOK

The effects of changing demographics are entered in the top row of table 9.4's top panel. As in table 9.3, the table's columns differ according to time period and whether low- or high-end estimates are used. The high-end estimates are the alternative demographic adjustments noted above, which assume that increasing education is a force toward increasing employment. The low-end estimates are the population-aging adjustment point estimate minus 0.003. The next row shows the long-term impact on aggregate hours per adult of the non-ACA tax effects shown in table 9.3. For any tax effect $d\tau$ in percentage points, the long-term impact on aggregate hours per adult is calculated according to formula (9.1):

(9.1)
$$\frac{\eta}{1+\eta}\ln\left(1-\frac{d\tau}{100-\tau_0}\right)$$

where τ_0 is the average marginal labor income tax rate (in percentage points) at the beginning of the time interval and η is the Frisch wage elasticity of the supply of aggregate hours.[21] I take τ_0 to be 40.2 and 44.5 percent for the interval beginning in 2007 and 2012–13, respectively.[22] Table 9.3 sets $\eta = 0.6$. The next row of the table adds the two,

TABLE 9.4. Forecasts of labor hours in 2016–17: building blocks and results

The Frisch wage elasticity of aggregate labor supply is assumed to be 0.6

Panel I: Long-run impacts on log aggregate hours per adult of factors that change during the specified time interval.

Potential causes of change	Ending in 2016–17 and beginning in:			
	2012–13		2007	
	Low	High	Low	High
Population aging and other demographic shifts	−0.018	−0.010	−0.042	−0.026
Non-ACA tax/distortion effects from table 9.3	0.020	0.048	−0.027	−0.008
Non-ACA total	0.002	0.038	−0.069	−0.033
ACA tax effects from chapter 6	−0.031	−0.031	−0.031	−0.031
ACA tax effects from table 9.1	−0.001	−0.001	−0.001	−0.001
ACA's effect on "employment lock"	−0.005	0.000	−0.005	0.000
ACA total	−0.038	−0.033	−0.037	−0.032
ACA and non-ACA totals combined	**−0.035**	**0.005**	**−0.106**	**−0.066**

Panel II: Estimate the part of the long-run impact that will be realized by 2016–17

	Time interval beginning:			
	2012–13		2007	
	Low	High	Low	High
Fraction of long-run impact realized in three years	0.92	0.92	0.92	0.92
Adjustment for ACA provisions taking effect after early 2014	0	0.20	0	0.20
Predicted change in log aggregate hours per adult	**−0.033**	**0.011**	**−0.098**	**−0.055**
Actual index of labor per capita at the beginning of the time interval	92.0	92.0	100.0	100.0
Index of aggregate hours per adult predicted for 2016–17	**89.0**	**93.0**	**90.7**	**94.7**

Notes: When the data becomes available, the bottom line in the table should be compared to an index of aggregate hours (including public sector workers and zeros for persons not working) per person that is not adjusted for age. At the time of writing, the latest available value for the index (April 2014) is 93.1.

showing how I expect the non-ACA factors to increase log aggregate hours per adult after 2012–13, including the effects of changing demographics. In other words, without the ACA the labor market would continue to slowly recover as measured by hours per adult. The last two columns in that row show that, even without the ACA, I would expect log hours per adult to remain below its 2007 values, primarily thanks to the aging effect but also owing to a lingering recession. As noted below, however, the numerical values in the third row of the table are not the exact amount I am predicting for the counterfactual because I still need to acknowledge the fact that only part of the long-term effects of a tax will be realized after the ACA subsidies begin but before 2017.

The next three rows of table 9.3 summarize the ACA effects and add them to the non-ACA effects. For the period 2012–13 to 2016–17, the ACA and non-ACA effects go in opposite directions, but the table shows that I expect the ACA effects will dominate. In other words, I expect the ACA to essentially stop the recovery as measured by hours per adult, if not significantly reverse it.

4. A NEW MINIMUM WAGE

At the time of writing, there is discussion of raising both federal and state minimum wages. Minimum wages by themselves reduce employment and increase the fraction of employment that is full time, with the amount related to the value for the minimum wage. However, if new minimum wages go into effect while the ACA is in place, it may be inaccurate to assume that their effects are similar to historical effects because the ACA influences the structure of wages especially among low-skill workers. The ACA also affects the composition of compensation and therefore the degree to which employers can adjust to higher minimum wages by restricting compensation.

I do not have estimates of minimum wage effects and their interaction with the ACA. If significant minimum wage changes occur before 2017, my forecasts will need to be adjusted for that.

5. THE ACA MAY CREATE A DEMAND FOR "STIMULUS"

To the extent that the ACA depresses the labor market, it may create demand for additional assistance for the poor and unemployed, which would further depress the labor market. The point here is not to critique such assistance—Mulligan (2014b) suggests that additional assistance might be a reasonable response—but to clarify that such a response to the ACA is not included in my impact estimates and needs to be added if such a response occurs. For example, if the EUC program were reinstated because of (or coincident with) the labor market effects of the ACA, then the 2.9 percentage points of compensation should be added to the marginal tax rate beginning at the time that the program started paying benefits again. For that matter, the same kind of calculation should be made for any change in the rules for assisting the poor, unemployed, and financially distressed, or any other change in marginal tax rates, regardless of what motivated the new policies. Mulligan (2012b) has the necessary ingredients for calculations related to food stamp expansions, additions to unemployment benefits, changes in the duration of unemployment benefits, and other policies.

The combination of the ACA and entitlement program growth may significantly increase payroll or income taxes. It seems unlikely that the federal payroll and income tax rates increase before 2017, but if those taxes did change then their effects should be added to the ACA's impact for the purposes of predicting labor market activity in 2016–17.

6. THE ACA IS REPEALED IN 2017 OR SOME TIME THEREAFTER

The long-term impacts of repealing the ACA (rather than letting the law continue) and replacing it with the policies in effect before the ACA was passed are the opposite of the long-term impacts of passing the ACA (e.g., as estimated in table 9.2's first column). A likely time for a repeal is in 2017 or some time thereafter, after the current administration has left office. However, the economic changes after repeal are unlikely to equal this long-term impact because the counterfactual of letting the law continue involves economic changes itself, especially to the extent that 2017 (or whatever is the year of repeal) is close enough to 2014 that the economic effects of the ACA will still be accumulating. For example, if, after the passage of the ACA but before its repeal, the capital stock is on a trajectory to fall 3 percent below trend in the long run because of the ACA (and no other factors are causing capital to deviate from trend), but the repeal occurs soon enough that it falls only 1 percent, then repealing the ACA will move the capital stock back to the trend it was on before the law took effect and therefore move capital back less than the amount of the ACA's long-term impact.

D. The Outlook for Capital and GDP Even without the ACA

The capital stock and GDP tend to increase over time with the amount of labor and with total factor productivity.[23] I assume that a permanent and unanticipated tax change that reduces the amount of labor per person (but does not affect total factor productivity) would, in the long run, reduce capital and production by the same percentage, relative to their trends. If the tax shock also affects the quality or efficiency of labor, then the long-term impact on the logs of capital and production (relative to trend) will be the long-term impact on the log of labor adjusted for quality and efficiency. As noted above, a number of tax or taxlike changes would occur between 2007 and 2017 even without the ACA, so I expect capital and output to deviate from their trends during those years.

Over a three-year horizon immediately after the tax change, though, capital would make only about one-third of its adjustment.[24] The adjustment of capital slows down the adjustment of labor somewhat. I assume that log labor makes 92 percent of its long-term adjustment during the first three years.[25] With log labor adjusting 92 percent over the three-year horizon and log capital adjusting 33 percent, log output adjusts about three-quarters over the same horizon.[26] To put it another way, labor adjusts more than output over the three-year horizon and therefore labor per capita and productivity move in opposite directions relative to their trend.

I focus on the three-year horizon because some of the largest impulses shown in tables 9.3 and 9.4, especially the ACA's subsidies, occur at the end of 2013 or the beginning of 2014, which is three years prior to the middle of 2016–17. Other events occurred earlier, the employer penalty occurs later, and aging is ongoing. The early effects of the ACA may (or may not) be prolonged somewhat as market participants adjust to the ACA's new incentives. For all of these reasons, the "high" columns in table 9.4 assume that an additional 20 percent (of the 92 percent) of the impact that the ACA's taxes are expected to have within three years is not yet realized before 2017. Regardless of how those issues are settled, I expect that a large majority of the labor adjustments, and a majority of the output adjustments, occur within three years of a tax change.

E. Summary of Predictions for 2016–17

1. LABOR HOURS PER ADULT

Panel II of table 9.4 shows the bottom-line predictions for labor per adult in 2016–17. I take the long-term log labor adjustment from Panel

I and multiply it by 0.92 to get the three-year adjustment of log labor and, when applicable, adjust for ACA provisions taking effect after early 2014. Notably, I predict that labor per adult in 2016–17 will not significantly exceed what it is at the time I am writing, even though the index has been increasing for the past four years. The bottom row of the table puts the predictions in terms of an index of labor hours per adult normalized to 100 in 2007. I predict that the index will be 5–11 percent below what it was in 2007, which is potentially as low as the trough of the recession. Without the ACA, the labor market would continue to slowly recover as measured by hours per adult, but the ACA reverses that recovery, and may reverse it to the point of testing the recession lows. Appendix 9.1 puts this forecast in the context of historical changes in the index.

The predictions for 2016–17 labor per adult are similar if they are built from the 2007 data (and thereby ignoring most of the recession) to what they are when built from the 2012–13 data.

2. ECONOMIC GROWTH

Using the long-term log labor impact estimates shown in table 9.4 (averaging the two "Low" columns and the two "High" columns), I estimate that the combination of ACA and non-ACA events occurring between 2012–13 and 2016–17 have a long-term impact on log labor hours per adult ranging from −0.029 to +0.012, which is shown in the top row of table 9.5. This range refers to labor per adult, but I want to forecast GDP per capita, so the second row of table 9.5 adjusts for the slow trend in adults per capita that derives from the fact that the number of children has fallen somewhat in recent years. Chapter 8 estimates that log labor hours adjusted for quality and efficiency increases 0.009 (relative to the log of unadjusted labor hours) in the long run as a consequence of the ACA. I therefore estimate that the long-term impact of both ACA and non-ACA events on the log of real GDP per capita relative to its trend is 0.009 plus the range of impacts for log labor hours per capita: the combination is the range of −0.012 to +0.029, as shown in the top half of table 9.5.[27]

As noted above, I expect GDP per capita to make about three-quarters of its adjustment by 2016–17, which means that by then the log of real GDP per capita will have deviated from its trend by −0.009

TABLE 9.5. Forecasts of economic growth between 2012–13 and 2016–17

The Frisch wage elasticity of aggregate labor supply is assumed to be 0.6

	Low	High
Long-run real GDP impact of all factors during time interval that change labor per capita		
Holding labor quality and efficiency constant (table 9.4)	−0.029	0.012
Increase in adults per capita	0.008	0.008
ACA impact on labor quality and efficiency (table 8.3)	0.009	0.009
Total	−0.012	0.029
Fraction of long-run deviation realized in three years	0.74	0.74
Deviation from trend realized by 2016–17	−0.009	0.021
Trend growth (four years)	0.016	0.040
Cumulative change in log real GDP per capita	0.007	0.061
Annualized growth rate of real GDP per capita	**0.2%**	**1.5%**
Addendum: Federal Reserve Board projection range	**1.2%**	**2.3%**

Notes: The Federal Reserve Board projections are from March 2014. I inferred their per-capita real GDP growth rates by subtracting 1 percent per year from their aggregate real GDP growth rates.

to +0.021. I take the trend (that is, non-ACA determinants of total factor productivity) between 2012–13 and 2016–17 to be in the range 0.016 to 0.040, which means my estimated log real GDP per capita change for this time interval is 0.007 to 0.061. As an average annualized rate of real GDP growth per person, that's about 0.2–1.5 percent per year.[28] Of course, the growth rate will fluctuate from quarter to quarter during that time, which means I predict there will be a quarter or quarters with negative seasonally adjusted real GDP growth per capita. Negative growth in quarterly real GDP per capita is fairly rare, about as rare as recessions are.

In March 2014, the Federal Reserve Board updated its projections for economic growth as far ahead as 2016. At an annualized rate, they expect aggregate real GDP to grow in a range between 2.2 and 3.3 percent per year (Board of Governors of the Federal Reserve System 2014). Because it has been at least 10 years since population growth most recently and significantly exceeded 1 percent per year, I infer that the Federal Reserve range for real GDP per capita projections are 1.2–2.3 percent per year, and maybe a bit greater. Their range of growth rate projections hardly overlaps with mine. I am not aware of the inner workings of the Federal Reserve, but on the basis of their speeches and papers I suspect they are paying little attention to the many implicit taxes that have emerged since 2007, including those contained in the ACA. I suspect GDP growth has continued to come in below their projections (Cochrane 2014) and will continue to do so over the next couple of years, because their current forecasts do not fully consider implicit taxes.

3. INSURANCE COVERAGE

Table 7.5 from chapter 7 predicts that 19 million more nonpoor nonelderly will be insured as a consequence of the ACA. Assuming that the Congressional Budget Office (2014a, table B-2) is correct that the propensity to be uninsured would have been pretty constant without the ACA, my impact estimate means that, adjusting for population growth, the number uninsured will ultimately fall 19 million after 2012–13.

Table 7.5 also predicts that 21 million fewer nonpoor nonelderly people will have employer coverage as a consequence of the ACA. Assuming that the CBO (2014a, table B-2) is correct that about 7 million people would have been added to employer plans without the ACA by 2017, my impact estimate means that the number of people insured through an employer will ultimately fall 13 million after 2012–13. As noted in chapter 7, the numerical coverage impact estimates in this book are less robust than the aggregate hours impact estimates.

4. SENSITIVITY ANALYSIS

Labor market change is the sum of the contribution of non-ACA factors—according to table 9.4, somewhere between 0.002 and 0.038 after 2012–13, largely owing to continued recovery from the recession—and the impact of the ACA. Thus, different models of the ACA's impact involve adding varying impact amounts to the non-ACA factors.[29]

One of the "different models" comes from Cutler and Sood (2010), who claimed that "modernization aspects" of the ACA would cut wasteful health spending by employer plans and by this mechanism "boost employment by 250,000 to 400,000 per year" over the next decade, beginning almost immediately. Over a four-year time frame, that is 1.0 to 1.6 million jobs, or about 0.7–1.1 percent of employment. If we take the midpoint of their range, 0.9 percent, the impact estimate from Cutler

TABLE 9.6. Forecasts as a function of impact model

for the period 2012–13 to 2016–17. The table shows adjustments to add to the forecasts in tables 9.4 and 9.5.

	Growth rate to be adjusted:	
	Real GDP per capita (annual average rate)	Aggregate hours (cumulative growth)
Benchmark model	0	0
Hours misreporting	0.1%	0.1%
Add 10 %-pts to non-ACA MTR	−0.2%	−0.5%
More elastic labor supply	−0.5%	−1.1%

Notes: In order to calculate an alternative forecast, take a forecast from the bottom line of table 9.4 (aggregate hours) or table 9.5 (real GDP per capita) and add the adjustment above. The alternative models are less different from the benchmark in terms of real GDP per capita because of the labor quality effects (see table 8.3). "More elastic labor supply" refers to a Frisch wage elasticity of aggregate hours of one, rather than 0.6.

and Sood is four percentage points greater than mine (−3.1 percent, or somewhat more negative with employment lock). In other words, employment per adult is supposed to increase somewhere between 1.1 and 4.5 percent between 2012–13 and 2016–17, mostly because of the ACA, whereas my table 9.4 predicts that it will decline and the decline may be more than 3 percent.

Table 9.6 shows how the forecasts from my alternative impact models are different from those based on my benchmark model (tables 9.4 and 9.5). For example, with an alternate Frisch wage elasticity of one, the forecast range for the annualized real GDP growth rate is 0.5 percentage points (bottom row of table 9.6) less than the benchmark range of 0.1–1.4 percent (bottom row of table 9.5). In other words, the alternate forecast range is −0.3 to 1.1 percent. Table 9.6 also shows that the aggregate hours forecasts are more sensitive to the various assumptions than real GDP growth is. Note that real GDP takes longer to adjust and depends on quality-adjusted labor, which is affected less by the ACA.

Appendix 9.1: The Index of Hours per Adult

The purpose of this appendix is to show how to construct the hours index that is being forecast. The index reflects a time series of aggregate hours paid per adult per week, including zeros for persons not employed during the week (people on paid vacation count as employed), with calendar year 2007 normalized to 100. The hours time series is itself the average of two series: one based on the household survey and the other (largely) based on the establishment survey. For the household survey series, I use the monthly Current Population Survey Merged Outgoing Rotation Groups public use microdata files for calendar years 2007–13, limited to persons age 16 and over. For each month, I calculate average hours worked from the week prior to the interview, weighted by the CPS "Final Weight," and then I average the months to a calendar year.

The U.S. government also conducts a monthly survey of employers (the "establishment survey"), which asks employers about their employees' paid work time (that is, including paid sick days and paid vacation days) during the reference week. The establishment survey omits unincorporated self-employed and agricultural workers (U.S. Bureau of Labor Statistics 2014a), who are about 8 percent of the workforce. I therefore measure the self-employed and agricultural workers (counting their overlap only once) from the household survey and add them to the payroll employees total from the establishment survey. The sum is multiplied by average weekly work hours per employee from the establishment survey and then divided by total persons age 16 and over to arrive at another estimate of weekly hours worked per adult.[30]

Figure 9.2 compares the two series. Their trends after 2010 have been close, but the correction for self-employed is important here because the unincorporated self-employed series has a significant downward trend over time. As another reference, figure 9.2 also shows a series from the American Time Use Survey (ATUS), but it is not used to form my hours index.[31]

Figure 9.3's red circles show the historical values for the aforementioned index, which combines the household and establishment surveys. The horizontal red line shows the average value of the index in 2012 and 2013, which is the starting period for the changes estimated in the left half of table 9.4. The wide and tall bar for 2016–17 is the forecast range shown at the bottom of table 9.4. The short bar is the rosy scenario without the ACA: what would happen to labor per adult if the "high" non-ACA labor changes were realized—the −0.033 entry in table 9.4—and the ACA impact was zero.

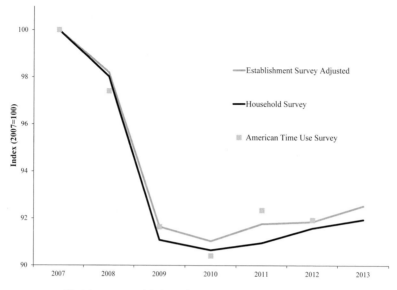

FIGURE 9.2. Work hours per adult, from three sources.

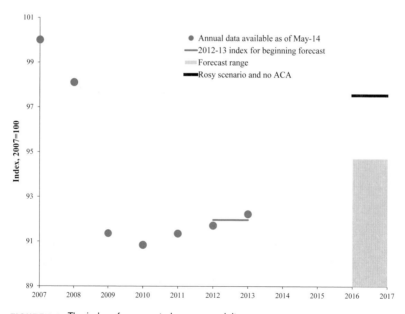

FIGURE 9.3. The index of aggregate hours per adult.

If the data shown in figure 9.3 are revised by the Bureau of Labor Statistics, then the predictions for the value of the index need to be revised accordingly.

Appendix 9.2: Measurement of the Employer and Employee Wedges

Labor wedges are quantitative diagnostics for, among other things, detecting the sources of labor market change (Mulligan 2005).[32] Table 9.7 shows some rough estimates and their components.[33] The employee wedge is one of those measures, and it tends to grow during a recession and contract during an expansion. Its formula is:

(9.2)
$$\Delta \ln(\text{comp}) - \Delta \ln(\text{hours}) - \Delta \ln(\text{consumption})$$
$$-\frac{1}{\eta} \Delta \ln(\text{hours per adult})$$

where Δ denotes a difference over time and η denotes an assumed value for the Frisch wage elasticity of the supply of aggregate work hours. "comp" and "consumption" denote aggregate employee compensation and per capita consumption expenditure, respectively. Consumption expenditure is the sum of private nondurable good expenditure, private services expenditure, and government nondefense consumption expenditure. "hours" denotes aggregate hours and is the ratio of hours per adult from figure 9.3 multiplied by adult population. Each of these components is shown in its own row in table 9.7 for the three time periods 2007, 2010, and 2012–13. The log changes for 2007 through 2012–13 and 2010 through 2012–13 are shown in the next two columns of the table. Like equation (9.2), the last column of the table shows how the components are combined to calculate the employee wedge.

The bottom two rows of the table show estimates for the employee wedge, depending on the time interval and on the assumed value for η. Both rows show that the labor market contracted significantly over the full time period relative to what was happening with wages and consumption. At the risk of oversimplifying, I will note that the 0.157 and 0.102 estimates say that much of the recession still lingered as of

TABLE 9.7. Measurement of labor wedges

Economic variable	Units	Amounts in levels:			Log change from:		Coefficient in wedge estimate:	
		2007	2010	2012–13	2007	2010	Employer	Employee
Consumption expenditure per person	$	33,953	35,510	38,033	0.113	0.069	0	−1
GDP	$ billions	14,480	14,958	16,522	0.132	0.099	1	0
Employee compensation	$ billions	7,899	7,967	8,736	0.101	0.092	−1	1
Aggregate work hours per week	Millions	5,330	4,966	5,169	−0.031	0.040	0	−1
Work hours per adult per week	Hours	23.0	20.9	21.1	−0.084	0.012	0	−1/η
Employer wedge					0.031	0.007		
Employee wedge: $\eta = 0.6$					0.157	−0.037		
Employee wedge: $\eta = 1.0$					0.102	−0.029		

Notes: Consumption expenditure includes nondefense government, but excludes durable goods. Work hours per adult are from figure 9.3 (not adjusted for population aging). Both log changes have 2012–13 as the ending date. η denotes the Frisch wage elasticity of aggregate hours supply.

2012–13. The −0.037 and −0.029 say that the employee wedge was moving slightly in the other "expansion" direction during the last part of the period, 2010 through 2012–13.

The employer wedge is discussed further in the main text. The wedge that emerged after 2007 remains as of 2012–13 (see the 0.031). Some of the growth of the employer wedge occurred after 2010 (see the 0.007). An online appendix at charts.acasideeffects.com further interprets employee and employer wedges, and relates them to labor market forecasting.

10 | Romneycare Times Eleven

One of Massachusetts's health reforms was passed in 2006 and implemented over the subsequent two years.[1] Romneycare, as it is called, specified that state residents must have health insurance, or potentially face a monetary penalty.[2] It created a couple of health plans with means-tested subsidized premiums.[3] The reform also penalized those employers that did not provide health insurance for enough of its employees, with the penalty amount linked to the number of employees on the payroll. Roughly speaking, the nationwide Affordable Care Act has the same three elements, which will take effect over the next two years.

The federal government and other advocates of the ACA have insisted that the federal law's negative impacts (that is, in the direction of a smaller labor market) will be hardly visible, by pointing to Massachusetts's experience with Romneycare. Because the Massachusetts labor market did not noticeably contract relative to the rest of the nation after Romneycare went into effect (Dubay, Long, and Lawton 2012), the U.S. Department of Health and Human Services said, "The experience in Massachusetts . . . suggest[s] that the health care law will improve the affordability and accessibility of health care without significantly affecting the labor market" (Contorno 2013). As an Urban Institute study put it, "the evidence from Massachusetts would suggest that national health reform does not imply job loss and stymied economic growth."[4]

This book begins with a warning against assuming that health coverage expansions are a "free lunch," let alone assuming that health coverage expansions can pay for themselves by growing the economy. It recommends instead a careful look at the law and its economic incentives. The same advice applies to Romneycare. The purpose of this chapter is therefore to describe Romneycare from a tax perspective and to replicate the key ACA calculations from chapters 3, 4, and 5 using the parameters from the Massachusetts law. Section A explains how Romneycare's penalty provisions created new, albeit small, taxes on work. The new implicit tax rates coming from new and expanded Romneycare subsidies, and from interactions with old subsidy programs, are examined in sections B and C. Section D concludes.

Although Western European countries have significantly higher payroll tax rates to pay for public health coverage for all of their citizens, Massachusetts need not have significantly higher payroll taxes after Romneycare than before. One consideration is that Massachusetts already had high taxes and high coverage even before the measure was passed. It was not designed to increase coverage as much as the ACA is. Also note that the federal government helped pay for much of Romneycare, whereas the ACA does not turn to any higher power for funding. As noted below, Romneycare encouraged employers in the state to help employees use pretax dollars to pay for health insurance, which means that the U.S. Treasury would be passively assisting employees in the form of reduced personal income and payroll tax receipts from Massachusetts. The state also had federal money that was attached to a Medicaid waiver from the federal Department of Health and Human Services (Powell 2012). Thus one should not assume that Romneycare would be elevating Massachusetts labor income tax rates to Western European levels, but instead carefully measure the law's incentives.

A. Romneycare's Employer Penalty

Romneycare included monetary penalties on employers that do not offer health insurance to their full-time employees and on individuals who fail to participate in the health plans that are made available to them. These penalties are known as the employer and individual responsibility provisions, respectively. The individual penalty is also described as the "individual mandate penalty."

Romneycare had two types of employer penalties. The first was a "Fair Share Employer Contribution" penalty of $295 per FTE (full-time equivalent) employee per year for large employers failing to offer health insurance and make a fair and reasonable contribution toward premiums.[5] FTEs are capped at the number of employees. Unlike the ACA's employer penalty, Romneycare's $295 is deductible from the employer's federal business taxes.

Massachusetts law defines FTE in terms of aggregate work hours so that the penalty creates an extra marginal cost on assessable employers for increasing those hours, so long as the hours are at or above the threshold for "large employer."[6] For large employers with more employees than FTEs, the penalty was proportional to aggregate hours and therefore neutral in terms of whether an employer changes labor hours by adjusting the number of employees or by adjusting the hours per employee. Thus, unlike the federal penalty, the Massachusetts penalty did not give employers an incentive to have twenty-niners. In a sense, the Massachusetts penalty was a smoothed version of the ACA penalty in that it increased linearly with hours per employee rather than jumping sharply at the thirtieth weekly hour.

For large employers with fewer employees than FTEs, for example, because the average employee works more than 40 hours per week, the Massachusetts penalty was just an employment tax and gave employers incentives to have fewer employees working more hours per week. For these reasons alone, it would be surprising if Massachusetts employers were responding to the state's employer penalty by cutting hours per employee.

The second "free rider" employer penalty applies to large employers failing to provide employees with "cafeteria plans," which are arrangements for buying health insurance (perhaps on the individual market) with pretax dollars and with the employer's administrative assistance in terms of withholding employee health payments and delivering them to the insurer. Employers are not required to contribute funds for payments for the insurance that employees obtain through the cafeteria plan. Large employers that fail to offer a cafeteria plan are liable for the health safety net (Massachusetts's system of uncompensated care) costs incurred by their uninsured employees. Despite the fact that a nontrivial number of employers do not offer a cafeteria plan, as of July 2011 no employer in Massachusetts had been held liable under this second employer penalty provision (Blue Cross Blue Shield of Massachusetts Foundation 2011). I therefore treat the free rider penalty as zero and expect that its primary function was to bring federal dollars into the state to help finance health insurance coverage for some of those who would otherwise be uninsured.[7]

Table 10.1's first column compares the Romneycare Fair Share Em-

TABLE 10.1. Employment taxes: 2010 Romneycare vs. 2016 ACA

	Employer penalty[a]	Subsidy forgone	
Amounts			
Romneycare[b]	0.3	3.0	
ACA[b]	4.0	5.5	
ACA as a ratio to Romneycare	12.3	1.8	
Frequency			
Romneycare	20%	4%	
ACA	26%	20%	
ACA as a ratio to Romneycare	1.3	4.8	
Frequency*Amount			Row sum
Romneycare[b]	0.1	0.1	0.2
ACA[b]	1.0	1.1	2.2
ACA as a ratio to Romneycare	**16.3**	**8.8**	**11.3**

[a] Romneycare's employer penalty was a tax on full-time equivalents (with a cap), whereas the ACA's is a tax on full-time employees.
[b] Measured as a weekly hours equivalent (work hours needed to pay off the penalty).

ployer Contribution penalty (as of 2010) to the ACA's employer penalty (as of 2016). As noted above, the former penalty is $295 per year. In 2014 dollars, and adjusting for employer payroll taxes, the salary equivalent of the penalty is $297.[8] By comparison, the salary equivalent of the federal penalty, $3,163, is 10.6 times greater.[9] People in Massachusetts also earn somewhat more per hour—16 percent more by my estimates—so they can pay off the same dollar penalty with fewer hours of work. Measured as an hours equivalent, the federal penalty (4.0 hours per week) is 12.3 times the Romneycare penalty (0.3 hours, or about 20 minutes, per week). Telling people in Massachusetts to work 20 minutes per week for their government is not the same as telling Americans to work more than four hours for theirs.

The Romneycare penalty also affects a lesser fraction of the Massachusetts labor market than the fraction of the U.S. labor market directly affected by the federal penalty. The Medical Expenditure Panel Survey (MEPS) reports national and region-specific propensities of employees to work at an employer that does not offer insurance to any of its employees. To be conservative about the differing propensities of the state and the nation, I assume that Massachusetts is comparable to the rest of the New England region and rescale the ACA employer penalty frequency from table 5.2 by the ratio of the MEPS New England propensity (9.5 percent) to the MEPS nationwide propensity (12.6 percent).[10] Thus the U.S. prevalence, so to speak, of the ACA's employer penalty is about 1.3 times that of the Romneycare penalty in Massachusetts. As discussed earlier in this book, the product of the prevalence or frequency and the penalty amount summarizes the aggregate importance of the penalty. The last row of table 10.1 shows that, in these terms, the ACA's penalty is 16.3 times greater than the Romneycare penalty.[11]

B. Romneycare's Not-So-New Implicit Employment Tax

Massachusetts adults not offered insurance by an employer in the last six months, not eligible for Medicare or Medicaid, and living in a family with income between 100 percent and 300 percent of the federal poverty line (FPL) are, under Romneycare, eligible to participate in Commonwealth Care (CommCare), which was a choice of four health insurance plans subsidized by the state and managed by Medicaid Managed Care Organizations (Blue Cross Blue Shield of Massachusetts Foundation 2011).[12]

As with the ACA's exchange subsidies, the CommCare subsidies contain two implicit taxes: a full-time employment tax (FTET) faced by ESI workers because their employment status renders them ineligible for subsidies, and an income tax faced by people who are insured by CommCare while they are working.[13] The amount of the implicit full-time employment tax depends on how much workers value the subsidy that they forgo by working full time. As a first step at valuing the CommCare subsidy, I looked at the program's cost, net of participant premiums and administrative costs, in fiscal year 2010: $717 million. Because aggregate enrollment during that year was 157,356 member years, the average subsidy for a full year of enrollment was about $4,900 in 2014 dollars. At a 25 percent marginal income tax rate the salary equivalent is about $6,600. The value of this subsidy depends on plan features, and CommCare has features that probably make it unattractive to a number of households in the eligible income range. CommCare is for adults only: parents who left ESI (or left the unsubsidized individual purchase market) for CommCare would have to put their children on Medicaid/CHIP, buy separate coverage for them, or leave them uninsured. CommCare is typically Medicaid-managed and does not have the same network of providers as do unsubsidized plans. Medicaid may carry a social stigma. People cannot join CommCare until they have been six months without the opportunity for affordable insurance. For these reasons, I take the participant value of CommCare coverage to be 60 percent of the tax-adjusted cost shown. Recall that most of this book uses a 75 percent valuation factor for the ACA's exchange plans, which have few if any of the unattractive features noted above.

CommCare's similarity to Medicaid and its low enrollment may help explain why Kolstad and Kowalski (2012) found that employees accepted lower wages when their employers began offering health insurance under Romneycare; employer insurance in Massachusetts (including the insurance workers obtain through cafeteria plans) is valuable to employees because the alternative is something like Medicaid, or no insurance at all. But this doesn't mean employers that begin to offer insurance under the ACA can be sure their employees will accept lower wages, because a significant fraction of those employees could obtain coverage, plus a subsidy, without employer assistance, and the coverage is supposed to be good enough for their congressman and senator (recall the Grassley amendment from chapter 2).

The features-adjusted salary equivalent of the ACA's implicit full-time employment tax used in most of this book is $6,297, which is 59 percent more than the aforementioned value of the CommCare subsidies. Moreover, people in Massachusetts also earn somewhat more per hour, so they can pay off the same dollar penalty with fewer hours of work. With this adjustment, the ACA's implicit FTET is about 1.8 times Romneycare's, as shown in the top part of table 10.1.

The novel parts of Romneycare's implicit FTET are far less prevalent in Massachusetts than the ACA's will be in the United States. The Romneycare eligible income range stopped at 300 percent of the poverty line, as compared to the 100–400 percent range under the ACA. I assume that Romneycare adds little value to the assistance available to households below 150 percent FPL, because Massachusetts already had Medicaid for adults up to 133 percent FPL and children up to 200 percent

FPL (Powell 2012).[14] Using the same data and procedures as I did to make table 4.1, except limiting the sample to Massachusetts and limiting the eligible income range to 150–300 percent of the poverty line, I found that only 10 percent of Massachusetts workers (in 2011) faced the implicit FTET. Moreover, if and when these people work less, many of them will do so by unemployment and CommCare does not have much to offer the unemployed compared to what they had before Romneycare. For many years, Massachusetts already had health insurance assistance for the unemployed through its MassHealth Medical Security Plan and MassHealth Essential programs.[15] I therefore further adjust the 10 percent incidence of the FTET by the fraction of work reductions that involve hours reductions or exits from the labor force: 42 percent (Mulligan 2012b, table 3.5).

As a result, the ACA's implicit FTET is almost five times more prevalent than Romneycare's, which is consistent with the fact that CommCare has so few participants (more on this below). The product of implicit FTET frequency and amount is almost nine times greater under the ACA. Table 10.1's bottom right entries add the two FTETs together and find that the ACA's employment taxes will be about 11 times more important for the United States than Romneycare's were for Massachusetts.

C. Romneycare's New Implicit Income Tax

Chapter 5 explains how the ACA's exchange subsidies are both an employment tax and an income tax, with the latter faced by persons who are insured on the exchanges with subsidies because the amount they pay for their participation increases with their income. CommCare subsidies have the same general character. As in chapter 5, the purpose here is to estimate the implicit marginal income tax rate faced by the non-ESI workers who are subject to one as well as the fraction of the potential workforce in that category of workers.

Figure 10.1's stair-shaped function shows the 2010 sliding scale payment schedule (Massachusetts Health Connector 2010), which ends at 300 percent FPL. Non-ESI workers from families above 300 percent of the poverty line have to buy coverage on the individual market, but under Romneycare they likely can do so with pretax dollars using their

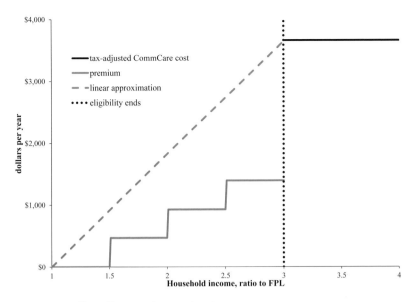

FIGURE 10.1. CommCare premiums and costs.

employer's cafeteria plan. The horizontal line in figure 10.1 therefore shows the average annual cost of CommCare, including both the government subsidies and premium payments by CommCare participants and multiplied by a tax-adjustment factor, in order to indicate what a person would pay for the same type of care once his or her income went above the 300 percent threshold and he or she was no longer eligible for CommCare's subsidized coverage.[16]

On a flat part of figure 10.1's payment schedule, premium payments do not change with a small change in family income. On the other hand, an income change that crosses a vertical part of the payment schedule triggers a comparatively massive change in the payment. As in chapter 5's figure 5.1, figure 10.1 approximates the step function with a straight dashed line whose single slope is equal to the average of the various slopes along the stair-shaped function, weighted by the width of the income interval in which the slope applies. With this approximation, the slope of the dashed line is the marginal income tax rate that derives from CommCare's premium schedule and eligibility rules. The slope varies with family size because the number of dollars represented by the federal poverty line varies by family size, with the maximum slope of 16.9 percent for a one-person family. Using the distribution of family sizes among the Massachusetts members of the March 2012 Current Population Survey with incomes between the poverty line and three times the poverty line, I estimate that the average slope among CommCare participants is 13.0 percent. In other words, CommCare participants typically face an additional 13.0 percent marginal tax on their income in addition to the usual personal income and payroll taxes. This does not count the implicit tax rate cut that comes from moving people off of means-tested uncompensated care, which I take to be 2.4 percentage points (as with the ACA). The combination of the two is 10.6 percent.

Recall from chapter 5 that the comparable average implicit marginal income tax rate for the ACA is 20.9 percent, which is almost double the implicit marginal income tax rate created by Romneycare.[17] Moreover, the ACA presents a larger share of potentially working nonelderly household heads and spouses nationwide with its implicit income taxes than Romneycare presented to the Massachusetts population: 11 percent and 6 percent, respectively. Even this understates the difference between Romneycare and the ACA in terms of implicit income taxes, because (1) some of the CommCare participants would, without Romneycare, have been on one of the longstanding Medicaid programs; and (2) the aforementioned 6 percent does not subtract nonworkers (e.g., housewives or early retirees) from CommCare enrollment. If two-thirds of the CommCare participants fit in one of these categories, then the aforementioned 6 percent would become 2 percent.[18] To a first-order approximation, I expect that the ACA's implicit income taxes will be 10 or 11 times more important nationwide than those of Romneycare were in Massachusetts.

D. Conclusion: Orders of Magnitude

Overall, the ACA erodes nationwide average work incentives about 11 times more than Romneycare did in the state of Massachusetts. Table 10.1 is a good summary of why the differences are so dramatic: the amounts involved and the fraction of the potential workforce presented with a new income or employment tax as a consequence of health reform. The primary difference between Romneycare and ACA employer penalties is the nominal amount: $295 versus $2,000 (plus health cost inflation), respectively. Also significant are the facts that the ACA penalty is not business-tax-deductible and that Massachusetts employers are especially likely to offer health insurance even without a penalty.

The subsidized coverage in Massachusetts has barriers to participation that are absent from the ACA and thereby make Romneycare's implicit FTET less significant. Romneycare came after other permanent forms of assistance for Massachusetts workers leaving ESI jobs,[19] whereas, before the ACA, the federal government had no significant and permanent program for assisting nonelderly nonpoor adults with health insurance while they are not working. Accounting for the prevalence of various taxes, I find that the ACA's implicit income tax (not shown in table 10.1) is about 11 times greater than Romneycare's.

As noted in chapter 9, the ACA has other provisions that affect incentives to work, such as a Medicaid expansion and relief from the individual mandate penalty. The same is true for Romneycare. Just as chapter 9 shows that the additional provisions are (collectively and individually) less than the incentives created by the employer penalty and the exchange subsidies, the same can be shown for Romneycare (Mulligan 2013b).

Advocates of the ACA have dismissed concerns that the law might be trading off labor market activity for more redistribution, citing the absence of a Massachusetts-specific labor market contraction when that state passed its law mandating health insurance coverage. However, their argument assumes that the Massachusetts reform increased marginal tax rates in the state by roughly the same magnitude that the ACA will increase them in the United States. The assumption is no longer necessary, because this book applies the same incentive-measurement methodology to both health reforms. Not surprisingly, Massachusetts reduced incentives to work as it attempted to target assistance to low-income families. However, the state-average disincentive added by the Massachusetts law was at least an order of magnitude less than it will be nationwide with the ACA.

The obvious conclusion from these data is to expect the ACA to depress labor markets by at least an order of magnitude more than the

Massachusetts reform did. If Romneycare had depressed the Massa-chusetts labor market by 0.2 or 0.3 percent, that would simultaneously be difficult for econometricians to detect in the Massachusetts data and be right in line with my estimates of the nationwide labor market consequences of the ACA.

11 | Conclusions

Making health care more affordable for a family means alleviating its need to finance health-care spending by way of less spending on non-health goods, more work hours, or more productive work. The European experience suggests, and careful measurement of the Affordable Care Act's provisions confirms, that subsidizing health insurance in order to make it more affordable for a significant part of the population—as the ACA does—requires large new taxes. Many of the relevant ACA provisions are not called taxes by politicians or journalists but nonetheless are the economic equivalent of taxes.

A. Taxes Identified and Measured

A number of opinions as to the economic impact of the ACA and the evolution of the labor market were offered during the years following the law's implementation. Yet rarely do they mention the law's implicit taxes, let alone properly quantify them. Excluding my own work, I am unaware of any economic analysis of the ACA's implicit full-time employment tax, which is arguably the law's single biggest tax, that was published online or in print prior to 2014, even though the law has been in effect since 2010. The first half of this book brings the ACA's hidden taxes out into the open and quantifies their importance.

The ACA's three largest taxes are illustrated in figure 11.1, which is based on chapter 5's table 5.2. The first and most surprising is an implicit tax on full-time employment derived from premium and cost-sharing assistance being withheld from the full-time workers at an employer that offers affordable coverage, while the same employer's part-time workers and former employees are typically allowed to receive subsidies at no cost to the employer. It is the economic equivalent of a tax because the law would hardly be different if it had allowed all people to receive the assistance and financed the extra spending (relative to the actual ACA) with penalty assessments on every employer—especially those offering coverage—in amounts equal to

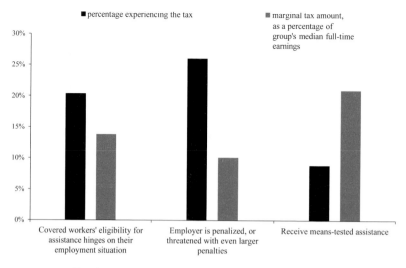

FIGURE 11.1. The size and prevalence of the ACA's three largest taxes in 2016.

the assistance received by full-time workers during the time of their employment.

The employer penalty is another full-time employment tax, but this one threatens employers that do *not* offer affordable coverage to their full-time employees. The third tax is a new implicit income tax experienced by potential workers who receive means-tested assistance while being covered on the ACA's new "exchanges" or "health insurance marketplaces."[1] The figure's black bars quantify the percentage of potential workers who experience each tax directly. Summing the black bars and subtracting eight percentage points for overlaps (many workers experience two of these taxes at the same time) shows that about half of the workforce will directly experience one of these three taxes.[2]

The red bars quantify the size of each tax among those included in the black bar as a percentage of what they would earn with a full-time schedule. The percentage varies among the workers facing any one of those taxes, so for the purpose of calculating figure 11.1's red bars I show a typical rate.[3] For the affected populations, all three new taxes have typical rates that are as high as or higher than payroll tax rates for employee and employer combined. The marginal income tax rate created by the ACA averages more than 20 percent among those who face it, and that is on top of the many longstanding federal and state taxes.

People normally work because it pays better than not working. Although figure 11.1 does not show it, the ACA puts millions of workers in a position where they have to pay for the privilege of working full time, meaning such workers would improve cash flow for themselves and their employer by working fewer hours per week, or not working at all. In 2016, as many as 80 million work hours per week, which is between 1 and 2 percent of all hours worked, will be rendered worthless to employers and employees because of the three taxes shown in figure 11.1.

Chapters 3, 4, and 5 show how the three disincentives are not experienced uniformly in the labor market. They are especially significant for low-skill workers. The disincentives are more significant for heads of households and their spouses than for working dependents. The disincentives can be largest for workers approaching age 65, but after age 65 only the employer penalty, if anything, directly affects them.

B. The Economic Consequences of the Health Reform

The ACA will have the nation working fewer hours, and working those hours less productively, such that its nonhealth spending will be twice diminished: once to pay for more health care and a second time because the economy is smaller and less productive than it would be without the law. I predict that the ACA's impacts—that is, the difference between the economy with the ACA and a hypothetical and otherwise similar economy without the ACA—will include about 3 percent less employment, 3 percent fewer aggregate work hours, 2 percent less GDP, and 2 percent less labor income (see chapter 8). During a typical week after the ACA is fully implemented, more than 50 million people (workers and dependents) will be experiencing significant labor market disruption, not to mention those experiencing lesser changes in their wages or work schedules.

The direction and order of magnitude of the employment and aggregate hours impacts are clear, but their precise magnitudes depend exactly on how the labor market responds to taxes generally, and the ACA's taxes specifically. In terms of the general tax responsiveness, I assume that the labor markets of the future will continue to respond as they have in the past as micro-econometricians have measured from "natural experiments" and other historical instances of tax changes. It would be going much too far to conclude that taxes do not matter, but one could reasonably assert that somewhat less, or somewhat more, responsiveness to taxes is consistent with the historical evidence. In addition, the ACA's taxes are unique: the politically precarious employer penalty is highly nonlinear as to the size of the employer, and avoidance of the implicit full-time employment tax requires participating in the law's new health insurance plans. Hardly any historical tax has been truly uniform across workers, but some of the concentration of the ACA's taxes is novel. This book analyzes the unique features of ACA taxes and displays sensitivity analysis, but without the luxury of as much historical evidence.

I do not assume that everyone has, or even that most people have, an intimate understanding of tax incentives. I use the historical experience from *actual* tax changes experienced by *actual* people, however knowledgeable or unaware people were during those episodes. The real question is whether taxpayers will be less knowledgeable than they have been in the past. Recall Mike Smith, introduced in chapter 1, who was able and willing to stop working once his district manager job was no longer necessary for getting health insurance. By retiring within 31 days of the start of the ACA's new insurance plans, Mike's actions reveal that he had advanced knowledge of the benefits contained in the law as they pertained to his situation. Or take Kathy Ezelle from Mobile, Alabama. In 2014 she was already thinking about how her new Social Security income would reduce her subsidy in 2015, and told AL.com that income "doesn't have to go up much for you to lose a lot of your subsidy" (Finch 2014).

People can also receive assistance and advice from others who are knowledgeable. Personal finance columnists began offering advice even before the exchanges opened in 2013 (Davidson 2013; Pender 2013), with headlines like "Lower 2014 Income Can Net Huge Health Care Subsidy." The federal and state governments have hired navigators—20,000 in California alone—to help people understand the exchanges and the application process (Bagley 2013). I also expect large employers to help their workers navigate the complexities of the ACA's health insurance plans. For example, Walmart is working "with a health coverage specialist to guide workers through the process of finding alternative coverage" (Tabuchi 2014). As noted in chapter 7, there are seasonal employers who perennially help their employees navigate the unemployment insurance system and, going forward, may find it to their advantage to help employees navigate the ACA's exchanges too.

The uncertainty of the ACA itself furthers the difficulty in assessing its ultimate impact. Will it be changed? How will the law be interpreted by those charged with enforcing it, who are not only the federal government but also state insurance regulators having to approve the plans offered on the exchanges? The labor market effects of the ACA will be less if the exchange plans are ultimately perceived to be more like Medicaid than like an employer-sponsored plan. If the employer penalty is repealed, indefinitely delayed, or weakly enforced, the ACA becomes less of an employment tax and more of an implicit income tax. As written, the ACA reduces the rate of growth of spending on Medicare, which is the longstanding public health insurance program for the elderly. If those reductions prove to be politically or technologically impossible, or the ACA otherwise turns out to be more expensive than anticipated, then one of the consequences of the ACA may be still more taxes on labor; the consequences of the additional taxes need to be added to the impacts estimated in this book.

A large majority of the workforce will work full time despite the two new full-time employment taxes. For them, the full-time employment tax is just an employment tax and thereby induces them to work fewer weeks and slightly longer weekly schedules than they would without the ACA. A smaller part of the workforce, the twenty-niners, makes a larger absolute change in their weekly work hours, in the direction of a shorter workweek, in order to avoid the full-time employment taxes. Perhaps contrary to the conventional wisdom, I predict an overall impact on average hours per employee of essentially zero.

The ACA reduces employment because it reduces the incentive for out-of-work people to accept jobs and because it subsidizes layoffs, quits, and early retirements. Before the ACA, people found health insurance to be less expensive when employed than it was when not working, and health insurance expenses were one reason unemployed people have been eager to get back to working in a position with coverage. But the ACA permanently reverses the calculus by giving people who do not work more opportunities for subsidized coverage than employed people will have. Employers and employees used to find layoffs, quits, and (before age 65) retirements to be financially costly because, among other things, many people want to have health insurance coverage even after their job ends. Employers have already realized that the ACA's exchange subsidies make early retirements less expensive (Dardick 2013). In effect, one of the easiest ways to get penalty-free assistance from the ACA is to be out of work.

The ACA also creates new incentives to underreport work hours and employment, or at least to find ways to avoid overreporting them. The ACA attempts to limit the ability of businesses to reorganize to avoid the employer penalty (National Federation of Independent Business 2011), but businesses may find other ways. Chapter 6 suggests that window dressing, reporting, and avoidance strategies are to be expected from employers, but it shows that the strategies do not significantly diminish the real labor market effects of the ACA's various taxes, and the two may reinforce each other.

The ACA will make workers less productive in terms of the market value of what they produce per hour, but the ACA also complicates the measurement of productivity and income. As noted above, the ACA gives low-skill workers the largest push out of the labor market, and their absence can give the illusion that labor has become more productive because their low productivity is no longer counted in the average. Changing reporting practices for hours and employment will also convey false impressions of productivity change. The employer penalty is new to national accounting, and chapter 8 explains how it can give the illusion of less labor income and how the anticompetitive effects (in the labor market) of the penalty by themselves may increase measured profits.

Observers will be surprised by how much the ACA reduces the number of people without health insurance, at least over the medium term before there are caps on enrollment or subsidy amounts intended to limit government spending on the programs. By 2016, the combination of the individual mandate and the subsidies for exchange coverage will put many of those at risk of being uninsured in the position where, in effect, they have to pay to be uninsured, even if they do not consume any market-produced health care. The employer penalty is not an important factor for moving people from uninsured to insured. The employer penalty primarily affects the composition of coverage;

eliminating it from the ACA would cause as many as 30 million people to move from employer-sponsored plans to taxpayer-sponsored plans through a combination of changes in employer benefit offerings, migration of workers away from employers offering coverage, and migration of consumers away from producers that offer coverage to their employees.

Uncompensated care, which refers to health care provided without reimbursement from the patient or an insurer, has been a real problem in the health sector. By moving people from uninsured to insured, the ACA will reduce (but by no means eliminate) the amount of uncompensated care. However, this reduction is dwarfed by the law's labor market distortions. The fundamental problem with using a massive law like the ACA to address uncompensated care is that the ACA directly affects the incentives of half of the workers in the economy (chapter 5), who far outnumber the people who will move from uncompensated care to insurer-financed care (itself financed largely by taxpayers).

Both the Smith and Winslett families, who were introduced in chapter 1, were paying for their own coverage before the ACA and therefore did not need to be part of any solution to uncompensated care. Yet the ACA added significantly to the longstanding subsidies for retirements like those that the Smiths have been enjoying since January 2014. By outlawing health plans like the Winsletts', the ACA has also "placed an enormous financial burden on normal, everyday people quite literally forcing us onto government assistance we didn't need before" (Winslett 2014). According to the methodology used in chapter 5, Mr. Winslett and his wife now each face marginal income tax rates that are 16 percentage points greater than they would have been without the law. A proper assessment of the ACA's success with alleviating uncompensated care costs would account for economic side effects like these using economic reasoning and representative samples.

My analysis suggests that, on average, the employer penalty is entirely passed through to workers in the form of lower wages, even among those working for an employer that is not penalized. The penalty has anticompetitive effects in the labor market: small employers who choose to grow their payroll beyond 50 employees are hit with the harshest penalties, and the threat of such penalties reduces their labor demand even though they may be profitable. However, chapter 7 shows that the employer penalty is passed through less than 100 percent on an employer-by-employer or industry-by-industry basis. Holding constant the ACA's subsidies, the chapter explains why employers paying penalties and cutting employee wages dollar for dollar would lose too many workers to employers that offer affordable coverage (and are thereby not penalized). But the other side of the coin is that the penalty by itself permits those employers offering affordable coverage to cut their workers' wages because the penalty increases their advantage, or reduces their disadvantage, in the market for employees.

C. Market Analysis Is the Right Tool for the Job

The labor market equilibrium perspective has a lot to say about health reform and other recent policies that redistribute incomes in the labor market, yet this perspective has been ignored in drawing conclusions about the policies' economic consequences. To name a few, MIT Professor Jonathan Gruber's Microsimulation Model (Gruber 2009), the Urban Institute's Health Insurance Policy Simulation Model (Urban Institute 2011), and the Congressional Budget Office's Health Insurance Simulation Model (Congressional Budget Office 2007) all fail to consider Adam Smith's theory of equalizing differences or otherwise put the employer-employee relationship in a market context. By assumption, nothing about health insurance policy affects where, when, or how people work, and nobody is affected unless the policy directly contacts them. One purported justification for these approaches is that labor market equilibrium is a highly esoteric theory with predictions that are hardly relevant for regular people and practical policy questions. This justification is readily contradicted: just look at your local barber, whose wages and living standards have been multiplied many times by economic events outside the industry (chapter 7), not to mention the many important consequences of the ACA for employment, wages, productivity, and insurance coverage that are highlighted in this book.

In principle, equilibrium-free policy simulation could be a first step toward a more complete analysis that considers the full marketplace. But too many incorrect policy conclusions have recently been the result of stopping at the first step, perhaps because labor market equilibrium analysis is perceived to be too difficult or too complicated to execute at the fast pace at which policy making can move in Washington. This perception is also shown to be incorrect in this book, where many of the labor market equilibrium calculations are nothing more than arithmetic, not to mention the fact that market equilibrium analysis is required training for any economics Ph.D.

Chapter 6's table 6.1 is a good example. It computes an estimate of the impact of the ACA on equilibrium aggregate hours as a sequence of five arithmetic operations, each of which is no more complicated than multiplying two numbers or adding three of them. The major barrier to this exercise is actually reading the law and the regulations that go with it, so that the proper incentives can be identified and measured. The purpose of chapters 2 through 5 of this book is to bring down that barrier by summarizing the ACA and its relationship to incentives in the labor market. Once we are confronted with results like those shown in figure 11.1, we can no longer be comfortable with the assumption that business as usual will continue in the economy while the ACA is rolled out.

The federal government and other advocates of the Affordable Care Act have dismissed concerns that the coming labor market contraction would be significant, or even noticeable, by pointing to Massachusetts's experience with a 2006 reform also designed to expand insurance coverage. Because the Massachusetts labor market did not noticeably contract relative to the rest of the nation after the reform went into effect (Dubay, Long, and Lawton 2012), the Department of Health and Human Services (HHS) said, "The experience in Massachusetts . . . suggest[s] that the health care law will improve the affordability and accessibility of health care without significantly affecting the labor market" (Contorno 2013). In their view, measuring taxes and incentives looks like a waste of time—even worse, misleading—when the nationwide adjustment to the ACA should be fundamentally similar to Massachusetts's adjustment to its 2006 reform.

Some observers may pigeonhole this book as trying to start a new battle in an ongoing war between equilibrium policy analysis and the "natural experiment" approach, which estimates policy impacts from the economic changes associated with historical policy implementations like that in Massachusetts, but the truth is that the two are inherently complementary. The second half of this book relies heavily on the natural experiments literature in order to translate estimates of the size and prevalence of the new taxes into estimates of labor market impact. Chapter 4 relies in part on a 2009 federal law that (temporarily) gave large health insurance subsidies to middle-class unemployed workers. Chapter 9 explains how experiences with state-level health reforms, especially two in Massachusetts, may be informative about the degree of substitutability between exchange plans and employer-sponsored coverage as well as some of the political and economic consequences of Medicaid expansions, employer penalties, and "employment lock." Chapter 10 shows in detail how the implicit and explicit taxes in the ACA are at least an order of magnitude greater than those in the 2006 Massachusetts reform, and in some cases they create fundamentally different incentives. The HHS mistake was to fail to mention and adjust for the differences. Although some of the leading economist practitioners of the natural experiment approach joined HHS in the mistake (see chapter 10), I see nothing inherent in the natural experiment methodologies that prevents classification of policy episodes according to the type, prevalence, and size of the tax incentives that are created.

D. Projections for Economic Change

The second half of the book primarily estimates the long-term economic impacts of the ACA, which refer to differences between our "actual" economy with the ACA in place for several years and an otherwise similar "counterfactual" economy with no ACA. In total, about one dozen labor market incentives created by the ACA are considered. But impact estimates are not the same as predictions for changes over time that will occur as the ACA is implemented because the change over time is the sum of the ACA's impact and the counterfactual change that would have occurred without the ACA. Chapter 9 quantifies several non-ACA causes of change over time—especially population aging and "recovery from the recession"—for the purpose of making predictions for changes over time between 2012–13 and 2016–17. As noted in

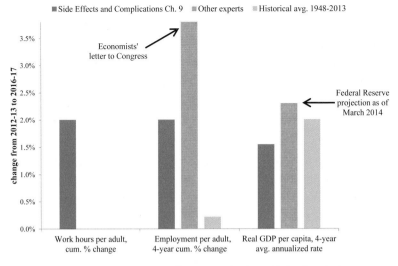

FIGURE 11.2. The economic outlook. Rosy scenarios from this book and other experts. Each source also has pessimistic scenarios (not shown).

the introduction, chapter 9 predicts changes so that readers in 2017 and beyond may compare them with the actual changes.

Figure 11.2 highlights a couple of the predictions and how much they deviate from those of some experts. Both this book and other forecasters offer a range of predictions; figure 11.2 shows only the rosiest scenario from the range. Chapter 6 explains that this book's quantitative predictions for aggregate hours worked per person are more robust than the predictions for employment rates because the ACA has offsetting effects on hours per employee. Chapter 9 predicts that aggregate hours per adult may increase over time, but only if the recovery from the recession is sufficiently strong (figure 11.2 shows a top-end cumulative increase of 2 percent, which is 4.5 percent from a strong recovery minus about 2.4 percent for the ACA's impact as of 2016–17). My projection for employment per person is essentially the same. As explained in more detail in chapters 2 and 9, almost 300 economists, including a few Nobel laureates, warned Congress that repealing the entire ACA would result in the loss of up to 400,000 jobs per year beginning almost immediately (Cutler et al. 2011). Over a four-year time frame, this is 1.6 million jobs, or about 1.1 percent of employment. In fact Congress did not repeal the ACA, so the ACA should be increasing employment per adult by 1.1 percent on top of a cumulative increase of, say, 2.8 percent due to a mediocre recovery from the recession.[4] Figure 11.2 also shows the historical average increase in employment per adult over four-year time frames, which is essentially zero (0.2 percent).

The Federal Reserve Board publishes economic projections as part of its Federal Open Market Committee meeting minutes. Their most recent publication, from March 2014, projects real GDP out through 2016. Over that period, and adjusting for population growth, their high-end projection is about 2.3 percent *per year*, which is well above my high-end projection of 1.5 percent per year. The Federal Reserve Board's projections do not indicate that economic growth would be below the average as a consequence of the ACA.[5]

E. Opportunities for Future Research

Very little work has been done on the ACA's taxes. There is room to have better estimates of the size of the employment and income taxes, and a better understanding of how they vary across groups, as well as the dynamic incentives they create. The employment situation of minimum-wage workers may be especially vulnerable to these taxes (Baicker and Levy 2008), and I have hardly begun to think about the kinds of adjustments that minimum-wage workers will have to make. The small-firm exemption from the employer penalty is complicated and has some anticompetitive effects in the labor market. As noted in chapter 2, additional taxes (not quantified in this book) will someday be needed if Medicaid and exchange subsidies ultimately prove to exceed the funding provided in the original law.

Moreover, jobs and incomes are not the only things the ACA taxes. The law creates new implicit taxes on marriage. It creates a variety of incentives for human capital accumulation: encouraging some health investments, discouraging others (Cole et al. 2012), discouraging young people from learning on the job by taxing full-time employment and by compressing the distribution of wages, encouraging young people to stay in school, and changing the types of investments students make while in school. All of these new taxes need to be quantified.

This book contains many details about labor taxes and health insurance premiums, and beyond that comparatively few details about health shocks, risk sharing, and the organization of the health insurance industry, because the people directly facing one of the ACA's significant labor taxes far outnumber the people who will be insured as a consequence of the law. But the latter group is still in the millions, which is why studies of the insurance industry and the ACA are important too; Aizawa (2014), Hai (2013), and Handel, Hendel, and Whinston (2014) are good examples. More work is needed to understand the interactions between health insurance markets and various labor taxes. More work is needed on the supply of physicians, nurses, and other health-care workers.

F. Intended and Unintended Consequences

Whether it be affordable health care in the early twenty-first century or French national security in the early twentieth, a good cause cannot defy the laws of economics any more than an unworthy cause can. Yet the Affordable Care Act has been passed and is being implemented with little attention to, or even acknowledgment of, the economic forces it creates. Many Americans would have liked to know about the full consequences of the law before embracing its advertised benefits. Perhaps it is too late for that now, and even irrelevant to the extent that the ACA delivers health benefits that ultimately warrant permanently contracting the economy 2 or 3 percent.

Regardless of whether the ACA was a step in the right direction, we can expect that its consequences will include fewer jobs and less income, simply because the law redistributes by taxing jobs and incomes. Anyone following economic change will want to know what is causing economic contraction or sluggish growth, and this book was written to precisely describe the connections between the ACA and economic change.

The book was also written to show that economics did not, and does not, have to be ignored or superficially considered at the policy-making stage. Quantitative economic analysis of market forces is possible even when legislation is complex and confusing. The standard economic toolbox permits prompt execution of the economics work without a large staff. The fundamental economic ideas, measurements, and conclusions of the analysis can be made accessible to audiences far beyond those professionally trained to carry it out.

Political pragmatists may claim that it is sometimes necessary to ignore economic consequences to support a worthy effort. Even without its pessimistic assessment of the ability of voters to receive information, this argument has been contradicted many times in history when unintended consequences overwhelmed promised benefits. Time will tell whether the health reform is remembered more for its intentions or its economic surprises.

NOTATION DIRECTORY

in order of first appearance

Description	Symbol	Chapter of first appearance	Description	Symbol	Chapter of first appearance
medical payroll tax rate	τ_{med}	2 (appendix)	employer penalty (hrs/week)	p	5 (appendix)
other payroll tax rate	τ_{other}	2 (appendix)	employer penalty ($/week)	pZ	5 (appendix)
medical payroll tax equivalent	τ_{eq}	2 (appendix)	unemployment benefit	UB	5 (appendix)
base mtr	t	4	uncompensated care	U	5 (appendix)
medexp at an annual rate	m	4	uncompensated care MTR	υ	5 (appendix)
medexp/FPL	M	4	consumption	c	5 (appendix)
critical compensation/FPL	E	4	ACA subsidy at an annual rate	s	5 (appendix)
hours per week	h	4	excess premium credit	z	5 (appendix)
cost-sharing discount rate	δ	4	fringe benefit factor	χ	5 (appendix)
premium cap/AGI	π	4	credit reconciliation schedule	G	5 (appendix)
other AGI/FPL	O	4	maximum part-time hours	P	6
other AGI	o	4	worker quasi-fixed cost	a	6
AGI/FPL	Y	4	aggregate hours	N	6
ACA MTR	τ	5	employer quasi-fixed cost	q	6
ACA subsidy/FPL	S	5	lump sum transfer	g	6
AGI	y	5 (appendix)	cost of hours deviations	f	6
index distinguishing individuals	i	5 (appendix)	low-skill labor	L	8
time	j	5 (appendix)	labor efficiency	Z	8 (appendix)
other taxes	T	5 (appendix)	capital used in production	k	8 (appendix)
weeks per year	n	5 (appendix)	production-function exponent	α	8 (appendix)

ABBREVIATIONS

ACA	Affordable Care Act
AGI	Adjusted gross income
ARRA	American Recovery and Reinvestment Act of 2009 (aka, "the stimulus")
ATUS	American Time Use Survey
CBO	Congressional Budget Office
CHIP	Children's Health Insurance Program
CMS	Centers for Medicare and Medicaid Services
COBRA	Consolidated Omnibus Budget Reconciliation Act
CPI	Consumer Price Index
CPS	Current Population Survey
CPS-MORG	Merged Outgoing Rotation Groups of the Current Population Survey
EITC	Earned income tax credit
ESI	Employer-sponsored (health) insurance
EUC	Emergency Unemployment Compensation
FPL	Federal poverty line
FTE	Full-time equivalent
FTET	Full-time employment tax
GDP	Gross domestic product
GGN	Garthwaite, Gross, and Notowidigdo
GMSIM	Gruber Microsimulation Model
HHS	Health and Human Services, Department of
HIPSM	Health Insurance Policy Simulation Model
IIT	Individual income tax
IRS	Internal Revenue Service
IW	Initial weight
KFF1	Kaiser Family Foundation premium calculator, mid-2013 edition
KFF2	Kaiser Family Foundation premium calculator, 2014 edition
MAGI	Modified adjusted gross income
NBER	National Bureau of Economic Research

PPACA   Patent Protection and Affordable Care Act (otherwise known as ACA)

PUMS   Public Use Microdata Sample

SNAP   Supplemental Nutrition Assistance Program

UI   Unemployment insurance

VW   Variable weight

NOTES

1. The Smiths' early retirement story was published and broadcast by a partnership between National Public Radio, Southern California Public Radio, and Kaiser Health News (National Public Radio et al. 2014). I estimated the Smiths' full premium (that is, what they would pay without subsidies) from coveredca .com and the Kaiser premium calculator (see chapter 4), assuming that two 64-year-olds would be insured in Los Angeles County. Ben Winslett's quotes (I corrected a one-character spelling error) are from his blog myobamacaretale .com (see also Walsh 2014). For more information about households that stop subscribing to cable television, see Ramachandran (2014).

2. Keynes (1919, p. 23) writes that "although the school of thought from which [the treaty] springs is aware of the economic factor, it overlooks, nevertheless, the deeper economic tendencies which are to govern the future." Keynes was also expecting larger economic effects from French Prime Minister Clemenceau's treaty than I am expecting from the ACA, championed by U.S. Senator Kennedy, President Obama, and their supporters.

CHAPTER TWO

1. The United States and other countries use general revenues to help finance public health insurance programs, such that their payroll tax rates alone do not fully reveal the labor market burdens of the programs. More important, this book does *not* use cross-country comparisons to estimate how the ACA will affect the economy. It looks directly at the ACA and carefully quantifies the incentives therein. The point of the America-Europe comparison is just to help readers quickly understand the magnitude of the fundamental tradeoffs involved with expanding health insurance coverage, and why it should not be assumed that coverage is going to be expanded without significant new taxes.

2. In response to a request from U.S. Senator Tom Coburn, the congressional Joint Committee on Taxation (2012) named a few ACA tax provisions "directly affecting" individuals earning less than $200,000 annually and families earning less than $250,000: the penalty on taxpayers who fail to maintain minimum essential health insurance coverage, the modification of the itemized deduction for medical expenses, and additional tax on health savings and related accounts. But the sum total of these provisions is on the order of the amount cited in the text. See also Klein (2012).

3. See, for example, Hausman (1969), Shoup (1969/2009, p. 183), Gruber and Wise (1999), or Mulligan (2012b).

4. The Bush administration created means-tested mortgage assistance programs in 2008 that implicitly taxed household incomes far beyond 100 percent (Mulligan 2012b), yet the implicit taxes were not discussed. The American Recovery and Reinvestment Act of 2009 (ARRA) was touted as "making work pay," yet it was full of implicit income and employment taxes (Mulligan 2012b) that economists ignored: see the ARRA comments by dozens of economists on the IGM panel of economic experts (IGM Economic Experts Panel 2012). Barro (2011) is a rare case in which implicit taxes were considered as part of assessing the ARRA's economic effects.

5. The Congressional Budget Office (2010, p. 48) mentioned implicit income taxes, and quantified rates of implicit income taxation in other work (Congressional Budget Office 2012a, p. 27), but implicit taxes were not part of their estimates of the quantitative effects of the ACA on labor markets until February 2014 (Congressional Budget Office 2014a).

6. See Gamage (2012). I am excluding my own papers and books from the document count. Prior to 2008, the implicit taxes associated with expanding health insurance coverage were openly discussed, as in Krueger and Reinhardt (1994).

7. The federal government now describes the health insurance exchanges as "health insurance marketplaces." For brevity, this book refers to the exchanges/marketplaces with the single word *exchange*.

8. Throughout the book, health insurance *coverage*, *plan*, and *policy* refer to the promise by an insurance company (private or public) to reimburse persons enrolled in the plan for many of their medical expenses if and when they are incurred. The persons enrolled pay a constant monthly health insurance premium for the opportunity to be reimbursed. Many times the reimbursements are paid directly from the insurance company to the health-care provider (physician, hospital, drug store, etc.).

9. Sellers are permitted to charge smokers more than nonsmokers.

10. CMS (2014) wrote: "Unlike the certification process for benefit year 2014, CMS will no longer simply utilize issuer accreditation status, identify states with review processes at least as stringent as those identified in 45 C.F.R. 156.230(a), or collect network access plans as part of its evaluation of plans' network adequacy. Rather, CMS will assess provider networks using a 'reasonable access' standard, and will identify networks that fail to provide access without unreasonable delay as required by 45 C.F.R. 156.230(a)(2)." See also Demko (2014) and Goozner (2014).

11. The out-of-pocket costs can be structured in various ways, e.g., as deductibles versus coinsurance rates.

12. Section 1312 (c)(1)(D)(i) of the ACA. See also Pear (2012).

13. Employer-sponsored insurance is purchased with "pretax dollars": that is, the purchase is subtracted from compensation for the purpose of determining payroll and personal income taxes. In effect, employer-sponsored insurance is not only a method of financing health care but also a vehicle for avoiding taxes. This advantage of employer-sponsored insurance continues under the ACA.

14. An offer of continuation coverage through a former employer, or through a family member's former employer, does not prevent an exchange plan participant from receiving premium tax credits (or cost-sharing subsidies) as long as the participant is not enrolled in the continuation coverage (U.S. Government Printing Office, 77 FR 30381). Employer coverage is considered affordable if self-only coverage under the plan costs the employee no more than 9.5 percent of household income (ibid., 77 FR 30380). I do not think the affordability criterion applies to continuation coverage that a person declined when leaving a former employer (see also Henry J. Kaiser Family Foundation 2014), but even if it did the criterion would usually not bind because continuation coverage is expensive and incomes of the unemployed are low.

15. As a transitional matter, families that purchased an exchange plan directly from an insurer (without using the ACA's exchange for their state) are also eligible for premium tax credits (Pear 2014a).

16. As discussed in chapters 4 and 5, the ACA-specified percentage depends on family income and the rate of health cost inflation.

17. A person who becomes eligible for government-sponsored coverage during the calendar year may wait up to three months to apply for that coverage and continue receiving premium tax credits until the government accepts an application (U.S. Government Printing Office, 77 FR 30379).

18. One economic prediction is that families informed about the rules for reconciliation will opt at enrollment to receive advance credits.

19. Gold and platinum plans are somewhat different (often with greater out-of-pocket costs) than silver cost-sharing-reduction plans for persons below 250 percent of the poverty line.

20. PPACA Sec. 1402(f)(3).

21. As far as I can tell, a participant who loses eligibility for premium tax credits during the coverage year can still receive the cost-sharing subsidies as long as the person continues to participate in the plan.

22. The full premium would be $13,886, and out-of-pocket costs would be $5,951. At 145 percent FPL, these are reduced $12,405 and $4,761 by premium tax credits and cost-sharing subsidies, respectively.

23. The exact salary equivalent of each $10,000 in exchange subsidies depends on the family's tax bracket.

24. Section 4980H(c)(2)(E) of the Internal Revenue Code, as amended by the ACA, says that the conversion factor from part-time employees to full-time employees is the ratio of the former group's monthly work hours to 120. For example, if February had exactly four work weeks, then every employee working 15 hours per week would count as a half of a full-time equivalent for the month of February.

25. The tendency of the employer penalty to shift employment to employers offering coverage (or shift employers' coverage decision) is in the opposite direction of the employment-composition tax implicit in the exchange subsidies. As shown in chapter 4, the exchange subsidies and the employer penalty have many

of the same compositional effects in terms of the distribution of jobs by length of the workweek.

26. $3,046 = $2,000/[1.0765*(1 – 0.39)], where 7.65 percent and 39 percent are the employer payroll and business income tax rates, respectively. Sections 4980H(c)(7), as amended by the ACA, and 275(a)(6) of the Internal Revenue Code of 1986 specify that taxes imposed by Chapter 43 of the Internal Revenue Code— among which is the ACA's employer penalty—are nondeductible for the purposes of calculating a business's federal income tax.

27. "Not affordable" means that employee premiums for self-only coverage exceed 9.5 percent of the employee's household's income.

28. Section 4980H(b)(1) of the IRC of 1986, as amended by the ACA. This employer penalty is capped at $2,000 (plus health cost inflation after 2014) times the total number of full-time employees, including those full-time employees who do not receive subsidized coverage. The cap calculation even includes the first 30 full-time employees.

29. The excise tax is not deductible for business income tax purposes (see the employer-penalty-deductibility endnote 26 for the relevant statutes).

30. The individual mandate penalty is less in 2014 and 2015. The total penalty for a year (even if coverage was lacking for just part of the year) is capped at the national average bronze premium; see section 5000A(c)(1)(B) of the Internal Revenue Code as amended by the ACA. For the purposes of calculating the penalty, only household income above the tax-filing threshold (ranging in 2014 from $3,950 to $20,300, depending on household composition and joint filing status: see U.S. Internal Revenue Service 2015) is considered.

31. The 133 percent threshold applies in states that did not expand Medicaid (Centers for Medicare and Medicaid Services 2013). The same threshold is sometimes referred to as 138 percent of the poverty line because of the two concepts of adjusted gross income used in the law (AGI and MAGI). Thresholds for parents are more complicated.

32. See Congressional Research Service (2010, p. 7), which also adds that "no additional limits are placed [by the ACA] on the IRS using correspondence or phone calls, either through its own employees or through private collection agencies, in an effort to collect the amount owed."

33. The cross-state average weights thresholds from Henry J. Kaiser Family Foundation (2012) by 2010 state population. The average threshold for children age one to five was 141 percent FPL.

34. Persons, such as pregnant women, who are eligible for limited Medicaid coverage are not necessarily ineligible for exchange subsidies because limited Medicaid coverage is not considered minimum essential coverage as defined by the ACA (U.S. Internal Revenue Service 2014a).

35. U.S. Government Printing Office (77 FR 30394). The Center for Budget and Policy Priorities (2013) reports that Medicaid eligibility does not prevent eligibility for exchange subsidies as long as "the Marketplace found [that the participant] was not eligible for Medicaid based on her *estimated* income, and her final income

is between 100 and 400 percent of the poverty line" (italics added). I have been unable to find the IRS or HHS rule that clarifies this situation.

36. For example, the transitional reinsurance program assesses a $63 tax in 2014 on every health insurance plan enrollee (including dependents, and including those enrolled in exchange plans) and uses the revenue to help sellers on the exchanges mitigate losses on high-cost cases (Carey 2013).

37. In early 2014 the Henry J. Kaiser Family Foundation released a premium calculator to illustrate possible pricing and subsidies on the ACA exchanges that would form later in the year, and their family premium estimates (before subsidies) matched closely with the average premiums charged by family plans obtained through employers, adjusting for the fact that silver exchange plans and the average employer plan have different actuarial values (Gabel et al. 2012). After the ACA exchanges were opened and exchange plan prices were published, the calculator was revised to reduce all premium estimates by the calculator by 16 percent (see chapter 4).

38. See U.S. Internal Revenue Service (2014b), which states that the income threshold for a widow with dependent child is $250,000 for the investment tax as opposed to the $200,000 threshold for the additional earnings tax (U.S. Internal Revenue Service 2013c).

39. The investment surtax is levied on the minimum of net investment income and the difference between total income (earned plus unearned) and the income threshold (see line 16 of IRS Form 8960 for tax year 2013). For taxpayers for whom the latter is the lesser of the two, the marginal earnings tax rate addition from the ACA's Medicare provisions is 3.8 percentage points because earned income adds to the investment surtax base (i.e., earned income adds to line 16 on Form 8960, from which the investment income tax is calculated by multiplying by 0.038). If, in addition, adjusted gross income includes some subtractions (e.g., deductions for IRAs or alimony), then it is possible that earned income is taxed by both of the new Medicare taxes at the same time, making the total marginal rate addition equal to 4.7 percentage points.

40. Herring and Lentz (2011) find that 94 percent of employer plans in 2008 and 2009 had premiums at least 30 percent less than the thresholds that would apply in 2018. It follows that an even larger percentage of 2008–9 plans had premiums less than the thresholds for the excise tax.

41. Medical-outcome-contingent payments from physicians to patients that are built into physician fees need not be wasteful, or have the characteristics of a tax, if the employees enrolled in health insurance plans value the contingent payments enough. The degree to which malpractice payments are wasteful is therefore an empirical question.

42. The American Medical Association is concerned that the ACA may increase malpractice payments by changing or establishing "standards of care" (Chirba and Noble 2013), although it can also be argued that the ACA's standards of care would somewhat ease the malpractice payments.

43. Baicker and Chandra (2006). See also Cutler (2011).

44. Cutler and Sood failed to note that the employer penalty is not deductible for business income tax purposes, and so its salary equivalent significantly exceeds its nominal value of $2,000 per full-time employee per year. They also did not include the labor demand effects of the $40,000 marginal penalty faced by employers with employment just below the threshold (see chapter 3), or account for the fact that the employer penalty is indexed to health cost inflation.

45. See also the survey conducted by Troy and Wilson (2014) in which employers indicated that the ACA would increase costs per employee, rather than reduce them.

46. I assume that the tax savings are 30 percent of the premiums and therefore $212 billion. Note that the Joint Committee on Taxation (2008) estimated the tax savings to be $246 billion in 2007, although their estimate includes the tax savings enjoyed by public sector employees. To the degree that table 2.1 underestimates employees' tax savings from health premiums, it overestimates what they would save by reducing those premiums.

47. Because Gabel et al. (2012) find that, on average, employer coverage (financed by premium payments) reimburses 83 percent of coverage medical expenses for persons enrolled, I assume that average out-of-pocket payments for persons enrolled are premium payments times $(1 – 0.83)/0.83$.

48. The Council of Economic Advisers (2009a, p. 30) obtained almost the same estimate with similar methods: it estimated that every 1.5 percentage points of health cost savings reduces employment costs by 0.12 percent, which translates to 0.40 percent employment cost savings for every five percentage points of health cost savings.

49. See, for example, Philipson et al. (2012) who find that an important part of the extra health spending in the United States (by comparison with Europe) results in longer life expectancy for cancer patients. If the ACA were to slow the growth of that type of spending, it would be reducing value received by patients.

50. Even if the ACA's spending were categorized as government purchases rather than transfers, their aggregate income effects would be minimal because those purchases are close (although not perfect) substitutes for goods and services that private citizens buy themselves. Military spending is a classic example of government spending with large income effects, precisely because military spending is so different from private spending (Barro 1981); the ACA does little to change military spending.

51. This eliminates Denmark, Ireland, Italy, Norway, Portugal, Spain, Sweden, and the UK, all of which pay for national health insurance with general tax revenues. Some of these countries may have an earmarked tax that is not reported by the Social Security Administration study.

52. Social Security Administration (2008, 2010, 2012) reports that Finland's medical payroll tax rate has varied over time. In 2008, 2010, and 2012, the employee rate was 1.24, 1.47, and 1.22 percent, respectively. The employer rates were 0, 2.23, and 0, respectively. All of these earmarked taxes were matched by general government revenues.

CHAPTER THREE

1. For this reason, chapters 3 and 4 are titled after the famous paper by Sargent and Wallace (1981).

2. Business income taxes are a legislated percentage of business revenue minus business costs, as defined by the tax law. As shown below, a business expense that the law deems to be deductible therefore has the added benefit of reducing the amount of business tax that is owed.

3. Employers who are organized as C corporations typically have a business income tax rate equal to the federal rate of 35 percent plus the applicable state rate, adjusted for the federal tax treatment of state business income taxes. For example, a 6 percent state rate puts the combined rate at about 39 percent. Employers who are organized as S corporations have a business income tax rate equal to their personal income tax bracket, which is their federal bracket (likely between 28 and 40 percent plus the Medicare surtax on net investment income, if any), plus their federal-adjusted state rate. Nonprofit employers do not pay business income tax. See also Mulligan (forthcoming).

4. Quoted from Section 1302(c)(4) of the ACA. See also Section 4980H(c)(5)(A) of the Internal Revenue Code of 1986, as amended by the ACA.

5. U.S. Department of Health and Human Services (2014c). For example, the secretary has decided to use projections of time series rather than historical time series, and to temporarily exclude observations of individual market premiums until "the premium trend is more stable."

6. Hourly employer costs are what the average employer spends on employees—including salaries, benefits, and penalties—per hour that they work.

7. Readers of the future who want to translate my 2014 dollar estimates into amounts measured in the dollars of the year in which they are reading will have to use inflation rates measured after 2014 to make the translation.

8. See also appendix 3.2.

9. 7.25 times 8 times 52 is only $3,016.

10. Appendix 3.1 explains how I estimate the likelihood of having an employer that offers coverage.

11. See also Baicker and Levy (2008).

12. The marginal cost of crossing the large-employer threshold can differ from $62,265. One complication is the look-back provision: large-employer status is based on employment in the year prior to the coverage year, whereas the penalty amount is based on employment in the coverage year itself. For example, the consequence of adding the one employee to the payroll in 2015 that puts the employer over the large-employer threshold could be $316,305 for 2016 if the 2016 payroll is going to have 130 full-time employees. Another consequence of the look-back provision is that part of the penalty serves as a tax on work hours rather than full-time employment because the look-back refers to full-time equivalent employees rather than full-time employees. For simplicity, this book ignores the look-back provision and discusses large-employer status as if it were determined in the coverage year on the same basis as the penalty amount.

13. The Congressional Budget Office (2007) uses a variety of sources, including the MEPS and Census Bureau data, although its 27 percent estimate may include some benefit-ineligible workers at the ESI employers (arguably these workers should be classified as non-ESI).

14. Perhaps a more precise description is that a full-time schedule would, for 26 percent of workers, create a penalty or a threat of penalty for their employer. As explained further in chapter 6, the actual penalties (with all of their complexities) may affect the structure of wages in much the same way as my assumed, but simpler, penalty structure does, in that employees in 2016 will get paid about $3,000 less for working 30 hours per week for an employer not offering coverage than for working 29 hours for the same employer, even if that employer is not liable for a penalty because of competition in the labor market for workers wanting to work more than 29 hours without coverage.

15. This example is for coverage year 2016; $61 is the $3,163 (noted above) divided by 52. The ACA penalties and exchange subsidies are determined monthly, even though the annualized subsidy amounts are a function of calendar year income. For simplicity, I assume that partial months of health insurance coverage are prorated in proportion to the number of weeks covered (and I ignore the fact that months usually do not have an integer number of weeks) so that I can refer to weekly amounts of penalties and subsidies.

16. As noted above, I am ignoring the more complex reality in which some employers that fail to offer ESI face zero marginal penalty and others face quite a large marginal penalty.

17. Because the purpose of this chapter is merely to assess the economic significance of the employer penalty before examining its behavioral consequences, table 3.3 does not adjust for the fact that some of the workers in the March 2012 CPS sample will not be working in 2016 because of the ACA.

18. For example, the hours calculation among the 6.9 million workers counts the 1.9 million of them with 30-hour schedules as one hour, the 0.009 million with 30-hour schedules as two hours, etc.

19. There are also about 5 million workers with exactly 35-hour schedules, and probably more than a million of them work for employers not offering coverage. Any of those (1 million plus) with hourly earnings less than $10 ($= 10 = 61/(35 - 29)$) would make more net of the penalty by working 29 hours.

20. Mulligan (2014a) found that estimates of the number of workers facing this 100 percent tax were 22 percent less when based on hours worked during the survey week (during March 2012) rather than usual weekly hours in 2011.

21. The independent variables are indicator variables for detailed industries and the interactions between indicators for employer size more than 100 employees and work schedule at least 40 hours. Part-time nonelderly heads and spouses that have ESI are assigned an indicator of zero, regardless of the fitted value that the probit equation assigns them. Results for the entire sample, or for specific groups of nonelderly persons, are not sensitive to variations on this procedure because dependents and the elderly are a small fraction of persons working at least 30 hours per week.

22. As noted in the text, I assume that premium adjustment percentages beyond 2015 will coincide with hourly employer cost inflation plus 1.6 percentage points, which is the historical average gap between health insurance premium inflation and hourly employer cost inflation.

CHAPTER FOUR

1. Recall that the exchange subsidies are the various kinds of federal assistance sometimes available to families who purchase health insurance on one of the "health insurance exchanges" created by the ACA. The details of these assistance programs are the subject of this chapter.

2. The length of figure 4.1's pink subsidy bars is the salary equivalent of the average subsidy forgone among the 64 million workers who work full time for an ESI employer, including zeros in the average for many of them whose employment status is not the only reason for their subsidy ineligibility. The measurement and composition of this average is explained further below.

3. To put it another way, the economics of the ACA's subsidies and penalties are fundamentally different from the economics of mandated employee benefits, which need not have much of a tax effect (Summers 1989). Under a mandated employee benefit, people must have a job in order to receive the benefit, whereas the ACA gives more benefits to people who are not employed.

4. I use the same March 2012 Current Population Survey sample as in chapter 3 and project 2016 population totals by multiplying by a factor of 1.01^4. Unmarried partners of household heads are treated as heads of their own one-person household. Foster children are analyzed as children. Any other person not related to a household head or spouse is excluded from my sample.

5. For the moment, I ignore the fact that changing employment status, even for a month, would affect calendar year income for the purpose of income eligibility. The amount of the income change depends on the duration of the employment status change and on the value of employer health premiums given up or received. In order to determine whether a worker who did not (in March 2012) obtain coverage through an employer nonetheless still works for an ESI employer (that is, an employer offering coverage to its full-time workers), I use the same method as in chapter 3.

6. Separate poverty lines apply to families in Alaska and Hawaii, but otherwise they are treated the same way in table 4.1. The federal poverty lines vary by family size and are adjusted for inflation from year to year (see also appendix 3.2).

7. The family coverage offered by a spouse's employer does not even have to be affordable, so long as the spouse's employer offers affordable (by ACA definitions) self-only coverage to its employees. See also Burkhauser, Lyons, and Simon (2011).

8. This ignores the full-time workers for ESI employers for whom coverage is not affordable in the sense that worker-only coverage is less than 9.5 percent of their family income. The number of these workers is likely small, unless employers significantly adjust the financing of ESI premiums (Burkhauser et al. 2011), but in any case they are still subject to an FTET in the form of an employer penalty

that is 50 percent larger than the penalty examined in chapter 3. Because this version of the employer penalty was not treated in chapter 3, I treat it here by including the affected workers among those facing an implicit FTET.

9. Gamage (2012) is the one exception.

10. Throughout the book, I refer to covered medical expenses (regardless of whether they are reimbursed by the health plan or paid as part of a deductible or copayment) as "medical expenses" and refer to cosmetic surgery and other expenses that are not covered by health insurance as "nonhealth expenses."

11. The comparison is at a fixed point in time. For example, among families for whom the ACA caps premiums at $3,000 (based on "affordability"), an $8,000 premium generates five times the subsidy ($5,000) that a $4,000 premium does. As premiums and medical expenses increase year to year, in principle both the premium assistance and cost-sharing subsidies increase proportionally.

12. This separate and additional effect has been widely discussed in the context of "employment lock": but for the ACA, people would be "stuck in their jobs" because individual coverage is unavailable. It is claimed that the ACA alleviates the problem by creating an individual market in which workers subject to employment lock would be willing to pay full price, or more, for exchange coverage (see also chapter 9).

13. One estimate says that general revenue contributions to the ACA's risk corridors program amount to a subsidy for exchange premiums at an average rate of 4 percent during 2014–16 (Chandler 2014). To the extent that the subsidies are front-loaded in 2014, they could easily depress 2014 premiums 6–10 percent relative to later years.

14. See, for example, Morgan and Humer (2014) and Viebeck (2014) citing insurance "industry officials and independent analysts." Also note that subsidies in each county are based on the second-cheapest silver plan available in the county. I expect that state insurance regulators, who have to approve sellers that participate in the exchanges, will learn over time how to make the second-cheapest plan more expensive and thereby enhance subsidies for the residents of their state at the expense of the federal government. Bronze plans may get cheaper over time (see chapter 7) and that trend may even reduce the average price of all exchange plans, but only the silver plans are relevant for my subsidy calculations.

15. Agency for Healthcare Research and Quality, Center for Financing (2013).

16. The actual cumulative health insurance premium inflation between 2010 and 2012 was 6.7 percent (Federal Reserve Bank of St. Louis 2014, series DMINR-G3A086NBEA.

17. "CBO and JCT expect that exchange plans will still have lower provider payment rates, more limited provider networks, and stricter management of care, on average, than employment-based plans but that the differences between employment based plans and exchange plans will narrow as exchange enrollment increases. That pattern will put upward pressure on exchange premiums over the next couple of years" (Congressional Budget Office 2014b, p. 8).

18. I have put many hypothetical families through both versions of the KFF calculator and found that KFF2 is always 16 percent less than KFF1. The latest edition of the calculator is available at http://kff.org/interactive/subsidy-calculator/.

19. However, PricewaterhouseCoopers Health Research Institute's analysis (2014) of the median 2014 premium for silver plans suggests that 2014 premiums are in between the KFF1 calculator and the KFF2 calculators. In order to have a sample comparable to PWC HRI's, I took the sample of household heads from the March 2012 CPS with coverage from their employer and ran all of them through both of the KFF calculators (single coverage for nonsmokers). The premium averages in this sample were $5,103 (KFF1) and $4,287 (KFF2), as compared to PWC HRI's average median silver premium of $4,742. PWC HRI also concluded that 2014 exchange plans were 4 percent cheaper than employer plans when comparably priced, as compared to the 16 percent differential between employer plans and KFF1 shown in table 4.3. None of the estimates in this note account for the possibility that 2014 exchange premiums are temporarily low.

20. If the average exchange features discount is 25 percent but varies around that percentage, then by assuming that everyone has the same discount of 25 percent I would overestimate take-up rates (that is, the fraction of the population with a positive subsidy net of the discount) but underestimate the value of subsidies among those who take up. However, I do not use the data from table 4.4 to project take-up rates: its purpose is only to estimate the average incentive of ESI employees to leave full-time work. Appendix 4.1 has a take-up rate estimate.

21. For example, a single-person household with income of $30,000 would typically get less than half of the premium subsidized, and no cost-sharing subsidy.

22. State income tax brackets vary across states and taxpayers vary in terms of whether they deduct state taxes when determining their federal personal income tax.

23. Ninety-five percent of the workers facing the implicit FTET have hourly compensation (including fringes) in this range.

24. In order to calculate the conditional averages, I took my CPS sample of those facing the implicit FTET and limited it to those who also had coverage through an employer and a work schedule of at least 30 hours per week. Using the remaining sample, I regressed either the full subsidy forgone or the value forgone net of the exchange features discount on a fifth-order polynomial in hourly compensation and used the regression fitted values as the conditional averages for figure 4.2. Note that the subsidy forgone conditional on family size is negatively correlated with hourly compensation; this is due to the subsidy's means test (see especially chapter 5), but family size is positively correlated with hourly compensation. As a result, the conditional averages do not vary much with hourly compensation.

25. The dollar amounts in table 4.8 are in 2014 dollars in order to facilitate comparison with the other tables in this book.

26. Because employer payroll taxes are excluded from the payroll base to which the 7.65 percent payroll tax rate is applied, the employer payroll tax amount can equivalently be calculated as in row (5) of table 4.8: (employer cost minus ESI premiums) times a factor of 0.0765/1.0765.

27. According to the KFF1 calculator, a family of four with one adult age 45 and the other age 41 (both nonsmokers) would have an exchange premium of very close to $12,110 before subsidies (to be exact, $12,120; the lesser amount used for the purposes of table 4.8's illustration avoids consideration of small additional tax terms).

28. In other words, the employer plan finances the $17,300 of covered expenses with premiums of $14,300 and out-of-pocket charges of $3,000 (Gabel et al. 2012) whereas a silver plan without subsidies finances with premiums of $12,110 and out-of-pocket charges of $5,190.

29. In other words, the silver plan with cost-sharing subsidies limits average out-of-pocket charges to 147-percent-of-poverty families to 6 percent of the average total expenses of $17,300. The cost-sharing subsidy that achieves this limit is shown in table 4.8's row (11): $4,152.

30. See Mulligan and Gallen (2013) for a fuller analysis of the incidence of the ACA.

31. Figure 4.2 already hints that, as I show carefully below, the average $26-per-hour worker (about $24 per hour after payroll taxes) will not earn more by cutting the work schedule by 11 hours per week because the exchange subsidy is not quite generous enough: figure 4.2 shows an average subsidy amount equivalent to about eight hours per week. Specifically, the table 4.8 worker's family income is not unusual but still somewhat below average.

32. The actuarial value of a family's medical expenditures is the average claims, loadings (e.g., costs for administration and advertising), and out-of-pocket costs that an insurer anticipates among health plan participants with the same family characteristics. For brevity, I refer to this actuarial value as "expected medical expenditures."

33. When referring to dollar amounts, I use a lowercase letter to denote the dollar value and the corresponding uppercase letter to represent the ratio of the value to the federal poverty line.

34. These schedules are described in detail in chapter 5. They include assumed health cost inflation (in excess of wage inflation) beyond 2014.

35. For simplicity, equation (4.1)'s $0.83tM$ term assumes that the household members who would be insured on the exchanges are also covered by ESI. In fact there are workers with ESI (and no spouse with ESI) who do not insure all nonelderly household members through their employer; for them I modify the $0.83tM$ term. The 0.83 reflects the average actuarial value of employer plans (Gabel et al. 2012). Because I hold hourly employer cost constant in making the comparison between (FT) and (PT), in effect I assume that full-time employees ultimately bear the cost of employer premiums and that there are no quasi-fixed costs of employment. Chapter 6's model does not make these simplifying assumptions.

36. Recall that $0.7M$ is the full premium, expressed as a ratio to the federal poverty line.

37. As explained below, I assume that the extra work expenses of adding eight hours per week to the work schedule is $20 per week.

38. Some of those discarded may also face a 100 percent implicit FTET because the full-time schedule that they would consider (as an alternative to their actual part-time schedule) is close enough to 30 hours per week that the earnings after the twenty-ninth hour are not enough to offset the exchange subsidies forgone. For this reason, I underestimate the total number of people who will face a 100 percent implicit FTET.

39. For simplicity, tables 4.9 and 4.10 assume that the only family members who would participate in an exchange plan as a consequence of the worker's taking the part-time position are those who were actually covered by the worker's ESI in March 2012.

40. For example, the hours calculation among the 3.8 million workers counts the 0.2 million of them with 30-hour schedules as one hour, the 0.002 million with 30-hour schedules as two hours, etc. The 2.7 million 40-hour schedules contribute 29 million of the 39 million hour total.

41. The subsidy amount shown in figure 4.1 is the average subsidy forgone among full-time workers at ESI employers, including in the average workers who do not face an implicit FTET (e.g., because their family income exceeds 400 percent of the poverty level). It is calculated as the average subsidy in table 4.4, adjusted to a salary equivalent and multiplied by the fraction of full-time ESI employees shown in table 4.1 who face an implicit FTET.

42. Figure 4.1's top employment category shows that the employer penalty is a kind of fee for using the exchange subsidies. But because the penalty/fee applies only to the top category, it also encourages workers from the top and bottom categories to move into the middle category where no fee applies—the focus of this chapter. Chapter 7 examines the role of the employer penalty as a fee for using the exchange subsidies.

43. The ACA may someday eliminate a small part of the ESI tax exclusion with its Cadillac tax. As noted in chapter 2, the Cadillac tax is yet another instance of the ACA's creating FTETs, on top of the FTETs examined in chapters 3 and 4.

44. The former employers received the ARRA subsidy by taking a credit on their payroll tax deposits.

45. Given that members of Congress and their staffs also have to obtain health coverage in the ACA exchanges, it is possible that the exchange plans will be perceived by consumers to be good-quality plans. Moreover, employer plans are converging with exchange plans, for example, as a number of employers are enrolling employees via "private insurance exchanges."

CHAPTER FIVE

1. As noted in chapter 4, neither component of M includes expenses, such as cosmetic surgery, that are not covered by health insurance.

2. The ACA slightly modifies the traditional AGI measure—its modification is called modified adjusted gross income or MAGI—but this book does not examine the differences between AGI and MAGI.

3. The premium charge is for the second-cheapest silver plan. Participants can choose a more expensive plan at their own expense, or choose a less expensive plan in order to reduce the premium they pay. Participants receive the same premium assistance regardless of which exchange plan they choose.

4. See Section 36B(b)(3)(A)(ii) of the Internal Revenue Code of 1986, as amended by the ACA. In any year after 2018 in which the aggregate exchange subsidies exceed 0.504 percent of GDP, the ACA also provides for an additional premium cap adjustment. The CBO's baseline forecast (Congressional Budget Office 2014a) does not have the additional adjustment taking effect before 2025, although they acknowledge the uncertainty in their forecast.

5. Algebraically, a plateau at income levels below 400 percent FPL reflects the max term in equation (5.1) evaluating to zero.

6. I use the exact expression in equation (5.2) rather than the approximation, but the latter helps for quickly seeing the economic significance of the implicit income tax rate.

7. Take, for example, a full-year participant for whom equation (5.2) evaluates to 20 percent. The worker would pay $200 extra for health coverage as a consequence of earning an additional $1,000 for the year, which is $50 extra for each quarter covered. If instead the participant were covered only three months of the year, then earning an additional $1,000 for the year would affect payments just for those three months of coverage, which is an extra $50.

8. Congressional Budget Office (2014a, table B-2). As explained in chapter 7, Trevor Gallen and I have our own estimates based on a tax-and-behavior analysis related to what is in this book (they span either side of the CBO estimate), but for the moment I start with the CBO's estimates, which incorporate fewer behavior changes.

9. Using the CPS sample described in appendix 3.1, I found that, among nonelderly persons who are privately insured, 52 percent are a working household head or spouse; 13 million is 52 percent of 25 million.

10. The 29.3 percent marginal earnings tax rate shown in the bottom row of table 5.2 is used to convert the average discounted subsidy (in after-tax dollars) to an hour equivalent. Note that, for the purposes of illustration, a 30 percent rate was used to construct chapter 4's figure 4.2, and the result there is a slightly greater hour equivalent (5.6).

11. Recent estimates include Congressional Budget Office (2012a) and Steuerle (2013).

12. For example, the 2014 federal personal income tax return (filed sometime during calendar year 2015) could provide the income estimate for the purposes of determining health expense discounts received during 2016. Reconciliation of the 2016 subsidies occurs sometime during calendar year 2017, when the family files its 2016 federal personal income tax return. In principle, documents avail-

able in late 2015, such as pay stubs or employer quarterly payroll reports, would be alternate sources of 2016 income estimates.

13. A fraction of 2.2 percentage points is entered in table 5.2, fifth row, because the workers represented in that row spend only a fraction of the year (if any) insured on the exchanges.

14. Kaiser Commission on Medicaid and the Uninsured (2008, p. 1). Section 1501(a)(2)(F) of the ACA cites a lesser amount of uncompensated care in 2008: $43 billion.

15. Many of the people insured on the exchanges would have had another kind of private insurance. Others would have been uninsured but not using uncompensated care.

16. Chapter 9 estimates the sum total of the ACA's incentives for families below the poverty line or above 400 percent poverty and finds it to be close to zero.

17. See Mankiw (2009) and D. Kessler (2011).

18. Also recall from chapter 4 that even more workers will face the implicit FTET if a significant number of employers stop offering health insurance coverage to the spouses of employees.

19. Here I have suppressed the notation indicating the amount M of medical expenditure; it is represented by the i subscript.

20. The square bracket term is not relevant for a worker who can be covered through a spouse's employer.

21. Z is a parameter converting hours to salary equivalent; it is explained further in chapter 6.

22. Recall that s' and U' are both negative because income reduces assistance.

23. Households have the option of forgoing advance credits and receiving their entire premium credit at the end of the year. For the reasons explained below, advanced premium credits will eventually be understood to be more valuable than end-of-year credits because only the former creates an opportunity for an excess credit.

24. For simplicity, this appendix ignores cost-sharing subsidies and the fact that the premium credit cannot be negative.

25. Aside from the unlimited cap for families above 400 percent FPL, the caps are six dollar amounts according to three income/FPL intervals—(0,2), (2,3), and (3,4)—crossed with two family types (individual and family). U.S. Government Printing Office, 77 FR 30394.

26. A tax unit whose annual income increased from $50,000 to $52,800 between years $j - 2$ and j would have an excess credit of about $600 (recall that the typical slope in figure 5.1 is about 21 percent), which is at or above the reconciliation cap for any family at less than 400 percent FPL.

CHAPTER SIX

1. The income and payroll tax exclusions of premiums paid for employer-sponsored health insurance are among the many longstanding policies affecting the incentives to work.

2. As noted in chapter 2, in theory a tax on labor might not reduce labor in the long term because of a large aggregate income effect of taking resources away from households (e.g., to fight a war). However, the offsetting income effect is not applicable to the ACA because the taxes in that law are used to finance redistribution: government transfers and/or purchases that are close substitutes for private purchases. In this regard, the ACA's effects on the amount of labor have a lot in common with the effects of a negative income tax.

3. The decision about weeks employed is sometimes called an "extensive margin" decision, as opposed to an "intensive margin" decision regarding hours worked per week. Unfortunately, much of the literature using this terminology fails to specify the time dimension that distinguishes extensive margins from intensive margins. For example, the extensive margin in a time diary study implicitly refers to the probability of working positive hours sometime during a particular day whereas the extensive margin in studies of the earned income tax credit studies refers to the probability of working positive hours sometime during a particular calendar year. I aim for additional clarity in this book by avoiding the two terms and instead referring explicitly to the relevant time dimension.

4. As explained further below, the ACA itself will reduce the fraction of workers who have a weekly schedule of 30 hours or more. In order to keep table 6.1's estimates slightly conservative, it measures the full-time fraction according to the fraction of employees who work 35+ hours, which is both a lesser fraction (than 30+) and one that is less affected by the ACA.

5. To be exact, 6.3 percentage points is 9.2 percent of 68.7 and 8.5 percent of 75.0; the –8.8 percent shown in table 6.1's row (8) is essentially the average of these two.

6. One difference between the ACA's FTETs and unemployment benefits is the treatment of people out of the labor force: they are eligible for ACA subsidies but not unemployment benefits.

7. This conclusion is for tax revenues that are spent on transfers or on goods and services that are close substitutes for household spending. Specifically, I take the Frisch elasticity of aggregate hours supplied with respect to the reward to work to be $\eta = 0.57$. The 0.36 "reward coefficient" cited in the text refers to $\eta/(1 + \eta)$, and can be interpreted as a substitution effect of 0.57 percentage points (per percentage point impact on the reward to work) partially offset by an income effect of about 0.21 percentage points associated with a negative effect of permanent marginal tax rates on aggregate consumption (note that, consistent with "balanced growth preferences," I assume that the household's reservation wage is proportional to household consumption). Chetty et al. (2011) survey and synthesize the microeconometric literature for the purpose of adapting it for aggregate analysis. They conclude that "micro estimates imply a Frisch elasticity of aggregate hours [with respect to the after-tax wage] of 0.78" and "it would be reasonable to calibrate representative agent macro models to match a Frisch elasticity of aggregate hours of 0.75." Using $\eta = 0.75$ instead would make the reward

coefficient equal to 0.43 rather than 0.36. However, I am not aware of any synthesis of the literature that properly adjusts for the reasons for which after-tax wages vary across observations (e.g., explicit taxes versus implicit taxes; I owe this point to economist David Phillips at the Institute for Fiscal Studies) and believe that proper adjustments might suggest that a Frisch elasticity of U.S. aggregate hours with respect to the reward to working of about 0.6 would be consistent with the studies surveyed by Chetty et al. (2011). See also Mulligan (2012b, p. 116) for estimates of the reward coefficient that are consistent with studies of the behavioral effects of unemployment benefits.

8. For example, if row (1) were 0.73 rather than 0.83, then the bottom line would be −2.9 percent rather than −3.2 percent.

9. Table 6.1 also shows that the 6.3 percentage points added by the ACA to work disincentives (row (6)) are composed of 2.2 percentage points employer penalty, 2.3 percentage points implicit FTET, and 1.9 percentage points implicit income taxation. In other words, the ACA's implicit income taxes are less than one-third of the law's work disincentives, and more than two-thirds is a full-time employment tax (either implicit or explicit).

10. With my reward coefficient, their −0.1 percentage points per year translates to an expansion of the labor market of about 0.05 percent per year, or about 80,000 jobs per year. Because they report at least 250,000 jobs per year, it appears that, in effect, they assume a larger reward coefficient.

11. As noted by Rosen (1978), a single hourly "wage" does not, by itself, clear the labor market in this model. Market clearing requires something like two-part pricing: a schedule of possible combinations of weekly earnings and hours as determined by both the marginal wage rate w and the quasi-fixed cost q.

12. Following much of chapter 5, equation (6.2) assumes, for the purposes of modeling the ACA's implicit income tax, that the income slopes of the net subsidy and non-ACA-tax schedules, $s − U$ and T, respectively, are constant and equal to τ and t, respectively. Equation (6.2) also assumes that a is independent of h.

13. See Rosen (1968) and Rosen (1978). See also Oi (1962), Calmfors and Hoel (1988), and Hart (1987).

14. My exposition ignores the "integer problem" and refers to the longest possible part-time schedule as "29 hours" and the shortest possible full-time schedule as "30 hours."

15. Among respondents with positive weeks worked and earnings in 2011, I averaged usual weekly work hours within detailed occupation, separately for government and private sector employees and using the March Supplement weight (the IPUMS detailed occupation variable included with the March 2012 file was not necessarily on the March questionnaire; it may have been asked of the respondent in a different month of CPS participation). I first selected occupations with average hours that were unusually above or below average and having at least 10 respondents sampled. Of those occupations, I selected those that either (a) had many respondents, (b) had a significant number of respondents and

closely related to the (a) occupations (hosts and hostesses, counter attendants, bus drivers and crossing guards), or (c) with characteristics obviously related to the cost analysis in the main text (ship operators and sailors).

16. Mower (2012) reports that large cities with a steady flow of emergencies schedule shorter shifts for firefighters because there is less time to rest between emergencies. The cost schedules represent this conclusion as a more rapidly increasing marginal hourly cost schedule for large-city firefighters than for other firefighters.

17. Chapter 9 looks at non-ACA policies and non-ACA factors affecting economic change.

18. Chapter 3 explains that, in terms of incentives to create, retain, and accept jobs, small employers that do not offer affordable coverage are effectively paying the employer penalty even though they are officially exempt from it because their adding to employment runs the risk of crossing the threshold defining large employers and thereby a prohibitive marginal penalty.

19. Or, in the last scenario, part-time workers do not forgo the subsidy represented by p.

20. This chapter's model is simulated by calculating equilibrium distributions of behavior separately for each tax scenario and then mixing the distributions using the frequencies shown in table 6.4. In other words, this chapter assumes that workers respond only to their own tax scenario and not the taxes levied on other workers. The purpose of chapters 7 and 8 is to estimate the additional behavioral effects that result from eliminating this assumption.

21. The shape of the average cost curve can be derived from the marginal cost curve and the various taxes.

22. Specifically, each worker is assumed to have a minimum average cost at their usual weekly hours in 2011. The mathematical details are shown in chapter 6 of Mulligan (2014c). My sample is all respondents in the March 2012 CPS who worked at least one week for at least eight hours per week during calendar year 2011 (weighted by weeks worked, less than 1 percent of the CPS sample has usual weekly work hours less than eight; among the remaining sample, 25 percent report usual weekly work hours less than 40 and 52 percent report exactly 40). I calculated nationwide weekly employment rates from the 2011 data by weighting each group of workers by the product of weeks worked during the year and the proportion of the workforce they accounted for.

23. To a first-order approximation, the slope of the marginal cost curve is unrelated to the magnitude of the employment effect of FTETs (see Mulligan 2014c).

24. For the purpose of preparing figures 6.1, 6.2, and 6.3, and the numerical estimates that follow, the slope of the marginal cost curve is taken from Mulligan's (2014c) comparisons of commuting times and weekly work hours in the 2000 Census Public Use Microsample. The idea is that commuting time has many of the economic characteristics of employment taxes and quasi-fixed costs: the daily commuting time is the same if working a six-hour day or a 10-hour day.

Those estimates suggest that an employment tax equivalent to five hours per week would increase weekly work hours by about one hour per week.

25. Hirsch (2005) finds that workers switching from a full-time position to a part-time one lose a full-time log hourly wage premium of about 0.09, but he also reports specifications with a premium that is statistically indistinguishable from zero. Cross-sectional hourly wage comparisons, controlling for various demographic measures, sometimes find a premium greater than 0.09, other times less. Most of these studies measure wages *without including fringe benefits*, and the little available evidence suggests that the log compensation premium for full-time work would be about 0.06 greater if fringe benefits were included because part-time employees are typically ineligible for the more valuable fringes such as health insurance (Hirsch 2005, p. 546).

26. A schedule for $\tau = 4.3$ percent is not shown because it is difficult to distinguish from the $\tau = 0$ schedule.

27. By themselves, two substitution effects tend to reduce the aggregate hours supplied by part-time occupations (i.e., those with part-time schedules regardless of the ACA): one effect as their wages vary directly with the hours supplied by full-time occupations and another because the ACA elevates their marginal income tax rate. Among the part-time occupations, I find that the income effect often dominates the substitution effects.

28. Owen's estimate (with macro data, 1979) of the substitution elasticity is 4.3.

29. Appendix 6.2 shows the results separately by scenario.

30. By convention, average hours per employee excludes from the average any person who is not on a payroll during the week.

31. The opposite composition effect can happen with the earnings tax, especially if low-hours workers are more sensitive to tax rates.

32. I use a slightly broader definition of twenty-niner to include those working 26, 27, or 28 hours per week because the threshold for salaried workers may be four days, rather than 30 hours, per week. The final rule issued by the U.S. Treasury states, "For employees paid on a nonhourly basis (such as salaried employees), an employer may calculate the actual hours of service using the same method as for hourly employees, or use a days-worked equivalency crediting the employee with eight hours of service for each day for which the employee would be required to be credited with at least one hour of service. . . . The proposed regulations prohibit use of these equivalencies, however, in circumstances in which their use would result in a substantial understatement of an employee's hours of service" (U.S. Department of Treasury 2014, pp. 22–23).

33. Time-diary studies offer an alternative technique for measuring hours worked, but the diaries usually measure minutes worked per day rather than hours per week. The ACA rules are based on hours per month, and not hours per day.

34. The 2011 distribution of weekly work hours by demographic group is shown in appendix 6.2. Throughout the chapter, I assume that all groups have the same utility parameter η that quantifies the wage elasticity of labor supply. If

women's labor supply were significantly more elastic than men's, then table 6.6 might understate the magnitude of the ACA's impact on women's employment and aggregate hours worked.

35. As explained in appendix 6.2, simulations by marital status assume hour equivalents of the penalty and forgone subsidies that are specific to marital status. Simulations by gender and age use the hour equivalents from table 6.4. I suspect, but have not yet confirmed, that the model predicts significantly greater ACA impacts on unmarried parents as compared to married parents.

36. The elasticity of substitution in production is 2 in the benchmark and 4 in table 6.7's fourth row.

37. As noted above, the CPS data show about half of workers working exactly 40 hours per week in 2011, and it gives little information as to how work schedule preferences might vary within that group. My model's quantitative predictions are therefore inaccurate when the gap between the full-time threshold and 40 is near, or less than, the hourly amount of the full-time employment tax, as it is with the 35-hour threshold.

38. In other words, I assume that, on average, ESI workers leaving their job need a premium discount of at least 25 percent to be willing to purchase an exchange plan, rather than going uninsured or paying full price to stay on their former employer's plan.

39. For example, the ACA does not require employers to offer coverage to new employees and gives employers up to a year to measure a new employee's work schedule to determine whether it is full time. During this period, the new employee can receive exchange subsidies even though the employer is not being penalized.

40. By just moving workers to the "subsidy phaseout and penalty" scenario from the implicit FTET scenario, I may have exaggerated the differences between rows (1) and (9), because some workers would be moving *into* the implicit FTET scenario from "no new incentives" as a consequence of employers' dropping coverage. An example of the latter shift would be ESI workers who would have access to coverage through a spouse if the spouse's employer retained coverage.

41. In other words, the sensitivity analysis with respect to the quasi-fixed costs is another way of demonstrating that the ACA's impact on aggregate hours, but not its impact on weekly hours, varies with the responsiveness of labor supply to incentives because higher quasi-fixed costs create additional responsiveness, holding η constant.

42. As explained by Mulligan (2014c), the model's reward coefficient varies somewhat across occupations. The benchmark reward coefficient of 0.36 corresponds to a Frisch wage elasticity of 0.57. The reward coefficient of 0.50 used in table 6.7's row (16) corresponds to a Frisch wage elasticity of 1.0. If the reward coefficient were 0.50 and the non-ACA earnings tax rate were 35 percent rather than 25 percent, then the ACA's impact on log employment and log aggregate hours would be −0.050 and −0.048, respectively (and not shown in table 6.7), rather than the −0.045 and −0.043 shown in row (16) of the table.

43. The U.S. Government Accountability Office reports that "in addition to

penalties under federal criminal law, PPACA imposes civil penalties up to $25,000 for failure to provide correct information due to negligence or disregard of applicable rules, and up to $250,000 for knowingly and willfully providing false or fraudulent information" (Bagdoyan 2014, p. 5).

44. There are also examples in the other direction. If we had two workers at 150 percent of the poverty line and just one of them hid $20,000, then the one who misreported would fall below the poverty line and not necessarily experience any of the ACA's marginal income tax rates.

45. For my purposes, it does not matter whether the employer or the employee is responsible for the misreporting, just that actual work hours can exceed the work hours that are reported for the purposes of compliance with the employer mandate.

46. A full analysis of multiple-job holders would also adjust the desired hours function f, which is not done in this book.

47. The 3 percent estimate is an impact and not an estimate of the employment rate change between, say, 2012 (before the exchanges and penalties took effect) and 2016. As explained in chapter 9, non-ACA factors, such as the aging of the workforce and the expiration of the Emergency Unemployment Compensation program, have also been changing between 2012 and 2016.

48. Some studies even find that raising the employer cost of weekly work hours reduces employment. See the literature surveyed by Hamermesh (1996a, chapter 3) and Hamermesh (1996b, pp. 106–7). See also Garicano et al. (2013) who show how employment taxes increase hours per employee.

49. Bovbjerg et al. (2010). Topel and Welch (1980) also explain how benefits for the unemployed are, in effect, layoff subsidies.

50. The ACA's employment impact can be understood as having two components: the impact that would occur if minimum wage laws automatically adjusted to labor demand and supply, plus the impact of having a fixed minimum wage rather than one that automatically adjusts. Both components are negative—in the direction of less employment—but only the former component is measured in this chapter: −0.033 log points. See also Baicker and Levy (2008) who estimate the low-skill employment effects of a hypothetical health insurance mandate (an analogue to the latter component), using data from a period when the federal minimum wage was $2.10 less than it is now, and find that it is about 0.2 percent of the full-time workforce. In other words, as a rough approximation one might revise my −0.033 log employment impact to be −0.035 in order to reflect the interaction between the ACA's employer penalty and minimum wage laws.

51. An alternative definition could put the after-tax value of the unemployment benefit in the quasi-fixed cost a and leave it out of q and g.

CHAPTER SEVEN

1. See Rosen (1986) for an overview of the theory. Many of the advances in the theory could be applied to the ACA's various taxes more fully than I have done in this book.

2. For example, the Chicago Barbers Association (2011) reports that the inflation-adjusted price of haircuts more than doubled from the 1920s to the 1960s, and more than doubled again in the subsequent decades. Also note that the average price of a men's haircut today is about $28 (http://www.usnews.com/news/blogs/data-mine/2014/02/28/what-america-pays-for-a-haircut), which would be $2.11 in 1925 prices (http://research.stlouisfed.org/fred2/series/CPIAUCNS). Legend has it that haircuts cost about $0.25 back then (the CBA data suggest closer to $0.50); we can be sure that 1925 haircut prices were far less than $2.11, and therefore sure that haircut prices far outpaced inflation 1925 to present, because $2.11 was about a day's wages for a laborer (U.S. Department of Labor 1939, and Wolman 1935) and regular people would not pay that much for a haircut and would seriously consider getting into the barber business if they could earn a day's wages in less than an hour.

3. For the sake of illustration, I do not consider the possibility that the two sectors have different weekly work schedules, so equalized compensation per employee is the same as equalized compensation per hour.

4. An alternative way to draw figure 7.3a would be to have the penalty paid by the non-ESI employer (that is, stacked above the dashed horizontal line), with penalized employers responding by letting employees go and lowering wages. The important point is that the sector-specific penalty is a force moving employees in the direction of the arrow.

5. In technical terms, the marginal revenue product of labor in the ESI sector falls as the sector absorbs additional employees. This may happen because the marginal product of labor is diminishing in the amount of labor in the sector or because the goods produced in that sector become less scarce and thereby less expensive.

6. Economics uses the phrases "compensating difference" or "equalizing difference" to describe the relationship between wage and nonwage attributes of a job as described by Adam Smith.

7. The modeling approach is not the only difference between table 7.1 and the Mulligan-Gallen estimates: the latter consider a somewhat lesser penalty, exclude poor and elderly workers from the analysis, and include fringe benefits.

8. Mulligan and Gallen (2013) show that estimates for low-income earnings impacts are sensitive to estimates of the value of the subsidies.

9. The individual mandate penalty is less in 2014 and 2015. The poor and those experiencing hardship are exempt from the penalty. For the purposes of calculating the penalty, only household income above the tax-filing threshold (ranging in 2014 from $3,950 to $20,300, depending on household composition and joint filing status: see U.S. Internal Revenue Service 2015) is considered.

10. The penalty for a year is capped at the national average annual premium for a bronze plan, even if the penalized taxpayer was uninsured for part of the year. Thus, the penalty for being uninsured part-year would likely exceed the cost of buying bronze coverage for that part of the year (note that the ACA permits coverage lapses of up to three months without penalty). On the other hand, a tax-

payer in a region with bronze premiums that significantly exceed the national average may find the penalty to be less than the premiums.

11. The plan premiums are due sooner than the individual mandate penalty, so a cash-hungry household might not sign up for coverage even if it were free by my definition. However, an even more cash-conscious strategy might be to sign up for coverage and miss or delay some premium payments, and thereby avoid the individual mandate penalty. Also note that health insurance plans have out-of-pocket payments too, but those can be avoided by refraining from using the coverage to access health care. In other words, a bronze plan could be purchased just for avoiding the penalty and not for its coverage.

12. As in chapter 4, I use the Kaiser premium calculator to estimate silver plan premiums and premium subsidies, if any. I estimate bronze plan premiums, before subsidies, to be six-sevenths of an unsubsidized silver plan premium, because bronze plans reimburse only 60 percent of covered expenses as compared to 70 percent by silver plans. The subsidized bronze plan premium is the difference between the unsubsidized premium and the premium for the silver plan. The plan premium is for the entire family, even if some of the members are otherwise insured. The uninsured population is measured from the March 2012 CPS.

13. Undocumented immigrants cannot receive exchange subsidies and are exempt from the individual mandate, and they should therefore be excluded from the first five rows of table 7.4. It is unclear which of the individuals represented in my CPS data are undocumented immigrants because documentation status is not measured by the survey. Table 7.4 does not have an adjustment for the uninsured who have access to affordable coverage through an employed person but turned it down; these uninsured still owe a penalty but are not eligible for premium assistance.

14. I take the share of but-for uninsured that becomes insured to be $2*\Phi[-1.253*\theta*\ln(\text{bronze premium ratio})] - 1$, where the bronze premium ratio is the premium ratio tabulated in table 7.4, Φ is the standard normal CDF, and θ is the magnitude of the price elasticity of insurance demand in the neighborhood of a price that equates the number insured to the number uninsured. Based on Lui and Chollet's survey (2006), the range of estimates shown in table 7.4 is derived from a range [0.2, 0.6] for θ.

15. If the head of family i was covered through an employer in March 2012, an estimate of the employer's premium payments are added to the worker's income for the purpose of calculating the income and therefore the available exchange subsidy had the employer stopped offering coverage.

16. The numerator in the ratio has been calculated in the literature on the "money's worth" of switching from employer coverage to exchange coverage (Rennane and Steuerle 2011).

17. Examples of insurance coverage simulators without labor market equilibrium analysis are the Gruber Microsimulation Model (Gruber 2009) and the Urban Institute's Health Insurance Policy Simulation Model (Urban Institute 2011). Almost 50 distinguished "economic scholars" certified to the U.S. Supreme Court

that "economist and MIT Professor Jonathan Gruber has developed a sophisticated economic model [GMSIM] that allows for a *robust prediction* of outcomes in the health care system, depending on various policy changes" (Aaron et al. 2014, italics and brackets added to the original). They added that "the GMSIM has been cited as one of the leading options for modeling health insurance reforms such as the ACA" but without mentioning that GMSIM fails to consider Adam Smith's equalizing differences or otherwise put the employer-employee relationship in a market context. See also Abraham's claim (2012, italics added) that, with these models, "differences before and after a policy change can be analyzed at the micro level and then aggregated to show the *overall effect* of a policy change." Gruber (2011, p. 518) cites "three major limitations" of the GMSIM model, but absence of marketwide employment analysis is not among them.

18. Workers covered in 2012 by plans from the individual market are included among "without employer or public coverage." Figure 7.4 weights each worker by the product of the number of persons in the family and the CPS weight.

19. The remainder of the 19 million is listed in table 7.5 as getting health coverage "on the individual market," but a few of those will find that their cheapest coverage is Medicaid.

20. In other words, ESI-advantage ratios between 0 and 0.4 are assumed to reflect inertia: those in the range without (with) ESI are assumed to stay without (with) it, respectively.

21. Note that the Gallen-Mulligan model does not consider the possibility that people from the individual market might have ESI as a consequence of the ACA, which is in part why their ESI impact estimate is more negative than table 7.5's.

22. I estimate that approximately 3 million persons, in addition to the 31 million shown in the top half of table 7.5, would not have ESI as a consequence of the ACA because the ACA stops them (or their household head) from working full time.

23. If the tax dramatically reallocates labor from one sector to another, there is also an additional issue of how to measure the share α.

CHAPTER EIGHT

1. Equivalently, total factor productivity is a change in value added per hour worked, adjusted for the contributions of labor and capital to that change.

2. More precisely, the two groups of workers "moving" in opposite directions are (1) relatively high-skill workers who would have been uninsured but for the ACA and (2) relatively low-skill workers who would have been insured through an employer but for the ACA.

3. Recall that "ESI employer" refers to one that offers coverage (employer-sponsored coverage) to its full-time employees.

4. This is closely related to the Diamond and Mirrlees (1971) result: that intermediate inputs should be uniformly taxed.

5. Figure 8.1 is typical of previous analyses of intersectoral tax distortions, such as Engen and Skinner (1996, figure 1).

6. Linear supply and demand curves deliver the 1:2 loss-to-tax-savings result. With nonlinear supply and demand, losses and tax savings can deviate somewhat from the 1:2 ratio, but nonetheless the 1:2 ratio is a common approximation used in tax analysis. Note that the productivity loss is related to the taxes *saved* by the workers changing their behavior, $(L^* - L)T_L$, and not the total amount of taxes LT_L (Restuccia and Rogerson 2008 examine the relationship between total taxes and productivity distortions).

7. Sixty-one percent of the twenty-niners face the implicit FTET ($4,422 per year after taxes), and the rest face the employer penalty ($3,163 per year).

8. The calculation from table 8.1 is closer to GDP per hour worked if the costs of deviating from the optimal workweek are considered as costs in accounting for GDP. It is possible that the costs are borne by households, in which case they would not be reflected in GDP as usually measured (recall the distinction between the two quasi-fixed costs q and a in chapter 6), and the impact on measured GDP per hour worked would be further from zero than is indicated in table 8.1. See also below on the average quality of the workforce and the effect of labor productivity on capital per worker.

9. The average amount of unemployment benefits per year added to non-employment is calculated as the product of the average benefit amount from Mulligan (2012b, table 3.9) and the propensity of persons leaving employment to receive unemployment benefits (Mulligan 2012b, tables 3.5 and 3.9).

10. Simulation of the benchmark parameterization of chapter 6's workweeks model shows that the ACA reduces value-added per hour worked by 0.2 percent (see also Mulligan 2014c), which is essentially the same as the approximate result shown in the first two parts of table 8.1.

11. The $1,416 is estimated as 25 percent of the average ESI premiums in chapter 7's CPS sample of persons likely to leave ESI under the ACA.

12. The sum is capped at the full premium for a bronze plan.

13. Specifically, the two penalty rows of table 8.1's bottom part are divided by two (the "triangle" approach) and the non-ACA tax subsidy row is not (the "rectangle" approach).

14. This effect on productivity through capital per worker is separate from the tax effects on the supply of capital noted below.

15. For the purposes of converting the percentage into an annual dollar amount, here I assume GDP of $18 trillion. Not all of the long-term GDP impact is a "loss"; to some extent there is more to be consumed in the short run because less capital is accumulated.

16. The ACA's effect on the composition or average "quality" of the workforce is related to the composition changes that occur during recessions, as documented by Bils (1985) and Solon, Barsky, and Parker (1994).

17. A small amount of production may be lost owing to the extra effort of accurately tracking hours, but in this example I assume that the hours-tracking costs are small.

18. I suspect it would be on the order of the productivity losses shown in

table 8.1. For example, if the investment surtax shifts 0.33 percent of the business capital stock into housing, and housing by itself does not affect the productivity of labor, then the shift will reduce labor productivity by about 0.1 percent.

19. If GDP in 2016 is $18 trillion (2014 prices), and 30 percent of that is capital income, then total capital income will be about $5 trillion.

20. About half of the gross marginal product is depreciation.

21. Mandel (2013). State and local government employer penalty payments will count against grants to state and local governments.

22. Value added and income are two of the ways in which national income accountants calculate gross domestic product (GDP).

23. For the same two reasons, the ACA will reduce some of the usual measures of labor's share of national income (see Karabarbounis and Neiman [2014] on measures of labor's share and its evolution over time). As of the time of writing, I do not have estimates of the likely magnitude or timing of the ACA's impact on measured labor's share. Regarding the timing, it is necessary to measure the evolution of employers' understanding and expectations about the employer mandate (e.g., the "look-back period," or whether the mandate will ever be enforced).

24. The economists' letter sent to Congress urging them not to repeal the ACA asserted, among other things, that "reform-induced expansions in insurance coverage would spur many talented Americans to launch their own companies" (Cutler et al. 2011). See also Bailey (2013), Gruber (2009), and Council of Economic Advisers (2009a, p. 38).

25. Workers who pick up the ESI will tend to be more skilled than those who drop it for individual coverage, so the ACA may end up reducing the average quality of entrepreneurs, if the word *entrepreneurs* is how we describe workers without ESI.

26. But see also the early computable general equilibrium tax models, such as Shoven (1976), that emphasize the role of nonuniform taxes in misallocating resources across sectors.

CHAPTER NINE

1. The ACA's Medicaid expansion is examined separately below.

2. The cross-state average weights thresholds from Henry J. Kaiser Family Foundation (2012) by 2010 state population. The average threshold for children age one to five was 141 percent FPL.

3. When Holahan and Headen wrote, states were required to expand Medicaid. Now it is optional.

4. This 4.3 percent is the product of the program weight of 0.47 (Mulligan 2012b, table 3.5) and the ratio of the $358 Medicaid benefit index to $3,885 monthly compensation (Mulligan 2012b, appendix 3.1 and p. 75; both these are FY 2010 dollars).

5. But note that workers leaving jobs that included health insurance already had access to unsubsidized coverage in the form of continuing coverage from their former employer. Access to this coverage lasted at least 18 months, and often

longer as with some early retirees. This is not to say that the ACA is identical to continuing coverage, but just that the alternative to ACA is not zero health insurance for people without jobs. Also note that the 1996 Health Insurance Portability and Accountability Act was intended to reduce job-changing frictions associated with health insurance, and was in effect long before the ACA was.

6. See also Heim and Lurie (2014), who look specifically at employment lock in Massachusetts after its 2006 health reform and did not find an increase in job separations, on average in the working population.

7. Their employment estimate, 0.4 to 0.6 percent (not percentage points), is 530,000 to 940,000 divided by nationwide employment of 146 million. The time horizon of their impact is approximately two years.

8. See also the related studies reviewed by the Congressional Budget Office (2014a) and by GGN.

9. Normative analyses of the ACA and alternatives include Goodman (2012) and Emanuel (2014). Presumably the best way to design health policy is with an understanding of its economic consequences; this book is dedicated to the task.

10. See also Liebman and Zeckhauser (2004), who argue that people are unaware of notches and cliffs and that their behavior is better explained with a model that approximates the nonlinear schedule with a linear one.

11. The sources for figure 9.1 are Paul-Shaheen (1998), McDonough (2000, chapters 4, 6, 7; and 2004), California Healthcare Foundation (2004), Walsh (2009), and Congressional Budget Office (2011).

12. I assume that the average subsidy valuation is 25 percent less than in the benchmark specification, which corresponds to an exchange-features discount factor of 39 percent rather than the 25 percent discount used in the benchmark specification.

13. If, for example, exchange subsidy enrollment were to be capped, then employers might rush to drop their coverage in order for their employees to enroll before enrollment is closed.

14. See appendix 9.1 for the measurement of work hours per adult.

15. The confidence interval of the sum of multiple random variables is not the same as the sum of each variable's confidence interval.

16. The ARRA refers to the 2009 American Recovery and Reinvestment Act, which paid states to "modernize" (that is, relax) their eligibility requirements for their unemployment insurance (UI) programs. See Mulligan (2012b) and Lindner and Nichols (2012).

17. Using state-level sales tax rates from taxfoundation.org, I found that the personal-income-weighted average sales tax rate increased less than 0.4 percentage points between 2007 and 2012–13, and this does not account for the fact that much consumption is not subject to sales tax.

18. This is the same measure as that in Mulligan (2012b, p. 278), except that now I have three more years of the CPS-MORG files.

19. The 2005–13 average monthly change of the log of the ratio of adjusted to unadjusted population is −0.000312, which is about 1 percent every three years.

20. Shimer (2014) estimates effects of changing demographics on employment rates, defining demographics in two ways: (a) age only and (b) the combination of age, education, race, sex, marital status. The latter demographic variables predict employment rates to fall two-thirds as much as the former variables. My alternative demographics effect is therefore 0.010 rather than the 0.015 based on age only. Also note that education could affect employment differently over time than it does in the cross-section.

21. Formula (9.1) reflects both substitution and wealth effects of the tax (see also endnote 7 in chapter 6).

22. The 2007 value is from Mulligan (2012b) as updated at http://marginaltaxrates.us. The 2012–13 value adds the marginal tax rate changes discussed in the text of this chapter and occurring during the relevant time interval.

23. This section contains an informal discussion of the neoclassical growth model, just to make the points that (1) the stock of capital adjusts more slowly than labor to a permanent and unanticipated change in the tax rate on labor and (2) the reaction of GDP is closer to labor's reaction than capital's.

24. The neoclassical growth model used in Mulligan (2012b, chapter 5) has a half-life of its capital dynamics of 5.2 years, meaning capital makes half of its long-term adjustment in that amount of time (the stable eigenvalue is –0.133).

25. For example, if the long-term impact of a tax change on the logs of labor and capital was –0.01, and so far log capital had adjusted only 0.003, then log wages would be elevated by $0.3^*(0.01 - 0.003) = 0.0021$ above its long-term value, where 0.3 is capital's exponent in an aggregate Cobb-Douglas production function. Using the same labor supply factor $\eta/(1 + \eta)$ as above, with $\eta = 0.6$, log labor would be 0.0008 above its long-term value, which means it still has 8 percent of its long-term adjustment (0.01) remaining.

26. $0.74 = 0.7^*0.92 + 0.3^*0.33$.

27. It is a coincidence that the first and fourth rows of the table have numerical entries that are mirror images.

28. This refers to the average growth rate over the four-year time frame. Throughout the book I assume that the ACA has no effect on the long-term growth rate of GDP per capita, just an effect on its level.

29. An exception: ACA impact models may also have something to say about the direction and pace of the recovery absent the ACA.

30. I make the entire calculation with the St. Louis Federal Reserve database (Federal Reserve Bank of St. Louis 2014): the sum of the three series PAYEMS, LNS12027714, and LNS12032184, times the weekly-hours series AWHAETP, divided by the population series CNP16OV. By using weekly hours from the employer survey, this measure adjusts for multiple-job holders.

31. The ATUS is dedicated to measuring time use. Participants in that survey are asked to account for all of their waking hours in a specific day with their various activities that day, including eating, watching TV, working, traveling, caring for children, etc. The BLS averages daily hours worked across ATUS respondents,

days of the week, and survey months to arrive at an annual average daily hours worked per person age 15 and over.

32. Gali et al. (2007) and Mulligan (2002) are two other papers using labor wedges to quantify labor market distortions over time; Hall (1997) uses them to quantify labor preference shifts.

33. For simplicity, table 9.7 uses expenditures rather than quantity (and sub-quantity) indices to estimate the employee wedge. The purpose of the table is just to get orders of magnitude.

CHAPTER TEN

1. As noted in chapter 9, one of the other Massachusetts health reforms was passed years earlier during the Dukakis administration. For further background reading on these reforms, see the book (2000) and a paper (2004) by McDonough chronicling health reform efforts as a Massachusetts legislator between 1985 and 1997, and the book by Joshua Archambault (2012) about the 2006 reform.

2. I use *Romneycare* to refer to the Massachusetts health law as implemented after 2006 (with special emphasis on 2010), regardless of whether the implementation details were determined under the governorship of Mitt Romney or that of Deval Patrick, who took office in early 2007. For brevity, I also refer to Massachusetts as a "state" rather than a "commonwealth."

3. Technically, the plans already existed and Romneycare just created the premium subsidies and put the plans for sale on a public exchange.

4. Dubay, Long, and Lawton (2012). See also Gruber (2011, 27:02). Most surprising is the recent study from the Center for Retirement Research at Boston College (Sanzenbacker 2014) that claims the differences between Romneycare and the ACA are "minor," without citing any prior research finding order-of-magnitude differences.

5. Commonwealth of Massachusetts, 188th General Court (2013) and Blue Cross Blue Shield of Massachusetts Foundation (2011). The penalty was recently repealed.

6. The Romneycare penalty has a couple of thresholds (11 and 50). Focusing on the 50-employee threshold, the marginal hiring cost of the fiftieth employee would be $14,750 and the marginal hiring cost zero for the first 49 employees. Following chapter 3's approach to the federal penalty, I treat the marginal hiring cost as $295 for all employers not offering health insurance, regardless of employer size.

7. The cafeteria plan itself is an employment subsidy because it allows employees to pay for individual-market coverage with pretax dollars, which is not an option available to people who are not working. But I presume that the failure of some employers to offer cafeteria plans prior to Romneycare is evidence that the administration of cafeteria plans is costly to employers.

8. $297 = 295*1.084/1.0765, where the numerator reflects inflation between 2010 and 2014 and the denominator reflects employer payroll taxes.

9. Dubay et al. (2012) note that one of the Romneycare thresholds for large employer is 11, as compared to the 50-employee threshold in the ACA, and that fewer employers fall under an 11-employee threshold. On the other hand, holding constant the per-employee penalty, the cost of crossing a 50-employee threshold is greater than crossing an 11-employee threshold because of the penalties levied on employees below the threshold.

10. CPS data suggest that, in 2006 (before Romneycare), the uninsurance rate among nonelderly working household heads and spouses was less in Massachusetts than in the New England region generally, which itself was less than the nationwide rate.

11. If, instead of assigning Massachusetts the New England average propensity of employees to work at an employer that does not offer insurance to any of its employees (9.5 percent), Massachusetts were assigned a propensity of 7.5 percent, then the ACA's employer penalty frequency times amount would be more than 20 times that of Massachusetts.

12. Recently a fifth plan was added that is managed by an insurance company (Blue Cross Blue Shield of Massachusetts Foundation 2011).

13. As in previous chapters, I refer to "ESI workers" as people working for an employer that offers health insurance coverage to its full-time employees and refer to "non-ESI workers" as the employees of all other employers.

14. Owing to a lack of precise data (e.g., small sample sizes, income and health plan definitions that differ between MassHealth and the CPS), I do not attempt to quantify the aggregate value of CommCare subsidies for adult health insurance going to Massachusetts households between 133 and 150 percent FPL.

15. MassHealth is the Massachusetts Medicaid and CHIP program.

16. Massachusetts Health Connector (2010, table 2) reports CommCare spending net of enrollee contributions, so I add back a $322 estimate of those contributions. The $322 is from the fiscal year 2013 annual report, which is the only one I have seen with information on funds received from CommCare members. The tax-adjustment factor is one minus an assumed 25 percent marginal income tax rate.

17. Recall table 5.2. Also note that Romneycare does not have means-tested reconciliation of the CommCare premium assistance.

18. One rough approximation of the fraction of CommCare participants who would have been served by Medicaid or are not working is the fraction of participants in families below 150 percent of the poverty line, which is about two-thirds.

19. "Massachusetts is the only state in the nation to offer a health care plan for unemployment insurance claimants, by providing assistance with the cost of existing health insurance premiums or by covering the cost of actual medical expenses" (Massachusetts Executive Office of Labor and Workforce Development 2013). An exception to this was a temporary federal COBRA assistance program under the American Recovery and Reinvestment Act (Mulligan 2012b).

CHAPTER ELEVEN

1. By potential workers, I mean those who would be working without the ACA.

2. Even though the ultimate objective is to understand how behavior is affected by policy, the first step in estimating the size and prevalence of taxes is to hold behavior fixed (see chapter 3), which I did for the purpose of preparing figure 11.1. Chapters 7 and 8 explain why many more workers experience figure 11.1's taxes indirectly. Recall from Chapter 3, however, that this book includes among its "direct effects" employer penalty payments and anticompetitive effects of the employer penalty (i.e., an employee at a small non-ESI employer is "directly" affected because his employment raises the threat of an exorbitant penalty for his employer).

3. For the two full-time employment taxes, the rate shown is the average dollar amount paid or forgone by the group, expressed as a ratio to compensation earned with a 40-hour weekly work schedule at the group's median hourly compensation. For the implicit income tax, it is the average marginal income tax rate from the distribution shown in figure 5.2, augmented to include uncompensated care and the reconciliation of tax credits as discussed in chapter 5.

4. The midpoint of the non-ACA effects estimated in table 9.4 is 2.8 percent. If I used the rosy scenario for that too, then the economists' letter prediction would be more than 4 percent.

5. The Federal Reserve projections are from Board of Governors of the Federal Reserve System (2014). I am frequently asked why the Federal Reserve and other economists appear to disagree with me about the negative growth effects of the ACA. I cannot answer because (1) I am not an expert on economists' opinions on current events and (2) economists have written so little that even acknowledges the possibility of the ACA's having large taxes, let alone explaining how their implementation is consistent with above-average growth. When the ACA's taxes are acknowledged, as in Gamage (2012) and Congressional Budget Office (2014a), the possibility of significantly negative growth effects is taken seriously.

REFERENCES

The reference list is available online at biblio.acasideeffects.com.

Aaron, Henry J., Stuary Altman, Susan Athey, et al. 2014. *Brief Amici Curiae for Economic Scholars in Support of Appellees. Halbig* v. *Sebelius*, U.S. Court of Appeals for the District of Columbia Circuit.

Abraham, Jean M. 2012. *Predicting the Effects of the Affordable Care Act: A Comparative Analysis of Health Policy Microsimulation Models.* Policy brief, State Health Reform Assistance Network.

Agency for Healthcare Research and Quality, Center for Financing. 2013. "Table II.D.1 (2012)." *Medical Expenditure Panel Survey.* http://meps.ahrq.gov /mepsweb/data_stats/summ_tables/insr/state/series_2/2012/tiid1.htm (accessed April 12, 2014).

Aizawa, Naoki. 2014. "Health Insurance Exchange Design in an Empirical Equilibrium Labor Market Model." Manuscript, University of Pennsylvania.

Americans for Tax Reform. 2013. "Full List of Obama Tax Hikes." atr.org. http:// www.atr.org/full-list-ACA-tax-hikes-a6996 (accessed May 20, 2014).

Archambault, Josh D. 2012. *Competing Visions for Massachusetts: Health Reform.* Boston: Pioneer Institute.

Bagdoyan, Seto J. 2014. "Patient Protection and Affordable Care Act." Testimony before the Subcommittee on Oversight, Committee on Ways and Means, U.S. House of Representatives, Washington, DC.

Bagley, Sharon. 2013. "Obamacare Rollout Requiring Tens Of Thousands of Workers: Analysis." *huffingtonpost.com.* June 21. http://www.huffingtonpost .com/2013/06/21/obamacare-rollout_n_3476261.html (accessed November 12, 2014).

Baicker, Katherine, and Amitabh Chandra. 2006. "The Labor Market Effects of Rising Health Premiums." *Journal of Labor Economics* 24 (3): 609–34.

Baicker, Katherine, and Helen Levy. 2008. "Employer Health Insurance Mandates and the Risk of Unemployment." *Risk Management and Insurance Review* 11, no. 1: 109–32.

Bailey, James. 2013. "Health Insurance and the Supply of Entrepreneurs: New Evidence from the Affordable Care Act's Dependent Coverage Mandate." Manuscript, Temple University.

Barro, Robert J. 1981. "Output Effects of Government Purchases." *Journal of Political Economy* 89, no. 6 (December): 1086–1121.

———. 2011. "Keynesian Economics vs. Regular Economics." *Wall Street Journal*, August 24. http://online.wsj.com/news/articles/SB100014240531119035969045 76516412073445854 (accessed June 19, 2014).

Barro, Robert J., and Chaipat Sahasakul. 1986. "Measuring the Average Marginal Tax Rate from Social Security and the Individual Income Tax." *Journal of Business* 59, no. 4 (October): 555–66.

Becker, Gary S. 1994. *Human Capital*, 3rd ed. Chicago: University of Chicago Press.

Bils, Mark J. 1985. "Real Wages over the Business Cycle: Evidence from Panel Data." *Journal of Political Economy* 93, no. 4 (August): 666–89.

Blue Cross Blue Shield of Massachusetts Foundation. 2011. "Massachusetts Health Reform: A Five-Year Progress Report." bluecrossmafoundation.org. November 17. http://bluecrossmafoundation.org/sites/default/files/Health%20Reform%20Implementation%20Massachusetts%20Health%20Reform%205%20Year%20Progress%20Report.pdf (accessed August 6, 2013).

Blumberg, Linda J., John Holahan, and Matthew Buettgens. 2014. "Why Not Just Eliminate the Employer Mandate?" rwjf.org. May. http://www.rwjf.org/content/dam/farm/reports/issue_briefs/2014/rwjf413248 (accessed May 14, 2014).

Board of Governors of the Federal Reserve System. 2014. "FOMC March 19, 2014 Projections Materials." federalreserve.gov. March 19. http://www.federalreserve.gov/monetarypolicy/fomcprojtabl20140319.htm (accessed April 18, 2014).

Bovbjerg, Randall R., Stan Dorn, Juliana Macri, and Jack Meyer. 2010. *Federal Subsidy for Laid-Off Workers' Health Insurance.* Washington, DC: Urban Institute.

Burkhauser, Richard V., Sean Lyons, and Kosali I. Simon. 2011. "The Importance of the Meaning and Measurement of 'Affordable' in the Affordable Care Act." NBER working paper, no. 17279 (September).

Calmfors, Lars, and Michael Hoel. 1988. "Work Sharing and Overtime." *Scandinavian Journal of Economics* 90, no. 1 (March): 45–62.

California Healthcare Foundation. 2004. "State Employer Health Insurance Mandates: A Brief History." Oakland: California Healthcare Foundation.

Campbell, John Y., and N. Gregory Mankiw. 1987. "Are Output Fluctuations Transitory?" *Quarterly Journal of Economics* 102, no. 4 (November): 857–80.

Carey, Mary Agnes. 2013. "What Is the ACA's 'Reinsurance Tax'?" *Kaiser Health News*, October 15. http://www.kaiserhealthnews.org/Stories/2013/October/15/FAQ-on-health-law-reinsurance-tax-and-Senate-compromise.aspx (accessed June 19, 2014).

Center for Budget and Policy Priorities. 2013. "Question of the Day: Coordination between Medicaid and Premium Tax Credits." healthreformbeyondthebasics.org. http://www.healthreformbeyondthebasics.org/wp-content/uploads/2013/12/Coordination-Between-Medicaid-and-Premium-Tax-Credits-FAQ.pdf (accessed May 30, 2014).

Centers for Medicare and Medicaid Services, Office of the Actuary. 2011. "Projected Medicare Expenditures under an Illustrative Scenario with Alternative Payment Updates to Medicare Providers." cms.gov. May 13. http://www.cms.gov/Research-Statistics-Data-and-Systems/Statistics-Trends-and-Reports/ReportsTrustFunds/downloads/2011TRAlternativeScenario.pdf (accessed May 2, 2014).

Centers for Medicare and Medicaid Services. 2012. "Early Retiree Reinsurance Program: Reimbursement Update." cms.gov. February 17. https://www.cms.gov/CCIIO/Resources/Files/Downloads/errp-posting_feb2012.pdf (accessed March 10, 2015).

———. 2013. "Fact Sheet: HHS Final Rule and Treasury Notices on Individual Shared Responsibility Provision Exemptions, Minimum Essential Coverage, and Related Topics." cms.gov. June 26. http://www.cms.gov/Newsroom/MediaReleaseDatabase/Fact-Sheets/2013-Fact-Sheets-Items/2013-06-26.html (accessed March 29, 2014).

———. 2014. "2015 Letter to Issuers in the Federally-Facilitated Marketplaces." cms.gov. March 14. http://www.cms.gov/CCIIO/Resources/Regulations-and-Guidance/Downloads/2015-final-issuer-letter-3-14-2014.pdf (accessed April 3, 2014).

Chandler, Seth. 2014. "CBO Implies Obama Regulation Shoveled $8 Billion to Insurers." acadeathspiral.org. April 17. http://acadeathspiral.org/2014/04/17/cbo-implies-obama-regulation-shoveled-8-billion-to-insurers (accessed April 25, 2014).

Chetty, Raj, Adam Guren, Day Manoli, and Andrea Weber. 2011. "Are Micro and Macro Labor Supply Elasticities Consistent? A Review of Evidence on the Intensive and Extensive Margins." *American Economic Review* 101, no. 2 (May): 1–6.

Chicago Barbers Association. 2011. "A History of Barbering in Chicago." chicagobarbersassociation.org. https://web.archive.org/20130310065846/chicagobarbersassociation.org/history-2/ (accessed May 17, 2014).

Chirba, Mary Ann, and Alice A. Noble. 2013. "Medical Malpractice, the Affordable Care Act and State Provider Shield Laws: More Myth Than Necessity?" Bill of Health Blog at Harvard Law. May 14. https://blogs.law.harvard.edu/billofhealth/2013/05/14/medical-malpractice-the-affordable-care-act-and-state-provider-shield-laws-more-myth-than-necessity/ (accessed April 3, 2014).

Cochrane, John H. 2014. "Groundhog Day." *The Grumpy Economist.* May 11. http://johnhcochrane.blogspot.com/2014/05/groundhog-day.html (accessed May 12, 2014).

Cohen, Robin A., Diane M. Makuc, Amy B. Bernstein, Linda T. Bilheimer, and Eve Powell-Griber. 2009. "Health Insurance Coverage Trends, 1959–2007." *National Health Statistics Reports*, no. 17 (July): 1–27.

Cole, Harold L., Soojin Kim, and Dirk Krueger. 2012. "Analyzing the Effects of Insuring Health Risks: On the Trade-Off between Short Run Insurance Benefits vs. Long Run Incentive Costs." NBER working paper, no. 18572 (November).

Cole, Harold L., and Lee E. Ohanian. 2004. "New Deal Policies and the Persistence of the Great Depression: A General Equilibrium Analysis." *Journal of Political Economy* 112, no. 4 (August): 779–816.

Commonwealth of Massachusetts, 188th General Court. 2013. "Chapter 149, Section 188." malegislature.gov. https://malegislature.gov/Laws/GeneralLaws/PartI/TitleXXI/Chapter149/Section188 (accessed August 6, 2013).

Community Resources Information. 2013. "Medical Security Program." mass resources.org. https://web.archive.org/web/20111229084947/http://www.mass resources.org/medical-security-program.html (accessed at massresources.org, August 9, 2013).

Congressional Budget Office. 2007. "CBO's Health Insurance Simulation Model: A Technical Description." *CBO Background Paper*, October.

———. 2010. "The Budget and Economic Outlook: An Update." August. http://thehill.com/images/stories/blogs/augustcbo.pdf (accessed April 9, 2013).

———. 2011. *CBO's Analysis of the Major Health Care Legislation Enacted in March 2010.* Testimony before the Subcommittee on Health, Washington, DC: Congressional Budget Office.

———. 2012a. *Effective Marginal Tax Rates for Low- and Moderate-Income Workers.* Washington, DC: Congressional Budget Office.

———. 2012b. *Illustrative Examples of Effective Marginal Tax Rates Faced by Married and Single Taxpayers.* Washington, DC: Congressional Budget Office.

———. 2012c. "July 24, 2012 Letter to John Boehner." July 24. http://www.cbo.gov/sites/default/files/cbofiles/attachments/43471-hr6079.pdf (accessed May 1, 2014).

———. 2013. "Effects of the Affordable Care Act on Health Insurance Coverage." May. https://www.cbo.gov/sites/default/files/cbofiles/attachments/43900-2013-05-ACA.pdf.

———. 2014a. "The Budget and Economic Outlook: 2014 to 2024." February. http://cbo.gov/sites/default/files/cbofiles/attachments/45010-Outlook2014_Feb.pdf (accessed April 3, 2014).

———. 2014b. "Updated Estimates of the Effects of the Insurance Coverage Provisions of the Affordable Care Act." April. http://cbo.gov/sites/default/files/cbofiles/attachments/45231-ACA_Estimates.pdf (accessed April 16, 2014).

Congressional Research Service. 2010. "The PPACA Penalty Provision and the Internal Revenue Service." Memorandum to Hon. Tom Coburn.

Contorno, Steve. 2013. "Localities Split on Providing Health Benefits for Part-Time Workers." washingtonexaminer.com. February 14. http://washingtonexaminer.com/localities-split-on-providing-health-benefits-for-part-time-workers/article/2521655 (accessed February 20, 2013).

Costa, Dora L. 1998. *The Evolution of Retirement: An American Economic History, 1880–1990.* Chicago: University of Chicago Press (for NBER).

Council of Economic Advisers. 2009a. *The Economic Case for Health Care Reform.* Washington, DC: Executive Office of the President, June.

———. 2009b. *The Economic Case for Health Care Reform: Update.* Executive Office of the President, December.

Crimmel, Beth Levin. 2012. *Trends in Offers, Eligibility, and Take-up Rates for Employer-Sponsored Health Insurance.* Statistical brief, Washington, DC: HHS, Agency for Healthcare Research and Quality.

Cutler, David M. 2011. Testimony for the U.S. House Committee on Energy and Commerce.

Cutler, David M., Harold Pollack, Henry J. Aaron, Jean Marie Abraham, et al. 2011. "Letter to the U.S. House Committee on the Budget." americanprogress action.org. January 26. http://www.americanprogressaction.org/wp-content /uploads/issues/2011/01/pdf/budgetcommitteefinal.pdf (accessed April 3, 2014).

Cutler, David, and Neeraj Sood. 2010. *New Jobs through Better Health Care.* Washington, DC: Center for American Progress.

Dardick, Hal. 2013. "Emanuel to Shift Retired City Workers to Obamacare." *Chicago Tribune*, May 15. http://articles.chicagotribune.com/2013-05-15/news/chi -emanuel-to-shift-retired-city-workers-to-obamacare-20130515_1_retired -city-workers-health-care-health-insurance (accessed June 19, 2014).

Davidson, Liz. 2013. "What 'Obamacare' Means for Early Retirees Next Year." *forbes .com*. May 30. http://www.forbes.com/sites/financialfinesse/2013/05/30/what -obamacare-means-for-early-retirees-next-year/ (accessed November 12, 2014).

Demko, Paul. 2014. "Flurry of New ACA Rules Adds to Insurers' Uncertainty." modernhealthcare.com. March 17. http://www.modernhealthcare.com/article /20140317/NEWS/303179949# (accessed March 25, 2014).

Diamond, Peter A., and James A. Mirrlees. 1971. "Optimal Taxation and Public Production I: Production Efficiency." *American Economic Review* 61, no. 1 (March): 8–27.

Don McNea Fire School. 2014. "Fireman Work Schedule." *fireprep.com*. http://fire prep.com/fire_man_firefighter_job_se.html (accessed October 21, 2014).

Dostal, Erin. 2012. "Restaurants to Mitigate Health Care Costs by Cutting Hours." *Restaurant News*. October 18. http://nrn.com/latest-headlines/restaurants -mitigate-health-care-costs-cutting-hours#ixzz2CCIVEKK3 (accessed November 7, 2014).

Dubay, Lisa, Sharon K. Long, and Emily Lawton. 2012. *Will Health Reform Lead to Job Loss? Evidence from Massachusetts Says No.* Washington, DC: Urban Institute.

Egan, Emily. 2013. "Primer: Cadillac Tax (High Cost Plan Excise Tax)." american actionforum.org. June 25. http://americanactionforum.org/sites/default/files /Cadillac%20Tax%20Primer%20Final.pdf (accessed April 2, 2014).

Emanuel, Ezekiel J. 2014. *Reinventing American Health Care.* Philadelphia: Public-Affairs.

Emanuel, Ezekiel J., and Victor R. Fuchs. 2008. "The Perfect Storm of Overutilization." *JAMA* 299, no. 23 (June): 2789–91.

Engen, Eric, and Jonathan Skinner. 1996. "Taxation and Economic Growth." *National Tax Journal* 49, no. 4 (December): 617–42.

Farenthold, Blake. 2013. "Investigating Obamacare Fraud at Texas Ground Zero for Abuse." *farenthold.house.gov.* December 22. http://farenthold.house.gov/news /email/show.aspx?ID=X726FTKFGV46DAP36AQIHXRV54 (accessed November 7, 2014).

Federal Reserve Bank of St. Louis. 2014. *Federal Reserve Economic Data.* http:// research.stlouisfed.org/fred2/ (accessed May 10, 2014).

Ferris, J. S., and C. G. Plourde. 1982. "Labour Mobility, Seasonal Unemployment

Insurance, and the Newfoundland Inshore Fishery." *Canadian Journal of Economics* 15, no. 3 (August): 426–41.

Finch, Michael III. 2014. "Mobile Woman Concerned about Losing Obamacare Subsidy, Navigating the Changes to Her Policy." *AL.com*. November 7. http://www.al.com/news/index.ssf/2014/11/mobile_woman_concerned_about_1.html (accessed November 12, 2014).

Friedman, Milton, and Anna J. Schwartz. 1963. *A Monetary History of the United States, 1867–1960.* Princeton, NJ: Princeton University Press.

Gabel, Jon R., et al. 2012. "More Than Half of Individual Health Plans Offer Coverage That Falls Short of What Can Be Sold through Exchanges as of 2014." *Health Affairs* 31, no. 6 (June): 1–12.

Galí, Jordi, Mark Gertler, and J. David Lopez-Salido. 2007. "Markups, Gaps, and the Welfare Costs of Business Fluctuations." *Review of Economics and Statistics* 89 (February): 44–59.

Gallen, Trevor S. 2013. "Size Provisions in the Affordable Care Act." Manuscript of Ph.D. dissertation, University of Chicago.

Gallen, Trevor S., and Casey B. Mulligan. 2013. "Wedges, Labor Market Behavior, and Health Insurance Coverage." NBER working paper, December.

Gamage, David S. 2012. "Perverse Incentives Arising from the Tax Provisions of Healthcare Reform: Why Further Reforms Are Needed to Prevent Avoidable Costs to Low- and Moderate-Income Workers." *Tax Law Review* 65, no. 4 (Summer): 669–721.

Garicano, Luis, Claire Lelarge, and John Van Reenan. 2013. "Firm Size Distortions and the Productivity Distribution: Evidence from France." NBER working paper, no. 18841 (February).

Garthwaite, Craig, Tal Gross, and Matthew J. Notowidigdo. 2014. "Public Health Insurance, Labor Supply, and Employment Lock." *Quarterly Journal of Economics* 129, no. 2 (May): 653–96.

Goldin, Claudia, and Lawrence F. Katz. 2008. *The Race between Education and Technology.* Cambridge, MA: Harvard University Press.

Goodman, John C. 2012. *Priceless: Curing the Healthcare Crisis.* Oakland, CA: Independent Institute.

Goolsbee, Austan. 2011. *Testimony at the Hearing on the Health Care Law's Impact on Jobs, Employers, and the Economy.* Washington, DC: Committee on Ways and Means, U.S. House of Representatives.

Goozner, Merrill. 2014. "The Coming Assault on Narrow Networks." *Modern Healthcare* 44, no. 11 (March): 25.

Graham, Jed. 2014. "ObamaCare Employer Mandate: A List of Cuts to Work Hours, Jobs." investors.com. February 3. http://news.investors.com/politics-obamacare/020314-669013-obamacare-employer-mandate-a-list-of-cuts-to-work-hours-jobs.htm (accessed February 10, 2014).

Gruber, Jonathan. 2009. "Documentation for the Gruber Microsimulation Model." MIT faculty website. http://economics.mit.edu/files/9906 (accessed August 2013).

———. 2011. "2011 Hewitt Health Care Lecture: The Budgetary Impact of Federal Health Care Reform." vimeo.com. March. http://vimeo.com/21114715#t =27m2s (accessed August 8, 2013).

———. 2012. "Will the Affordable Care Act Kill Jobs?" *New Republic*, July 9.

Gruber, Jonathan, and Brigitte C. Madrian. 2004. "Health Insurance, Labor Supply, and Job Mobility: A Critical Review of the Literature." In *Health Policy and the Uninsured*, edited by Catherine G. McLaughlin, 97–178. Washington, DC: Urban Institute Press.

Gruber, Jonathan, and David A. Wise. 1999. *Social Security and Retirement around the World*. Chicago: University of Chicago Press (for NBER).

Hai, Rong. 2013. "The Determinants of Rising Inequality in Health Insurance and Wages." Manuscript, University of Chicago.

Hall, Robert E. 1997. "Macroeconomic Fluctuations and the Allocation of Time." *Journal of Labor Economics* 15, no. 1, part 2 (January): S223–50.

Hamermesh, Daniel S. 1996a. *Labor Demand*. Princeton, NJ: Princeton University Press.

———. 1996b. *Workdays, Workhours, and Work Schedules*. Kalamazoo, MI: Upjohn Institute for Employment Research.

Hancock, Jay. 2013. "'Narrow Networks' Trigger Push-Back from State Officials." kaiserhealthnews.org. November 25. http://www.kaiserhealthnews.org /stories/2013/november/25/states-balk-at-narrow-networks.aspx (accessed May 10, 2014).

Handel, Ben, Igal Hendel, and Michael D. Whinston. 2014. "Equilibria in Health Insurance Exchanges: Adverse Selection vs. Reclassification Risk." Manuscript, MIT.

Hart, Robert A. 1987. *Working Time and Employment*. Winchester, MA: Allen & Unwin.

Hausman, Leonard J. 1969. "Potential for Financial Self-Support among AFDC and AFDC-UP Recipients." *Southern Economic Journal* 36, no. 1 (July): 60–66.

Heim, Bradley T., and Ithai Z. Lurie. 2014. "Does Health Reform Lead to Increased Job Mobility? Evidence from Massachusetts." Manuscript, Indiana University, February.

Henry J. Kaiser Family Foundation. 2012. "Income Eligibility Limits for Children's Regular Medicaid and Children's CHIP-Funded Medicaid Expansions as a Percent of Federal Poverty Level, January 2012." kff.org. https://web .archive.org/web/20130120035535/http://statehealthfacts.org/comparereport .jsp?rep=76&cat=4 (accessed at kff.org in October 2012).

———. 2013. "Key Facts about the Uninsured Population." kff.org. September 26. http://kff.org/uninsured/fact-sheet/key-facts-about-the-uninsured-population/ (accessed February 2014).

———. 2014. "Health Reform FAQs." kff.org. http://kff.org/health-reform/faq /health-reform-frequently-asked-questions/#question-im-leaving-my-job -and-will-be-eligible-for-cobra-can-i-shop-for-coverage-and-subsidies-on -the-marketplace-instead (accessed May 4, 2014).

Herring, Bradley, and Lisa Korin Lentz. 2011. "What Can We Expect from the 'Cadillac Tax' in 2018 and Beyond?" *Inquiry* 48, no. 4 (November): 322–37.

Hicks, Josh. 2012. "'Obamacare' Tax Hikes vs. Tax Breaks: Which Is Greater?" washingtonpost.com. July 6. http://www.washingtonpost.com/blogs/fact-checker/post/obamacare-tax-hikes-vs-tax-breaks-which-is-greater/2012/07/06/gJQAx6AyPW_blog.html (accessed May 2, 2014).

Hirsch, Barry T. 2005. "Why Do Part-Time Workers Earn Less? The Role of Worker and Job Skills." *Industrial and Labor Relations Review* 58, no. 4 (July): 525–51.

Holahan, John, and Irene Headen. 2010. *Medicaid Coverage and Spending in Health Reform*. Henry J. Kaiser Family Foundation.

Hopkins, Nicole. 2013. "ObamaCare Forced Mom into Medicaid." *Wall Street Journal*, November 20. http://online.wsj.com/news/articles/SB10001424052702303531204579207724152219590 (accessed June 19, 2014).

Hsieh, Chang-Tai, and Peter J. Klenow. 2009. "Misallocation and Manufacturing TFP in China and India." *Quarterly Journal of Economics* 124, no. 4 (November): 1403–48.

Huemer, Michael. 2012. "In Praise of Passivity." *Studia Humana* 1, no. 2: 12–28.

IGM Economic Experts Panel. 2012. "Economic Stimulus." igmchicago.org. February 15. http://www.igmchicago.org/igm-economic-experts-panel/poll-results?SurveyID=SV_cw5O9LNJL1oz4Xi (accessed April 3, 2014).

Janicki, Hubert. 2013. *Employment-Based Health Insurance: 2010*. Washington, DC: U.S. Department of Commerce.

Joint Committee on Taxation. 2008. *Tax Expenditures for Health Care*. Public Hearing, Washington, DC: Senate Committee on Finance.

———. 2012. "Letter to Honorable Tom Coburn." Washington, DC, March 20.

Jorgenson, Dale W. 2009. "Introduction." In *The Economics of Productivity*, by Dale W. Jorgenson, 9–28. Northampton: Edward Elgar.

Kaiser Commission on Medicaid and the Uninsured. 2008. *Covering the Uninsured in 2008: Key Facts about Current Costs, Sources of Payment, and Incremental Costs*. Menlo Park, CA: Henry J. Kaiser Family Foundation.

Karabarbounis, Loukas, and Brent Neiman. 2014. "The Global Decline of the Labor Share." *Quarterly Journal of Economics* 129, no. 1 (February): 61–103.

Kennedy, Edward M. 1978. Democratic National Convention, Health Care Workshop Speech. December 9.

Kessler, Daniel P. 2011. "How Health Reform Punishes Work." *Wall Street Journal*, April 25. http://online.wsj.com/news/articles/SB10001424052748704628404576265692304582936 (accessed June 19, 2014).

Kessler, Glenn. 2013. "Does 'Obamacare' Have $1 Trillion in Tax Hikes, Aimed at the Middle Class?" *Washington Post*, March 12. http://www.washingtonpost.com/blogs/fact-checker/post/does-obamacare-have-1-trillion-in-tax-hikes-aimed-at-the-middle-class/2013/03/11/1e685f4c-8a9b-11e2-8d72-dc76641cb8d4_blog.html (accessed June 19, 2014).

Keynes, John Maynard. 1919. *The Economic Consequences of the Peace*. London: Macmillan (also http://www.gutenberg.org/files/15776/15776-h/15776-h.htm).

King, Christopher. 2014. "Privately Employed Seasonal Workers Fight to Keep Unemployment Benefits." *cbs46.com*. March 7. http://www.cbs46.com/story /24666695/privately-employed-seasonal-workers-fight-to-keep-unemployment -benefits (accessed November 14, 2014).

Klein, Ezra. 2012. "No, 'Obamacare' Isn't 'the Largest Tax Increase in the History of the World.'" *washingtonpost.com*. July 2. http://www.washingtonpost .com/blogs/wonkblog/wp/2012/07/02/no-obamacare-isnt-the-largest-tax -increase-in-the-history-of-the-world-in-one-chart/ (accessed July 2, 2014).

Kolstad, Jonathan T., and Amanda E. Kowalski. 2012. "Mandate-Based Health Reform and the Labor Market: Evidence from the Massachusetts Reform." NBER working paper, no. 17933 (March).

Krueger, Alan B., and Bruce D. Meyer. 2002. *Labor Supply Effects of Social Insurance*. Vol. 4, in *Handbook of Public Economics*, edited by Alan J. Auerbach and Martin Feldstein, Elsevier, 2327–92.

Krueger, Alan B., and Uwe E. Reinhardt. 1994. "The Economics of Employer versus Individual Mandates." *Health Affairs*, Spring, 34–53.

Liebman, Jeffrey B., and Richard J. Zeckhauser. "Schmeduling." Manuscript, Harvard University, October 2004.

Lindner, Stephan, and Austin Nichols. "How Do Unemployment Insurance Modernization Laws Affect the Number and Composition of Eligible Workers?" Manuscript, Urban Institute, 2012.

Lui, Su, and Deborah Chollet. *Price and Income Elasticity of the Demand for Health Insurance and Health Care Services: A Critical Review of the Literature*. Washington, DC: Mathematica Policy Research, 2006.

Lynch, Matthew. 2014. "Need a Reason to Cut Costs at Your Business? Blame Obamacare." *huffingtonpost.com*. February 26. http://www.huffingtonpost.com /matthew-lynch-edd/need-a-reason-to-cut-cost_b_4856283.html (accessed November 14, 2014).

Malkiel, Burton Gordon. 1973. *A Random Walk Down Wall Street*. New York: Norton.

Mandel, Benjamin A. 2013. "Accounting for Changing Impact of the Federal Government Including the Affordable Care Act." May. http://www.bea.gov /about/pdf/Gov_ACA.pdf (accessed March 7, 2014).

Mankiw, N. Gregory. 2009. "Supply-Side Ideas, Turned Upside Down." *New York Times*, November 1, BU14.

Massachusetts Executive Office of Labor and Workforce Development. 2013. Medical Security Program. https://web.archive.org/web/20130223055549/www.mass .gov/lwd/unemployment-insur/programs-and-services-for-claimants/medical -security-program-msp/ (accessed February 20, 2013).

Massachusetts Health Connector. 2010. "Implementation of Health Care Reform. Fiscal Year 2010." Report to the Massachusetts Legislature.

McDonough, John E. 2000. *Experiencing Politics: A Legislator's Stories of Government and Health Care*. Berkeley: University of California Press.

———. 2004. "The Road to Universal Health Coverage in Massachusetts: A Story in Three Parts." *New England Journal of Public Policy* 20, no. 1: article 9.

Mercer, Marsha. 2014. "Is Your Medicare Safe?" *AARP Bulletin*, January. http://www
.aarp.org/health/medicare-insurance/info-12-2013/medicare-and-affordable
-care-act.html (accessed June 19, 2014).

Moffitt, Robert. 2015. "The U.S. Safety Net and Work Incentives: the Great Recession and Beyond." *Journal of Policy Analysis and Management* 34, no. 2 (Winter):
458–65.

Montgomery, Mark, and James Cosgrove. 1993. "The Effect of Employee Benefits
on the Demand for Part-Time Workers." *Industrial and Labor Relations Review*
47, no. 1: 87–98.

Morgan, David, and Caroline Humer. 2014. "Insurers See Double-Digit Obamacare Price Rises in Many States Next Year." bangordailynews.com. March 23.
http://bangordailynews.com/2014/03/23/health/insurers-see-double-digit
-obamacare-price-rises-in-many-states-next-year/ (accessed April 12, 2014).

Mower, Lawrence. 2012. "Firefighter's 24-Hour Shifts Get Close Look." *Las Vegas
Review-Journal*, May 6, online edition.

Mulligan, Casey B. 2002. "A Century of Labor-Leisure Distortions." NBER working paper, no. 8774 (February).

———. 2004. "What Do Aggregate Consumption Euler Equations Say about
the Capital Income Tax Burden?" *American Economic Review* 94, no. 2 (May):
166–70.

———. 2005. "Public Policies as Specification Errors." *Review of Economic Dynamics* 8, no. 4 (October): 902–26.

———. 2012a. "The ARRA: Some Unpleasant Welfare Arithmetic." NBER working
paper, no. 18591 (December).

———. 2012b. *The Redistribution Recession.* New York: Oxford University Press.
www.redistributionrecession.com.

———. 2013a. "Average Marginal Tax Rates under the Affordable Care Act." NBER
working paper, no. 19365 (November).

———. 2013b. "Is the Affordable Care Act Different from Romneycare? A Labor
Economics Perspective." NBER working paper, no. 19366 (November).

———. 2014a. "The ACA: Some Unpleasant Welfare Arithmetic." NBER working
paper, no. 20020 (March).

———. 2014b. "Uncertainty, Redistribution, and the Labor Market since 2007."
IZA Journal of Labor Policy 3, no. 8: 1–16.

———. 2014c. *Side Effects: The Economic Consequences of the Health Reform.* Self-
published e-book.

———. Forthcoming. "The New Full-Time Employment Taxes." *Tax Policy and
the Economy*, 29.

Mulligan, Casey B., and Trevor S. Gallen. 2013. "Wedges, Wages, and Productivity
under the Affordable Care Act." NBER working paper, no. 19771 (December).

National Bureau of Economic Research. 2012. *Marginal Tax Rates, Federal and
State.* March 30. http://users.nber.org/~taxsim/marginal-tax-rates/at84.html
(accessed May 10, 2014).

National Federation of Independent Business. 2011. "Employer Mandate Penalties Cribsheet." nfib.com. November 11. http://www.nfib.com/Portals/0/PDF/AllUsers/research/cribsheets/employer-mandate-penalties-nfib-cribsheet.pdf (accessed May 7, 2014).

National Public Radio et al. 2014. "Obamacare Enrollees Embolded to Leave Jobs, Start Businesses." *Health News Florida*. April 30. http://health.wusf.usf.edu/post/obamacare-enrollees-emboldened-leave-jobs-start-businesses (accessed November 8, 2014).

Nurin, Tara. 2012. "Denying Unemployment to Seasonal Workers at Jersey Shore." *njspotlight.com*. May 17. http://www.njspotlight.com/stories/12/0516/1936/ (accessed November 14, 2014).

Oi, Walter Y. 1962. "Labor as a Quasi-Fixed Factor." *Journal of Political Economy* 70, no. 6 (December): 538–55.

Owen, John D. 1979. *Working Hours: An Economic Analysis*. Lexington, MA: Lexington.

Pagliery, Jose. 2013. "For Fatburger and Others, Obamacare Delay Came Too Late." *money.cnn.com*. July 8. http://money.cnn.com/2013/07/08/smallbusiness/obamacare-fatburger/index.html (accessed November 7, 2014).

Paul-Shaheen, Pamela A. 1998. "The States and Health Care Reform: The Road Less Traveled and Lessons Learned from Seven That Took the Lead." *Journal of Health Politics, Policy, and Law* 23, no. 2 (April): 319–61.

Pear, Robert. 2012. "Brawling over Health Care Moves to Rules on Exchanges." *New York Times*, July 7, A14.

———. 2014a. "New Health Fix Offers Subsidies for Insurance Policies Bought Outside Exchanges." *New York Times*, February 28, A10.

———. 2014b. "Public Sector Cuts Part-Time Shifts to Bypass Insurance Law." *New York Times*, February 20, A12.

Pender, Kathleen. 2013. "Lower 2014 Income Can Net Huge Health Care Subsidy." *sfgate.com*. October 12. http://www.sfgate.com/business/networth/article/Lower-2014-income-can-net-huge-health-care-subsidy-4891087.php (accessed November 12, 2014).

Philipson, Tomas, et al. 2012. "An Analysis of Whether Higher Health Care Spending in the United States versus Europe Is 'Worth It' in the Case of Cancer." *Health Affairs* 31, no. 4 (April): 667–75.

Piotrowski, Julie. 2013. "Health Policy Briefs: Excise Tax on 'Cadillac' Plans." *Health Affairs*, September.

Powell, Jennifer Heldt. 2012. "Competing Visions for Massachusetts: Health Reform." In *The Great Experiment*, by Josh D. Archambault. Boston: Pioneer Institute.

PWC Health Research Institute. 2014. "Health Insurance Premiums: Comparing ACA Exchange Rates to the Employer-Based Market." pwc.com. May. http://www.pwc.com/en_US/us/health-industries/health-insurance-exchanges/assets/pwc-hri-health-insurance-premium.pdf (accessed May 13, 2014).

Ramachandran, Shalini. 2014. "Pay-TV 'Cord Cutting' Accelerates." *Wall Street Journal*, November 6, online edition.

Rennane, Stephanie, and C. Eugene Steuerle. 2011. "Health Reform: A Four-Tranche System (Updated and Revised)." www.urban.org. February 22. http://www.urban.org/publications/901408.html (accessed March 15, 2013).

Restuccia, Diego, and Richard Rogerson. 2008. "Policy Distortions and Aggregate Productivity." *Review of Economic Dynamics* 11, no. 4 (October): 707–20.

Rosen, Sherwin. 1968. "Short-Run Employment Variation on Class-I Railroads in the U.S., 1947–63." *Econometrica* 36, no. 3 (July): 511–29.

———. 1978. "The Supply of Work Schedules and Employment." In *Work Time and Employment*. Washington, DC: National Commission for Manpower Policy.

———. 1986. "The Theory of Equalizing Differences." In *Handbook of Labor Economics, vol. I*, edited by Orley C. Ashenfelter and Richard Layard, 641–92. Amsterdam: North-Holland.

Sanzenbacker, Geoffrey T. 2014. *What We Know about Health Reform in Massachusetts*. Boston: Center for Retirement Research at Boston College.

Sargent, Thomas J., and Neil Wallace. 1981. "Some Unpleasant Monetarist Arithmetic." *Federal Reserve Bank of Minneapolis Quarterly Review*, Fall, 1–17.

Shimer, Robert. 2014. "Historical and Future Employment in the United States." CBO Advisory Board presentation, June, https://sites.google.com/site/robertshimer/cbo-employment.pdf (accessed November 1, 2014).

Shoup, Carl S. 1969/2009. *Public Finance*. New Brunswick, NJ: Transaction.

Shoven, John B. 1976. "The Incidence and Efficiency Effects of Taxes on Income from Capital." *Journal of Political Economy* 84, no. 6 (December): 1261–83.

Smith, Adam. 1776/1904. *An Inquiry into the Nature and Causes of the Wealth of Nations*. Edited by Edwin Cannan. London: Methuen.

Social Security Administration. 2008. *Social Security Programs throughout the World: Europe, 2008*. Washington, DC: Office of Research, Evaluation, and Statistics.

———. 2010. *Social Security Programs throughout the World: Europe, 2010*. Washington, DC: Office of Research, Evaluation, and Statistics.

———. 2012. *Social Security Programs throughout the World: Europe, 2012*. Washington, DC: Office of Research, Evaluation, and Statistics.

Solon, Gary, Robert Barsky, and Jonathan A. Parker. 1994. "Measuring the Cyclicality of Real Wages: How Important Is Composition Bias?" *Quarterly Journal of Economics* 109, no. 1 (February): 1–25.

Sonier, Julie, Michael H. Boudreaux, and Lynn A. Blewett. 2013. "Medicaid 'Welcome-Mat' Effect of Affordable Care Act Implementation Could Be Substantial." *Health Affairs* 32, no. 7 (June).

Steuerle, C. Eugene. 2013. *Statement on Labor Force Participation, Taxes, and the Nation's Social Welfare System*. Testimony for the Record, U.S. House of Representatives, Committee on Oversight and Government Reform.

Summers, Lawrence H. 1989. "Some Simple Economics of Mandated Benefits." *American Economic Review* 79, no. 2 (May): 177–83.

Sweetwater Now News Desk. 2014. "Sweetwater County School District #1 Extends Work Year to Reduce Impact of Affordable Care Act on Employees." *sweetwaternow.com.* May 16. http://www.sweetwaternow.com/sweetwater -county-school-district-1-extends-work-year-reduce-impact-affordable-care -act-employees/ (accessed November 7, 2014).

Tabuchi, Hiroko. 2014. "Walmart to End Health Coverage for 30,000 Part-Time Workers." *New York Times,* October 7, B9.

Tetlock, Philip E. 2006. *Expert Political Judgment.* Princeton, NJ: Princeton University Press.

Topel, Robert, and Finis Welch. 1980. "Unemployment Insurance: Survey and Extensions." *Economica* 47, no. 187 (August): 351–79.

Troy, Tevi D., and D. Mark Wilson. 2014. *The Cost of the Affordable Care Act to Large Employers.* Washington, DC: American Health Policy Institute.

Urban Institute. 2011. "Health Insurance Policy Simulation Model Methodology Documentation." *Publications.* December 14. http://www.urban.org/Uploaded PDF/412471-Health-Insurance-Policy-Simulation-Model-Methodology -Documentation.pdf (accessed January 1, 2013).

U.S. Bureau of Labor Statistics. 2014a. "Employment from the BLS Household and Payroll Surveys: Summary of Recent Trends." bls.gov. http://www.bls.gov /web/empsit/ces_cps_trends.pdf (accessed May 10, 2014).

———. 2014b. "Firefighters." *Occupational Outlook Handbook.* http://www.bls.gov /ooh/protective-service/firefighters.htm (accessed October 21, 2014).

U.S. Census Bureau. 2014. "Statement by Census Bureau Director John H. Thompson on Improved Health Insurance Questions in the Current Population Survey." census.gov. April 15. http://www.census.gov/newsroom/releases/archives /directors_corner/cb14-67.html (accessed May 21, 2014).

U.S. Department of Agriculture, National Institute of Food and Agriculture. 2014. "About Us: Extension." March 28. http://web.archive.org/web/20130422034544 /http://www.csrees.usda.gov/qlinks/extension.html (accessed at usda.gov on May 16, 2014).

U.S. Department of Health and Human Services. 2014a. "Am I Eligible for Coverage in the Marketplace?" healthcare.gov. https://www.healthcare.gov/am-i -eligible-for-coverage-in-the-marketplace/ (accessed March 25, 2014).

———. 2014b. "ASPE Issue Brief." aspe.hhs.gov. February 12. http://aspe.hhs.gov /health/reports/2014/MarketPlaceEnrollment/Feb2014/ib_2014feb_enrollment .pdf (accessed March 25, 2014).

———. 2014c. "HHS Notice of Benefit and Payment Parameters for 2015." gpo.gov. March 11. http://www.gpo.gov/fdsys/pkg/FR-2014-03-11/pdf/2014-05052.pdf (accessed April 11, 2014).

———. 2014d. "How Do I Choose Marketplace Insurance?" healthcare.gov. https://www.healthcare.gov/how-do-i-choose-marketplace-insurance/ (accessed March 25, 2014).

U.S. Department of Labor. 1939, "Wages and Income of Farm Workers, 1909 to 1938." *Monthly Labor Review,* July, 59–71.

———. 2012. "All Special Extended Benefit Programs." Employment and Training Administration. http://www.oui.doleta.gov/unemploy/spec_ext_ben_table.asp (accessed July 26, 2014).

———. 2013. "FAQs about COBRA Continuation Health Coverage." Employee Benefits Security Administration. http://www.dol.gov/ebsa/faqs/faq-consumer -cobra.html (accessed November 20, 2013).

U.S. Department of Treasury. 2010. "COBRA Premium Assistance." Interim report to Congress.

———. 2014. "Treasury and IRS Issue Final Regulations Implementing Employer Shared Responsibility under the Affordable Care Act for 2015." treasury.gov. February 10. http://www.treasury.gov/press-center/press-releases/Pages/jl2290 .aspx (accessed February 11, 2014).

U.S. Internal Revenue Service. 2013a. "Medical Device Excise Tax." irs.gov. November 27. http://www.irs.gov/uac/Newsroom/Medical-Device-Excise-Tax (accessed April 2, 2014).

———. 2013b. "Notice of Rulemaking: Shared Responsibility Payment for Not Maintaining Minimum Essential Coverage." irs.gov. February 1. http://www .irs.gov/PUP/newsroom/REG-148500-12%20FR.pdf (accessed August 14, 2013).

———. 2013c. "Questions and Answers for the Additional Medicare Tax." irs.gov. December 2. http://www.irs.gov/Businesses/Small-Businesses-&-Self-Employed /Questions-and-Answers-for-the-Additional-Medicare-Tax (accessed April 1, 2014).

———. 2014a. "Questions and Answers on the Individual Shared Responsibility Provision." irs.gov. May 13. http://www.irs.gov/uac/Questions-and-Answers -on-the-Individual-Shared-Responsibility-Provision (accessed May 15, 2014).

———. 2014b. "Questions and Answers on the Net Investment Income Tax." irs .gov. March 5. http://www.irs.gov/uac/Newsroom/Net-Investment-Income -Tax-FAQs (accessed April 1, 2014).

———. 2015. "Individual Shared Responsibility Provision—Reporting and Calculating the Payment." irs.gov. February 25. http://www.irs.gov/Affordable -Care-Act/Individuals-and-Families/ACA-Individual-Shared-Responsibility -Provision-Calculating-the-Payment (accessed February 28, 2015).

Viebeck, Elise. 2014. "O-Care Premiums to Skyrocket." thehill.com. March 19. http:// thehill.com/blogs/healthwatch/health-reform-implementation/201136 -obamacare-premiums-are-about-to-skyrocket (accessed April 12, 2014).

Viscusi, W. Kip, and Joseph E. Aldy. 2003. "The Value of a Statistical Life: A Critical Review of Market Estimates throughout the World." *Journal of Risk and Uncertainty* 27, no. 1 (August): 5–76.Walsh, Alex. 2014. "Who Hates Obamacare? Increased Costs Are a Common Story." *AL.com*. January 21. http://blog .al.com/wire/2014/01/who_hates_obamacare_increased.html (accessed November 8, 2014).

Walsh, Kaitlyn Kenney. 2009. *Deadlock: A Political Economy Perspective on the Massachusetts Health Policy Reform Experience*. Ph.D. dissertation, Boston: Northeastern University Public and International Affairs.

Winslett, Ben. 2014. *myobamacaretale.com*. January 22. (accessed via google cache November 10, 2014).

Wolman, Leo. 1935. *Wages and Hours under the Codes of Fair Competition*. New York: National Bureau of Economic Research.

Yellen, Janet L. 2014. "Speech." federalreserve.gov. April 16. http://www.federal reserve.gov/newsevents/speech/yellen20140416a.htm (accessed May 20, 2014).

Yelowitz, Aaron S. 1995. "The Medicaid Notch, Labor Supply, and Welfare Partici-pation: Evidence from Eligibility Expansions." *Quarterly Journal of Economics* 11, no. 4 (November): 909–39.

INDEX

The letter *f* or *t* following a page number denotes a figure or a table, respectively.